STATES OF TRANSITION

States of Transition takes a deep dive into the multiple roles states are playing in supporting transitions to a more sustainable world and where there is scope for their transformation. Going beyond unhelpful binaries – which cast the state as the central problem or the all-encompassing solution to ecological and social crises – it explores diverse current state practice across key domains: military, democracy, welfare, entrepreneurial, industrial and foreign policy. It builds on theoretical resources from a range of disciplines, as befits the challenge of making sense of these diverse aspects of state power. It moves beyond existing analysis of the 'environmental state' to explore scope for a 'transition state' to emerge, capable of corralling and transforming all aspects of state power behind the goal of responding to the existential threat of planetary collapse. The book will be invaluable to students, academics and practitioners concerned with environmental policy and sustainability.

PETER NEWELL is Professor of International Relations at the University of Sussex. He has been involved in the politics of sustainability for more than 30 years, working with several governments and for international organisations such as the United Nations Development Programme (UNDP), Global Environment Facility (GEF), United Nations Conference on Trade and Development (UNCTAD) and the Inter-American Development Bank. He has served on the boards of Greenpeace UK and Carbon Market Watch.

'Rather like remaking the ship while at sea, *States of Transition* offers a timely analysis of the crisis and opportunities we face as requiring the reconfiguration and restructuring of the state and its complex and contradictory institutionalised capacities as ineliminable and unavoidable features of how humanity navigates the uncertainties and turbulences it now faces on a destabilised Earth.'

Professor John Barry, Queen's University, Belfast

'*States of Transition* is a superb exploration of what it will take for states to move from governing for the transition to sustainability to governing for more radical transformations. In his much needed book, Peter Newell provides a critical examination of state power that exposes its contradictions and assesses prospects for transformative change.'

Professor Jennifer Clapp, University of Waterloo

'As we hurtle towards accelerating polycrises, the battle over the role of the state has never been more important. *States of Transition* is therefore essential reading. Rigorous and forensic, Newell makes a compelling case that, if we're to rise to the threat of planetary collapse, the state must move beyond enabling transitions within and for capitalism, to supporting the necessary deeper transformations in the economy, politics and society. There could be no better guide through the complexities and contradictions of the role of the state at this critical time.'

Caroline Lucas, former MP, Green Party of England and Wales

STATES OF TRANSITION

From Governing the Environment to Transforming Society

PETER NEWELL
University of Sussex

CAMBRIDGE
UNIVERSITY PRESS

CAMBRIDGE
UNIVERSITY PRESS

Shaftesbury Road, Cambridge CB2 8EA, United Kingdom

One Liberty Plaza, 20th Floor, New York, NY 10006, USA

477 Williamstown Road, Port Melbourne, VIC 3207, Australia

314–321, 3rd Floor, Plot 3, Splendor Forum, Jasola District Centre, New Delhi – 11002, India

103 Penang Road, #05–06/07, Visioncrest Commercial, Singapore 238467

Cambridge University Press is part of Cambridge University Press & Assessment, a department of the University of Cambridge.

We share the University's mission to contribute to society through the pursuit of education, learning and research at the highest international levels of excellence.

www.cambridge.org
Information on this title: www.cambridge.org/9781009590112

DOI: 10.1017/9781009590129

When citing this work, please include a reference to the DOI 10.1017/9781009590129

First published 2025

A catalogue record for this publication is available from the British Library

A Cataloging-in-Publication data record for this book is available from the Library of Congress

ISBN 978-1-009-59013-6 Hardback
ISBN 978-1-009-59011-2 Paperback

Contents

Figures and Table

Figures

Table

Acknowledgements

It feels somewhat ironic writing a book which places the state at the centre of analysis. This is because I dedicated my PhD work and spent much of my early career exploring the role of non-state actors in global environmental politics as a conscious attempt to challenge and move beyond state-centric accounts of global politics that predominated in International Relations at the time (in the early 1990s) and, to some extent, still do today. From there, I started researching questions of civil regulation: attempts by civil society to provide informal and social regulation of the corporate sector to make up for the absence of, or limited and often weak nature of, regulation of the environmental impacts of business in an increasingly globalised economy. More recently, I have been involved in projects with colleagues on transnational climate change governance and citizen-led energy transitions, again seeking to explore and explain political life beyond the state. The role of private business actors in shaping and, more often than not, obstructing efforts to build a more sustainable society has been another key focus of research throughout my career.

By centring the state in this book, my intention is not to 'bring the state back in' for the sake of it, something many others have done in distinct ways at different points in time. Nor is it to reify or universalise the state as a political construct. Neither is it to redeem it as the magic bullet that will deliver strong sustainability when there is so much evidence to the contrary. It is rather to advance critical conversations about the multiplicity of forms and types of state power, authority and governance which require our attention as scholars and activists working on sustainability transitions and to explore the prospects (and limits) of their reform. Hence, it seeks to engage with critiques of the undemocratic, unsustainable and repressive nature of state practice in order to assess what needs to change and whether and how that might happen. It seeks to find a path through representations of the state as monolithic, universal, benign or unyielding to recognise the complex reality of actually existing states with which we need to work and coexist, but also contest, in a context where sweeping short-term change is imperative and where few actors other than the state can command the sorts of power and resources to meet the scale of the polycrisis we now face.

The research which underpins the book draws, in different ways, on fieldwork, research projects, practitioner and activist engagements and reflections over the whole course of my career. For the same reason, I have accumulated numerous debts and been lucky enough to work with many wonderful people. For ongoing collaboration across multiple projects, inspiration and friendship, I would like to thank: Harriet Bulkeley, Angela Carter, Mat Paterson, Harro van Asselt, Caroline Kuzemko, Marie-Claire Brisbois, Gurminder Bhambra, Benjamin Sovacool, Olivia Taylor, John Thompson, Joachim Peter Tilsted and Matthew Lockwood; the team working with me on my research project on supply-side climate policies (SUS POL): Freddie Daley, Daniela Soto Hernandez and Lukas Slothuus; and the Rapid Transition Alliance team: especially Andrew Simms, Freddie Daley, Sophie Marsden and Nicky Saunter. For translating an idea in a newspaper article into the successful global campaign for a Fossil Fuel Non-Proliferation Treaty, I would like to thank Tzeporah Berman, Rebecca Brynes and Alex Rafalowicz in particular. Finally, I have to thank the legendary scholar, activist and musician Phil Johnstone from the Science Policy Research Unit (SPRU) for the title of this book, which was the original title of our journal article on the state and sustainability transitions, but which the editors objected to on the grounds that they didn't like a play on words. Well, I guess I do. States of transition is also the title of a sometimes band made up of Phil (guitars and vocals) and me (cajón drum) that has had the privilege of playing at the celebration of our (now former) local Green MP Caroline Lucas' re-election (something that gives me some faith that there are decent politicians out there willing to do the right thing) as well as at a solidarity event for the Yukpa people in Colombia struggling against extractivism by mining companies in which the state is complicit: a reminder of the darker side of state power.

For his support for this and my many other books with Cambridge University Press, I am grateful to my editor Matt Lloyd, the production team at the Press and the six reviewers of the book proposal and draft chapters for such positive and constructive feedback. I hope they recognise the ways in which their suggestions have helped to improve the book.

On a personal level, I would like to thank my family in the UK and Argentina, in particular my parents Helen and Brian, my partner Lucila, my children Ana and Camilo and, in the spirit of interspecies love, my dog Sunny.

Abbreviations

AI	artificial intelligence
ASEAN	Association of Southeast Asian Nations
BEE	Black Economic Empowerment
CA	Climate Assembly
CBAM	Carbon-Border Adjustment Mechanism
CCS	carbon capture and storage
COP	Conference of the Parties
DoT	Department of Transport (UK)
ECT	Energy Charter Treaty
EPE	ecological political economy
EU	European Union
GDP	gross domestic product
GEF	Global Environment Facility
GM	genetically modified (crops)
GND	Green New Deal
GSI	Global Subsidies Initiative
IAEA	International Atomic Energy Agency
IEA	International Energy Agency
IISD	International Institute for Sustainable Development
ILO	International Labour Organization
IMF	International Monetary Fund
IPCC	Intergovernmental Panel on Climate Change
IRA	Inflation Reduction Act
IRENA	International Renewable Energy Agency
ISDS	Investor–State Dispute Settlement
ITER	International Thermonuclear Experimental Reactor
JETP	Just Energy Transition Partnership
JOCCA	Joint Oireachtas Committee on Climate Action

LINGO	Leave it in the Ground Initiative
LMICs	low- and middle-income countries
LNG	liquefied natural gas
MIC	military-industrial complex
MNC	multinational corporation
MNE	multinational enterprise
NAFTA	North American Free Trade Area
NATO	North Atlantic Treaty Organization
NDC	nationally determined contribution
NIMBYism	Not-In-My-Backyard-ism
NPT	Nuclear Non-Proliferation Treaty
NUM	National Union of Mineworkers
OECD	Organisation for Economic Co-operation and Development
PPA	Power Purchase Agreement
R&D	research and development
REIPPPP	Renewable Energy Independent Power Producer Procurement Programme
RTA	Rapid Transition Alliance
SDGs	Sustainable Development Goals
SRA	strategic relational approach
TCCG	transnational climate change governance
TOA	technology-oriented agreement
UCD	uneven and combined development
UK	United Kingdom
UN	United Nations
UNCTAD	United Nations Conference on Trade and Development
UNFCCC	United Nations Framework Convention on Climate Change
UNIDO	United Nations Industrial Development Organization
US	United States
VoC	Varieties of Capitalism
WTO	World Trade Organization

1

Introduction

The State We Are In

By its presence or absence, the state features centrally in discussions about collective responses to the ecological crisis currently enveloping the world, often understood as sustainability transitions. Increasing expectations and demands are placed on the state from citizens, businesses, social movements and regional and international institutions to restructure economies, strengthen governance systems, as well as make them more inclusive and transparent, and deal with the social justice challenges that arise from the pursuit of a 'just transition'. But, at the same time, states both face and create unprecedented pressures from multiple sources in the form of the polycrisis observable in a series of short- and longer-term intersecting and social, economic and environmental crises (Lawrence et al. 2022),[1] or what Moore describes as a 'singular crisis' with 'manifold expressions' (Moore 2015: 298). These fault lines are magnified by political crises induced by populism and the erosion of democratic institutions which enable social demands to be articulated and addressed.

The need to simultaneously innovate, regulate, consult, redistribute, police and globalise transitions confronts the state with a series of tensions and trade-offs in its approach to sustainability transitions. This places the state squarely at the centre of the contested politics of disruptive and accelerated transformative change. Whether examined in their entrepreneurial, regulatory, competitive, developmental, military or welfare form, states are one of the key arenas of struggle in which social actors negotiate how and by whom transitions should be governed, and on whose terms, and are therefore the target of competing social demands about the future. While hopes might be invested in the idea of a 'transition state', whereby key state functions and capacities are increasingly corralled behind the task of tackling the existential threat posed by a deepening ecological and social crisis, our understanding of how, when taken together, different but interrelated aspects of state power enable or impede the capacity of the state to rise to this challenge remains limited.

Despite a number of important contributions, critical thinking and conceptualisation of the role of the state in both more narrowly defined sustainability transitions as well as deeper transformations remains underdeveloped. The distinction between transitions and great transformations is significant, as Eckersley argues, because of its implications regarding the nature and extent of state agency and 'the depth and direction of change towards ecological sustainability' (Eckersley 2021: 246). Transition and transformation (co)exist on a spectrum, nevertheless, from narrow 'plug-and-play' changes to technology adoption and patterns of behaviour through to a deeper and more profound recasting or re-embedding of the state and market within broader frameworks of social and democratic control (Polanyi 1980 [1944]), which require key shifts in power to secure planetary survival (Newell 2021a). It is a distinction to which we will return throughout the book (see Table 1.1).

There is now a burgeoning literature on sustainability transitions, some strands of which are increasingly recognising the centrality of questions of governance and, by default or by extension, acknowledging the role of the state as enabler or barrier to sustainability transitions (Duit 2016; Craig 2020; Hatzisavvidou 2020; Hausknost and Hammond 2020). This turn towards governance and politics in the study of transitions (Meadowcroft 2008; Johnstone and Newell 2018; Silvester and Fiske 2023) is partly a function of political scientists and political economists increasingly engaging with transition debates (Meadowcroft 2009; Kuzemko et al. 2016; Bernstein and Hoffman 2019; Newell 2021a). But, more recently, it also reflects an increasing return to state interventionism, heightened under Covid, and a belated recognition of the vital role of states across arenas such as innovation, regulation and diplomacy, witnessed in debates about a Green New Deal (Pettifor 2019) and just transitions (Swilling and Annecke 2012; Newell and Mulvaney 2013). Geopolitically, the increasing salience of 'rising powers' in the global economy has brought to the fore models of state capitalism and the developmental state (Leftwich 2000; Nem Singh 2024) that have yet to gain traction in the 'Lockean heartlands' of the global economy (van der Pijl 1998) with important implications for models of transition, while questions of war and the military state are never far from view and are actively constitutive of the form and possibilities of transition pathways.

Yet while philosophers and large bodies of social science scholarship have sought to make sense of the state and its role in society over centuries, critical thinking about diverse aspects of the state's role in sustainability transitions is underdeveloped. It often starts and ends with narrower discussions of governance and the institutional arrangements required to manage and steer sustainability transitions. It also often remains siloed in relation to individual state functions (whether environmental, industrial or innovation policy, security and foreign policy or welfare) rather than grounded in a wider and deeper understanding of what I am calling 'states of transition': the uneven and contradictory ways in which state power is currently being deployed to seek to manage and control socio-ecological change and disruption. Such a siloed approach makes it harder to assess the overall prospects of a 'transition state' emerging where one of the overriding objectives and logics of the exercise of state power becomes the collective management of societal transitions or, more ambitiously still, to support deeper transformative change.

In this sense, the book departs both from discussions about the emergence, form and limits of an 'environmental state', which, through ecological modernisation, seeks to reconcile environmental management with overriding growth imperatives (Mol et al. 2010; Duit et al. 2016; Hausknost and Hammond 2021), and from normative enquiries into the form a 'green state' might take (Eckersley 2004; Barry and Eckersley 2005). In the case of the former, an environmental state is 'a state that possesses a significant set of institutions and practices dedicated to the management of the environment and societal-environmental interactions … [with] specialised administrative, regulatory, financial and knowledge structures that mark out a distinctive sphere of government activity' (Duit et al. 2016: 5–6). Largely dedicated to managing the 'externalities' of industrial society and dealing with the contradictions this generates, the limits of this project of environmental statehood are becoming ever more visible and manifest themselves in the legitimacy crises environmental states now face regarding their inability (and unwillingness) to generate responses of the nature, speed and scale required to adequately respond to ecological crises and therefore afford citizens the protection they need. In part, this relates to the fact that the environmental state, as Hammond and Hausknost (2021) show, derives it 'functional logic' from the paradigm of ecological modernisation: 'the strategy of increasing the effectiveness and efficiency of environmental management through means of technological and administrative innovation without at the same time questioning the basic structures of the capitalist mode of production or industrialism more generally' (Hammond and Hausknost 2021: 2). A transition state has thus far failed to address the causes of the polycrisis and underlying drivers of our current predicament where a more fundamental reset of the goals and functions of contemporary life is required. As Hammond (2021: 174) suggests:

> The failure of environmental states to move beyond piecemeal reform suggests transformability is woefully lacking: even societies fully intent on responding to the environmental crisis have hit a 'glass ceiling' that prevents change of the depth required to adequately respond to the ecological realities at hand. These societies have created environmental government departments, significantly reduced levels of pollution, incentivised green technology and seen widespread environmental concern among the public. Yet despite full awareness that this has not been effective as a response to existential threats like climate change, the deeper culprits of consumer capitalism, industrialism and resource overuse remain in place, in fact continuing to intensify.

To move the discussion forward, this book seeks to build a broader understanding of the role of the state in sustainability transitions by bringing to bear interdisciplinary perspectives on key dimensions of state power with an assessment of how those dimensions relate to sustainability transitions, before assessing the prospects of their transformation. It follows and applies this approach to each dimension of state power explored in the book from the entrepreneurial, industrial and military state to the democratic, welfare and global state. Though the principal focus of this book is the role of the state in enabling and frustrating sustainability transitions, the approach I take is to understand the state as a whole in order to understand the interrelationships and cumulative effects of diverse state functions on the prospects of pathways to change. This is because the entrepreneurial, industrial, military, welfare, democratic and foreign policy functions of states have at least as much impact upon the ability of states to build a sustainable society as more narrowly defined and bespoke environmental policies (where most scholarly attention has been focussed to date) but whose traction and impact will be minimum in the absence of change in these other areas of state policy. This distinction is captured in the subtitle of the book: from governing the environment to transforming society.

Moreover, although the state frequently appears as saint or sinner, saviour or devil in political debate – caricatured as too big, too powerful, too small, too inefficient, too ineffective, too unsustainable – the reality is more complex, nuanced and contingent on the historical and geographical context, prevailing social relations and the state function and issue in question. Understanding the varieties of states in all their (in)glorious guises helps to challenge these unhelpful binaries and to counter dominant narratives about market-led transitions which obscure and negate the role of the state. This is important because past cases of large-scale and rapid socio-technical change reveal that new technological systems require significant public support in the form of state investment, regulation and establishing and enforcing property rights, for example (Mazzucato 2011; Vogel 2018). Despite claims to the contrary, transformations in markets are always embedded to different degrees in state–society complexes. The notion that transitions unfold as a result of the 'natural' operations of the market guided by (an often elusive) 'invisible hand' or that they will be unproblematically imposed from above and accepted below seems fanciful at best, missing the messy and contingent nature of actually existing transitions, while being historically illiterate about the conditions in which previous periods of transition have taken place. As Polanyi reminds us, 'the market has been the outcome of a conscious and often violent intervention on the part of government which imposed the market organisation of society for non-economic ends' (Polanyi 1980 [1944]: 250).

Likewise, however, the notion that the scale of change now required and the time frames in which it has to happen will be achieved solely through citizen-led innovations and grassroots resistance in ways which bypass or do away with the need for the state, however appealing, seems naïve. As Hausknost and Hammond put it, 'A rapid, purposeful and comprehensive decarbonisation of modern society without the force of law and without adequate institutions of deliberation, will-formation, decision-making, policy coordination and enforcement seems highly unlikely' (Hausknost and Hammond 2021: 4). Or as Eckersley reminds us, 'no other institution can match the state's regulatory capacity' and 'nor is there any other institution with the resources and financial transfer mechanisms to provide social welfare and address inequalities and injustices on the scale of states, and this makes them central to managing the unavoidable dislocations that will occur in the transition process' (Eckersley 2021: 248). The same challenges face those supportive of degrowth. Writing on the role of the state in degrowth transformations, Buch Hansen et al. (2024: 76) argue:

> [M]ost of the eco-social policies that are typically suggested to initiate and deepen degrowth transformations – be it in relation to respecting ecological ceilings or social floors would require a great deal of intervention by states and/ or international organisations ... Degrowth advocacy has therefore suffered from a tension between viewing the state as incapable of initiating transformational change and appealing to it to do precisely that.

We are left, therefore, with the challenging political task of contesting, as well as reworking, the state in ways which make it more likely to be able to perform the critical political work of coordinating and orchestrating collective social change in ways that respond to a notion of the planetary common good.

1.1 Locating the State

So, what then is the state? What independent agency does *it* (whatever that *it* may be) exercise? 'No definition of the state is innocent' (Jessop 2008: 2) and every definition is inevitably partial and selective. In some renditions, it appears as an almost empty vessel without autonomous agency whose significance derives only from the rulers, classes or bureaucrats that work within it and control its structures. This is why some prefer to talk about governments and executive branches, rather than the more general category of the state. But state structures and institutions outlive particular ruling coalitions, governments and regimes and even many of the people that occupy them (such as civil servants) do not change when governments come and go. Nor do other key pillars of power such as the military, police and the legal system, nor the entrenched ties and relationships which bind the state as a global actor. Nor, absent a coup, do basic democratic functions. Neither do they stand above or apart from the social relations which they seek to govern but at the same time crystallise.

Bob Jessop, the author of many classic texts on the state, suggests 'the core of the state apparatus can be defined as a distinct ensemble of institutions and organisations whose socially accepted function is to define and enforce collectively binding decisions on a given population in the name of their "common interest" or "general will"' (Jessop 2008: 9). Though this provides a broad definition, it does exclude certain activities such that 'not all forms of macro-political organisation can be classed as state-like nor can the state simply be equated with government, law, bureaucracy, a coercive apparatus or another political institution' (Jessop 2008: 9). The extent to which that function is 'socially accepted', adequately serves the 'common interest' and the means by which decisions are made 'binding' and enforceable provide the terrain of contestation in many societies about whose interests are served by state policies and how much legitimacy surrounds the law, policing and foreign policy interventions used to enforce them.

This is the backdrop to critical questions about the scope for change, transition and transformation in the role of the state regarding the multiple and intersecting social, economic and ecological crises that the world now faces. There are many varieties of states and statehood, embedded in turn within varieties of capitalism and non-capitalist economies (Hall and Soskice 2001). As Jessop notes, 'The basic features of capitalism as a mode of production and object of regulation assume different patterns in different varieties and stages of capitalism' (Jessop 2002: 1) as accumulation regimes and political regimes couple, uncouple and co-evolve. Deciphering what it is about the state that is structural, fixed, inevitable and impervious to change, and what it is, on the other hand, that might be reformed or transformed as part of broader projects of social and ecological transformation, is a vital contemporary task. Might it be possible, for example, to expand state functions of protection, radical innovation and environmental stewardship while reducing, better regulating or subjecting to social control the industrial and military functions of the state as part of a vision pursued by a 'transition state' or a more transformative successor? Or is such an endeavour fruitless and naïve given the core functions of a state in a competitive capitalist and anarchical international society where there are few constraints on the use of force and violence? Other scholars have referred to a 'glass ceiling' on the capacity of the state to support the sorts of transformations required for sustainability whereby there exists 'a structural barrier that marks the line until which environmental reform is compatible with functional requirements of the state and beyond which its compatibility gives way to functional tension, conflict and outright contradiction' (Hausknost and Hammond 2021: 3). Notions of degrowth and sufficiency propose to transgress that ceiling by reducing consumption and production and impacting employment and state revenues which are 'toxic for all but the sustainability imperative' (Hausknost 2020: 22). These tensions and contradictions exist in relation to extractivist and growth-oriented economies whose consequences are apparent in ever increasing social and environmental crises which states struggle to manage.

But they also find expression in the crisis experienced by modern forms of democracy which give rise to a profound crisis of legitimation (Blühdorn 2020) around who states represent and how in the context of a fraying social contract, where their ability to provide basic protection and secure citizens' rights is compromised by a refusal to reverse the economic processes driving ecological and societal collapse. This points to the distinction between an environmental state with 'specialised administrative, regulatory, financial and knowledge structures that mark out a distinct sphere of government activity' (Duit et al. 2016: 5–6) and a 'transition state' whose overarching goals are supporting the necessary deeper transformations in the economy, politics and society (see Table 1.1). The shift is from managing environmental change within and for capitalism to supporting transformative social and economic change compatible with a sustainable society where fundamental shifts (and reductions) in patterns of production and consumption are the goal rather than substituting technologies and energy sources in

Table 1.1 *A state typology*

Type of state	Key features
Environmental state	Environmental states are those actually existing states which through processes of ecological modernisation are 'greening' key state functions which they seek to reconcile with conventional state priorities such as growth, welfare provision and militarism. Informed by ecological modernisation, it reaffirms the ability of states to adapt their core functions to ecological imperatives.
Transition state	Less narrowly focussed on the environment per se, a transition state is one whose primary purpose becomes the management, orchestration and steering of multiple transitions across society. It seeks to effectively manage key transitions in critical sectors of the economy without questioning dominant rationales and modes of statehood nor the material base of the economy which sustain them.
Green state	Definitions and visions of a green state vary, but in essence a green state (of which there are not yet fully fledged models in practice) would embody key Green values of sustainability, decentralisation, ecological democracy and non-violence.
States of transformation	Less a dominant state form and more an actor, *primus inter pares*, the state uses its power and authority alongside that of other actors to address the sources and drivers of unsustainability as part of a wider project of societal transformation including of key state functions. Sustainability moves to the centre of state practice and logics whereby the state plays an active and enabling role in addressing the multiple sources of unsustainability in economic, political and social systems as part of a broader project of transformation.

a 'plug-and-play' fashion (Newell 2021a). Indeed, as Hausknost (2020: 21) suggests, 'the logic of state imperatives is cumulative ... Previous transformations of the state thus expanded state functions rather than replacing them.' Any such reconfiguration would require broader shifts in power within and between states, driven and accompanied by deeper shifts in cultures and values to presage and embed that change and to sustain structures of governance with a very different view of the responsibilities of the state in pursuit of a radically distinct view of the good life. Change of this nature and scale is unlikely to come from within the state, though support for such shifts from key allies within the state may well be critical to their success.

This landscape of power is not a static one. The roles, functions, capacities and landscapes of power in which states are embedded (but at the same time reconfigure) are in flux, as expectations of states and views about how to assess their effectiveness evolve and change. From mercantilist to competition states, colonial to postcolonial states, developmental and post-developmental states, Keynesian to neoliberal and postliberal, the functioning, organisation and purpose of states are always in a process of rearticulation and realignment in the face of shifting global and domestic pressures from social forces and external events. Securing domestic legitimacy is vital to maintaining some measure of control and order amid this shifting terrain where ecological crises further test the ability of states to protect their citizens and dispose of their duties. For Machiavelli (2020 [1532]: 48), states' strength should be assessed according to their ability

> to keep the lower classes satisfied, and without loss to the public, they have always enough means to give them work for one year in these employments which form the nerve and life of the town, and in the industries by which the lower classes live; military exercises are still held in reputation and many regulations are in force for maintaining them.

Though written long before the advent of the environmental crisis which presents a new order of challenge for statecraft, the essence in his comments about states being pulled in competing directions to shore up their legitimacy and maintain power through 'soft', 'hard' and performed means resonates today.

Crises of course precipitate change and have the potential to give rise to legitimacy crises for states. The global Covid pandemic shifted ground in fundamental ways by giving the lie to long-cherished neoliberal myths about the inability and incapacity of the state to intervene in the economy: to determine which sectors, industries and people are more in need of protection than others and to prioritise protection over profit. In some parts of the world, we saw states requiring industries to convert their production to respond to the Covid crisis as breweries started repurposing alcohol for use in hand sanitisers and vacuum cleaner manufacturers were instead required to produce ventilators for hospitals. These moments of disruptive change showed that industries can be repurposed much more quickly than dominant narratives had led us to believe. 'Magic money trees', said not to exist, turned out not only to exist but to be constantly bearing fruit (in the wealthier centres of the global economy at least) in the form of furlough and state-sponsored bailouts to workers and key sectors affected by the constraints imposed on our patterns of work, travel and social interaction by the lockdown. Reflecting on responses to the pandemic, Andreas Malm (2020: 7) notes:

> In the emergency, the fences around private property blew away like a thatched hut in a hurricane: Spain nationalised all private health facilities in one stroke and instructed companies with potential capacity for producing medical equipment to align with state plans. Britain all but nationalised its railway system and the Italian state took over flag carrier Alitalia.

In the face of an emergency, state action was decisive, wide-ranging and effective. Parallels with, and speculation about, whether such interventions might presage similar efforts to tackle the climate emergency inevitably followed. But the experience of this period, to some extent, helped to correct the dominance of anti-statist neoliberal ideology whose ascendance coincides with vastly increased emissions and the obvious need for herculean state-led efforts to decarbonise the global economy, what Naomi Klein calls 'an epic case of bad timing' (Klein 2015: 73).

The contested role of the state solicits a spectrum of strong reactions and counter-reactions from activists, businesses and governments themselves amid calls for a Green New Deal (Green New Deal Group 2008; Pettifor 2019), for strengthened forms of global governance and planet politics (Burke et al. 2016) or for critiques of the extractivist, ecocidal nature of the capitalist or industrialist state (Dunlap and Brock 2022). To some extent, these conflicting views of the state reflect the multifaceted nature of state power and its consequences, something I suggest in this book that we need to appreciate, differentiate, conceptualise and engage with more systematically in studies of sustainability transitions. They bring into focus some of the core tensions and contradictions in the ways states both support and frustrate sustainability transitions: between functions of protection (of society and the environment) and promotion (of industry), between innovation (bringing technologies to market) and exnovation (taking them out of production), between providing security but doing so through militarism and violence (which renders others insecure) or more broadly still between legitimation (for social acceptance) and accumulation (of capital).

These raise, in turn, more fundamental questions that political economists and political ecologists have long wrestled with about the relationship between labour exploitation and industrial expansion, securitisation and democratic freedoms and the compatibility of infinite economic growth with a finite planet. In this sense, the state can be thought of as the concentration, centralisation and embodiment of some of the key contradictions and tensions which inhere in capitalism: the reproduction of inequalities which circumscribe consumption for growth (the first contradiction); the ways in which growth diminishes the resource base upon which accumulation is premised (the second contradiction); and the tensions this produces between capital and labour and between humans and more-than-human nature (O'Connor 1998). These contradictions are manifest across the different dimensions of state power and the performance of diverse state functions, which reflect not just a plethora of societal demands and human needs but conscious political attempts to manage these deeper contradictions through the use of the institutional and material power of the state and to both maintain social order and protect elite and incumbent power from challengers to their authority. This often takes the form of ensuring that discussions about transitions are kept on the terrain of techno-managerial management and not allowed to spill over into calls for deeper economic, social and political transformations: *trasformismo* rather than transformation (Newell 2019).

The state is at the heart of navigating, obscuring and seeking to appease these tensions but does so not in isolation or devoid of historical context. Social, economic and ecological interdependencies bind the collective fates of states and their citizens together. How they resource their economies and create and distribute wealth is the product of intra- and inter-societal inequalities and their racialised, gendered and class-based manifestations. This is why the book includes a chapter on the global state to reflect the reality of the state's location in a world economy characterised by multiplicity and uneven and combined development (Rosenburg 2013) to push beyond the national focus of many transition studies. Levels of development are relational and interdependent, whether viewed as part of a world system (Wallerstein 2014) or a product of global relations between the core and the periphery (Cardoso and Faletto 1979). This means that sustainability transitions in one part of the world are often only possible because of transitions elsewhere – and thus need to be understood in relation to (since they are dependent upon) these other transitions. Appreciating this deep inter-relationality is vital. Whether this is visible and understood through analysis of political and economic relations between 'rival states and rival firms' (Stopford and Strange 1991), along global wealth chains (Seabrooke and Wigan 2017), by following the money or from an appreciation of the patterns of 'ecologically uneven exchange' that underpin modes of extraction and trade in the global economy premised on the availability of ostensibly 'cheap' labour and nature (Patel and Moore 2017), this intimate relationality between transitions, mediated in direct and indirect ways by states, needs to be comprehended. It also poses huge practical and political challenges to the possibility and effectiveness of the global governance of just transitions across spaces, scales and social groups (Newell et al. 2023) while disorienting methodologically nationalist accounts of transitions which treat them in isolation from one another.

But a more historical account is vital too. Colonialism forms the basis of the resource wealth of many industrialised nations in Europe (Rodney 2018; Bhambra 2021; Newell 2021b) that style themselves as transition leaders, and the term 'new colonialism' is invoked to describe dominant patterns of extractivism between China and sub-Saharan Africa, for example, as part of a 'new scramble for Africa' (Ayers 2013) around land, energy and water. Yet clearly colonial patterns of extraction, uneven exchange, land grabbing, dispossession and the use of violence extend far beyond relations between 'rising powers' and African states. Historical legacies cast long shadows over the current politics and pathways to sustainability (Sultana 2022) and colonial imaginaries, circuits of capital and practices of power continue to operate today. It is important also to situate the very practice of sovereignty itself historically (Bartleson 1995) as the foundation of the state system. As Jessop notes, drawing on Teschke's work (2003) on 'The Myth of 1648', 'a system of territorially exclusive, mutually recognising, mutually legitimating national states exercising formally sovereign control over large and exclusive territorial areas is a relatively recent institutional expression of state power that is historically contingent rather than an inevitable and irreversible result of social development' (Jessop 2008: 5). States continue to operate as just one institutional ensemble among others within a broader social formation but remain nevertheless 'peculiarly charged with overall responsibility for maintaining the social cohesion of the social formation of which it is merely a part', *primus inter pares*, meaning the state is 'continually called upon by diverse social forces to resolve society's problems and is equally continually doomed to generate "state failure"' (Jessop 2008: 7).

Given the central role of the state at the intersection of these historical and contemporary processes and as a vital node in circuits of economic and ecological exchange, it is unsurprising that there is a growing recognition that 'from protecting niches, nurturing research and technological innovation through to industrial policy, regulation and enforcement, the range and depth of powers that only the state can call upon will be required if radical and rapid transitions are to be achieved which allow humanity to operate within planetary boundaries' (Johnstone and Newell 2018: 72). What is also often missing from such discussions, however, is a more historically grounded, global and geographically sensitive account of which states are playing roles in which transitions, where, when and why and on whose behalf, as well as a more granular account of the variety of state forms, functions and practices which, when taken seriously (and together), provide a richer account of the potential and limitations of state-led transitions to sustainability. Starting to build such an account is crucial, I argue, as part of an attempt to mobilise key intervention and leverage points, to inform social theories of change, to build more effective coalitions and alliances for change and to hardwire urgency and equity into state responses to our collective predicament, as well as dispel myths about lack of agency and the absence of precedents for change.

On the one hand, a wider and richer account of different aspects and dimensions of state authority might be thought to introduce unwelcome complexity by pointing to additional sites of power and resistance that have to be overcome in order to accelerate just transitions and sow the seeds of transformative change. In other words, it is hard enough shifting innovation and industrial policy or strengthening environmental policy. Why also take on the might of the military state or the complexity of the welfare state or bring foreign policy into the equation? On the other hand, unless we attend to each of the multifaceted aspects of the state and their role in enabling or frustrating sustainability transitions, we will likely fail in endeavours to build a more socially just and sustainable society, since continuing with a predominant focus on one set of state activities (around innovation and regulation or environmental policy narrowly conceived) obscures other, often more powerful, state functions (in relation to welfare, foreign policy and militarism) which, whatever the merits of the former, are outweighed by lock-in to unsustainable pathways produced by the latter. From education, health and welfare, innovation and representation to defence and foreign policy, all aspects of state activity impact positively or negatively (and nearly always both) upon the prospects of sustainability transitions. Getting within, amongst and beyond the state helps to identify the cracks, fragilities and vulnerabilities in state power, as well as reveals some of the potential ways in which state power could be mobilised for more progressive and sustainable ends. It affords at least the possibility of moving beyond binary accounts of the states' role in transitions – interventionist/laissez-faire, neoliberal/social democratic, liberal/coordinated and so on – by forcing us to hold these different latent and actual potentialities simultaneously in our analysis.

1.2 Understanding the State

How then can we best understand, conceptualise and engage with the complexity and contradictions that derive from the diverse ways in which states govern and un-govern sustainability transitions?

Specifically:

- How can we best account for the role of the state in sustainability transitions?
- What roles are states currently playing with respect to those transitions?
- What prospects are there for the transformation of key state roles in sustainability transitions?

Each chapter in the book first introduces an aspect of state power. It then applies this to the question of sustainability transitions before finally exploring the prospects of transforming that aspect of state power. This structure reflects the core argument of the book that the dominant role of most states at the current conjuncture is one of *trasformismo*: enabling transitions *within* and *for* capitalism rather than transformations *of* it and which move *beyond* it. Rather than addressing key contradictions within capitalism and industrialism which produce unsustainability, current transitions are for the most part aimed at managing them, displacing them and moving them around through spatial and temporal fixes. In so doing, dominant transition responses further entrench social, economic, racial and gendered inequalities: the very antithesis of just transformative change. Indeed, it would be surprising if deeply unjust economies and societies produced just transitions if what shifts is only a technology or system of service provision and not the power relations which determine access to that system, the labour conditions which prevail in their production and who bears the ecological costs which result from it. Though often described as national plans and experiments, contemporary transitions are intimately interconnected because of the ecological flows, social and labour relations and networks of production and finance that bind them together.

This is the 'deep relationality' explored in the book which requires a more global and holistic account not only of the state but of the contexts in which states are seeking to address sustainability challenges. Relationality is key to understanding the social, spatial and ecological organisation of transitions, as well as the potential for deeper transformations. It has many dimensions that are explored in this book, including the state and social relations (of which it is a part and, at the same time, crystallises); the state and its relationship to its own society and citizens (where relationalities are bounded by the duties and obligations that flow from being bound by sovereign borders and the fabric of the social contract that underpins citizenship); relationalities between state functions and within and across the state (which, because they are in tension with one another, produce the conflicts and contradictions explored in the book); relationalities across societies (the state as a nodal point in a global system of states and transnational relations which shape that relationship); the state's relation to nature (the ecologies of statehood) and the materialities of the state and the ways in which it is both grounded in and seeks to manage the ecologies and material base which its fate is intrinsically bound to.

In this book, I show how the role of the state cannot just be reduced to one of governance and governing transitions. The notion that states neutrally steer, corral and manage different elements of transition towards stated goals is to neglect the deeply political nature of transitions and the social relations in which they are embedded. States do much more than govern. The causes of unsustainability are hardwired into our economic, political, social and cultural systems, infrastructures and behaviours, over which states have significant degrees of direct and indirect influence and control and are frequently centrally placed. To grapple with this reality adequately requires a broad notion of the state which extends way beyond its executive functions, to the multiple levels and arenas in which its authority is exercised and its reach felt across political and civil society (Gramsci 1971). To understand the tensions, contradictions and injustices that flow from how these (often competing) roles are performed – or neglected – requires a more political account and one which roots the state in broader social relations of which it is a part and helps to reproduce drawing on theoretical resources outlined in Chapter 2. This means being attentive to the networks and relations of power in which the state is situated and which it seeks to enrol to achieve collective social ends and manage the tensions and contradictions it is confronted with.

I argue in this book that we need to see deeper and more radical shifts across all sites of state power and not just those which have been the focus of debate about the environmental state so far (though those need to change too), namely technology, innovation and environmental policy, and to a lesser extent industrial and tax policy. Rather, we need to address how the state conducts foreign relations, its monopoly on the use of violence through war, imperialism and policing, its industrial, extractivist and centralising tendencies and exclusionary dynamics which mean most of the world's citizens are unable to actively shape their collective destiny. Hence, as well as analysing emergent, embryonic and unfolding transitions in the contemporary world, I also refer to historical transitions with a view to better appreciating and foregrounding the ways in which neglected dimensions of state power had a bearing on the direction, form, nature and speed of previous transitions: whether foreign policy and its military iterations, industrial and welfare policy or the degree of democracy prevailing in those transitions that states have overseen in the past. This requires a deeper, more rounded, more political, geographical and historical account of the state.

The chapters that follow do not end with a fatalistic and pessimistic account derived from an analysis of contradictions and limits, however, as is often common in critical political economy scholarship. They rather point to examples, precedents, parallels and emergent state practices which show, for example, that demilitarisation is possible because it has happened before; that rapid conversion of industries has been achieved; that welfare can be prioritised by states; that drives towards reducing consumption and waste can be overseen by governments that normally seek to fuel it; that democracy can be deepened through new forms of engagements with citizens traditionally excluded from politics; and so on. Highlighting these examples gives lie to the notion that states cannot change or lack the agency and will to tackle major global challenges. But neither should it provide the basis of a naïve optimism that the state will save us from ecological collapse and deepening social inequalities. Far from it. Many of the transitions and shifts described in the book derive from intense social struggle, often over decades, in preparing the ground for progressive state action and once in place it still has to be fought for against attacks from those wanting to roll back or otherwise control the state for their own purposes.

State forms, functions and capacities vary hugely, resulting from different histories and locked into different patterns of uneven development. As Weber (1948) noted, there is no activity that states always perform and none that they have never performed. We can observe then different views of the state and its role in regulating markets and the appropriate role of business in societal transitions. From a political culture seemingly at ease with a command and control and centralised model of planning which produces visions and missions (such as India's solar mission reflecting a particular Nehruvian legacy of state planning or reflected in Kenya's Vision 2030) to transitions largely focussed on private sector–led innovation and investment (such as Jet Zero in the UK or the Breakthrough Agenda agreed at the Glasgow climate Conference of the Parties (COP) in 2021 to advance business-led sectoral transitions), the politics and practice of transitions are not immune from deeper ideological currents and worldviews. Likewise, there are diverse views of the role of business in policy, from the lack of perceived need to negotiate with business in China (Newell 2008c) to state complexes deeply entwined with capital (such as the Minerals Energy Complex in South Africa) (Baker et al. 2014) to more tripartite bargaining in social democratic and more coordinated economies such as the Netherlands and Denmark where business associations and trade unions both have a central role (Greene and Carter 2024). Regulatory ideologies also diverge around, for example, the political acceptability of tax measures (harder in the US than Northern Europe) and the extent to which regional institutions such as the European Union (EU) should be allowed to shape transition pathways (resisted in the UK and more embraced in France and Germany for example). Different levels of democratisation and scope for civic engagement and deliberation create more openings in settings like Denmark, the UK, Ireland and France, where climate assemblies have been held, but are unavailable in China for example.

Globally, shrinking civic space sharply constrains scope for popular engagement with transition pathways and the deepening of the democratic state (Newell, Shankland et al. 2022). Political party systems make a difference too. Where proportional representation (PR) voting systems have amplified the influence of Green parties whose role in government has been crucial to Germany's *Energiewende* energy transition (Lockwood 2015), first-past-the-post systems have inhibited effective voice in many other democracies such as the UK. Different degrees of integration and incorporation into the global economy in relation to trade, aid relations and levels of indebtedness all structure scope for autonomous action in pursuit of sustainable development. For many countries in the Global South especially, the relevant model might be what some scholars in the varieties of capitalism tradition call DMEs (dependent market economies) (Hall and Soskice 2001) with important implications for levels of policy autonomy and independence from incumbent actors. Meanwhile, dominant economic models such as the finance-led 'regime of accumulation' in the UK accounts for its eagerness to use its structural advantage as home to the City of London and it is no coincidence early voluntary carbon trade centred around the Chicago exchange in the US.

Amid this diversity, there is commonality. Achieving and replicating rapid transitions that are both far-reaching and unprecedented in terms of scale – which, as the Intergovernmental Panel on Climate Change (IPCC) Special Report on Global Warming of 1.5°C (SR15) suggests, are required to keep warming below 1.5°C (IPCC 2018) – means engaging with the deep politics of transition and transformation across different societal and institutional settings. As Hammond and Hausknost (2021: x) put it: 'Posing a systemic challenge to the very structure of modern industrial states – their fossil fuel dependent economies, their consumerist culture, their individualist, interest-driven model of democracy – the climate crisis in particular revealed the inability of previously successful "environmental states" to engender the social change needed to adapt to the reality of rapidly escalating climate change.' I argue here that this implies supporting political and institutional innovations that disrupt incumbent power within and beyond the state and enable new actors and voices to drive socially just transitions. I suggest such innovations and disruptions are a prerequisite for effective innovations in technology and for rapid decarbonisation that does not entrench social inequalities (Sovacool et al. 2022). This goes beyond questions of good governance and policy design for sustainability, which imply more incremental realignments of socio-technical systems, and centres instead questions of how to disrupt the dominant political economies that frustrate the possibility of both rapid and just transitions required by the Paris Agreement as well as the Sustainable Development Goals (SDGs).

Not only do incumbent industries resist required changes; the speed and scale of interlinked shifts required also demand simultaneous changes in the larger social order and material base of society. This includes shifts in finance, production and technologies, consumption patterns, infrastructures, governance, social behaviours and culture. It reframes the debate from being one about environmental governance more narrowly conceived and instead centres it as a project of economic transformation: a reset of economic goals, institutions and values and the societies and political systems they create in their guise. Prescriptions for change cannot be formulaic, as it will take different forms around the world, where state capacity, the nature of markets and finance and the form of civil society engagement are diverse and uneven, suggesting the need to consider the scope and inter-relationality of change within an ecosystem of transformation. To complicate matters further, there are few direct historical parallels to turn to for answers about how to realise transformations of this nature. While transitions have occurred in specific sectors or regions that point to the possibility of rapid transitions (Newell and Simms 2020), none have occurred at the speed and scale now required to keep warming below 1.5°C or even 2°C compared with pre-industrial levels (IPCC 2018) nor to live within planetary boundaries. In many ways, therefore, we are in uncharted territory.

Disruptive politics is a crucial dimension of both transitions and more transformative change and deserves more attention compared to the ongoing dominance of work on disruptive technologies and finance. It raises key questions of democracy and accountability which are the focus of Chapter 6. While recognising the central importance of technology and finance in rapid transitions, plugging in alternative technologies or mobilising new flows of finance is unlikely to produce the sorts of accelerated and transformational changes now required without rethinking the purposes for which they are deployed and without generating shifts and realignments in the distribution of political power and influence which keep an unsustainable economic order in place and continue to shape the direction and deployment of that technology and finance. A 'plug-and-play' approach reinforces and reproduces incumbent power: plugging in new technologies or energy sources, for example, but without disrupting the systems in which they are embedded (i.e., the way in which electric cars reproduce systems of auto-mobility where public transport is key), and thereby undermining our collective ability to attend to questions of inclusion and social justice that are prerequisites for lasting and deeper transformations (Newell and Martin 2020). It reduces the challenge to one of technological substitutability rather than shifts in production, consumption and political power. As Pickering et al. (2022: 4) suggest:

> Institutions … are crucial for resolving collective action problems and offering durable frameworks to safeguard societal values such as environmental protection. Yet, paradoxically, the very durability of institutions may present an obstacle for transformation because of the strong path dependency in societies' existing dominant institutions, including states and markets that systematically disregard their environmental impacts. Likewise, prevailing institutions perpetuate inequalities of gender, race and socioeconomic status that are reflected in disparities in access to benefits from social-ecological systems and in exposure to environmental harms.

This highlights the need to go beyond questions of institutional change and governance reform associated with the environmental state. It is about power shifts, expressed in part in a reconfiguration of the state: from an environmental state (which finds expression in the ecological modernisation of existing state structures), or broader transition state which increasingly adopts the goal of transition as a meta-project of statehood but without addressing the underlying drivers of unsustainability, to states of transformation where core state goals, functions and modes of operation are reimagined (see Table 1.1). Going beyond narrow questions of governance and the processes of aligning and steering key actors in critical domains brings us to the deeper politics and social relations which make governing possible and privilege some ways of organising politics over others. Despite recent advances, we continue to lack a deeper theorisation or examination of state practices or a fuller political, sociological or historical treatment of the state in the study and practice of sustainability transitions. This is important because existing governance innovations and incremental policy shifts are clearly not up to the challenge of bringing about transitions at the speed and scale required by the SDGs. This is partly about preventing further technological and infrastructural lock-in given that new projects and infrastructures approved today lock in decades of emissions growth and ecosystem depletion. But it is also about political lock-in and the reproduction of incumbency. Challenging this implies power shifts and more transformative change in the very modus operandi and core functions of the state.

The need for speed and acceleration called for by the IPCC (2018), or the 'code red' warning issued by UN Secretary-General António Guterres, does not just recentre the state; it also changes the conduct of politics. It is scientists, not revolutionaries, calling for 'transformative' and 'systemic' change within the next 10–20 years. But as Naomi Klein (2015) notes, it is unfortunate (to say the least) that at the height of our awareness about the severity of climate change, neoliberal ideology is paramount and governments in many contexts exercise only indirect control over their energy, transport and food systems that need to be transitioned. Hence, at the very time we most need the steering capabilities of states, the power (or perhaps more pertinently, willingness) to intervene has been diminished in many contexts (notwithstanding the glimpse of what state intervention could look like afforded to us by the pandemic). Ignoring, dismissing or dismantling democratic states as the primary arena for the negotiation of sustainable futures threatens to further delay transition and transformation.

Indeed, some of the greatest resistance to more ambitious climate action comes from fossil-fuelled autocratic states not subject to democratic pressures to act more responsibly. China, Russia, Iran, Venezuela and Saudi Arabia have been amongst the most laggard states when it comes to climate action and are, in many instances, actively seeking to delay the energy transition. But even in more established democracies, populist and reactionary groups have brought climate and ecological questions into the so-called culture wars through the spread of fake news and conscious, well-funded and increasingly internationally organised efforts to derail progressive social and environmental causes through front groups and industry-funded 'astro-turf' organisations posing as representatives of concerned publics (Beder 1997; Jacquet 2022).

The perspective developed in this book posits the state as neither an inherently good or bad actor nor an intrinsically captured one but rather as a site of conflict and an arena (one among many) of negotiation and social contestation. It is within the state that the demands of capital and the demands of a broader society produce contingent social frictions across what we broadly consider to be 'the market' (Polanyi 1980 [1944]; Burawoy 2003) apparent in the tension between accumulation and legitimation (Paterson 2010). States in capitalist democracies balance this tension between industry's demands for growth and collective concern for the environmental and social risks generated by that growth through a complex, differentiated and contested state apparatus – one that is not inherently reducible to any particular class or faction but is, at least partially, 'open' to political mobilisation (Prudham and Morris 2006). As Buch Hansen et al. (2024: 79) suggest, while 'the state facilitates the stabilisation and maintenance of the social order via its force, laws, regulations, curricula, resources and its discourses of legitimation … concrete state strategies are the results of the material and symbolic struggles and tensions between social forces within and beyond its institutional borders, which may take the form of contradictions between different state apparatuses and branches'.

The state is best understood then not as one, unitary, rational entity but rather a large web of governance relations and forms of authority, albeit with key foci, nodes and concentrations of power. Key decision-making sites within the state shift constantly as the agenda-setting, law-making and rule-implementing arms of the state respond to the pressure of non-state actors (including private individuals, interest groups and specific firms) as well as the specific political culture of the state (the norms, values and identities of a particular society), outsourcing and delegating governance tasks or extending their authority in new directions. The implications that flow from this view of the state are important for understanding how societies can pursue action across what I call 'ecosystems of transformation'. Ecosystem here refers to interdependencies between multiple pathways to transformation – the intertwined routes to change mobilised by various segments in society, including the financial sector, the productive capacities of the 'real economy', civil society and the state. This provides a more circular and relational understanding of the ecology of change than the hierarchies of levers and agency implied by analysis of 'leverage points' (Meadows 1999) and 'tipping points' (Otto et al. 2020). It affords a more eclectic theory of change as befits the complex political landscape within which responses to sustainability challenges have to be conceived. In some settings, where civic space, a free media and a functioning legal system exist, direct efforts to engage and reform the central state might constitute the key route to change. Elsewhere, targeting cities or businesses directly or working through social movements to amplify voice below or beyond the state forms a more viable option. Questions of strategy and political manoeuvring always have to be guided by a sense of the chain reactions and multiplier and boomerang effects that might be achieved by triggering change in one part of the system in the hope that this leads to change elsewhere, including of course in the state. The windows of opportunity to effect such change are also shaped by political opportunity structures and the shifting 'strategic selectivity' of the state (Jessop 2016).

A more ecosystemic approach also recognises the polycentric and fractal nature of contemporary governance (Ostrom 2010; Gadinger and Scholte 2023; O'Brien et al. 2023). Writing about oil politics in Africa, Phillips (2018: 104) notes 'the links between the sub-national spaces and transnational circuits of resource production somewhat defy a state-based territorial internal-external logic'. More helpful, he suggests, are 'relational understandings of sovereignty' that question 'the presumption that state actors exercise agency in opposition to capital, describing instead conditions of hybrid or shared sovereignty made through the conditions that state and capital place upon one another to commodify resources and enable extraction' (Phillips 2018: 104). Other work on transnational climate governance initiatives shows how sub-state and non-state actors that seek to reduce greenhouse gases (GHGs) have an important role to play in achieving just transitions by plugging governance gaps, creating novel linkages and generating momentum where multilateral efforts to mitigate climate change, biodiversity loss and many other issues are seemingly in gridlock and the current global political landscape far from conducive to ambitious action underpinned by radical innovation and experimentation (Bulkeley et al. 2014). These initiatives include networks of cities committed to climate mitigation, voluntary corporate reduction targets and disclosure processes and efforts to promote nature-based solutions and to rewild key ecosystems. Nevertheless, many scholars continue to emphasise nation-states and intergovernmental organisations as the primary actors capable of orchestrating such transnational governance initiatives. According to one estimate, this strategy accounts for nearly one-third of transnational climate governance initiatives, for example (Hale and Roger 2014). Hence, there is a complex interplay of public and private authority across a muti-level governance system which presents a conceptual challenge for scholars but also reveals multiple entry points for seeding transformative change.

It is also important to reiterate that the state itself is in transition. In its wide variety of geographically and institutionally distinct forms, the state is not a static or universal entity. As part of broader ecosystems of transformation, states are intertwined with changes in technological, productive, financial and social movement arenas which they both create and are affected by. In helping to bring about socio-technical change, the state itself will have to oversee transformations in political institutions and shifts in relations of power. Indeed, histories of energy statecraft (Yergin 1991; Gore 2017) show that particular forms of energy production and infrastructures (Bridge et al. 2018) require, or at times make possible, particular types of politics. For example, nuclear energy requires a more centralised and militarised state. Indeed, concerns around the 'plutonium economy' (Patterson 1984) and the 'nuclear state' (Jungk 1979) required a level of secrecy due to the nature of materials being handled which had the effect of reducing democratic control and crowding out alternative energy imaginaries (Sovacool et al. 2019).

Extending the argument to the materiality of resources and how this shapes statecraft, Mitchell's work on carbon democracy shows how struggles over fossil fuel infrastructures played a defining role in the articulation of social democratic demands on the state (Mitchell 2011), while the relationship between oil and authoritarianism and large bodies of work on the 'resource curse' (Watts 2008; Ross 2012) lend further weight to the notion that all aspects of statecraft are imbued with energy and resource politics. Selby (2022: 338) suggests: 'Oil revenues have fed authoritarianism and militarism – what are often, if somewhat problematically, referred to as "rentier state" dynamics' (see also Beblawi and Luciani 1987). While recognising the materiality of energy sources, it is important here to avoid resource determinism: 'there is no singular model of how hydrocarbon rents affect state-building' (Selby 2022: 339). Indeed, as Phillips et al. (2016: 27) note, 'Through associated policy prescriptions and interventions, the resource curse thesis has power not only as a set of management norms, but as an "economic device" that shapes how resource development is constructed'. In other words, energy shapes, but does not determine or proscribe, state politics. The desire by many states to maintain tight central control over energy systems in particular is seen by some as a form of 'state paternalism'. Szabó and Fabok (2020: 4) suggest: 'energy has been a centralised provision that has been foundational in the state pursuing and disseminating the idea of state paternalism'. Drawing on examples from Hungary and Poland, they suggest this is manifest in 'growing the state's ownership of key energy firms to maintain its paternal role in society' (Szabó and Fabok 2020: 5).

1.3 Just Transitions

Yet, despite growing attention to state transformation in debates about sustainability transitions, the state is often reduced to enabler, regulator and manager of transitions, without sufficient attention to the ways in which the state itself transforms as it attempts to disrupt and manage transformative change in technological and socio-political systems. Choreographing deep structural change on an urgent timeline calls for new distributional and procedural capacities in states to balance, mitigate and manage transition and its impacts across society. Distributional capacities must attend to the spatial and temporal dimensions of just transitions, given that transition initiatives in one community can redistribute risks and benefits in undesirable ways elsewhere in another: both locally and globally, through the uneven distribution of costs and benefits within and between countries (Newell 2021a). Examples include the effect on food security of land grabs driven by the expansion of biofuel consumption and the demand for offset programmes (Fairhead et al. 2012) or scrambles for lithium and cobalt to sustain battery production for increased electrification (Sovacool et al. 2019; Soto Hernandez and Newell 2022). The need for managed and orderly transitions that can attend to some of these intra- and inter-societal injustices speaks to the need for coordinated and sequenced regional and multilateral responses – as proposed for example by advocates of a Fossil Fuel Non-Proliferation Treaty (Newell and Simms 2019) – and the need for the strengthened global governance of just transitions (Newell et al. 2023).

The disruptive and contested nature of transitions can have profound impacts on some social groups (Sovacool et al. 2019), underscoring how transitions can create new vulnerabilities or worsen existing ones if led by dominant incumbent actors and visions (Newell, Sovacool and Geels 2022). Developing the distributional and procedural capacities needed to achieve just transitions requires greater participation and representation from civil society. Civil society operates at the core of 'ecosystems of transformation', often forming the connective tissue across sites and scales of contentious politics and uniquely positioned to pressure public and private sectors to propel forward mutually supportive and virtuous cycles of change around transitions. For instance, divestment pressures can trigger actions in both the public and private sectors, such as institutional investors excluding fossil fuel stocks from their portfolios and governments using procurement programmes to support non-fossil fuel products. These, in turn, can trigger larger shifts in global value chains, rendering fossil fuel leases 'stranded assets'. Civil society can also hold the public and private sectors to account in pursuing desired justice-oriented outcomes (Newell 2008b).

This raises the question of what constitutes legitimate participation in decision-making and who has a right to a seat at the decision-making table: a key challenge for the democratic state explored in Chapter 6. Strengthening procedural justice (fairness in decision-making) requires opening up what are often considered the domains of experts, bureaucrats and elected representatives to civil society, including lay people and those who represent groups historically denied adequate representation, or who will be disproportionately impacted by environmental change (such as Indigenous groups). More challengingly perhaps, this means creating de facto representation for future generations through governance innovations such as ombudspeople for future generations. Strengthening procedural justice also means ensuring basic protections for civil society, a significant challenge in the face of diminishing civic space (ICNL 2020). A civil society that is capable of autonomous action and provides subordinate groups the possibility of collective action lies at the core of democratic governance (Evans and Heller 2015). This, in turn, requires effective electoral competition to hold those who control the state accountable to electoral majorities. It also assumes basic rights to speech and social movement organising, which have come under attack in the face of attempts to delegitimise and criminalise protest movements (Brock et al. 2018).

1.4 Structure of the Book

The remainder of the book is organised as follows. Chapter 2 explores a range of theoretical and conceptual resources for making sense of the state, with an accent on those most relevant to the role of the state in sustainability transitions. It first looks at how the state has been addressed to date in literatures on socio-technical transitions, before assessing broader analysis of the 'environmental' and 'green state' which helps to understand the potential and limits of a transition state and scope for more transformative state-led change. Finally, it draws on conceptualisations in disciplines as diverse as politics and political theory, political economy and international relations, geography, sociology and development studies which can be combined to provide a more multifaceted, historical, global and sociological and political account of the state in all its dimensions as they relate to the challenge of sustainability transitions. Thereafter, the book is structured around key aspects and dimensions of state power: the entrepreneurial state, the industrial state, the military state, the democratic state, the welfare state and the global state.

The choice of which aspects of the state to focus on reflects a conscious effort to foreground neglected dimensions of state power and practice which I argue are critical to appreciating both the potential and the limitations of the state as an effective and inclusive agent of change in accelerating just transitions and broader transformational change. I start with those aspects of the state that have received most attention in transition studies. Chapter 3 looks at the entrepreneurial state where the bulk of transitions scholarship has focussed to date. Chapter 4 looks at the industrial state and the ways in which state strategies for managing the economy through industrial policy, tax and regulation have a significant bearing on sustainability transitions. This includes a discussion of the developmental state as one approach to securing the aims of the industrial state. Chapter 5 then moves on to the military state whose activities, power and influence over techno-imaginaries, resources and the ecological impacts it generates make it a central yet problematic actor in the politics of transitions. Chapter 6 analyses the democratic state, increasingly under strain from populist movements and the intensity and scale of challenges presented by the polycrisis but critical to including diverse citizen voices in transition pathways. Chapter 7 then explores the neglected role of the welfare state in providing social protection and advancing just transitions both within and between states. Chapter 8 goes beyond the national context to explore the global state: the state's uneven imbrication in global networks, institutions and relations of power which shape and reshape transition pathways, currently inadequately captured by their categorisation in the transition literature as 'landscape' factors. I then conclude with overall reflections on future directions for the transition state and its potential successor as part of a project of 'reimagining the state' as a facilitator of more transformational change.

Of course, there are many other dimensions or typologies or categories of state which, though discussed in the book, could easily have warranted standalone chapters in their own right. These include, for example, the 'regulatory state' (Majone 1994; Pildes and Sunstein 1995; Moran 2002): an idea developed in a European context but subsequently applied elsewhere (Dubash and Morgan 2012). This focusses on competition law, the redefinition of the state in the wake of privatisation and centring regulation as a distinctive mode of state intervention in the economy and society. Discussion of the 'developmental state' meanwhile is subsumed under the chapter on the industrial state but equally could warrant deeper enquiry since it is clear that proactive developmental states will be required to radically reorient economic development pathways towards sustainability. Each of these are covered in different chapters rather than analysed as standalone 'state functions'. It is also the case that these aspects of state power analysed distinctly here are, in practice, deeply intertwined. Whether it is the overlap between the military and industrial state, captured in the notion of the military-industrial complex, or the 'military welfare state' (Mittelstadt 2015), or imperatives to democratise the entrepreneurial state or to pursue 'democratic defence' (Tatchell 1985), different state functions overlap, collide and converge in response to the multifaceted nature of the policy challenges they seek to address and the nature of the networks which run through the state, transgressing these distinct functions. This presents both analytical challenges for an adequate understanding of the transition state and its potential successor but also increased opportunities to intervene and reshape the ecosystem of transformation to generate positive change. It is to the conceptual and analytical challenge of understanding the state that we now turn our attention.

2

Theorising the State and Transitions

As we have seen in Chapter 1, the state increasingly features in policy discussions and political debates about sustainability transitions. Yet, in the academic literature on this subject, the state is often treated either abstractly in more theoretical accounts or superficially and atheoretically in more empirically driven analysis. This often results in analysis which ends up being apolitical (analysing the performance of managerial and governance functions over deeper relations of power and politics), asocial (separated from the social relations in which the state is both imbued and reproduces), ahistorical (without reference to the historical constitution and changing forms of state power over time) and amaterial (in abstraction from the ecologies and resources that sustain it), each of which, for different reasons, is problematic.

One of the key purposes of the book is to start to begin to remedy that situation. This chapter first outlines some of the ways in which current literatures on transitions address the state. It then explores insights and debates from broader bodies of scholarship on sustainability as they relate to the state, before turning to theories of the state from different theoretical and disciplinary traditions including political theory, political economy, sociology and geography. From there, the chapter seeks to build a more rounded, multidimensional and adequate theory of the *transition state* and the prospects of it playing a more enabling role as an actor, *primus inter pares*, supporting states of transformation.

2.1 The State in Literature on Socio-technical Transitions

Within debates on transitions the state appears in a number of different guises: as barrier, innovator, visionary, incumbent, hegemon, leader and laggard. Thinking about the state's role in transition scholarship (Meadowcroft 2011; Andrews-Speed 2016; Kuzemko et al. 2016; Lockwood et al. 2017) ranges from transition management approaches (Loorbach et al. 2015) to work on the governance of transitions

(Verbong and Loorbach 2012) and work on specific state functions in relation to transitions, such as the entrepreneurial state (Mazzucato 2011), the use of industrial policy (Altenburg and Pegels 2012; Pegels 2014) and to a lesser degree the welfare state (Koch 2022). Alongside this, there is interest in the role of the state in broader 'green transformations' (Barry 2012; Scoones et al. 2015; Avelino et al. 2016; Hausknost and Hammond 2021) including most ambitiously in projects of degrowth (Buch Hansen et al. 2024).

But there continues to be a neglect of more systematic and comparative thinking about the relationship between distinct forms of state and statehood and different approaches to transition and transformation. As Koch (2021: 123) notes, 'the transformational change literature has as yet hardly engaged with the possible role of the state'. This is notwithstanding important inroads from scholarship focussed more narrowly on transitions. Transition scholars have explored how the types and depth of democracy produce different types of pathways, for example (Johnstone and Stirling 2020); as well as the role of electoral and party systems and specific policy processes and styles of decision-making (Kern and Rogge 2018), through to different political economies constituted by an array of state–society complexes captured in part by the notion of varieties of capitalism (VoC) (Ćetković and Buzogány 2016; Benney 2019) and the politics of which states are best able to accelerate transitions (Roberts et al. 2018). As Argyriou and Barry (2021: 3) note, however, the VoC literature tends to reflect a form of 'rational choice institutionalism' whereby different varieties of capitalism 'produce policy landscapes dictated by the specificities of their institutional configuration', rather than capture the broader alignments of social forces which make change possible, and often provide a nationally constrained account of the basis of comparative advantage which obscures its historical and global constitution.

The role of the state has also been discussed more narrowly in predominantly economic approaches to sustainability. Here the emphasis is on the role of the state in enforcing property rights, establishing pricing mechanisms and articulating minimum standards, frequently reduced to its role in enabling the 'smooth' operation of markets, where a theory of the state tends to be implied rather than articulated (Stern 2006). Instead, a set of normative recommendations are proffered about what a 'night watchman' state should do to achieve 'optimal policy outcomes' (Mabey et al. 1997) assumed to be achieved by facilitating the functioning of a notionally self-regulating market. Neo-institutional and evolutionary economics approaches, meanwhile, allow for a greater appreciation of the active and potentially positive role of the state in shaping policy outcomes (Foray et al. 2012; Mazzucato 2015; Jacobs and Mazzucato 2016), while stopping short of analysis of the social bases of state power and how this affects the strategic selections that states make with regard to policies and priorities (Jessop 2008).

The state is also being brought back through the renewed attention to 'industrial policy' where the state plays a more active role in directing policy instruments towards addressing 'market' and 'coordination' failures as part of a more long-term strategy to support industry (Stiglitz et al. 2013; Pegels 2014; Pegels and Lütkenhorst 2014). In many renditions, 'the state is typically portrayed as a progressive, collaborative, "facilitator-stimulator-controller-director" of the transition management process' (Lawhon and Murphy 2012: 359), overlooking the more malign and predatory exercises of state power expressed through policing, prisons, militarism and the closing of civic space, for example, which are explored later in the book.

More attentive to questions of power, increasing attention is being paid to questions of incumbency (including 'deep incumbency') and the role of elites in transitions, often subsumed under the broader umbrella of 'regime resistance', as well as questions of regime destabilisation, disruption and discontinuity (Turnheim and Geels 2012; Geels 2014; Johnstone and Stirling 2015; Johnstone and Kivimaa 2018; Kivimaa et al. 2021). The notion of a regime in studies of socio-technical transitions is not reducible to the state, though the state is often assumed to be a central arena for both contesting dominant regimes and socio-technical configurations and accommodating threats to them. Insights from historical institutionalism, meanwhile, show how path dependencies and institutional lock-in can frustrate the pace of change (Lockwood et al. 2016). Early work on the multi-level perspective (MLP), which predominates in the study of transitions, incorporated a conception of power in which individual and collective actors with 'conflicting goals and interests' bring about change through 'conflicts, power struggles, contestations, lobbying, coalition building and bargaining' (Geels and Schot 2007: 415), but falls short of providing the theoretical resources to advance such an account of the exercise and bases of that power.

In order to understand the politics of sustainability transitions, scholars have instead focussed on explaining specific strategies and effects of power on the policymaking process. To do this, they have drawn on a range of policy process theories such as advocacy coalitions theory (Markard et al. 2016), a policy networks approach (Normann 2015, 2017), a political coalitions framework (Hess 2014, 2019), historical institutionalism (Lockwood et al. 2017; Roberts and Geels 2019), Bordieuan insights (Husu 2022) and discursive politics (Kern 2012; Bosman et al. 2014). These bodies of work seek to account for the policy process through reference to the role of coalitions and networks and feedbacks, for example; in other words, *how* policy is made (or networks formed around a particular discourse, for example). The emphasis is more on specific manifestations (feedbacks) or strategies of power (coalitions and networks) than explaining the basis and (deeper) nature of state power: how, *in spite of* different policy styles, policy arenas, varieties of capitalism and so on, common power dynamics are discernible that warrant the type of conceptualisation I propose here. Dominant approaches, it has been suggested, reflect the epistemological roots of transition scholarship in science and technology studies 'that essentially conceive of the state as a homogenous, undifferentiated and non-conflictual "landscape" influence' (Argyriou and Barry 2021: 3).

Indeed, many assumptions are made and not scrutinised. In particular, the explanations for observed patterns of influence are often underdeveloped. It is one thing to note the mobilisation of bias, structured and privileged patterns of access or the activation of veto points in political systems. It is another to furnish an explanation of the power relations that make such outcomes both possible and likely. In this regard, Swilling et al. (2016) develop the idea of a 'socio-political regime' to advance existing typologies of politics in sustainability transitions which has four dimensions. The first is 'how power relations are arranged and reproduced within the regime, that is, how political power is constituted, distributed and maintained by those who have power' (Swilling et al. 2016: 656), especially the governing party and its allies within and outside government. The second is the 'underlying policy paradigm': the beliefs which shape the way policy problems are understood by 'actors engaged in the everyday business of politics' (Swilling et al. 2016: 656). The third is 'the way government and state institutions are organized and operated', which reflects the power relations, 'but without them being entirely determined by these power relations' (Swilling et al. 2016: 656). Finally, there are the policies themselves which are debated and adopted by policy actors 'within a given socio-political regime' (Swilling et al. 2016: 656). This typology, linking policies and paradigms to the organisation of institutions and the distribution of power, moves beyond the narrower focus on governance.

But where an account of the socio-political moves us forward, lack of attention to the economic sphere limits its explanatory value in relation to transition processes which inevitably need to disrupt and realign economies and the social relations which they reflect, uphold and benefit. Moreover, while attention to policy, the organisation of the executive and the role of the governing party is important, this constitutes just one aspect of what the state does and stops short of providing an account of the social relations underpinning the state which find expression through its practices of power across multiple domains, beyond those that have attracted most attention by transition scholars to date. Most accounts fail to furnish an explanation for how and why states behave the way they do, and how different components and functions of the state compete and collide, less still with regard to multifaceted processes of transition with which we are concerned here. Efforts by transition scholars such as Geels (2014) and Avelino (Avelino and Romans 2009, 2011; Avelino and Wittmayer 2015; Avelino 2017) have sought to articulate different dimensions of power, while not proffering a deeper account of the state. Although much of this work is focussed on particular sites and strategies of resistance to socio-technical change, there have been attempts to draw on more critical social and political accounts of state power (Johnstone and Newell 2018; Ford and Newell 2021) by emphasising the importance of hegemony and a relational understanding of the state. These provide a more helpful analytical entry point, I will argue, for a fuller, more historical, relational, global, geographical, social and ecological account of the role of the state in transitions. The fact that 'transitions scholars have largely shied away from explicitly integrating state theory in the analytical frameworks that guide empirical work' (Silvester and Fiske 2023: 1) suggests such an account is still very much required.

2.2 The Environmental and Green State

While under-conceptualised in the transition literature in the ways described in Section 2.1, the state figures centrally in debates within environmental and green political theory regarding the prospects and possibilities of a move towards an ecological, 'Green' or post-capitalist society (Eckersley 2004; Newell 2019): a bolder and more ambitious project than the reconfiguration of socio-technical regimes and construction of a transition state. This is true across the spectrum of environmental and Green political thought from anarchist traditions (Kropotkin 2022 [1955]; Bookchin 1980; Bahro 1986) which advocate stateless self-governing communities, to long-standing commitments to decentralisation of the state and subsidiarity, through to the multi-level or transnational eco or environmental state (Barry 1999; Eckersley 2004; Meadowcroft 2004; Death 2016; Bäckstrand and Kronsell 2015; Hausknost and Hammond 2021).

Depending on which version of Green politics is drawn upon, the state is viewed, variously, as too large, too small, too captured and compromised by incumbent actors, elites and classes, or too exploitative, violent or hierarchical and bureaucratic. For some, it represents too large and distant an institution to build an ecological society, especially one that aspires to have grassroots democracy at its heart. Yet, for others, it is too small a unit to deal with ecological challenges (Ophuls 1973). This concern lies behind proposals for a transnational ecological state (Eckersley 2004). Alongside the issue of the scale and centralisation of state power is the question of whether the enforcement and coercive powers of the state can (or should) be used for the achievement of a sustainable society, eliciting punishments, fines and imprisonment for unsustainable behaviour by corporations and individuals, suspending freedoms and civil liberties where 'freedoms to' (travel, trade) have an impact on 'freedoms from' (environmental degradation, ill health, poverty) for others.

A similar degree of 'anarchic splendour' is attributed to political ecology and the multitudinous ways in which it conceives of the state (Bryant 2015). Despite some important contributions to understanding 'the political ecologies of the modern state' (Whitehead et al. 2008), political ecology's treatment of the state is ambiguous, despite the fact, as Loftus (2020: 140) suggests, 'With most environmental regulation being traced back to the state, and with the relations embodied within the state appearing central to a variety of environmental conflicts, it seems crucial to take this "actor", this "scale", this "relation" or this "institutional form" seriously'. He further highlights that while some path-breaking works on political ecology 'afford the state a central role in environmental decision-making' there are many 'inadequacies' when it comes to 'questions of policy and when it comes to interpretations of the instruments of the state' in particular in relation to 'how state power functions' (Loftus 2020: 139). In his application of insights from political ecology scholarship to transitions, Sovacool (2021) identifies four key processes: enclosure (capture of land or resources), exclusion (unfair planning), encroachment (destruction of the environment) and entrenchment (worsening of inequality or vulnerability), all of which implicate or centre the state.

The 'environmental state', meanwhile, has attracted significant interest from scholars of environmental governance. It refers to 'a state that possesses a significant set of institutions and practices dedicated to the management of the environment and societal-environmental interactions … [with] specialised administrative, regulatory, financial and knowledge structures that mark out a distinctive sphere of government activity' (Duit et al. 2016: 5–6). It is far from clear, however, that 'a sustainability transformation could follow from an intensification or enhancement of the strategy of ecological modernisation that is inherent to the environmental state' (Hausknost and Hammond 2021: 6). The slow 'greening' of different parts of the state in so far as, and as long as, they can be rendered compatible with modernist visions of development is clearly not of a speed, scale or depth as to be proportionate to the transformative interventions societies are now called upon to undertake. Indeed, existing patterns and practices of state authority may be incompatible with such shifts – a theme to which we will return throughout the book. It would be unsurprising to scholars of critical political economy that when the material and productive base of the economy changes, the social relations and institutional arrangements they give rise to also undergo change as power shifts and that the dominant ideas that currently reflect and reify a growth-based economy of abundance will also have to be transformed around an alternative notion of the good life. This might include, for example, efforts to sever the chord which binds economic growth to state legitimation by advancing dematerialised notions of prosperity (Jackson 2011). As Hammond and Hausknost (2021: x) put it: 'If the very structure and apparatus of environmental governance – the environmental state – is locked into an unsustainable productivist, growth-based trajectory, how can the urgently needed "Great Transformation" of modern societies come about?' The issue here is not just capitalism's inability to adequately deal with ecological crisis but the tensions inherent in growth-oriented industrial systems whether socialist or capitalist (Newell 2019; Hickel 2020). Hence, from many critical Green perspectives, a centralising, extractivist growth-oriented state is part of the problem and a key obstacle to the prospects of more radical and progressive transitions.

Given the clear limits to the environmental state's ability to manage these tensions and contradictions in the long term, the notion then that a more fully fledged 'Green state' is an oxymoron is perhaps unsurprising given that, historically speaking, core state imperatives include defence of state territory and sovereignty, the pursuit of national security through military means and the exploitation of economic resources for development, defined narrowly as economic growth (themes we return to in Chapters 4 and 5 on the industrial and military state). The state, in this rendition, is a primary driver of unsustainability and a prima facie barrier, therefore, to the achievement of a sustainable society. It is seen as the embodiment of 'materialism, institutionalized violence, centralization, hierarchy' (Porritt 1989: 216–217). Many more critical accounts seek explicitly to move beyond the state because of its destructive potential to destroy humanity whether through the 'industrialisation of war' (Hoffman 1995) or as a function of the ecocidal tendencies of the state (Dunlap and Brock 2022).

Historically speaking, as Conca (2005: 181) notes: 'The emergence of the centralising, industrialising, national state, with its capacity to centralise decision-making, concentrate capital, strip local communities of their historical property rights in nature, supply coercive power and protect elite interests, has been a key social innovation along the road to global planetary peril.' Indeed, allocating and defending property rights, intrinsic to liberal Lockean notions of the state and, as noted, more economistic understandings of the state, is also a prerequisite for the functioning of capitalism and extractivism. When combined with the policing of territories, duties and responsibilities between nations and citizens and non-citizens along insider/outsider lines (Walker 1993), the basis for resource competition and unsustainable patterns of development can be clearly deciphered. The centralisation of state authority is crucial to this. Historically, as Marx and Engels (1988 [1848]: 4) note, the bourgeoisie has

> agglomerated population, centralized the means of production, and has concentrated property in a few hands. The necessary consequence of this was political centralization. Independent, or but loosely connected provinces, with separate interests, laws, governments, and systems of taxation, became lumped together into one nation, with one government, one code of laws, one national class interest, one frontier, and one customs tariff.

Lane and Lane (1976: 58) suggest similar dynamics pertain to socialist states in their account, *The Socialist Industrial State*, where, 'The value system of an industrial system puts great emphasis on the instrumentality of work, a striving for a mastery of the environment, for individual enhancement and status differentiation. Large scale production required central planning, state control and greater power to technocrats at plant level.'

Beyond these questions of scale and the design of the state, a related question is whether the problem of unsustainability is one of a lack of state capacity and resources, as opposed to more structural constraints, or political interest in securing a transition to a more secure and ecologically sustainable future. This raises the question not only of whether the state alone has the power, authority and resources to bring about the transitions so urgently required but also of whether it has the autonomy of action and political interest in pursuing and accelerating deeper transformations towards sustainability and away from an economy organised in ways which often enrich state elites and their class allies in society. While political borders, organised along sovereign lines, make little sense ecologically, and provide a poor starting point for envisaging forms of political community that best respond to the needs of global publics and the notion of a global common good, there are scholars willing to counter this view in proposing that sovereignty can be a force for good. Eckersley (2004: 232–233) suggests, for example:

> [T]he territorial dimension of sovereignty might be made to work *for* the environment insofar as it might enable political communities to resist certain aspects of economic globalization or to censure and possibly halt practices in other states that threaten to undermine domestic ecosystem integrity. In these circumstances at least, territorial sovereignty – including self-determination and the associated principle of non-intervention – can serve as a bulwark against anti-ecological practices that encroach upon the territory and policy-making powers of particular nation-states.

Indeed, in relation to transitions, the ability of (some) states and regional blocs (such as the EU) to protect ambitious transition plans (such as the European Green Deal) rests on their ability to defend a territorially defined economic and political community from competitors imposing less ambitious environmental requirements on their firms through, for example, trade measures such as the EU's Carbon-Border Adjustment Mechanism (CBAM) that discriminates against carbon-intensive imports from other states and regions.

For Dryzek (1992), it is when capitalism, liberal democracy and the administrative state work together that environmental crises are compounded, inhibiting the prospects of more transformational change. Indeed, there is often a mismatch between the level at which ecological contradictions are generated (based on the growth imperative of globalised capital accumulation embodied in the functioning of the industrial state) and the level at which political responsibility and crisis management is allocated (the democratic state and to a lesser extent the global state through global managerialism), though often then passed down to individuals. Following this logic:

> [W]ithout a transformation in the role and functions of the liberal capitalist state and capitalist society, the contradictory requirements of legitimation and accumulation cannot be solved (as distinct from politically managed) by changes in the policy tools, policy setting, and even the hierarchy of policy goals. It is the character of the system (the mutual dependencies of the capitalist economy and the liberal capitalist state) that set limits to the effectiveness of such state interventions. (Eckersley 2004: 81)

This critical account of the prospects of state-led sustainability transitions underscores the need to engage with the multifunctionality of states and their deep embeddedness in broader structures of social power if we are to articulate theories of change and pursue strategies that will bring about lasting change. In this understanding, the democratic and industrial state take centre stage, but I will argue in this book that their interplay with many other state functions also demand our attention. This requires a more nuanced account of and engagement with the plurality in state forms and the very different contexts in which they function and the uneven scope for their reform.

This brings us to the diverse geographies and political economies of statehood and the question of which state we are talking about. The European focus that characterised many early studies of environmental policy and socio-technical transitions makes assumptions about a well-resourced, functioning, autonomous state able to act independently of private or foreign actors (Power et al. 2016; Johnstone and Newell 2018). This is not a description that adequately accounts for the reality faced by many states in the Global South where, perhaps more so than in other areas of the world, any greening of the state would have to be supported, or at least tolerated, by a range of other internal and external actors upon which it is dependent for political and financial support (Death 2016). It is not for nothing then that much of the early work on ecological modernisation drew from Northern European examples and was criticised for being Eurocentric, even if subsequent work sought to broaden the geographical focus (Weale 1992; Mol et al. 2010; Bailey et al. 2011). States are embedded within a wide variety of political economies and models of more or less state-based capitalism such that there is significant variation in the role different models of political economy are likely, or even able, to play in sustainability transitions (Ćetković and Buzogány 2016). This has implications in terms of state capacity, autonomy and willingness to support transitions, let alone deeper transformational change where shifting alignments of social forces will also be necessary.

Beyond these spatial and regional differences, a related common conceptual and political challenge is the constitution of public and private and the assumed separation between the political and economic functions of the state in its democratic (and non-democratic) and industrial guises. The state is often associated with governance of the public realm. And yet in reality there is a blurring of the public and the private in ways that elude conceptual abstractions and distinctions between public and private (Saurin 2001). State control over natural resources and systems of service provision across sectors such as water, forests, energy and transport exists on a spectrum from full to partial ownership, and even where private responsibility ultimately rests with the state, raising a series of tensions and contradictions with regard to the state's role in sustainability transitions outlined in Chapter 1. We can see this blurring of public and private power clearly in the experience of botched and partial water privatisations around the world which in all instances rely on combinations of state resources and authority (Bakker 2010). Likewise, given the abundance, centrality and power of state-owned enterprises (SOEs) in the energy sector, distinctions between producer, regulator and manager are fragile at best and checks and balances between these functions are often weak to non-existent even when they do not function as 'vessels of rent-seeking interests' (Nem Singh and Chen 2017: 1077). Reflecting on energy transitions in South Africa, Hochstetler shows how the energy major 'Eskom was treated quite generously with little meaningful oversight for years' despite its poor performance because of 'Eskom's central role in directing rents to the Zuma government and its allies' (Hochstetler 2021: 120). Likewise, the environmental and social performance of SOEs is often less subject to critical scrutiny in many settings, even in the face of widespread local protests about their harmful effects (O'Rourke 2004; Newell 2005).

Appreciating the peculiarities of particular constellations of public and private power is crucial to critiques of contemporary and historical forms of statehood and state practices and alternative envisionings of the state. This helps to discern what is fixed, universal and given about the characteristics and functioning of states and what can be reversed and reformed in other historical, regional, political and economic circumstances. Looked at in this way, we can repose the question as one about a plurality of state forms and forms of statehood rather than in terms of the characteristics we attach to a supposedly monolithic and universal state form and a tendency to 'fetishise' particular state formations. This reflects criticism of much of the scholarship on the environmental and green state, that it has 'largely been developed from normative ideas about what states ought to be while paying less attention to what states are and how they work' (Silvester and Fiske 2023: 3).

2.3 Theories of the State

> The state is a complex phenomenon and no single theory or theoretical perspective can fully capture and explain its complexities. (Jessop 2008: 1)

Without engaging in a systematic or exhaustive review of literature on the state which would take many volumes, let alone multiple chapters of this book, and where existing scholarship covers many of the key bases (Jessop 1990, 2008, 2016; Eckersley 2004; Death 2016), here I review selectively bodies of work and theoretical perspectives that I argue provide useful analytical insights regarding the role of the state in enabling and frustrating both transitions and deeper transformations towards sustainability. This reflects my view, building on the quote at the start of this section from Bob Jessop, that there is no single theory that adequately accounts for all dimensions of state power, less still the ways in which they interrelate with questions of sustainability. Each chapter introduces and engages with literatures directly relevant to the aspect of state power in question (innovation, industrial, military, democracy, welfare and foreign policy). These theoretical resources come from different strands of political science, political theory and sociology, comparative politics and political economy, geography, development studies and international relations. They help to generate required insights respectively regarding the global politics of statehood and how these are shaped by international relations, the geographies and ecologies of statehood in a highly unequal and uneven global system and the social and institutional bases of state power and authority across varieties of capitalism.

Political theories from more liberal, marxist, constructivist, feminist, anarchist, green and decolonial traditions have each explored the question of state power – its sources, manifestations and problems – in different ways. With the exception of Green political thought as noted earlier, however, very few theories explore the implications of their account of the state for sustainability transitions broadly conceived. Where Feminist, Anarchist and Marxist scholarship overlaps with Green political thought, there is greater engagement as noted earlier (Pepper 1995; Shiva 1998; Dunlap and Brock 2022) and Indigenous scholarship rightly centres the state's role in extractivist development and the denial of citizenship that this often implies for Indigenous communities (Yashar 2005; Gilio-Whitaker 2019). But I agree with Quastel's (2016: 337) observation about political economy accounts that 'Most approaches posit a capitalist economy freely exploiting resources and waste-sinks. Yet these leave out many societal forces that can and do shift the law and regulations that shape the commodification of nature.' Hence 'EPE [Ecological Political Economy] needs a theory of transition – how we move from the present to more desired futures' (Quastel 2016: 337). This indeed is the line of critique leading transition scholar Frank Geels pursues of political economy approaches to transition: that they are 'too grand, abstract and distanced from the experiences of real world actors in particular production-consumption systems' (Geels 2024: 8). Leaving aside the numerous contributions from political economy scholars engaging precisely with the details of those systems (Baker et al. 2014; Argyriou and

Barry 2021), it is also notable that narrowing the criteria for assessing the value of approaches to theorising transitions only to those able to account for change 'in the next few years' not only forecloses approaches interested in transforming the capitalist system and cultural values as he acknowledges but is misplaced given what we know from transition studies about the temporality of transitions and the often slow pace at which values and institutions change, infrastructures are repurposed and political power is reconfigured.

Here, I briefly and selectively review different strands of classic state theory in relation to their relevance to transition debates. I follow Jessop's sentiment that 'the aim of state theory should be to demystify the state' and that 'the state is a complex and polymorphous reality that is best analysed from several entry points and standpoints rather than by focusing one-sidedly on just one of its elements and possible crystallizations' (Jessop 2016: 51). Given the emphasis in this book on questions of power and transformation, classic understandings of the liberal state and its claimed separation of the economy (often reduced to 'the market') from politics and the sphere of collective decision-making provide a partial and limited account of the reality of state power. Constructions of the former as a place of neutral exchange elide the social and power inequalities which produce unsustainability and social injustice as a matter of course while erasing the question of agency which is a precondition for assessing the prospects of transformative change. Naturalising the alleged separation of state and market also de-historicises the social struggles that have assembled and dissembled, dis-embedded and re-embedded the economy within broader frameworks of collective social control and democratic oversight (Polanyi 1980 [1944]) which are once again required to realign the economic system with the imperatives of a liveable planet. Such moves challenge the theoretical structural separation in capitalism between processes of production and wealth creation from the political processes of exercising coercive power and administrative control (Koch 2021: 117) through the use of law, the allocation and enforcement of property rights and other means to create 'equivalence' between capitalists.

The same is true of the separation of the state from the society in which it exists but also creates in its guise. As Jessop (2008: 1) suggests, 'there can be no adequate theory of the state without a theory of society' since the former is embedded within a broader ensemble of social relations and itself constitutes a social relation (Poulantzas 1978). This is an argument against the fetishisation of the institutional functions and practices of the state and a preoccupation with governance as opposed to relations of power which transgress the state even if they are crystallised within it (Mann 1986). More sociological accounts such as Badie and Birnbaum's (1979) book *The Sociology of the State* build an account drawing on Marx, Durkheim and Weber to explore the state, society and culture as well as the role of bureaucracies and civil societies. Though Giddens (1994) is critical of Weber for defining the state 'in such a way as to make it difficult to distinguish some of the specific characteristics of the nation-state' (Giddens 1994: 116), at the same time he seems to argue the opposite: 'All states are pyramids of power; there is no point in differentiating between them in terms of their specific qualities or characteristics' (Giddens 1994: 118; see also Giddens 1985). Some accounts fuse insights from different theoretical accounts grounded in Foucauldian and Marxian analysis, for example relating notions of 'biopower' and the power of capital to the ethnographies of particular 'energopolitics' (Boyer 2019), highlighting the importance of uncovering how particular socio-technical imaginaries – the 'collectively imagined forms of social life and social order reflected in the design and fulfilment of nation-specific scientific and/or technological projects' (Jasanoff and Kim 2009: 120) – circulate and land in particular places.

For many Marxist scholars (Miliband 1973; Jessop 2002) the state is a key site in the struggle between capital and labour where in Marx and Engels' classic formulation the 'The executive of the modern state is but a committee for managing the common affairs of the whole bourgeoisie' (1998 [1848]: 2). In some renditions, the state is reduced to an instrument of power without independent autonomy of action. Robinson (2004: 98) suggests: 'States do not do anything per se. Social classes and groups acting in and out of states (and other institutions) do things as collective historical agents. State apparatuses are those instruments that enforce and reproduce the class and social group relations and practices embedded in states.' Such accounts, as Quastel (2016: 339) notes, focus on 'capitalism as an economic system rather than as coupled to a social system and the state. This implies that the state remains subordinate to, or controlled by, capitalist firms rather than also being open to influence by civil society or other forces.' In Gramsci's understanding of the 'integral state', however, the 'State = political society + civil society' (Gramsci 1971: 263). Jessop evolves the Gramscian definition of the integral state to 'government + governance in the shadow of hierarchy' thereby shifting attention 'from the state as a juridico-political apparatus towards the modalities of the exercise of state power' (Jessop 2016: 176). Yet there is a tension between the conception of the state apparatus as an institutional ensemble (Jessop 1990) and Gramsci's broader conception of the integral state as a terrain of contestation (Silvester and Fiske 2023).

The key point here is that key 'contradictions are not only internal to capitalism, but also stem from how capitalist economies relate to other societal sub-systems' (Quastel 2016: 345). In ways which resonate with neo-Marxist regulation theory's emphasis on how 'sustainability is a new way capitalist institutions move to contain and manage capitalism's contradictions to secure accumulation and prevent a crisis' (Quastel 2016: 342), I explore in the book the multiple ways in which states seek to manage and accommodate tensions between accumulation and legitimation imperatives (Habermas 1975; Paterson 2010). Akin to what Regulation School theorists refer to as the 'mode of regulation' required to stabilise and socialise a regime of accumulation (Aglietta 2000), Jessop suggests 'institutional fixes' are provided by law, policy and other institutions to provide a temporary, partial and relatively stable solution to regulatory crises and dilemmas (Jessop 2008). These operate as 'an ensemble of socially embedded, socially regularized and strategically selective institutions, organisations, social forces and actions organised around (or at least involved in) the expanded reproduction of capital as a social relation' (Jessop 2002: 5).

Such approaches help move us beyond abstract discussions of state functions and towards questions of strategy and agency: 'not so much a theory of the state as it is a theory of state power, how it is exercised, how it succeeds, and how it fails' (Silvester and Fiske 2023: 3). The focus on praxis and analysing particular sites and manifestations of state power across functions and diverse geographies moves beyond methodological nationalism because it quickly becomes apparent that the seemingly bounded nature of state autonomy and the power relations which enable and circumscribe state strategies are often a function of deeper social relations of class, race and gender which the state condenses and crystallises at particular moments through procedural and distributional choices (strategic selectivity), but which are not contained by the state and play a critical role in understanding the prospects of transformative change. Hence although hegemonic historic blocs are those which succeed in consolidating a historically contingent and 'unstable equilibrium of compromise among different social forces around a given economic, political and social order' (Jessop 2002: 6), their very contingency in the face of shifting circumstances that the state encounters and the precarious political work of securing and maintaining compromises and social compacts across diverse and conflictual actors is generative of openings for change.

Each of the subsequent chapters of the book is organised in this way: starting with a discussion of a key aspect of state power, exploring its practices and politics in relation to sustainability transitions, before concluding with a discussion of transformational possibilities. The latter aspect, in particular, requires attention to the way in which the state itself is in transition, subject to shifting alignments of power and configurations of social forces which can both frustrate and enable radical change. As Poulantzas (1978) and others argue, social classes and forces compete to represent and advance their own interests (often seeking to present them as collective ones) and the role of the state is to stabilise these social relations and manage conflict between groups, suggesting a greater degree of both autonomy and agency, simultaneously 'structured' and 'structuring' (Bourdieu 2014). Building on the notion that the state is a social relation (and not just an instrument or subject) reflecting dominant relations of production, Poulantzas (1978: 40) argues, for example, that the state 'concentrates, condenses, materializes and incarnates politico-ideological relations in a form specific to the given mode of production'. It seeks to give form and unity to this ensemble and is not, therefore, a 'mere assembly of detachable parts' (Poulantzas 1978: 136) guided by the imperative to organise the bourgeoisie as the dominant class. This means the state is

> a strategic field and process of intersecting power networks … traversed by tactics which are often highly explicit at the restricted level of their inscription in the state: they intersect and conflict with one another, finding their targets in some apparatuses or being short-circuited by others, and eventually map out that general line of force, the state's policy, which traverses confrontations within the state. (Poulantzas 1978: 136)

How does this inform sustainability transitions? Historically, Abramsky (2010: 10) notes '[s]truggles for control of energy (broadly along the lines of interstate, interfirm, and inter (and intra) class struggles) have had a crucial impact on the historical development of capitalism as a global set of social relations'. For this reason, '[a] discussion of energy cannot be separated from a discussion of capitalism, crisis and class struggle' (Abramsky 2010: 11) such that 'the transition process to a new energy system is, in effect, the next round of global class struggle over control of the means of production and subsistence' (Abramsky 2010: 10), in which, following the logic of such an analysis, the state is centre stage. As examples throughout the book show, such an analysis can be extended to struggles over related resource domains such as land, forests and water.

Taking seriously the class base of the state has a number of permeations for the prospects of more radical state interventions aimed at unsettling incumbency or reallocating power to disenfranchised groups as part of just transitions. Put bluntly, as the popular expression goes, 'turkeys don't vote for Christmas': how likely is it that state elites will wrestle finance, technology, infrastructure or control over production necessary for transformation from the very class allies that keep them in power or from which they themselves directly benefit? In other words, there are shared interests and a common endeavour among ruling classes in maintaining (and expanding) their rule and the concentration of their power over systems of wealth generation and distribution which makes them unlikely candidates to limit or place constraints on that control, let alone concede it to others in the interests of sustainability. Accumulation and legitimation imperatives can be reconciled through an ever-expanding circle of consumerism: whereby mass access to the latter softens criticism of the unequal nature of accumulation through dispossession and its ecocidal consequences, which 'blurs the convenient distinction between capital interests and "society"' (Hausknost 2020: 23). Hausknost (2020) explores this through the distinction between 'systemic sustainability' and what he calls 'lifeworld sustainability': where the imperative for states of enhancing the lifeworld and short-term welfare of their citizens is in tension with the sorts of policies and measures that would support 'systemic' or strong sustainability. The limits of current models of state-based democracy (explored further in Chapter 6) serve, according to Blühdorn (2020), to perpetuate this 'politics of unsustainability'.

In Gramscian terms, this is not just about the exercise of power by the executive but also the outer reaches of the state in political and civil society where state legitimation and class rule are secured and reproduced through the media, the church and systems of education which are key to reproducing the labour force (Gramsci 1971). In some contexts, the church has played a key role in generalising and legitimating state power (even to the extent of supporting military regimes such as in Latin America and Islamic republics) (Miller and Moraw 1996). Given this social, cultural and moral power, social movements have sought to ally with the church as a means to put pressure on states to act on key sustainability issues such as climate change. Building on lessons from campaigns for debt relief and the divestment movement, the more recent global campaign for a Fossil Fuel Non-Proliferation Treaty has successfully garnered the support of key religious leaders in the Vatican as well as his holiness the Dalai Lama for their campaigns. In more populist versions, the idea of 'the establishment' is invoked which brings into view the courts and the legal system, the police and the informal social clubs and networks through which elite power circulates and is maintained (Jones 2014). Perspectives such as these help to strengthen and deepen an understanding of the social in accounts of socio-technical change but as part of a web of social power in which the state is embroiled through political and civil society.

In environmental terms, an understanding of the operations of the ruling class reveals the ways in which decisions get made that systematically distribute risk and hazard to the poor while at the same time preserving the privilege and property of the bourgeoisie. The economic incentives for the ruling class to behave in this way are clear. Haynes (1999: 224) notes: 'Political elites are very likely to be major wealth holders with interests in a variety of activities, some of them environmentally damaging, including commercial logging, mineral and oil exploitation, plantation cropping and large-scale irrigated farming.' This intensifies the tension between production and protection, accumulation and legitimation and relates to Marx's and Engel's contention that the capitalist state is 'based on the contradiction between public and private life, on the contradiction between general interests and private interests' (Marx & Engels 1975: 46). Its role is to maintain market discipline and mediate between the contradictions of general and particular interests even within capital, such that, as Newell and Paterson (1998) show, competing fractions of capital seek to present their interests as consistent with those of capital in general in environmental as in other issue areas. The state then is not seen as a separate sphere with its own logic, not 'suspended in mid-air' as Marx noted, but giving form to economic institutions and production relations. An analysis of class allows us to locate the state within those larger relations that are implied in the production of environmental degradation.

What makes the use of state power for these ends a class project is the shared interests in a particular form of managing the economy, protecting wealth, power, property and private privilege. While others claim 'the ruling class does not rule' (Block 1987: 51) especially in a context of post-industrial development, it is nevertheless the case that property relations, control of finance and concentrations of land ownership are all critical in terms of the actors states have to negotiate with (or are linked to) to secure change. This is so because transitions imply shifts in infrastructures and financial and business models as well as questions of ownership and power in more transformational models. Following an account of the multiple bases of power associated with 'the establishment' (Jones 2014), class power is premised upon and can be reinforced through aristocracies and monarchies given the amount of resources and land over which they have control and their ability to fetishise and project the desirability of order and tradition in the public imagination, as well as the ways in which class rule can be enforced through the policing of dissent (Brock et al. 2018). To take an example, the monarchy in the UK is exempt from hundreds of laws, including ones which relate to energy use at their numerous properties (Carrell et al. 2022). In one instance, it was revealed that the lawyers to the late Queen Elizabeth II 'secretly lobbied Scottish ministers to change a draft law to exempt her private land from a major initiative to cut carbon emissions' (Evans et al. 2021). Attention to the ways in which incumbent regimes ossify and benefit from hierarchies of social and economic power pushes us to look at the social foundations of the state, whereby the state is often a crystallisation of dominant social relations. The work of Poulantzas (2014) and Jessop's strategic relational approach (SRA) (Jessop 2016) enable such a shift from conceiving the state as a distinct, unified entity or actor toward a conception of the state as a social relation.

Though Marxist theorists have thought about this predominantly in terms of class, less attention has been paid, for example, to critical race theory of the state which explores how the state both 'shapes and is shaped by racial conflict' (Bracey 2015: 555). Appreciating the wider social relations underpinning the state makes it easier to understand how economies and interventions for transition are racialised, gendered as well as class-based (Lennon 2017; Hooper et al. 2021; Newell 2021b) since they both reflect the preferences of dominant social actors, hierarchies and power structures based on patriarchy and racism, for example, and produce racialised and gendered governmentalities. This brings to the fore core questions about who the state represents and serves. Attention to the racialised nature of the state exposes the uneven treatment of citizens (and non-citizens) through migration policy and policing as well as distributions of resources for welfare and the uneven levels of environmental protection afforded to communities of colour that activists and environmental justice scholars have long pointed to (Agyeman et al. 2003; Bullard 2005; Baker 2016). Such work on environmental justice and environmental racism offers one obvious entry point in advancing our understanding of racialised governance, including the experience of Indigenous groups in contesting siting decisions such as the positioning of nuclear waste dumps on Native American reserves (Brook 1998; Powell 2018) and struggles for recognition justice by Aboriginal communities in Australia (Hulbert and Rayner 2018). In India, up until 2013, the Land Acquisition Act, a piece of colonial legislation dating from 1894, was frequently invoked to override objections to new projects, allowing the union or a state government to acquire private land for the purpose of industrialisation and the development of infrastructural facilities, often leading to the dispossession of tribal communities (Newell 2005). Such place-based accounts of racial injustice benefit from being embedded, however, within a more historical, social and racialised account of the state and how richer European colonial states acquired their wealth and continue to concentrate and distribute it in racialised ways (Gilio-Whitaker 2019; Bhambra and Newell 2022). Though still less explored in the literature, the use of state power to police and enforce a hierarchy between humans and more-than-humans which makes torture, exploitation and destruction of the latter legal and devoid of rights claims constitutes another axis of exclusion which upholds speciesism (Newell 2024a).

In this regard, the law as a central instrument of state power is also a key validating and legitimating mechanism in upholding incumbent power and dominant social structures and anthropocentric hierarchies. Critical scholars suggest that legal systems are not neutral towards the inequalities they produce but rather exist, and are invoked, in order to preserve such injustices (Cutler 2002). In this reading, legal relations cannot be divorced from the material conditions in which they are produced and seek to preserve through the exercise of state power. As Rupert and Smith (2002: 10) suggest: 'Legal rules are a crucial constituent of property relations and privatized class power, and also form the "legal culture" of a transnational bloc advancing a globalizing neoliberal agenda under the guise of naturalized representations of property, market and capital.' I explore in Chapter 8 how some scholars argue for the emergence of a transnational state in response to the globalisation of the economy and the shifting preferences of transnationally organised capitalist elites (Robinson 2004) who play a key role in shaping the form of earth systems governance (Albert 2020). This posits a very different view of the assumed benign role that regulation plays in supporting and directing transitions in debates about their governance (Lawhon and Murphy 2012).

Understandings of blocs, elites and hegemony have also been explored at national level in relation to sustainability transitions. Both Haas (2019) and Ford and Newell (2021) draw on Gramscian scholarship to explore key dynamics of incumbent power in relation to regime resistance to transitions and transformations: how hegemonic groups control dominant ways of realising societal functions. Drawing on Gramsci, Jessop (2002: 6) suggests hegemonic rule is maintained through 'political, intellectual and moral leadership with and over a given political space in such a way as to bring social forces and institutions into conformity with the requirements of capitalist reproduction'. The concepts of 'historical bloc' and 'integral state' meanwhile are applied to identify a broader range of relevant regime actors, including policymakers and civil society organisations, who play a key role in maintaining hegemony. Rather than describing a static landscape, for Jessop, a historical bloc is constituted by 'the mutually implicated, structurally coupled and historically co-evolving ensemble of economic, political and socio-cultural relations' (Jessop 2008: 46). From a neo-Gramscian perspective, civil society plays an important role in (re)producing the legitimacy of a particular set of interests by helping to present them as the general interest. Given its relative autonomy from industry and government, civil society is a key site of political contestation and often appears in transition debates as a counterbalancing force, or what Gramsci would call 'counter-hegemonic movements'. Gramsci's notion of a 'war of position' has been applied to understand the resistance of dominant firms in a regime and their industry organisations to niche developments and government policy supportive of potential competitors to incumbent interests. Ideas around 'passive revolution' and '*trasformismo*', meanwhile, have been applied to understand the accommodation of niche developments by incumbent firms and their industry organisations while controlling the direction and pace of transitions (Newell 2018). Hence while Gramscian accounts point to the importance of counter-hegemonic power, they are also alert to the ways in which more conservative elements of civil society can lend legitimacy to dominant policy responses and sideline calls for more ambitious action. This is a phenomenon we can see today in organised right-wing pushback against measures to tackle the climate and ecological emergency such as charges for polluting vehicles or support to low-traffic neighbourhoods or 15-minute cities on the grounds they allegedly infringe civil liberties.

Nevertheless, activist mobilisations can open up possibilities to contest dominant articulations of 'common sense' and prevailing political grammars and sow the seeds of alternative visions in the fallout of the legitimation crises that states increasingly face: 'a political conjuncture that bottom-up mobilisation of social movements can exploit to initiate change' (Hammond and Hausknost 2021:11). As with Polanyi's 'moves' that precede counter-movements, Gramsci wrote about 'molecular transformations' where, as Marchi shows, the concept of the 'molecular' (*molecolare*) is 'fundamental to shedding light on the potentially transformative implications of everyday contentious actions' (Marchi 2021: 67) or what Foucault (2019) calls the 'microphysics of power'. Hence, while, as Poulantzas suggests, the state operates as a strategic field 'formed through intersecting power networks that constitutes a favourable terrain for political manoeuvre by the hegemonic fraction' (Jessop 2008: 123), hegemony is never complete and cracks, contradictions and fragilities in elite power create openings for change as condensations of power fragment and reconfigure.

Scope to comprehend this exists within Jessop's strategic relational approach (SRA) which emphasises the flexibility of capitalism, its modification through the state and civil society and the potential for social agency (Jessop 1990, 2002). This is distinct from the notion of relationality introduced in the previous chapter since it does not seek to incorporate (as I do) relations within and across the state, between states, citizens and ecologies. It rather explores how institutions and practices 'reflect the power of dominant social actors' (hence 'relational'), but they can be remade by new strategies or 'projects', which work across different sub-systems (hence 'strategic'). The dynamism of the approach and attention to shifting historical (and material) configurations of social forces based on relations between states and economies is helpful, nevertheless, to understanding the role (and limits) of the state in transitions and transformations and in understanding current forms of the state as the product and crystallisation of numerous previous rounds of struggle over the depth and reach of key state functions (around the military, welfare and democracy, for example).

Other scholars have sought to use the SRA approach to bring in ecological dimensions with Robertson suggesting 'the coordination and provision of stable articulations between the state, the economy, and natural science is perhaps one way of describing the task of environmental governance' (Robertson 2006: 371) while Quastel (2016: 344) uses the SRA approach to address 'the relationship of all societal sub-systems to nature'. Silvester and Fisker (2023) develop a framework grounded in the SRA approach to understand the following dimensions of the state: forms of representation, internal organisation, forms of intervention, social basis, state projects and hegemonic formation. Attention to shifting landscapes of power affords a more optimistic account of the possibility of state transformation for, as Argyriou and Barry (2021: 3) note, 'This means that while state structures have inbuilt biases that make them more or less accessible to certain social (especially economic) groups, a particular group's prospects of accessing state capabilities, resources and influencing state policy is shaped by the strategy that they adopt towards the state'. Hence, 'whether, how, and how far these biases are actualized depends on the changing balance of forces and their strategies and tactics' (Jessop 2016: 54). Scope to be successful in this endeavour is provided by the state's search for legitimation, the 'strategic selectivity' it employs as it attempts to reconcile competing goals and imperatives and which is contingent and has to adapt to shifting social demands and economic and geopolitical pressures in a highly integrated capitalist political economy.

How best to account for these concentrations and formations of power has produced theoretical differences between elite theory, Marxism and neo-pluralism (Dunleavy and O'Leary 1987). Writers from a more neo-pluralist perspective emphasise the diversity of business interests (consciously not using the term capital), find less evidence of systematic privileges being afforded to capital and attribute less structural power to capital (Falkner 2008; Meckling 2011), reflecting different understandings of the state and its degree of autonomy from class and industrial interests (Evans 2012 [1995]; Domhoff 1996). Thinking of forms of material or structural power in terms of elites (as the agents that embody that power) offers another analytical entry point (Reinhard 1996; Sovacool and Brisbois 2019) for understanding intra- and inter-elite competition, different in emphasis from the category of a 'ruling class' used in Marxist accounts.

Others have emphasised the way in which different fractions of capital (including finance capital, productive capital and commercial capital) compete to assert their preferences and to attract the backing of the state: the 'competing and contingent logics of capital' (Jessop 2008: 33) which the state has to negotiate as the 'custodian of accumulation … primarily concerned with responding to market imperatives as well as preserving the broader capitalist tenets upon which the status quo rests' (Da Costa Vieira 2024). Newell and Paterson (1998) show with respect to energy in particular, at least to date, it has been easier for fossil fuel productive capital to represent their sectoral interests as convergent with the interests of 'capital in general'. Their ability to continue to do this might start to appear more tenuous as the impacts of the climate and ecological crisis make themselves felt in ways which impact the profits of capital and elites. It forms the starting point of civil society strategies to engage fractions of finance capital that have a material interest in more ambitious climate action. In this way, as Jessop (2008) suggests, hegemonic projects privilege interests compatible with their conception of the general interest while derogating other competing or contradictory interests. Such an account allows for state autonomy, strategic selectivity and conflict among elites given 'the state is neither a unified subject nor a neutral instrument but an asymmetrical institutional terrain on which various political forces (including state managers) contest control over the state apparatus and its distinctive capabilities' (Jessop 2008: 31). This supports Block's (1977) notion that 'the ruling class does not rule' as such but rather a governing class can be distinguished from the capitalist class where 'state managers' are those who run the governmental and state apparatus, who are often not capitalists themselves.

This type of perspective opens up the question of *who* and *what* constitutes an elite. Regarding sustainability transitions, the question is not just how elites exercise power and what forms the basis of their shared (material) interests but the direct and indirect impacts they exercise over sustainability pathways. Whichever way the boundaries are drawn, beyond their political influence manifest in (lobbying, party donations and representation on key committees) and financial power demonstrated through (ownership of companies, stocks and shares), the direct impacts of what Kenner (2019) calls the 'polluter elite' through emissions associated with their lifestyles (owning large homes and multiple cars, flying frequently, often owning yachts, etc.) are significant. For example, one study found the richest 10 per cent of the world's population accounted for more than half of the emissions added to the atmosphere between 1990 and 2015, while the richest 1 per cent were responsible for 15 per cent of emissions during this time – more than all the citizens of the EU and more than twice that of the poorest half of humanity (Gore 2020). Political work is, nevertheless, required to hold elite alliances together and find common ground in the face of commercial and political differences layered upon shared core material interests in organising the economy in ways which privilege the rule of capital, and this creates cracks and openings to disrupt incumbent power.

These more general accounts of the sources and manifestations of political and social power within and beyond the state, can be complemented by attention to the everyday work of statecraft: the work of assembling different actors, coalitions and networks, managing dissent, building narratives (as well as infrastructures), engaging (or managing) publics and balancing competing interests. This is the quotidian work of getting by in the face of competing demands and ever shifting 'external' contexts (often described by transition scholars as 'landscape pressures') by building advocacy coalitions and creating feedback effects that benefit advocates for change as noted earlier. Political settlements are not just configured around bureaucratic units and functions, however, but rather imply going with the grain of where power lies within and beyond the state in order to garner and sustain support for change (Khan 2010). Scott's (2020) emphasis on 'Seeing like a state', meanwhile, invites attention to the ways in which the state renders messy and multifaceted transitions involving a multitude of actors and agents across scales 'legible' as a governance strategy: herding disparate actors behind common visions and discursive enterprises, mobilising finance as the catalyst and providing structure through disclosure, law and regulation. It can imply using convening power and authority to establish the terms of engagement and the direction of change, however hollow those appeals to order are in reality, while often avoiding accountability for the consequences of transition strategies. What this points to in practice is modes of steering and governing networks of networks. Gamble (2014: 15) describes states as complex associations with their own governance rules but which 'sit in judgement on the governance rules of others', recognising the fact that 'Representation in the modern state is indirect since the people cannot govern themselves, but the state acts in their name and is assumed to possess a single will and personality'.

Taking a broader and more relational view of the state means recognising not just that the state crystallises intersecting and dominant forms of social relations but that different elements of the state are related to one another (such as military and industrial functions captured in the notion of a military-industrial complex) guided by an overarching ideology and vision of the purpose and function of the state in a competitive and unstable capitalist world economy. As we will explore in Chapter 5, the role of militarism in preserving state power and privilege has important implications for transitions. The police, prisons and military are key means by which elite power is maintained from threats within and from without. Such approaches are critical to an understanding of the role of the state in sustainability transitions because they move us beyond an understanding of the state as an administrative unit, a unitary, autonomous, rational, neutral and independent actor reducible to the executive branch of government – and rather help to identify and excavate the deeper social and political foundations of state power. Points of intersection with transition scholarship include the fact, as Johnstone and Newell (2018: 78) put it, 'who sets the terms of transition and how, is often a product of broader configurations of social, economic and military power that are crystallised in the state in particular patterns of representation and privileged access to decision-making'.

2.4 Towards a Political Economy of the Transition State

So how might we draw on these very different strands of theoretical work in order to make holistic sense of the state's ability to respond to the crisis of unsustainability? As argued thus far, a more rounded account of the role of the state in transitions requires *a more relational account* both across functions and dimensions of power and scale and in relation to the social and the ecological. In concrete terms, this is only possible by following the transition: appreciating the complex assemblages of power and the flows of labour, resources and finance that make particular interventions or transformations viable or which inhibit them. In this sense, I would recommend using the conceptual and theoretical resources drawn upon here in a selective and instrumental way, as and when they appear relevant to the sites of transition, contestation and emergent transformations being explored. Methodologically, this implies starting with particular sites and configurations of micro-politics and working outwards conceptually as and when following the transition requires it but always attentive to the fact that seemingly micro and site-specific articulations of power reflect, embody and are related to broader structures and relations of power operating across levels and historically constituted. This is vital to avoiding the 'local trap' scholars of political ecology have been accused of (Brown et al. 2005) while taking seriously specific sites of contestation and what is unique about particular assemblages rather than force them into existing macro conceptual categories.

To develop such an account of the state, here I build on some elements of the framework I initially developed with Phil Johnstone (Johnstone and Newell 2018). I first make the case for historicising the role of the state in transitions which shapes so much of the terrain on which the contemporary politics of transition play out and cautions against a fetishisation of current political developments. Second, I flesh out a basis for understanding the political economy of the state drawing on the critical literatures engaged with in this chapter which understand the state as both a key site of condensation of dominant social relations and forces and an arena in which they are contested. Third, I attend to the geographies of statehood, offering a global and spatial reading of state–society complexes, given the diverse and uneven geographies of statehood that exist around the world and the need to connect the 'local' and 'global' in light of the intimate relationship between the two. Finally, I explore the geopolitics of transition in which states, some more than others, are intimately entwined, but taking seriously the ecological and material constitution of states and their relations with one another. Taken together, I suggest these approaches offer an improved account of diverse configurations of the transition state and prospects of it playing a more active role in supporting transformative change.

2.4.1 Historicising the State

The position of the state in global and regional hierarchies of power and wealth, which shape states' power and influence as agents of transition, is historically constituted: often through war, colonialism and extractivism (Bhambra 2021). State formation is a product of war and violence in various forms (Mann 1987; Tilley 1993) and state power and wealth are often built on extractivism – from labouring classes within (and beyond) its borders, from historical inheritances of plundered wealth (Rodney 2018; Tharoor 2018) and from ongoing relations of uneven social and ecological exchange (Hornberg 1998) maintained as we will see in Chapter 8 in 'soft' (diplomacy and commercial pressure) and 'hard' ways (sanctions, violence, withdrawal of aid). The contemporary legacies of these historical relations are observable in current climate debates about loss and damage, controversies around the double standards of richer countries demanding that African countries not tap fossil reserves while they expand their own supplies (Okereke and Sokona 2022) and concerns among states in the Global South to bypass models of dependency on Northern technology by building local and indigenous capacity for renewable energy development, for example.

Ideologies and strategies of governance have also been shaped by broader historical shifts in capitalism, particularly during its neoliberal phase, regarding the role of the state and the rescaling of the global economy through processes of globalisation. In the former case, critiques of the role of the state as a provider of energy services have driven a wave of power sector reform in large parts of the majority world enforced by actors such as the World Bank and the International Monetary Fund (IMF) (Tellam 2000). Meanwhile, water scarcity is presented as a problem produced by inefficient state institutions and a failure to incentivise conservation by allocating property rights, such that privatisation becomes the obvious solution (Bakker 2010) while mobilising private finance and public–private partnerships are advanced as the means to support 'climate smart agriculture' (Newell and Taylor 2018). From this perspective, transitions are, therefore, part of broader attempts to deepen and extend neoliberal discipline and market society over time: opening up new investment opportunities for capital through access to investments in infrastructures in energy, water and land.

Even the recent wave of Just Energy Transition Partnerships (JETPs) negotiated by donors with South Africa, Indonesia, Vietnam and Senegal have come under fire from activists for serving as 'trojan horses' for opening up the energy sector to private capital. Dominant ideologies which get globalised and socialised through global (neoliberal) institutions and their evolving sense of how best to deliver capitalist growth enable or frustrate particular projects of transition and deeper transformation. We see this in shifting ideologies around neoliberalism and the development of a 'Wall Street Consensus' (Gabor 2021) about the role of private capital in fostering development alongside a return to state developmentalism and capitalism (Singh and Chen 2018; Alami, Babic et al. 2022; Alami, Dixon et al. 2022) in emerging economies and 'rising powers' of the world; each driven by the evolving requirements of global capital and shifting expectations on states about how best to provide the enabling conditions to facilitate accumulation. Glatzer et al. (2024: 463) suggest: 'The Wall Street Consensus marks the global North's recent attempt to make development in the global South investable.'

Forms of governance bear the hallmark of the historical period in which they are conceived, therefore, the national and regional context in which they were developed and for which they were designed, and of the actors, institutions, social forces and ideologies that shaped their emergence. This implies attention to disparate and uneven statecrafts, contests between national and global capitals, the fluctuating power of labour and the role of civil society and social movements. We can observe a process of a shifting balance of power between public and private control over governance from state control to privatisation and the neoliberalisation of governance of key sectors such as water and energy. In the early 1970s, for example, there was a trend towards states asserting control over energy supply. This came in the form of expropriations of assets (Libya, Algeria), unilateral decisions to fix maximum rates of production (Kuwait) or the unwillingness to accept production expansions which had been scheduled by the companies (Saudi Arabia) (Odell 1981). Energy nationalism was then challenged with neoliberal reform programmes for the power sector throughout the 1980s and 1990s, though in many contexts the state retained a key role (Baker et al. 2014). In Africa, though arguably elsewhere, McDonald (2009) suggests that this political shift took the form of 'electric capitalism'. Likewise, with water we have seen both the rollout of water privatisation schemes (Bakker 2010) and subsequent attempts to re-common water and assert public control over its access, pricing and distribution (Balanyá et al. 2005).

Contemporary state practices reflect the effect of these historical and political legacies and attempts to balance and accommodate global pressures for reform with the need to address historical inequalities. For example, South Africa adopted Black Economic Empowerment (BEE) measures to create jobs and economic opportunities for racialised marginalised groups to address the historical legacy of apartheid (Baker et al. 2014). These modes of governance are not fixed but rather reflect different political economies and models of organising state–market relations. Sometimes dramatic recalibrations of governance occur in the wake of crises which call upon the state to intervene. Examples include the abandonment of Bolivia's experimentation with water privatisation in the wake of social protests or the rapid transitions in Cuba's energy sector (the Revolución Energética) where the country moved to a more efficient, decentralised system with smaller generator stations and shorter distances to transmit energy as part of a forced drive towards energy conservation in response to US-imposed oil embargos (Simms 2013: 209).

2.4.2 Political Economy of the State

The ability of states to create the historical conditions for change and to adapt to them in ways of their own choosing is unevenly shared across the international system. I noted in the previous chapter the different degrees of developmental space and policy autonomy that states have to chart their own pathways to sustainability which reflect historical relations of uneven development and the contemporary structure of the global economy. State-led programmes (such as India's solar mission), visions (such as Kenya's Vision 2030) and programmes of technology innovation and development can and do flourish within a neoliberal global political economy which questions the efficiency, desirability and effectiveness of such interventions, demonstrating ongoing processes of accommodation and diverse attempts by states to intervene strategically to secure their objectives. For example, the Chinese state has driven a series of energy transitions reflecting its increasing power as a global energy leader, building capacity around wind and solar much faster than other countries in the world. By 2016, China had installed more than twice the wind capacity of the US, making up 36 per cent of the capacity installed globally. In the case of Brazil's biofuels programme (Proálcool), introduced in November 1975 to increase ethanol production and substitute ethanol for petroleum in conventional vehicles, by 1981, six years later, 90 per cent of all new vehicles sold in Brazil could run on ethanol (Sovacool 2016). The Inflation Reduction Act (IRA) in the US, the heartland of global capitalism, seeks to lever huge amounts of state funding for 'green' investments in renewable energy and infrastructure for electric vehicles. By default, or by design, competing pathways can coexist even under common 'landscape' pressures.

The relations of power at play require a more dynamic and multi-level analysis: following the transition by mapping the articulations of power across spaces and arenas of contestation. At every level – from local, city, national, regional and global governance – political systems reflect and are imbued with the structural and material power of incumbent providers and interests, reinforced by institutional power through high levels of access and representation of incumbent actors in the key centres of decision-making and further entrenched by discursive power to frame their needs as congruent with those of the state and wider society as a form of 'common sense' and their preferred pathways as the most viable and attractive (Ford and Newell 2021). Conceptually, the exercise of power in these ways has been described in a diversity of ways from the community power debates of the 1960s (Bachrach and Baratz 1962), which drew attention to the power to keep threatening issues off public and political agendas, from discussions about the 'captive' and 'shadow' state (Monbiot 2000; Chipkin and Swilling 2017) to the capture of political systems (democratic and undemocratic) by private interests and indeed the fragility of the division between the interests of state and capital (Holloway and Picciotto 1978). Nationally, transition scholars have narrowed this down to regime resistance and the role of incumbent actors, but the sources of power those actors wield to resist change are multi-sited. Globally, such power finds expression in what some scholars have referred to as 'oil hegemony' in the international system (Bromley 1991) or 'private empires' (Coll 2012).

In this sense, the state is positioned at the interface between the evolving demands of systems of provision and the dynamic nature of capitalism, using its power to mould delivery of the former to the evolving needs and structural requirements of the latter. Capital becomes entwined with the state through a tightly bound complex which takes different forms in distinct contexts. We can see this in the disproportionate weighting of the demands of the mining and energy industries in South Africa as part of the minerals-energy complex (Fine and Rustomjee 1997), or as part of a private resource boom as in Chile's copper industry, but also in the extraordinary levels of state support given to nuclear power in the UK (Cox et al. 2016), for example, at a time of austerity and fuel poverty for many in the population at large, while elsewhere efforts to extend energy services to the poor are often also undermined by aggressively pursued cost recovery programmes (McDonald 2009).

Taking political economy analysis of patterns of inclusion/exclusion down a level, analysis of the state can also explore informal practices and patterns of power – clientelism, patronage and corruption at local levels of the state (Blair 2000). Alongside ministries and institutions with formal mandates and responsibilities for making official policy, there is often an informal political economy at work of service provision: delivery, installation, repair and upkeep of technology and a 'murky' political economy of deal brokering and rent extraction around market access provided by state actors and control over and procurement of contracts which shape outcomes and questions of access in important ways (Newell and Daley 2022). The political economy literature on rent-seeking and clientelism points to collusion between elites and business groups over lucrative deals funded by public money (Hicken 2011) and the phenomenon of 'crony capitalism' which took hold in the wake of the privatisation of state assets in many former socialist regimes which were shared among key state allies. The emergence of Russia's oligarchs who became spectacularly wealthy by acquiring former state-run energy assets is a case in point (Aslund 2019). There is also often a lack of transparency around procurement and contracting for services that incentivises centrally negotiated deals which governments can control as Newell and Phillips (2016) show in the case of Kenya's 'neoliberal' energy transition. But rather than assume instances of collusion between state and private actors are exceptional and abnormal, political economy accounts would expect such outcomes given the tight social networks and shared material interests which bind state and corporate actors.

2.4.3 Geographies of Statehood

State power and the roles it plays are not static and fixed (Greenberg and Mayer 1990) in the way more structural accounts in International Relations (IR) might suggest, describing either an anarchial international system that forces all states to compete for power in particular ways (Morgenthau 1948; Waltz 1959), captured in the classic 'billiard-ball' model of how states are assumed to interact with one another, or accounts which fix states into particular positions within an economic order defined by 'core' and 'periphery' for example (Cardoso and Faletto 1979). States face shifting geopolitical configurations, economic, social and ecological shocks (not to mention health ones) and internal threats and challenges (revolts, uprisings, revolutions) to their authority, legitimacy and ability to act.

There is a huge variety of forms and typologies of statehood from 'rogue', 'liberal', 'predatory', 'failed', 'social democratic', 'authoritarian' and many other political labels or academic constructions often employed by states themselves to discipline, discredit or else reward other states. Narratives of failed states (Starr 2009) often serve as a pretext for intervention by foreign powers. There are of course many 'contested states' around the world from Somalia to Palestine and Western Sahara to Northern Cyprus whose right to govern is disputed and fought over (Geldenhuys 2009), as the current war in Gaza makes graphically clear, or 'stateless societies' as anthropologists refer to them (Glenhill 2000). As noted earlier, there is also a diversity of political economies in which states are embedded: coordinated, liberal and dependent market economies (Hall and Soskice 2001).

As will become clear in Chapter 8 on the global state, statehood does not sit in isolation from broader geographies of power and geopolitics which shape its contemporary form and continually recast it through uneven processes of global exchange premised on colonial relations. Questions of state autonomy run through many literatures on the state. Insights from literatures exploring state autonomy from industrial actors (Evans 2012 [1995]) and from external actors and institutions in the form of 'developmental space' (Wade 2003; Gallagher 2005) have been drawn upon to account for energy transitions in particular contexts (Newell and Phillips 2016; Power et al. 2016). The boundaries between state and non-state, public and private are also often very fragile in practice, therefore. Marxist scholars highlight this in terms of the fusions of state-capital complexes, as noted earlier, but in practice governance roles and functions, sometimes referred to as 'governmentality' (the conduct of conduct), reveal an array of hybrid, partnership, synergistic arrangements which characterise governance in practice and the 'accomplishment' of climate governance, for example (Bulkeley 2016). Scholarship on transnational climate change governance (TCCG), for example (Bulkeley et al. 2014), points to a growing role of local councils and the city level of the state playing (at times complementary and at times contradictory) roles. In such scenarios, states often play key roles as orchestrators of climate action across scales (Hale and Roger 2014).

Recognising the interconnected nature of transition processes across scales and spaces presents an analytical challenge in terms of how to 'follow the transition'. This presents practical and political challenges for local, national and global governance systems accustomed to dealing with these issues in isolation rather than addressing the ways in which they impact one another: the 'triple disconnect' that can occur between the global, national and local scales as the trade-offs inherent in dealing with the political and ecological connections between competing goals (around the SDGs, for example) are negotiated across levels of authority. Thus, despite an international policy arena saturated with rhetoric around integration, evidence suggests this rarely happens in practice (Newell et al. 2018).

2.4.4 Geopolitics

I have already noted the ways in which state-led transitions and pathways are co-constituted and shaped by evolving geopolitical configurations. So, how should we understand and engage with the geopolitics of transitions? How do we conceptually capture the diverse elements that link transitions across time and space? These include circulations of energy, water, resources and minerals to capture seriously the 'geo' in politics; but also circulations of capital, value, labour, resistance to transitions, as well as state power and the role of global governance institutions in shaping transition pathways in enabling and coercive ways. These elements make up the global assemblages of sustainability transitions.

Transition scholars deal with these levels and the connections and relations between them in terms of emergent 'niches', dominant 'regimes' and shifting 'landscape' pressures (Geels and Schot 2007). Although transition literature has not yet paid enough attention to geopolitics (Goldthau et al. 2019; Blondeel et al. 2021), historically transitions in key sectors such as energy, water and transport have had important geopolitical dimensions. Think of the importance of the Suez or Panama canals to global shipping which prompted the 'Suez war' in Egypt. Likewise, Thompson (2022) argues:

> For nearly 200 years, fossil-fuel energy has been central to geopolitics. The relationship between western Europe and China changed decisively in 1839, when Britain deployed coal-fired steam ships in the First Opium War. This move opened up China to a succession of imperial powers. The turn to oil in the twentieth century made the United States the world's dominant power and began the decline of Europe's great powers. For the past decade, the United States and Russia have competed with each other to sell gas to Europe, as they did oil at the start of the past century (Hill 2004). Energy makes for dramatic geopolitical conflicts with after-effects that last decades.

A fuller account of agency, power and the social means not just documenting financial and ecological flows and circuits of capital but accounting for unevenness and injustice in the co-constitution of pathways and the social relations which constitute the global order. Contemporary (and in different guises historical) geopolitical configurations are driven by dominant growth and accumulation imperatives and often combined with the use of both violence and soft power to secure and maintain access to resources to sustain high levels of production and consumption in metropolitan centres and core regions of the economy and among wealthier classes. Transitions from one system of provision to another recalibrate socio-technical configurations and can disrupt and alter geopolitics by enhancing the power of states with the greatest access to key resources (such as rare earth minerals) or technologies to access new resource frontiers (in oceans, for example), while not unsettling the overriding rationale and drivers of geopolitical competition in the way more radical visions of sustainability would propose around degrowth and a reduced need for militarism for extractivism (Newell 2019).

This is an opportune moment to re-engage with the geopolitics of transitions (Bazilian et al. 2019; Blondeel et al. 2021). Not only have contemporary events such as the invasion of Ukraine and the rise of populism and resource nationalism pointed to the key role of geopolitics in determining the viability of different sustainability and particularly energy pathways but scholars are struggling to make sense of the interconnection between transitions unfolding in different parts of the world. This is especially so in the light of renewed appreciation of the consequences of resource interdependence (of gas and oil and water but also lithium, cobalt and rare earth minerals) when supplies are disrupted, as well as in the context of net zero commitments which imply resource acquisition by richer countries and companies in poorer parts of the world (Sen and Darbi 2021) as well as through what have been referred to as 'green grabs' (Fairhead et al. 2012). Recent examples include the oil company Total's controversial offset project in the Democratic Republic of Congo (DRC): a major tree-planting offsetting project which the company claims will sequester more than 10 million tonnes of CO_2 over 20 years. An investigation by Unearthed, however, revealed how communities lost access to the lands they have farmed for generations which were requisitioned by the Congolese government over a year before consultations with local communities finished. Some families received a payment of about $1 per hectare of land, while others received nothing (Quashie-Idun and Howard 2022).

A geopolitical lens provides a potentially usefully way to empirically and conceptually connect the uneven and combined nature of transitions as they unfold simultaneously and relationally. There are many ways then of understanding the geopolitics of transitions. Existing work looks at (i) how the growth of 'rising powers' impacts on transitions in energy (Power et al. 2016); (ii) how the pursuit of decarbonisation reconfigures economic relations around trade and finance and so on (Goldthau et al. 2019); or (iii) the geopolitics associated with particular technologies or energy sources such as renewable energy (IRENA 2019). In more traditional perspectives, geopolitics are a function of 'great power' manoeuvring and the 'balance of power' in Realist renditions or normative shifts in English School versions (Falkner and Buzan 2022). Though not focussed on transitions, IR scholars have explored the geopolitics of key resources such as oil (Bromley 1991,

2005; Bridge and LeBillon 2013) but increasingly also of renewable energy and hydrogen (Van de Graaf et al. 2020). Older analytical categories of imperialism (Harvey 2003), applied to previous wars in the Middle East and Afghanistan (Rees 2001) and quasi-imperial states (Shaw 2000), informal empires (Brown 2009) and spheres of influence between the Lockean heartlands (Van der Pijl 1998) and contender states, might continue to have value in making sense of the 'new cold war' in which access to gas plays such a central role. Marxist perspectives associate such manoeuvres with imperialist ventures and the global rule of capital (Desai 2013) in general, or specific strategies which employ spatial and temporal fixes to pass on the costs of transition to other societies or social groups (Harvey 1981). Critical geopolitics, meanwhile, gives a post-structuralist take where geopolitics is about performative representations of space (Tuathail et al. 1998).

On another level, however, geopolitics can also be understood as a continuation of colonial relations (Bhambra 2021) and patterns of underdevelopment (Mhango 2018). Attention to resource plunder and ecologically uneven exchange in such accounts helps to underscore the ecological and material dimension of this uneven development (Bhambra and Newell 2022). Though not couching it in terms of geopolitics, work in international political economy (IPE) on chains of wealth creation, global value chains (Gereffi et al. 2005) and more critical versions of such work (Selwyn 2019) and on global production networks (Baker and Sovacool 2017) afford other ways of understanding the connective tissue of transitions within the contemporary global political economy (Szabó and Newell 2024). Blondeel et al. (2021) propose a 'whole systems' approach to energy geopolitics to provide a global account of the interactions between high- and low-carbon energy transitions. But the role of the state as a critical node in these networks and assemblages warrants further attention.

An alternative Marxist-informed approach would view states as embedded within social relations, challenging IR's ahistorical abstraction of geopolitics from wider social processes and relations which help to constitute 'the international' (Teschke 2003). A less state-centric account, and one distinct from Realism, would concentrate the analytical focus on the international and relational unevenness of these social formations which reflect different developmental stages and dynamics of incorporation into an international system of capitalist relations. Approaches drawing on uneven and combined development (UCD), expanding on insights from Trotsky's reflections about the Russian Revolution (Trotsky 2019 [1942]), understand unevenness resulting from the historical evolution of capitalism and the 'whip of external necessity' (Rosenberg 2013). But the combined element is key. Applied to sustainability transitions, it would seek to understand, for example, the different nature of sustainability pathways as non-coincidental and in so doing challenge accounts that are more methodologically nationalist in orientation assuming they derive from discrete national transition processes and plans. Unevenness would be understood as a necessary and inevitable feature of global relations because resources are extracted unevenly: wealth and poverty are relational and co-constituted, reliant on patterns of uneven exchange development and underdevelopment between the core and the periphery (Smith 2010). By foregrounding the specifically *inter-national* element of this process, such a perspective would depart from the work on 'deep transitions' which also aspires to provide a more global and historical overview of meta-transitions (Kanger and Schot 2018).

For Wallerstein (2007), it is the coexistence of a singular world economy and a political system divided into competing nation states which allows powerful actors, such as capital, to play states off against one another to benefit from uneven exchange between unequal regions. Analysis such as this usefully highlights some of the limits of liberal 'win-win' understandings of the possibilities of just transitions in deeply unequal economies characterised by widespread social injustices (Szabó and Newell 2024). As Wallerstein (1979: 73) puts it,

> [T]he framework of the capitalist world-system limits critically the possibilities of transformation of the reward system within it since the disparity of reward is the fundamental motivating force of the operation of the system as it is constructed. To be very concrete, it is not possible theoretically for all states to develop simultaneously. The so-called 'widening gap' is not an anomaly but a continuing basic mechanism of the operation of the world economy.

These theoretical resources provide an important means of understanding the geopolitics of transitions: the realignments, accommodations and manoeuvres by which states seek to adjust to changes in the structure of resource production and provision which shape material life. Siebert (2021) explores the potential of a more ecologically inflected rendition of UCD which, while not directly addressing questions of transition, does provide the means for understanding the geopolitical aspects of transitions. For her, 'the value of UCD for IR theory and historical sociology lies in its unique ability to simultaneously internationalize the social and socialize the international by redefining development as inherently multilinear and interactive – that is, uneven and combined' (Siebert 2021:167). This means extending 'the causal implications of the inter-societal to the metabolic relations between society and nature' (Makki 2015: 492).

Concretely, questions of just transition bring these geopolitical questions to the fore: how, why and by whom costs and benefits of sustainability transitions are distributed within and between countries. Looking at the spatio-temporal dimensions of this might go beyond Harvey's (1981) account of spatial and temporal fixes to the structural problems and contradictions of capitalism. A critical addition to such an approach to understanding the geopolitics of transitions would be to bring in the significance of the ecological element of this unevenness (Hornberg 1998). Taking ecology seriously, ecologically uneven exchange captures transborder flows of resources, value and capital. Attention is drawn to the ecologies that connect resources and systems of provision in practice which, in turn, are a function of different socio-natures and how these are ordered within and between societies. Such an approach could not only connect local sites with global processes, as others have done using global political ecology (Newell and Bumpus 2012), but also more meaningfully ecologise geopolitics. Geopolitical ecology might provide one useful point of departure in this regard (Hoffmann 2018). What this suggests is the need for an account that integrates these different dimensions, as Shaw (2000) does, writing of the relationship between the 'state, geopolitics and industrial society'. As we will see in Chapter 8 on the global state, this reflects the systemic political power wielded by powerful and hegemonic states in the global system, with critical implications for the course and nature of transitions.

3

The Entrepreneurial State

3.1 Introducing the Entrepreneurial State

In neoliberal mythology, the notion of an entrepreneurial state is an oxymoron. Slow-moving and bureaucratic and likely to distort the 'natural' operations of the market or pick the 'wrong' winners, its preferred role in such accounts is reduced to bystander and observer of the historical waves of creative destruction, innovation and technological breakthrough orchestrated by restless global capital (Friedman 2009 [1962]). In this reading, beyond making and enforcing rules and property rights for market actors, the state is not the engine of innovation. In standard accounts such as this, it is individuals and entrepreneurs that drive change in technology and markets. This bias is also reinforced in classic academic accounts. For example, Shane's (2003) 'general theory of entrepreneurship' centres on the 'individual–opportunity' nexus, while economic historians celebrate the ingenuity of enterprising elites (Dalzell 1987).

In transition studies, however, it is the entrepreneurial function of the state that has perhaps received most attention, reflecting the dominance to date of innovation studies in analysis of transitions. Indeed, technological change is clearly a vital component of successful transitions and deeper transformations. Yet historical analysis of 'technological revolutions' (Perez 2002) shows that 'Most of the radical, revolutionary innovations that have fuelled the dynamics of capitalism – from railroads to the internet, to modern day nanotechnology and pharmaceuticals – trace the most courageous, early and capital-intensive "entrepreneurial" investments back to the state' (Mazzucato 2015: 134). State support for innovation can take a number of forms. Attention has often focussed on how support can be provided to 'niche' technologies and innovations that might ultimately disrupt dominant socio-technical 'regimes' (Geels and Schot 2007), in part through building markets for new products and services through financing, provision of infrastructures and the generation of demand. Such 'strategic niche management' (Schot and Geels 2008), when combined with landscape pressures (which refer to combinations of factors and drivers external to the regime), is thought to be able to disrupt existing socio-technical configurations and enable the development of new ones. So, for example, subsidies to renewable energies, or the building of innovation networks, when combined with clear targets and timetables to help mobilise finance and set the direction of change through missions, can help accelerate key tipping points that enable niche technologies to become mainstream.

The extent of state involvement in supporting innovation speaks to classic concerns with which technological options should be supported and by whom, when (at which stage in the cycle) and what incentives should be provided to speed up development, deployment and scaling from research and development (R&D) to prototyping and demonstration through to commercialisation. Traditionally, this implied a key role for the state in 'picking winners' from competing options. But this view came under attack in the late 1990s and early 2000s from bodies such as the International Energy Agency (IEA) and leading governments such as the UK that sought, as stated in their 2003 Energy White Paper, 'policy that is not about picking winners, but which allows the market to provide appropriate incentives' (cited in Watson 2009: 126). Discursive moves such as these reflect a dominant neoliberal narrative about the shortcomings of state intervention and corresponding caricatures of the public sector as slow, undynamic, unresponsive and inefficient, whose investments are alleged to 'crowd out' private investment when the key function of a competition state is to 'crowd in' private investment (Cerny 1995). Through these means, as Mazzucato (2015: 134) notes, 'Business is accepted as the innovative force, while the state is cast as inertial – necessary for the "basics", but too large and heavy to be the dynamic engine'.

These narratives have helped prepare the grounds for reform programmes in electricity markets and the power sector led by institutions like the World Bank (Tellam 2000; McDonald 2009), the drive towards water privatisation (Bakker 2010) and initiatives such as 'Grow Africa' which seek to make private actors the leading drivers of transitions in food and agriculture in the region and thereby 'accelerate the execution and impact of investment commitments'.[1] The dominant framing of market failures produced by state intervention leads relatively seamlessly to the privileging of market-based solutions such as pricing and carbon trading, privatisation and private financing schemes increasingly under the meta-narrative of 'de-risking' private finance. Though justified in terms of greater efficiency in bringing down emissions or delivering services than traditional 'command and control' approaches, ongoing support for them in the face of their lack of success in either supporting innovation or bringing down emissions suggests an ideological element is also at play (Stephan and Lane 2015).

Such claims are amplified by wealthy entrepreneurs and thought leaders such as Bill Gates who emphasises a combination of finance and technology as the key to avoiding climate collapse (Gates 2021) and reflect a reluctance on the part of many states to be seen to be directly intervening in their economies, even in the face of an all-compassing energy crisis, such as that which faced Europe in the wake of Russia's invasion of Ukraine. Amongst leading capitalists, 'breakthrough coalitions' such as the 'Breakthrough Energy Coalition' of 25 leading investors (Milman 2015), private philanthropy and mobilising 'coalitions of capital' are regarded as a substitute and preferred alternative to state intervention. This has become a new model of cooperation in climate governance with the launch of a series of 'Breakthroughs' at the Glasgow COP26 summit focussed on 'hard to decarbonise' sectors such as power, steel, road transport, hydrogen and agriculture in line with the goals of the Paris Agreement. It is suggested: 'This international plan for sectoral decarbonisation includes action to align on standards to favour low-carbon alternatives, coordinate government procurement to stimulate demand, and scale up production through support for finance, demonstration projects and R&D.'[2] The role for states in this imaginary is to harmonise standards and coordinate procurement to create the right enabling environment for private capital to deliver the necessary innovations.

Accounts of the entrepreneurial and 'green entrepreneurial state' (Mazzucato 2015) usefully confront some of the hubris about the state as an obstacle to innovation and contest dominant neoliberal myths by exposing the centrality of the state even to purportedly market-led breakthroughs and innovations. From a proactive entrepreneurial state investing in research and innovation, de-risking and 'crowding in' investment and supporting technology diffusion through to the work of other arms of the state such as donors building innovation networks and capacity in the countries where they operate (Ockwell and Bryne 2017), there are few innovations in which the state is not to some degree involved. Even a moment's consideration of the extensive political work involved in convening and coordinating responses across sectors and sites of governance in assembling the socio-technical elements underpinning transitions from finance to infrastructure to training and education, regulation, trade rules and behaviour change leads to the conclusion that the state is an inescapable actor in processes of technological (and social) change. The model of the solitary individual and the private pioneer that is so favoured by narratives of private sector–led development disguises and diminishes the extensive labour, resources and support from all actors that are required for innovations to succeed. From enabling infrastructures such as health and education which provide a trained and socially protected workforce, to transport networks to import and export goods and components and bring them to market, to tax incentives, regulations, procurement and the provision of financial, legal and institutional support which is a prerequisite for a functioning (market) economy, private business has always relied heavily on and benefitted from the state. This explains why private actors invest so much in lobbying the state to ensure these forms of support and regulatory frameworks benefit their business and sector. As Swilling et al. (2016: 653) point out, ‘The private sector always under-invests in human capital, innovation and networks because the direct returns to the investor are impossible to predict. Without state-led investment in these sectors facilitated by an appropriately configured socio-political regime via universities, NGOs and developmental partnerships/compacts, knowledge-based, innovation-led economic development in the era of the network society may be impossible’. Mazzucato (2015: 134) further notes:

> [W]e find that across the globe the countries that are leading in green transformations (solar and wind are the paradigmatic examples explored) are those where the state is playing an active role. And the public sector organisations involved, such as development banks in Germany, Brazil and China, are not just proving counter-cyclical lending. but are even ‘directing’ that lending towards the innovative, risky and uncertain parts of the ‘green’ economy.

Figure 3.1 shows how major economies all have higher levels of R&D spending as a share of GDP than smaller ones since it is considered to be key to their economic

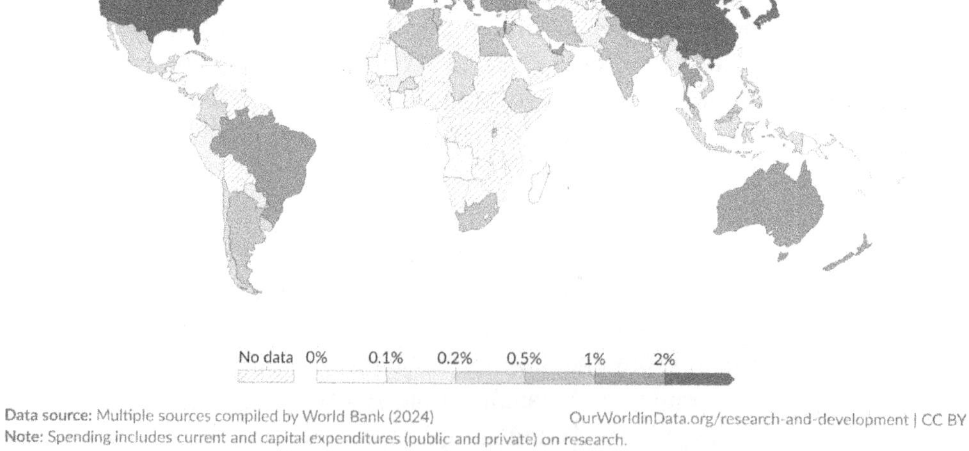

Figure 3.1 R&D spending as a share of GDP. Source: Our World in Data.

success. One key role envisaged for the state is to see start-ups through the 'valley of death' as companies seek to move technologies from the demonstration or prototype stage to commercial deployment. In the UK, for example, the Carbon Trust was set up to fulfil that role (Watson 2009). Without this, they rely on venture or vulture capital and its attendant demands for high-risk, high-gain, fast-return products and services. These may not be those which would the priority for a just and rapid transition which would need to focus on social and environmental objectives when targeting particular technologies and sectors. Mobilising and de-risking 'patient' capital, through measures such as feed-in-tariffs and support from state development banks, means sending 'long, loud and legal' signals about the direction of change (Hamilton 2009) and is critical to creating the enabling conditions for transition. This more affirmative and directional form of intervention goes beyond popular notions of 'nudging' business or leaving change to the operation of the 'invisible hand' of the market as Adam Smith (2014 [1776]) put it. In political economy terms, this reflects Polanyi's (1980 [1944]: 144) argument that 'the road to the free market was opened and kept open by an enormous increase in continuous, centrally organized and controlled interventionism'. This forms an important counter to the myth of the self-regulating transition fuelled principally by private finance and entrepreneurialism while obscuring the role of the transition state all the way down.

Beyond the unhelpful binaries of public and private and caricatures of their respective roles, histories of transitions reveal shifting patterns of public–private collaboration and partnership to be key to 'actually existing transitions', what Mazzucato (2015: 145) calls the 'ecosystem of innovation'. This recognises the collective nature of innovation in practice where 'Different types of firms (large and small), different types of finance and different types of state policies, institutions and departments interact sometimes in unpredictable ways' (Mazzucato 2015: 151). Empirical evidence suggests extensive blending and blurring of roles by public and private actors. Moberg et al. (2021) review shifts in consumption of three food commodities (farmed tilapia, milk and chicken) after the Second World War and find evidence of collaboration and synergy in practice: 'large-scale shifts in commodity systems and diets have taken place when public-funded technological innovation is scaled-up by the private sector under supportive state and international policy regimes' (Moberg et al. 2021: 282). Some scholars argue that the rate of innovation has declined since around 1970, observable when comparing key innovations since the 1970s in computing, mobile phones and digital platforms with the period 1870–1970 which saw advances in electricity, sanitation, pharmaceuticals, plastics, concrete, steel and computers. Ironically, therefore, Vinsel and Russell (2020) argue 'innovation speak' rose just as major innovations started to stall.

With regard to energy, many scholars have pointed to the central role of the state in supporting innovations around lower-carbon technology. Hochstetler (2021: 79) writes, 'Market forces alone did not generate the dynamic wind and solar power sectors that exist around the world today … Much of the existing wind and solar electricity has therefore depended on specific governmental policies to encourage it, including both demand- and supply-side industrial policies.' The rapid expansion of solar energy in Spain was also strongly supported by the state. Key to this, the Rapid Transition Alliance (RTA) suggests, is 'National leadership combined with local flexibility: The new Spanish government has been steadfast in its dedication to the energy transition, setting out a variety of national policies. The sophisticated level of devolution through Spain's 17 autonomous regions has provided much-needed flexibility so governments can match policy with local needs' (RTA 2022). Crucial were policies such as the 'sunshine tax' introduced in 2018 whereby self-generating consumers were obliged to give their surplus energy back to the grid free of charge while paying a toll to cover the costs of distribution and maintenance. To boost this, the Spanish government overhauled the regulatory regime in 2020 by introducing a 'pay-per-bid' mechanism that applies to new renewable projects and the refinancing of existing facilities alike. A second policy which has also helped scale up solar capacity throughout Spain is Power Purchase Agreements (PPAs): long-term contracts between renewable generators and large companies or wholesalers to secure supply at an agreed price from a specific source. According to the RTA, in 2021, approximately 23.7 GW of renewable energy contracts were signed by more than 130 companies using PPAs (RTA 2022).

Underlying rationales and justifications for this state role include correcting market failures such as the underpricing of carbon (Stern 2006), supporting niches and market choice and, by implication, addressing market concentration, monopolies and imbalances in markets accumulated through tax support, subsidies and privileged regulatory structures. Tools that flow from this, therefore, include fiscal and industrial policy and competition policy as well as innovation policy. This also implies using infrastructure and investment to address (regional) social and economic inequalities such as the much feted 'Northern Powerhouse' and 'levelling up' agenda in the UK aimed at using transport links (such as HS2) to improve access to poorer regions of the country.

But the military has also played an important role as an incubator and innovator of new approaches, demonstrating again the porous nature of the boundaries between public and private innovation and the fragile nature of distinctions between state roles (entrepreneurial, military, industrial, etc.) discussed in Chapter 1. For example, a key reason for accelerating the shift from coal to oil was because of military preoccupations with naval supremacy at the time of the First World War

(Ediger and Bowlus 2018). More recently, Watson (2009: 128) notes the key role of governments in supporting solar photovoltaic (PV) and gas turbine technologies which 'transformed many electricity industries in the 1990s' and 'simply would not exist without indirect state support through military budgets'. Military actors are also at the forefront of current efforts to develop geoengineering solutions to climate change and provide 'antecedents to many key geoengineering technologies' (Stoddard et al. 2021: 664).

There is nevertheless a danger of a narrow appropriation of the notion of an entrepreneurial state in discussions about its role in supporting sustainability transitions. As Goldstein and Tyfield (2018: 74) suggest:

> The entrepreneurial state represents a neoliberal re-appropriation of Green Keynesianism, where dominant financial actors (in Silicon Valley, as opposed to on Wall Street) are tapped as the visionaries who can and should set our collective innovation agenda. Although there is a need for large-scale, coordinated techno-social efforts to address sustainability challenges, supporting 'green' innovation cannot simply be framed as maximizing 'innovation' while taking the 'state' for granted. Instead, it must entail a careful assessment of the specific trajectories of innovation being enabled and the underlying socio-natures that they maintain and promote.

This implies greater attention to the sorts of politics and critical social engagement discussed in this chapter aimed at democratising the entrepreneurial state and the struggles between competing interests and social forces within and beyond the state over which future innovations should be supported for competing development trajectories. As Godfrey-Wood (2016) puts it, 'although entrepreneurial state-type institutions are often framed as operating by harnessing high degrees of cooperation between different actors according to commonly-held long-term objectives, achieving the right types of institutions is likely to require a high degree of contestation in order to overcome existing vested interests'. What sorts of entrepreneurial states are viable and appropriate in what sorts of contexts requires further documentation and reflection.

3.2 The Entrepreneurial State and Transitions

The role of the state in facilitating and frustrating technological innovation has received significant attention, not least because of the roots of a lot of transition studies in technology and innovation studies, as noted earlier. Kuzemko et al. (2016: 101) emphasise, however, that there is a need to bring political perspectives to bear: 'By understanding governing for sustainable innovations as part of a more complex political whole this allows us to question which interactions between governance actors and actors in energy systems are delivering sustainable practice change and which constrain such change.' Indeed, as Laird (2003:

27) notes, technology policy often serves as 'an arena for political conflict about the future of the body politic. Debate about technology became debate about the future.' Technologies cannot be abstracted from social relations, nor social worlds understood without an appreciation of the role of technology in (re)shaping them. It is at this interface between technology, society, governance and the environment that we explore the enabling (and constraining) role of an entrepreneurial state in supporting the conditions in which deeper sustainability transitions or more transformative change might take hold.

3.2.1 Actually Existing Innovation

Governments can shape both 'technology push' and 'demand pull', but increasingly there is recognition of the 'coupled' and networked nature of innovation (Watson 2009) and the role of a multiplicity of actors in enabling it – documented through innovation histories. This methodology helps to challenge accounts of heroic private entrepreneurs and overly simplified accounts of entrepreneurial states. In the case of the success of Solar Home Systems in Kenya, for example, such accounts overlooked years of donor support to networks of innovation which preceded the market entry of private business actors who feature highly in the histories constructed by actors such as the World Bank (Ockwell and Byrne 2017).

At the same time, it is important not to exaggerate what states can do alone. Governments can steer and herd, but '[e]xpecting governments to single-handedly enable the green transformation would be unrealistic, given the complexity of this undertaking, its effects on the economy and society at large, and the political dynamics that such a process unleashes' (Pegels et al. 2018: 30). Innovations can be both more incremental and radical and bottom-up or grassroots as opposed to top-down (Seyfang and Haxeltine 2012; Smith et al. 2016). The latter are often explicitly aimed at taking control back from the state (and sometimes the market) over the purpose and direction of innovation. The Lucas Plan to re-employ workers in armaments factories in socially useful alternatives in the UK is a pertinent example in this regard (Smith 2014). Informal spaces of repurposing, reusing and recycling, such as repair cafes, perform an important and subversive role in the context of the relentless drive for consumerism, in prolonging the life of goods, sharing skills and saving energy involved in producing and transporting new products (Cole and Gnanapragasam 2017). The Dutch journalist Martine Postma ran an experiment in her hometown of Amsterdam in 2009, what she called a 'Repair Café' – a free event where people could bring their broken belongings and volunteers would help to try and fix them. This has inspired the creation of 1,700 repair cafés offering their services in 35 countries around the world (RTA 2019). My own experience of using these cafés is that they provide a much valued and convivial space where skills in danger of being lost are valued and appreciated, people can save money and the life of consumer goods is prolonged, reducing waste and unnecessary consumption. For some involved in this movement, as Figure 3.2 makes clear, there is a clear political agenda at work too, invoking the language of consumer rights as well as ecological notions of entropy guided by principles of connection, creativity, independence and sustainability.

The state has a potentially positive role to play too, however, in challenging planned obsolescence. From the EU to the US, new laws are being developed to support the 'right to repair' to radically reduce waste, make things last longer and make them easier to repair. Kate Raworth (2017) describes the degenerative nature of industrial design within our current economic model as 'the industrial caterpillar' – a linear model based on extracting natural resources, employing them in industrial processes, using the final output and, eventually, throwing it away. She highlights instead the need to transform this linear logic of 'take, make, use, lose' (or 'make, break and throw away') into a regenerative 'butterfly economy' where resources are used and reused within the economy and waste is radically reduced. Ideas about sustainable design and architecture have a long legacy (Irwin 2015). Victor Papanek's (1971) *Design for the Real World: Human Ecology and Social Change* was one earlier pioneer in this area, but such visions need to move centre stage once again in enabling sustainable innovation. Underpinning them, as with Ivan Illich's (2009 [1973]) path-breaking thinking, is a desire for social and cultural shifts towards 'conviviality' in contrast to industrial productivity where autonomous needs can be articulated and met. But there is a role for an emboldened state in 'choice-editing': in neither supporting nor approving for commercialisation products and services of minimal social use whose primary purpose is fuelling consumerism as an end in itself.

3.2.2 The Return of Industrial Policy

Over time, attention has moved from support to specific niche technologies and innovations towards the role of industrial policy as a means of attracting and supporting industries key to building a more sustainable economy (Allan and Nahm 2024; Pegels 2014). In particular, a growing recognition of the scale of decarbonising the economy has helped re-legitimise government coordination of markets (Hildingsson et al. 2019). But it also derives from a recognition that supporting integrated and coherent transitions across multiple sectors and sites of political authority, as action across 17 Sustainable Development Goals (SDGs) demands for example, requires the convening and coordination powers of the state, as well as providing comparative institutional advantages for leading economies able to do this well. The global recession and coronavirus pandemic have also helped to

Figure 3.2 Repair café manifesto. Source: iFixit, Repair Manifesto, 2024. Retrieved from iFixit.com. Used with permission from iFixit.

demonstrate the willingness of governments to coordinate resources and investment for public policy goals, as discussed in Chapter 1, in ways that may hold lessons for sustainability transitions, putting pay once again to the myth of the powerless state (Weiss 1995).

Feed-in tariffs are one such tool of industrial policy. They are perhaps one of the most successful examples of how policymaking designed to promote the uptake of small-scale renewable and low-carbon electricity generation can herd venture capital and private equity funds towards certain technological winners (Bürer and Wüstenhagen 2009). To facilitate the transition in the renewable energy sector, a small number of ambitious actors, in particular governments, introduced policies such as feed-in tariffs and were followed by a critical mass of early movers (Sterl et al. 2017). Broad policy toolkits or mixes are now available for addressing these issues, such as production tax credits and renewable portfolio standards, that can hasten the adoption of preferred technologies within a positive enabling environment. To play a continued positive role, however, such interventions need to be sustained to avoid policy fluctuation and mixed signals for investors. In the UK, for example, when the Feed-in Tariff (FIT) export tariff scheme ceased from March 2019, small-scale generators lost the guarantee that they will be paid a fair price, or any price at all, for electricity that they export to the grid (Chapman 2018). Likewise, the auction for new wind power in the UK in September 2023 received no bidders because the price was set too low (Race 2023).

The need for the state to intervene also derives from underinvestment on the part of the private sector through concerns about being unable to reap the full rewards of upfront investments. In part, this results in pressure on the state to de-risk investments, largely by absorbing the risks itself in terms of building infrastructures and clearing the way for new investment opportunities. Amongst other things this, in turn, leads to demands for stronger Intellectual Property Rights (IPR) protection, though as Ockwell et al. (2008) have shown, overly stringent IPR regimes often suffocate innovation. For the renewable energy organisation IRENA (International Renewable Energy Agency), policies required as part of a 'fair and just transition' instead include 'industrial policies that support the creation of domestic supply chains' where governments provide 'preferential access to credit, land and buildings' as well as the creation of 'economic incubators and industry clusters' (IRENA 2018: 73). IRENA also stresses the importance of 'educational and training policies' as part of a just transition that includes 'an assessment of the occupational patterns and skill profiles in rising and declining industries' and 'interim support such as unemployment insurance and other social protection measures' (IRENA 2018: 73).

Proactive procurement provides another route to constructing a preferred industrial base. Independent power producer (IPP) agreements offer one way to build infrastructures, investment opportunities and supply chains. For example, markets can be opened up to competition and supporting niches through IPP agreements. To address issues of social inclusion, conditions can be attached to these such as with South Africa's Renewable Energy Independent Power Producer Procurement Programme (REIPPPP) agreement that included Black Economic Empowerment (BEE) criteria to help address historical and racialised inequalities (Baker et al. 2014). Recognising the political economy dynamics that inevitably flow from any attempt to redistribute finances and power, a key challenge is to try to create policy 'feedback effects' through such measures which build political support for them to help embed them in the policy landscape and ensure their political sustainability. This is important to deal with the fact state policies can create concentrated benefits or rents for a limited number of sectoral firms leading to claims of 'capture' or clientelism (Hochstetler 2021). When those beneficiaries are associated with historically uneven (and racialised) incumbent power, as in South Africa, resistance can be particularly acute as they seek to maintain their tight hold over the energy sector (Baker et al. 2014).

At a bolder level still, visions and transition plans can also set the direction of change and create targets and timetables around which finance, technology and infrastructure can be mobilised. This is the rationale behind both Europe's Green New Deal (GND) and the Inflation Reduction Act (IRA) in the US (Brusseler 2022). Energy security or economic competitiveness considerations are often the key drivers of such policies rather than sustainability per se (Schmitz 2017), but the effect nevertheless is to drive transitions forward. Visions of independence from imported oil drove India's solar mission (Phillips and Newell 2013) and Brazil's drive for bioethanol. Brazil today is home to the world's largest fleet of cars that use ethanol derived from sugarcane as an alternative fuel to fossil fuel–based petroleum. Twenty-seven million cars, 73 per cent of the total, can use a mix of ethanol and gasoline. What is more extraordinary than the scale of the transition to ethanol fuel in Brazil is the speed at which it occurred. In only six years from when the Brazilian government introduced the National Alcohol Programme (Proálcool) in 1975, 90 per cent of all new vehicles sold in the country could run on ethanol. Proálcool was a government-led initiative that spurred rapid action across multiple stakeholder groups: national and international auto manufacturers, sugarcane farmers, ethanol distillers and Brazilian consumers. As the RTA note, 'This extraordinary rapid transition involved cooperation between sugarcane farmers, ethanol distillers, national and international automobile manufacturers and environmental groups, spurred to action by radical public policy that was initially a response to the oil price shocks of the 1970s, but was extended and expanded for the environmental benefits of transitioning away from petroleum' (RTA 2018).

Such targets, timetables and visions can be critical to meeting the desire of investors for 'investment grade policy' by sending 'long, loud and legal' signals about the direction of travel: long time frames, powerful market support and backed by legal frameworks (Hamilton 2009). As Foxon et al. (2005: 2123) note, reviewing evidence of UK government innovation support to renewable energy, 'a stable and consistent policy framework is required … aimed at improving risk/reward ratios for demonstration and pre-commercial stage technologies. This would enhance positive expectations, stimulate learning effects leading to cost reductions, and increase the likelihood of successful commercialisation.' Because they are driven by geopolitical, energy security or competitiveness concerns, however, such state-led industrial policy drives can be very much elite-driven processes often aimed at managing the pace of change or accommodating criticisms of the sustainability credentials of incumbents, as with the dominance of carbon capture and storage (CCS) provisions, calls to continue supporting fossil gas as a 'transition fuel' and the 'Jet Zero' programme to project the sustainability of the aviation industry in the UK (DoT 2022).

Recognising the integrated and globalised nature of these sectors, state-led partnerships with key industries can take the form of global industrial partnerships and cooperative agreements on innovation. Initiatives such as the Asia-Pacific Partnership on Climate and Energy to enable the exchange of low-carbon technology or technology sharing agreements provided an early example of this form of foreign innovation policy by the entrepreneurial state (McGee and Taplin 2006). Despite criticisms and concerns about them drawing political momentum away from multilateral efforts, De Conick et al. find that technology-oriented agreements (TOAs) aimed at knowledge sharing and coordination, research, development or demonstration 'could increase the overall efficiency and effectiveness of international climate cooperation but are likely to have limited environmental effectiveness on their own' (De Coninck et al. 2008: 335). They identify four clusters of roles that TOAs can perform: (i) meeting, planning and exchange of information: an example being the Carbon Sequestration Leadership Forum and the coordination and harmonisation of research agenda and measurement standards; (ii) research, development and demonstration (RD&D) agreements such as jointly agreed RD&D activities and funding commitments (such as the International Thermonuclear Experimental Reactor (ITER) fusion project) or mutual agreements to expand or enhance domestic RD&D programmes; (iii) technology-transfer agreements that include commitments for technology and project financing (e.g., the Global Environment Facility), particularly flowing from developed to developing countries, as well as potentially facilitating international licensing and patent protection; (iv) international agreements encouraging technology deployment by establishing deployment mandates for a specific technology or group of technologies (e.g., renewable portfolio standards), international technology performance standards (e.g., automobile fuel economy or appliance efficiency) or technology deployment incentives (e.g., renewable subsidies). Alongside this, of course, are the private to private, inter- and intra-firm patterns of technology diffusion (Keller 2004).

There are number of global institutions of which states are members with relevant mandates in this area such as the United Nations Industrial Development Organization (UNIDO), International Atomic Energy Agency (IAEA) and International Renewable Energy Agency (IRENA) which engage in different ways and to different degrees either with specific technologies (IAEA, IRENA) or with key aspects of transitions (UNIDO, United Nations Conference on Trade and Development (UNCTAD), World Bank) (Newell et al. 2023). To some degree, IRENA is a one of a kind, however: the only international organisation with a specific mandate to facilitate cooperation, advance knowledge and promote the adoption and sustainable use of renewable energy through policy. However, as IRENA plays no role in implementation of funding or capital investment into alternative sources of energy, it has been labelled an 'epistemic' organisation, with a focus on promoting the deployment of renewable energy, and with a specific focus on capacity building and technical support within the least developed countries (Urpelainen and Van de Graaf 2013). Positively, through IRENA, least developed countries can secure access to a wide range of information and expertise on renewable energy, putting themselves in a better position to benefit from financing and technology transfer (Urpelainen and Van de Graaf 2013) even if richer, more industrialised nations can also use their membership of IRENA to shape and influence the renewable and industrial policies of those lesser developed nations that rely on IRENA for support (Urpelainen and Van de Graaf 2013). This means that they can promote the technologies in which they may have a competitive advantage in order to boost exports and trade links in emerging markets. Despite being premised on a partnership model, such arrangements are inevitably characterised and shaped by these broader power dynamics.

In global terms, it is critical to respect and enhance the ability of Southern states to pursue innovation strategies tied to their national development needs to help reverse some of these inequities. A key concern is that when it comes to global transitions richer countries are repeating the historical tendency to use their power to 'kick away the ladder' (Chang 2002) by not allowing states in Africa, Asia and Latin America to make use of the very policy tools and instruments that were so critical to supporting their own industrial and innovation pathways. For example, constraints on the use of support for infant industry, restrictive trade policies, limits on the use of conditionalities around sourcing of local materials and labour and overly stringent IPR protection are inhibiting the ability of poorer countries to build the capacity of their own renewable energy industries and compete globally. But without a more supportive external enabling environment, and the policy tools to develop their own renewable energy industries, countries faced with the opportunity to extract newly found reserves of gas or oil, for example, may be tempted to do so to avoid being dependent on the acquisition and transfer of renewable energy technologies from richer countries.

There is clearly uneven state capacity in geographical and sectoral terms to act like a 'developmental state' (about which more in Chapter 4) in using instruments of tax, trade and industrial policy to advance core state objectives, with major powers such as India, China and South Africa in a very different situation to many sub-Saharan African or South American states. There are varieties of green industrial policy taking hold across so-called emerging markets (Harrison et al. 2017). Duckett (1998) describes how the entrepreneurial state in China emerged under radar as part of a quiet transformation whereby, 'Since the 1980s, but especially in the 1990s, individual departments across the state system have been setting up new profit-seeking, risk-taking businesses', concluding that 'After almost two decades of reform, the Chinese state has become entrepreneurial' (Duckett 1998: 3). The emergence of this dimension of the state in China confounds caricatures and assumptions about clientelistic state officials embedded in neo-patrimonial networks resisting state reform when there is evidence to the contrary even in the most centralised of settings (de Graaff 2020).

3.2.3 Financing Transitions

Whichever way they are envisioned and supported through industrial and other policy instruments, transitions still need to be financed. Indeed, without deliberate and proactive attempts to redirect and regulate flows of public and private finance, achieving the goals of the Paris Agreement and the SDG goals will remain elusive. This finance needs to be governed by state and international institutions to mobilise, steer and redirect finance to where it is most needed. The poorest regions of the world, such as sub-Saharan Africa, received only around 15 per cent of investment in 2018 even though they account for 40 per cent of the global population (IEA 2019) while increased investments in clean energy finance have largely been captured by China, the US, Europe, Brazil, Japan and India who together have received 90 per cent of increased funds (CPI 2023). The IEA estimates that 85 per cent of the required investments in non-fossil-fuel-based energy will need to come from private sources (IEA 2019). This gives rise to dominant discourses about mobilising and de-risking private finance as the principal means by which transitions will be financed.

A key role is imagined for and demanded of public institutions and financiers to lever private finance through de-risking, largely by the 'de-risking state' (Carruthers and Stinchcombe 1999). Indeed, at the heart of the Wall Street Consensus is 'the reconfiguration of state institutions' for the purpose of 'building the basis for accumulation organized around development asset classes and industrial policies' (Glatzer et al. 2024: 467–468). The verb to 'de-risk' was one of a flurry of new words entering the lexicon of the financial sector in the aftermath of the credit crisis, referring to the process of removing or minimising risk in financial operations and de-risking new asset classes through subsidies, guarantees and securitising bank energy loans. Steckel and Jakob (2018), for example, suggest that financing costs can be lowered by either addressing the underlying sources of investment risk (policy de-risking) or shifting risk away from private sector investors (financial de-risking) on the domestic and the international level. O'Boyle (2018) further specifies three types of risk: technology risk, development risk and pricing risk. Addressing each of these risk profiles helps investors such as utilities, banks or other institutions find the necessary will to invest. For example, renewable energy is especially capital-sensitive because, while renewable energy technologies have high initial costs, they then cost very little to operate because they do not require fuel. One consequence of this capital-intensive nature is that renewable energy is very sensitive to the cost of capital: to the interest rates or return rates demanded by those who lend or pay for renewable energy technology up front. So, for example, high interest rates can significantly increase the overall cost of a wind farm. If public policy can drive down risk, it can drive down cost and the difference can be dramatic, cutting overall costs by close to 50 per cent in some cases (O'Boyle 2018).

What de-risking can also do, however, is shift risk back to cash-strapped governments that are expected to set up entities to undertake surveys, secure land rights, mobilise financial guarantees and deposits and put in place 'enabling regulation' to make the extraction of profit as risk-free and painless as possible. In the case of the development cooperation agreement in Ghana, power sector liberalisation was sought through 'an enabling environment that reduces barriers and levels the playing field for private sector investment' (Glatzer et al. 2024: 478). The example of the Geothermal Development Corporation in Kenya provides a further case in point where scoping work, securing land and undertaking impact assessments were all done by the state to clear the way for private investors to capture those investment opportunities identified as most lucrative (Newell and Phillips 2016). Similar dynamics have been observed in other sites of de-risking green finance in Zambia and Senegal, for example (Elsner et al. 2021; Haag 2022). Key risks for private investors include interest rates, grid integration issues, political risk insurance, as well as protection against revenue shortfalls. But they also include environmental risks, such as climate, where risk guarantee schemes have been used whereby the state compensates investors for losses in case of severe climate 'events' (Glatzer et al. 2024). Among the many PPPs Ghana has been targeted for across social and health infrastructure, agriculture and housing, Gabor (2021) highlights the example of Ghana's PPP energy project backed by the World Bank for the exploitation of Sankofa offshore gas which includes a 'take or pay' clause that obliges the Ghana National Petroleum Corporation to purchase 90 per cent of the gas whether it can use it or not, leading to high costs and indebtedness for the state. Mazzucato (2015: 149) meanwhile cites the case of General Electric who 'inherited' the prior investments of the state in wind turbine manufacturing, while studies of agricultural biotechnology policy reveal a similar pattern of state agricultural research institutes leading the way with pioneering applications and private actors engaging at the point at which commercial applications become clear and scalable (Scoones 2006). Moving from a 'parasitic' to a 'symbiotic' model of partnership (Mazzucato 2015) is far from straightforward, however. Placing capitalist development in Zaire in a colonial and global context of core and periphery regions, Macgaffey (1987), shows how commercial classes organised around oil and cotton production resisted state policies limiting 'parasitic' extraction regarding controls on wages, prices, taxation, licensing and protection for local industry that would have captured more of the benefits. This lends weight to arguments about the way in which colonial dominance has been prolonged by the 'longue durée' of financial power structures' (Koddenbrock et al. 2022) which lock in financialisation (Glatzer et al. 2024).

Equally, when commercial success and niche breakthroughs are not forthcoming, there is a one-sided politics of blame allocation. As Mazzucato (2015: 151) notes, 'when wind or solar markets faltered following retraction of US support for renewables in the late 1980s, the tendency has been to focus on how government investment is flawed, while the role of business in contributing to that failure is ignored or written off as part of the "natural" behaviour of competitive markets'. At the same time, leading states and the finance they provide to global bodies continue to lock in high-carbon trajectories, increasing the risk of stranded assets even if delivering short-term profits for some fossil fuel majors. Bloomberg recently reported that the ratio of clean energy lending and equity underwriting relative to fossil fuels needs to hit 4 to 1 by the end of the decade to achieve the goals of the Paris Agreement. That ratio was roughly 0.8 to 1 at the end of 2021. Since the Paris Agreement, about $4.6 trillion of bonds and loans have been committed to businesses focussed on fossil fuels, roughly double the $2.3 trillion arranged for renewable projects and other low-carbon solutions (Quinson 2023).

The allocation and direction of support for particular technology and innovation pathways are sharply determined by both the availability and nature of finance and the scale of anticipated profits. Hence, as well as offsetting, sharing or de-risking the upfront costs of investment, states have a key role to play in sending signals about the direction of change and its permanency. State investment banks (SIBs) such as the Clean Energy Finance Corporation (CEFC) in Australia, the Kreditanstalt für Wiederaufbau (KfW) in Germany and the Green Investment Bank (GIB) in the UK, for example, have also played a critical role in this regard. SIBs can take a broader approach to mobilising finance than capital provision and de-risking, as well as signal trust and 'crowd in' private finance (Geddes et al. 2018). At the same time, given the growing financial power of state development banks, whose loans often dwarf those of multilateral development banks (MDBs), there is also a clear need to coordinate climate safeguards in lending practices between banks. For example, the stock of outstanding loans made by the China Development Bank was $1,635 billion in 2017, much larger than the total loans by the World Bank (UNCTAD 2019). Some forms of state support are about addressing market failures produced by the underpricing of pollution or seeing technology developers through the 'valley of death' as they move from demonstration stage to commercial deployment. With energy, there are added issues because of the long-lived nature of the capital assets and the high potential for lock-in (Unruh 2000).

The approach to thinking about the state and state power outlined in the previous chapter also points to the need to question the assumed neatness of the distinction between state and capital, public and private, however. Indeed, approaches adopted by entrepreneurial states around the world reflect varieties of decarbonisation and varieties of climate capitalism (Newell and Paterson 2010; Lachapelle et al. 2017). Examples include Germany's *Energiewald* and India's solar mission where the state positions itself as the enabler of private investment. India's Five-Year Plans and various policy 'missions' such as the National Solar Mission are based on a model of state-led development that dates from the era of Nehru (Phillips and Newell 2013: 657). Amongst the varieties of decarbonisation, we can observe a return of state capitalism (Alami, Dixon et al. 2022): Green New Deals in Europe; bailouts in the wake of the pandemic; industrial conversion along the lines discussed in Chapter 1; and a large role for state development banks in China, Brazil, and South Africa among others (Geddes et al. 2018). Multiple drivers are at play and include a desire to reduce state expenditure in the case of India's solar mission and to reduce dependency on imported oil; savings from fossil fuel subsidy reform; reducing geopolitical vulnerabilities such as the shift away from dependence on Russian gas in Germany, the UK and elsewhere in Europe; the drive for energy efficiency and renewable energy after the OPEC crisis; and building a global export model around biofuels in Brazil and wind and solar in China (Hochstetler 2021).

3.3 Transforming the Entrepreneurial State

As Schumpeter (2011 [1947]) and Marx before him showed, dynamic and transformative change is inherent to capitalism. He suggests:

> [I]n dealing with capitalism we are dealing with an evolutionary process … Capitalism, then, is by nature a form or method of economic change and not only never is but never can be stationary. And this evolutionary character of the capitalist process is not merely due to the fact that economic life goes on in a social and natural environment which changes … they are not its prime movers … The fundamental impulse that sets and keeps the capitalist engine in motion comes from the new consumer goods, the new methods of production or transportation, the new markets, the new forms of industrial organisation that capitalist enterprise creates … industrial mutation … incessantly revolutionises the economic structure *from within*, incessantly destroying the old one, incessantly creating a new one. This process of creative destruction is the essential fact about capitalism. It is what capitalism consists of and what every capitalist concern has got to live in. (Schumpeter 2011 [1947]: 82–83; emphasis in original)

The question then is *where* and *how* and *for whom* will capitalism evolve next? What will be creatively (or uncreatively) destroyed, by whom and on whose terms? Will it be the transformation of economic structures 'from within' as Schumpeter suggests with shifts in production, markets and transport leading the way, or will it be more directed and regulated by public institutions to ensure it is guided by ambitious sustainability targets and social justice principles as part of global just transitions? There may be growing recognition that the state is heavily implicated in even allegedly market-led transitions, though the extent to which this is the case and the way it manifests itself will vary by region. But are there seeds within the existing order of more progressive, profound and transformational change or is such a prospect delusional? More convivial post-growth economies are unlikely to be supported by advanced, industrialised, modern capitalist states and yet they might flourish anyhow precisely because of the inability of the state and other institutions of modern governance to deliver the public goods people need and to protect the commons in ways vital to sustaining life, triggering forms of mutual aid, self-help and community organising, the like of which proliferated during the Covid pandemic.

What emerges might well be a polycentric model of governance of innovation in which the state plays an enabling role, steering a range of actors, *primus inter pares*, rather than mission-oriented leviathan. Rather than a new project of state-ordering or capital-led innovation, for De Schutter and Dedeurwaerdere (2021) this implies a reconstitution of social capital and a project of democratic renewal from below. This is not to deny the vital role of the state in providing key services, affording social protection and discipling the market but to also engage the state as an actor that can help to support and cross-fertilise citizen-led experimentation. It is a vision of social innovation in which businesses can also mobilise finance and activate their supply chains in support of such endeavours.

In specific terms, our focus here is the question of the potential and means for transforming the entrepreneurial state, that part of the state centrally concerned with innovation. It means rethinking the purpose and means of innovation: what it is for, how it occurs and who innovates. The question of *who* and *what* is defined (and *by whom*) as entrepreneurial and worthy of state support, what sorts of innovation are most urgently needed and *how* they can be enabled requires a reimagining of the economy since so much innovation is aimed at replicating and expanding an economic system which, from the point of view of more radical notions of sustainability, is no longer fit for purpose, or put more bluntly, is driving us towards social and ecological collapse.

It also requires an opening up of imaginaries and possible futures on the part of researchers of innovation who have traditionally imagined their task to be serving the growth machine. Malerba and Brusoni's (2007) expansive volume *Perspectives on Innovation* establishes that understanding economic growth is 'the central task of economic analysis' in the book's opening section on 'Innovation and Economic Growth' (Malerba and Brusoni 2007: v). But it also requires a more honest, dynamic and inclusive account of 'actually existing innovation' distributed across multiple sectors and sites within society where attempts to reconfigure production, technology use and development are commonplace and not the exclusive preserve of industrial actors with state backing. Everyday innovations take place in social, cultural, political, economic as well as technological arenas to save, share, repurpose goods, resources and technologies and enhance welfare. The task of a more sustainable state is to support those processes and practices.

3.3.1 Rethinking Innovation

A progressive entrepreneurial state needs to shift from supporting innovation and growth for the sake of it towards supporting innovation and incumbent disruptions that fundamentally reorganise systems of production and consumption in line with ecological limits. This implies more than a shift in the 'techno-economic paradigm' (Perez 2002) and ideologies of governance (Gamble 2014). It rather implies a role for choice-editing (not issuing licences for destructive forms of production rather than leaving it to consumer choice in the market), accelerating the managed decline of polluting industries and rescaling economies: a shift from transition to transformation (Akenji 2014; Newell 2018). It means contesting and reversing the logics and practice of a 'make, break and throwaway economy' (Porritt 1989; Raworth 2017) and planned obsolescence. As Vinsel and Rusell (2020: 14) note, 'The innovation mindset has led to a devaluation of maintenance and care with disastrous results'. Innovation has come to be juxtaposed with maintenance which Buck (cited in Vinsel and Rusell 2020: 80) suggests refers to the 'overlooked and underpaid work of keeping daily life going, caring for people and things, sustaining what we've collectively inherited'.

Given finite resources and competition for R&D funding, tough choices have to be made. This means abandoning the notion of 'technological neutrality'. In the face of a climate and ecological emergency to not take sides, or to explicitly or implicitly support pathways which lock in global heating, is to be directly culpable for the devastating consequences. To some extent, the choices are zero-sum in a context of limited state resources: one technology or sector's gain will be another's loss. It is not a question of 'lifting all boats' with climate change when expanding one boat (fossil fuels, for example) will lead to sea-level rise that will sink all others (Daley and Lawrie 2022). Indeed, ongoing support to the fossil fuel sector, which for fossil fuel subsidies alone runs at $11 million a minute (IMF 2021), is adding social and environmental costs to the rest of society in health and climate impacts, while slowing the pace of much-needed transitions in related sectors such as transport and agriculture.

Radical demand reduction through support to social innovation is key: shared housing, public transport, community energy and food systems can be supported through policy and economic instruments and more individualised, exclusive, commercialised and private modes of provision disincentivised. Patterns of demand and behaviour are shaped through policy and planning and can recast the landscape of innovation in profound ways as innovators and entrepreneurs adapt business models to new ways of working, travelling, consuming energy and water and eating. Social innovation can drive shifts in business practice, technology development and innovation to support sustainable lifestyles (Westley and Antadze 2010; Hiteva and Sovacool 2017). This needs to be accompanied by policies and interventions to restrict the generation of demand for unsustainable products and services by advertisers, as highlighted by the Badvertising campaign and taken up by cities such as Chennai, Amsterdam and Grenoble (Simms and Murray 2023). Indeed, in their analysis of the transformation of the industrial state Ashford and Hall (2011: 12) call on the state 'To regulate deceptive and inaccurate advertising, as well as to provide counteracting government messaging to discourage unsustainable consumption'. Such moves, though seemingly utopian in today's consumer society, have historical precedents in the time of the Second World War. As Newell and Simms (2020: 12) reflect:

Amazingly, from today's standpoint of rampant mass consumerism, efforts were invested by the state in de-legitimising wasteful consumption. Railway companies advertised that needless travel is a crime. The Railway Executive Committee produced a poster which read 'Is your journey really necessary?' 'War gardens' were promoted 'for victory', while the UK Ministry of Fuel and Power appealed to people not to 'squander electricity' and to 'save fuel', 'mend, sew, repair'. In the US the Food Administration urged citizens not to 'waste food' and issued a list of instructions about how to do it which included: 'buy it with thought, cook it with care, use less wheat and meat, buy local foods, serve just enough, use what is left'.

These are not the traditional activities of an entrepreneurial state in a capitalist economy and there are legitimate questions about whether retraction rather than expansion of economic activity is a realistic expectation of the state given its core functions in industrial society (which we explore further in Chapter 4). And yet it is clearly necessary and imperative in light of the fair division of global responsibilities guided by notions of contraction (for richer countries) and convergence (for poorer ones) towards equal per capita entitlements for example (GCI 2018) as part of the global just transition discussed in Chapter 7 in relation to the welfare state. In this regard, there is an important role for undoing destructive innovations, or what some scholars have called 'exnovation' (Martin 2017): taking destructive innovations out of existence. For Martin (2017: 138), 'Exnovation is a process in which a given technology is currently no longer used because its physical infrastructure has been deliberately removed; this distinguishes exnovation from concepts of discontinued use'. Exnovation is 'the removal of unsustainable technologies and associated actor and value structures from extant socio-technical regimes', or as Kimberly first defined it, 'the removal of an innovation from an organization. Exnovation occurs when an organization divests itself of an innovation in which it had previously invested' (Kimberly 1981: 91). This points to the limits of innovation and Schumpeterian notions of 'creative destruction' through innovation for engendering fundamental changes (Heyen et al. 2017; Davidson 2019) or what Shove (2012) calls 'the shadowy side of innovation'. Exnovation can be a driver of innovation and makes space for the development and maturation of novel sustainable technologies (David 2017). It can be achieved through bans, taxes and product standards which constrain the production and consumption of harmful products and have been adopted before, such as the creation of emissions standards, animal welfare standards (bans on caged chickens) or bans on chlorofluorocarbons (CFCs) or asbestos which address production processes or final products with the aim of taking them out of circulation, as well as controls on advertising as discussed earlier. It can be viewed as part of a growing trend towards the use of phase-out policies, plans and supply-side policies which seek to manage the removal, decline or early retirement of key technologies and infrastructures whose social and environmental impacts can no longer be justified (Trencher et al. 2023).

Hence, while such a transformation implies a shift in state behaviour and modus operandi, as emphasised throughout the book, it is important to recognise that the state itself is in transition. The nature of agency and leadership expected of the state may be expected to shift once again in the face of the climate and wider environmental crisis and the crisis of state legitimation to which these may give rise. As Pegels et al. (2018: 29) note, '[w]hile innovation has been supported, technology diffusion has been left to the market. Supply and demand have largely been taken as given, and market dynamics have led to the selection of certain technologies. In contrast, environmental pressures are now making it necessary to deliberately disrupt established pathways and replace them with new, sustainable ones.'

It will also require deliberate disruption, managed decline of incumbent industries and supply-side policies aimed at limiting production and demand-side policies to reduce unsustainable consumption. As Geels (2002: 1258) notes, 'reconfiguration processes do not occur easily, because the elements in a socio-technical configuration are linked and aligned to each other. Radically new technologies have a hard time to break through, because regulations, infrastructure, user practices, maintenance networks are aligned to the existing technology.' Indeed, the flip side of not picking winners is disparate, diffuse and unfocussed support, none of which is sufficient to meaningfully bring to market any one technological innovation/pathway and the antithesis of the 'long, loud, legal' frameworks required by investors to guide future pathways (Hamilton 2009). In reality, distinct types and levels of support are required at different times for distinct technologies in a diversity of markets, a fact which inhibits the relevance of one-size-fits-all proscriptions and supports arguments for 'picking problems' as the target of state action rather than specific technologies (Mazzucato 2022). This is partly also because ambitious temporal targets around net zero by 2050, for example, limit the number of technological options. 'This deadline means that public investment can no longer be limited to long term R&D in risky technologies. Instead, the technologies included in the net-zero mix must be testable and deployable within three decades' (Arcand and Meadowcroft 2024: 11). But, as argued throughout the book, it is ultimately power relations that need to be reconfigured if more just and sustainable outcomes are to be achieved as part of a more far-reaching reset of the economy and the values which govern it and not just systems of support for one technology over another.

3.3.2 Bolstering Industrial Policy

These same environmental pressures driving a rethink of innovation have led to renewed interest in the return of state-led industrial policy, as noted, and a shift away from a predominantly laissez-faire model of industrial development towards various versions of a green new deal (Klein 2019; Pettifor 2019; Chomsky and Pollin 2020) as seen in Europe and the US and proactive 'developmental state' strategies pursued by China, India, South Africa and Brazil. Drawing on examples from Chile and Brazil, Nem Singh (2024) proposes hybrid development strategies formulated through SOEs as a means to move beyond extractivist growth models. This will be vital to transforming the nature, purpose and ambition of the entrepreneurial state. For Pegels et al. (2018), the available instruments of what they call 'green energy policy' can be grouped into mandating, incentivising and nudging instruments. Moreover, they need to be designed under conditions of technological uncertainty, to be more selective and directional by narrowing technological development corridors, and to cover long periods to support long-term transformation processes. Conditions for the success of such policies include efficiency, effectiveness and legitimacy, yet capacity to produce such conditions varies hugely across societies. As Rodrik (2007) has argued, effective policy first and foremost needs an institutional setting that balances embeddedness and autonomy of governments vis-à-vis the private sector. The nature and scale of this challenge should not be underestimated when considering, as I do in Chapter 4, the way in which the industrial state is organised and its systematic privileging of the priorities of industry over other social goals and the extent to which the interests of capital are hardwired into state decision-making (Miliband 1973).

In relation to energy, we can see the concrete importance of this in relation to competition and contestation over subsidies to renewable energy and around the Non-Fossil Fuel obligation that was introduced in the UK, or in relation to the vast subsidies for nuclear energy where in the UK the Hinkley Point nuclear power plant is now the most expensive piece of infrastructure on record and its developers are negotiating a model whereby costs can be recovered up front (Watt 2017). Political and institutional lock-in around industrial policy can also be observed in the contracts to provide tariff-free electricity to mining companies in South Africa that were negotiated in the apartheid era when the government was desperate to attract investors amid international ostracism for its racist regime (Baker et al. 2014). Returning to themes of policy autonomy and development space, it is also important to emphasise the scope for states to adopt industrial policies such as infant industry measures and procurement policies that are sometimes circumscribed by World Trade Organization (WTO) rules (Lewis 2014) to avoid kicking away the ladder (Chang 2002) which, as noted, will be critical to supporting just transitions. There is a role for the global state discussed in Chapter 8 to use its influence to support policy change in key global governance institutions such as the International Monetary Fund (IMF), WTO and World Bank to make this possible (Newell et al. 2023).

Returning to the theme of rethinking innovation as it relates to industrial policy, whereas there are now many technology and innovation hubs ostensibly aimed at driving green innovation, many of these are aimed at bringing new technologies to market without addressing the need to reduce demand for more resources. In other words, they add to the mix of available technologies but do little to shift resource trajectories if business-as-usual demands continue to rise and nothing is done to discontinue existing incumbent technologies. Most dramatically perhaps, we observe this in the way in which renewable energies are adding to the energy mix but, as yet, not displacing fossil fuels (Fressoz 2024). Green industrial policy, however, might move towards more bottom-up planning and needs assessment as well as a rebalancing of the respective roles of state and market actors. This would mean addressing the allocation of direct and indirect subsidies from the state to capital: how to move beyond public subsidies and risk-taking for technologies and innovations that the private sector then develops for commercial and exclusive ends and not the 'common good' where the definition and pursuit of the common good should not be the prerogative of the state alone. It would also imply an active embrace of exnovation as discussed earlier – accelerating the obsolescence of particular technologies and production processes combined with more choice-editing.

3.3.3 Democratising Innovation

The current situation in which governments by default or by design 'pick winners' from among technologies and solutions proposed by existing incumbents is often hidden from public view, behind outward-facing rhetoric about 'letting all flowers bloom' and allowing the market's logic to work its magic by letting competition determine where demand is greatest. Since the 1970s, many governments have shifted the sites of developmental and industrial policymaking away from legislative bodies and public debate to the halls of regulatory agencies and government ministries, from where the state steers markets through the funding of basic science, R&D projects, demonstration plants and public procurement programmes and less obvious marketing strategies (Block 2008; Mazzucato 2011). In the case of natural gas and biofuels, for example, government laboratories not only provided key technologies such as hydraulic fracturing demonstration projects, 3D geologic mapping technologies and cellulosic conversion processes but also helped create markets for gas through deregulation and for biofuels through national consumption mandates. Restricting government support for high-emitting and polluting industries is one thing.

But there is clearly also a need for greater emphasis on radical as opposed to incremental innovation in both the technological and social spheres, where Freeman (1992) suggests 'incremental' innovations lead to improvements in existing products and services and 'radical' ones bring about new inventions and methods of production. But to be successful and sustained, such shifts need to challenge and reverse the power dynamics in terms of who controls technology and whom has access to finance and is involved in decision-making and the evaluation of proposed innovations. In this regard, there is growing interest in 'grassroots innovation' (Smith et al. 2016): citizen inclusion in shaping the form and direction of technological innovation through more participatory technology needs assessments, for example. As Watson (2009: 146) notes, 'the deliberative features of these processes need to be strengthened and adapted to widen participation. Without such an open approach, there is an increased risk that historical inertia due to technical and institutional "lock-in" will prevail, and that the plurality of new and existing technologies required for a more sustainable energy future will not be deployed.'

In terms of democratising technology, a key issue is the risks and trade-offs they may pose for other societal values. From newer technologies such as carbon capture and storage (CCS) and solar geoengineering (such as solar radiation management) to older ones such as nuclear, there are key challenges around citizen engagement. This is particularly so around openness on the direction, purpose, ownership and control and compatibility of technological innovations with other social goals and pathways rather than public selection of options being predetermined by incumbent actors. Around energy, for example, the challenge is that 'Contemporary energy systems are highly technocratic, managed by experts, who in many countries frame the challenge of energy change within the contours of competitive markets. Accordingly, dominant framings of energy transformations or transitions continue to largely exclude the possibility of public involvement in how the sector may evolve' (Pickering 2022: 9).

Nevertheless, past experience suggests that if innovation and experimentation are to deliver social as well as environmental benefits, it is vital to open up decision-making to potential beneficiaries as well as groups that may be impacted negatively. The use of citizens' assemblies and other participatory approaches have been used to help chart out socially acceptable decarbonisation pathways, as can more proactive deliberations on specific innovations such as genetically modified (GM) crops (Pimbert and Wakeford 2002; Newell 2010). Climate assemblies are being trialled in France and the UK and existing frameworks for doing this in the European context are available through the Aarhus Convention (Bryant and Stone 2020). Such political innovations can help to avoid the imposition of unpopular policy measures, thereby improving the chances of lasting success with deeper social ownership and public acceptance.

But states must now be pushed to envision futures and pick winners more democratically, in ways that go beyond backing drop-in 'plug-and-play' solutions that substitute or add technologies without shifting the patterns of production and consumption associated with them (Newell and Martin 2020). Such strategies maintain the conditions of accumulation for dominant firms, especially when those firms engage in activities that undermine sustainable transitions away from fossil fuels through strategies of hedging, delay and resistance (Green et al. 2021). How participation and representation take shape around policy initiatives affects which pathways are pursued (Scoones et al. 2015). Greater citizen engagement in technology needs assessment, evaluation and priority setting around R&D might help to steer science, technology and innovation in more sustainable directions. It would do this by encouraging consideration of a broad range of social concerns or, at the very least, making them less subject to capture by private and vested interests. There are many examples of 'Citizen-led innovation for a new economy' from community-owned enterprises and social innovation to efforts to construct a 'conservation economy' around issues of land, energy, health and housing (Mathie and Gaventa 2015).

There are opportunities to build deliberative, inclusive spaces that encourage social learning and persuasion. This is a difficult task, but it may be more straightforward and easier to accomplish in some arenas than others. As all the examples explored in this chapter make clear, the state has leverage and makes strategic selections (Jessop 2002). Industry already heavily depends on publicly provided resources to access the resources, markets, technologies, infrastructures and relationships that enable their accumulation strategies. Fundamentally, then, the state must craft policy agendas around subordinating short-term profits and investor returns to innovations that help to achieve the most sustainable outcomes, those which address widespread inequality and those which help communities become more resilient to multiple ecological and economic crises. This can mean making public policy support and procurement conditional on meeting social and environmental criteria or making public resources contingent on participation in a broader policy plan developed through an inclusive, deliberative process that can strengthen a collective ability to build consensus around desirable ways forward. It can also mean bringing decision-making about permit allocations, science funding, R&D policy, innovation hubs, regulatory science, the design of market incentives, technology transfer and the entrepreneurial state more generally out into the open and inviting public critique and engagement with them.

Politically, this is challenging and is unlikely to happen without sustained advocacy and mobilisation to support any such moves in that direction grounded in rights-based claims to information and participation on the part of citizens in decisions which affect them. But the overarching goal is to open up decision-making to learning and deliberation, inviting a wider range of affected publics to partake in imagining what futures are desirable and what means are justified to realise those ends. This requires stronger democratic institutions to guide the practice of 'picking winners', alongside a broader understanding of what 'winning' means, revisiting policies around tax breaks and the vast amount of subsidies that still go to polluting industries. Questions of 'transition to what, for whom, and when?' must be publicly debated and democratically framed, not only in the policy process but in the larger visions a society assembles.

States are needed that can support 'socially embedded entrepreneurialism': transitions that are moulded according to the visions of a broader range of social actors. And institutional innovations are needed that enhance transparency and accountability, as well as more traditional 'good governance' checks on the regulation of party funding and the representation of lobbyists in policy processes that work so hard to preserve and expand incumbent power. Though challenging, shifts in political power are a prerequisite for transformative change that can carry society beyond plug-and-play approaches to realigning socio-technical configurations (providing services differently) while keeping the power relations intact in terms of who provides those services and on what terms. At the moment, 'Ecopreneurial' companies and actors create 'new products, services, techniques and organizational modes that substantially reduce environmental impacts and increase the quality of life' and thus go beyond incremental improvements, which are frequently characteristic of environmental management in large companies (Schaltegger et al. 2015: 46), but of their own volition they have limited capacity to deliver wider change (Hörisch 2015).

The pace and depth of innovation and experimentation are often frustrated by dominant incumbent actors who seek to protect their market share. Hockerts and Wüstenhagen (2010) show how incumbents resist radical, transformative sustainability-oriented innovations because of investments in existing (and often unsustainable) assets. As incumbents are usually reluctant to bring about their own sustainability-oriented innovations, they are challenged by the new products and services of entrants. Their access to decision-making must be restricted to create space and demand for new forms of innovation. In practical terms, this means enacting policies and measures that restrict party funding, minimise the revolving door between governments and incumbent industry actors and enlarge the representation of beneficiaries of ambitious action for sustainability, including younger people (Newell and Martin 2020). Greater de facto representation of future generations and efforts to lower voting ages might be further ways to do this.

Dominant approaches to innovation and experimentation assume an 'as well as' model of adding to existing forms of innovation and experimentation rather than an 'instead of' approach. The latter requires abandoning the strategies, tools and business models of existing consumption and production that are no longer compatible with building a more sustainable society and achieving just transitions. Disruptive approaches need to actively enable new social and economic actors to lead transitions that redesign transport, food and waste systems, for example, so that they meet broader social and human needs. Concretely, this means expanding the 'Green entrepreneurial state' (Mazzucato 2015) and strengthening green industrial policy (Pegels 2014). As former Green MEP Molly Scott Cato (n.d.) put it:

> [W]e would propose the introduction of a number of Ecological Enterprise Zones, in areas where the resources necessary for a sustainable economy to succeed are present, but which have not thrived in the competition for financial investment. These EEZs would be supported by government grants to become hot-houses for the innovation of green technologies and sustainable lifestyles. In return, they would be expected to achieve significant cuts in carbon emissions, resource usage, and levels of waste production. Government should enable local authorities in such areas to experiment with policy tools, such as carbon taxation and import and export duties. The aim would be for the EEZ to become a prototype of the self-reliant local economy that a green economy requires.

Disruptive innovation in politics is a prerequisite for ambitious and progressive approaches to sustainability through finance, technology and other means. It requires challenges to incumbent control over transition pathways. Given their central role in key nodal points within them, governments are particularly well placed to activate and orchestrate a variety of levers and tools at their disposal within an ecosystem of transformation. Interventions in one area have knock-on effects elsewhere, amplifying their overall impact. Taking the case of energy transitions, supply-side policies that restrict access to remaining reserves of fossil fuels and redirect finance in new directions can shift business practices away from fossil fuels when combined with new rules on disclosure and corporate governance. Necessity is the mother of all invention. Governments must seriously consider supply-side policies by placing clear limits on further fossil fuel reserves extraction. The only way to redirect finance towards lower-carbon technologies, infrastructures and services is to make clear that some models of wealth creation that have reached their sell-by date are off limits. In practice, this implies using bans and moratoria, active phase-downs and clear timelines for managed decline. Businesses need a clear and consistent signal that the end game for fossil fuels has arrived. Likewise, tax and fiscal measures to help local businesses and cities raise their level of ambition can trigger change from below, setting off waves of change among transnational city networks. Alongside such economic policies that withdraw state support to fossil fuel industries, policies that enhance the participation and representation of beneficiaries of climate action in decision-making can tilt the balance of power towards even more ambitious action.

Building multi-level and multi-actor alliances is key to engaging different parts of the state in ambitious and progressive innovation and experimentation. It is important not to treat 'the state' as a monolithic entity, not to fetishise the agency and power of those arms of the state ostensibly charged with directing and supporting innovation while neglecting other areas of state activity (as discussed in Chapters 1 and 2). By design or by default, most parts of the state enable or frustrate innovation pathways in the sectors they oversee. Support for innovation and experimentation cannot be siloed in particular sectors. Governments around the world have signed up to the SDGs and so need to simultaneously address questions of climate change, food security, access to water and energy, economic inequality, the need to avoid conflict and more. This poses a huge challenge for conventional policymaking. But the more inclusive and participatory processes we have, the better the chances of sustainability initiatives identifying and acting on potential synergies in action across these domains while not passing on the costs and burdens to poorer and more vulnerable members of society (Alcamo et al. 2020).

As we saw in Chapter 1, states are also not neutral with respect to the actors they are meant to be regulating, nor with respect to particular innovation pathways. States can have large stakes in incumbent systems and be incumbent actors themselves – classically through state-owned enterprises – making them reluctant to support niche innovation and experimentation. Some states also clearly have more power than others to enact ambitious policies for sustainability or to facilitate and finance global transitions, and within the state, certain ministries and levels of office more inclined to support transformative action than others. This points to the need for creative multi-actor alliances that work with central and local governments, business, civil society groups and trade unions. Coalition building among these groups can help rally support for bolder interventions and involve important actors who have often been excluded from decision-making. Recognising the different geographies of innovation, there is a key role for cities, municipal and regional governments and supranational institutions in supporting more ambitious forms of innovation and experimentation by creating positive enabling environments through regulation, participatory planning, fiscal policy and other measures (such as tax breaks, preferential rates for local businesses) to support niche business and community actors. Sub-national experimentation can create positive practice that is shared across networks and amplified by coalitions of business and civil society actors, showcasing what is possible and generating demand for positive change elsewhere.

Around technological innovation, too, an ecosystemic approach is required to build 'connections between innovation intermediaries, such as incubator and accelerator centres, niche actors, such as green champions, and regime actors, such as policy entrepreneurs [which] show potential to contribute to a green economic development strategy' (Gliedt et al. 2018: 1247). These connections have to be built and sustained. As Newell, Daley and Twena (2022: 72) note:

> Identifying and leveraging the impact of transition intermediaries can have profound impacts on consumption pathways and emissions lock-in. In the case of housing, for example, urban planners can integrate sustainable practices into the built environment (Capstick et al., 2019). Similarly, a car salesperson who advises a customer to purchase an EV is helping to prevent further emissions lock-in within the mobility sector (Sovacool et al., 2020). Utilising intermediaries is by no means a substitute for public policy interventions, which can be far more targeted, but they provide opportunities to access and shape key junctures and moments of change within all of our lives.

Such actors can help navigate the complex geographies of innovation. All aspects of transition are produced, in reality, across scales. Some scholars have found, for example, that 'core processes of innovation systems show distinct scalar relations that vary between development phases' (Dewald and Fromhold-Eisebith 2015: 110). For example, the innovation path of photovoltaic technology is shaped by 'scale-transcending and multi-scalar dynamics'. Key to effective innovation in this instance was 'Temporal and spatial coherence within a national frame' (Dewald and Fromhold-Eisebith 2015: 110).

This requires a political economy account that can traverse these levels, linking macro landscape trends with small-scale and rooted innovations and niches in disparate locations and varied contexts, often far removed from the political centres of gravity. This is a classic case of multi-level governance: trying to govern from local to global across states, as well as regional, national and global bodies using different levers of power in different spaces for diverse ends. Successful transitions will require shifts in culture and practice, in financing and business models, in models of innovation and service, as well as in the regulatory and policy environment. How these socio-technical, and political, elements combine is a key focus of transitions research.

A more holistic or systemic view of transformation also highlights, however, the need not just to fetishise particular environmental problems but rather to look at the range of social and ecological impacts associated with different pathways consistent with a more holistic and ecological approach. Achieving the SDGs requires this. Hence, it is less a question, for example, of only taking carbon out of systems, as much as innovating, experimenting with and supporting and scaling up technologies, infrastructures and practices that build resilience and regenerate ecosystems rather than deplete them. An ecosystemic perspective also helps to keep in mind the global nature of transition processes. Experimentation and innovation in one part of the world have impacts for the pathways and policy options available elsewhere. As discussed in Chapter 2, relationality is key. As we have seen with respect to natural gas, biofuels, electric vehicles and climate smart agriculture, the costs of adjustment and decarbonisation can be passed on to other societies and social groups in the search for 'low-carbon' energy, food and transportation, for example (Newell and Taylor 2018; Soto Hernandez and Newell 2022). 'Just transitions' have to be socially just in global and temporal ways, and not just in relation to particular places and transitions. The conversation about justice has to be opened up to its global and even intergenerational dimensions in ways that go beyond the national focus of most discussions and dialogues on energy transitions and current trends towards the negotiation of Just Energy Transition Partnerships (JETPs). One country's transition choices cannot be seen in isolation from their global effects, in terms of shifts in demand for land (e.g., for biofuels) or for minerals (e.g., for car batteries or photovoltaic panels) or the waste they generate (e.g., nuclear) given the nature of uneven and combined development described in Chapter 2. This places pressure on regional and global institutions to coordinate, oversee and manage the spillover effects of different transition pathways in support of just transitions.

This is clearly also about building innovation and diffusion networks, not just R&D policy and the provision of subsidies. As critics of the entrepreneurial state approach have suggested, 'the exclusive focus on knowledge creation through R&D and different forms of firm subsidies ignores the equally important mechanisms of knowledge dissemination and creation through commercial exploitation in markets' (Karlson et al. 2020: 81). It also feeds into wider discussions about what, beyond support to innovation, might be required of an 'entrepreneurial developmental state' (Pacheco Pardo and Klingler-Vidra 2019). There are also the unintended consequences – or political fallout – of policy strategies driven by an entrepreneurial state. These include the fact that the entrepreneurial state can 'inadvertently crowd out entrepreneurship' through 'coordinated policies that prioritize and target capital, knowledge, and human capital accumulation in particular industries, sectors, technologies, and firms have created a formidable societal knowledge filter, which in turn can impede endogenous entrepreneurial activity' (Audretsch and Fiedler 2022: 573). The overall effect can be to slow the transition to an entrepreneurial society. Ultimately, the entrepreneurial state, however ambitious and radical in its orientation and strategies, needs to be supported by a set of overarching state strategies promoting an altogether different, and more sustainable, model of industrial development. It is to the industrial state that we now turn our attention.

4

The Industrial State

4.1 Introducing the Industrial State

What is the purpose of the state in industrial society and what implications does that have for the prospects of industrial transformation for sustainability? Or, put differently, what is the significance of the organisation of the state along industrial (primarily capitalist) lines for the nature and prospects of sustainability transitions?

As we saw in Chapter 2, a key function of the state in a capitalist society and central to its ability to secure legitimation is its ability to facilitate capital accumulation. Even in socialist societies, growth and extractivism remain both the goal and the way to achieve it, even if the means of production are held in state hands and the wealth generated publicly shared (in theory at least). Hence industrial development and expansion is a key *raison d'être* of the modern state and should not be confused with particular historical expressions of this core function around dominant regimes of accumulation such as with regard to the 'neoliberal state' for example which emerged from the late 1970s onwards (Plant 2010) and its increasing reliance on a finance-led regime of accumulation (Aglietta 2000; Arrighi 2010). It is, nevertheless, the case that the terms on which, and the conditions in which, the state is able to secure the advancement of its industrial objectives are shaped by continual reconfigurations of social forces, a shifting geopolitical economic context and evolving notions of what counts as an attractive 'investment climate' to mobile private capital. Thus, in order to attract mobile transnational capital, states recast themselves as 'competition states' (Cerny 1995) to secure advantages over 'rival states and rival firms' in an integrated global political economy (Stopford et al. 1991) in which competition is the driving force of capital accumulation. In terms of securing the extra-economic conditions for a post-Fordist accumulation regime, Jessop (2002) suggests a 'Schumpeterian competition state' has emerged around a new techno-economic paradigm. He defines the competition state as: 'a state that aims to secure economic growth within its borders and/or to secure competitive advantages for capitals based in its borders, even where they operate abroad, by promoting the economic and extra-economic conditions that are deemed vital for success in competition with economic actors and spaces located in other states' (Jessop 2002: 96). What makes it Schumpeterian per se is a concern with technological change, innovation and enterprise, and rather like the entrepreneurial state described in Chapter 3, the Schumpeterian competition state seeks to 'develop new techniques of government and governance to these ends' from institutions and regulation to the provision of capital, subsidies, infrastructures, technical assistance and research and development. In this sense 'States engage in the pursuit of technological rents on behalf of capital' (Jessop 2002: 132). The ways in which economic and non-economic conditions for capital accumulation are secured by states beyond their borders is a theme we return to in Chapter 8 on the global state.

A more contemporary example of a techno-economic paradigm in the service of a new accumulation strategy is the 'Wall Street Consensus' which conscripts states into 'risk-proofing' assets as part of a project of making development 'investible' (Gabor 2021). There is then a spectrum of approaches and tools for enhancing state competitiveness underpinned by competing ideologies about the role of the state and which fractions of industrial and financial capital it should serve. These range from a Ricardian emphasis on static comparative advantage and effective exploitation of factors of production to a Listian preference for protection, state support and steering of the economy, a Keynesian emphasis on full employment as the goal, through to Schumpeterian strategies which centre on enhancing capacities for 'permanent innovation' (Jessop 2002: 121). These strategies are reflected in the institutional underpinnings and modes of regulation of accumulation regimes, what scholars in the varieties of capitalism tradition might refer to as the institutional sources of comparative advantage (Hall and Soskice 2001). These are observable in regulatory frameworks across levels of governance to produce lock-in, enabling spatial fixes to delay and displace crises from the domestic sphere and socialise the conditions of production.

Powerful states both generate those disciplinary pressures and apply them to other states (directly and through firms based in their jurisdiction) and extend their reach through the control and resourcing of global institutions which act on their behalf (as we will see in Chapter 8). While around energy transitions, for example, the International Energy Agency (IEA) has emphasised on many occasions, 'governments hold the key to changing the mix of energy investment' (IEA 2009: 41), they also need to manage industrial relations and in such a way that squares competing pressures towards accumulation and legitimation (Paterson 2010), bringing to the fore tensions between their ability to serve finance and industrial capital simultaneously and to balance both domestic and international pressures and economic, social and environmental goals. The state then is a key mediator of conflicts between and within capital, labour and other social forces.

Through inactions and actions, interventions and non-interventions, the state is centrally anchored in the production, maintenance and reproduction of industrial life. It is against this background that key dilemmas, tensions and contradictions arise that were discussed in Chapter 1: between accumulation and legitimation, between labour exploitation and industrial expansion and social protection and social justice (the distribution of costs and benefits within and beyond the state), between securitisation and militarisation, between economic growth and resource depletion and between national and global priorities. The starting point here for an analysis of the industrial state then is the problematic, compromised and complicit role of the state in the very processes of accumulation that are degrading the planet and producing social and economic injustices. As Michael Saward (1998: 345) asks, 'Could it be that the contemporary state is simply not the type of entity which is capable of systematically prioritizing the achievement of sustainability?' In one sense, this derives from a key set of contradictions and functional interdependencies between the capitalist state and the capitalist economy to secure the conditions of accumulation which serve both, and the 'grow-or-die' imperatives of capitalism. As Koch (2021: 116) argues, in the environmental state, 'State-led environmental policies are feasible as long as these do not undermine the overall growth orientation and are therefore largely reduced to the provision of 'green growth'.

The need for legitimation may constrain the pursuit of those goals, but perceived or alleged public legitimacy and access to state power can also be mobilised for the purposes of elite plunder under the guise of state-led industrialisation strategies (Salah Ovadia 2018). There is plenty of evidence of elites ransacking the state to serve patronage and clientelist networks and cronies, hence the term 'crony capitalism' or references scholars make to 'parasitic' forms of capitalism (Macgaffey 1987). The privatisation and selling off of state assets to the allies of ruling elites in Central and Eastern European 'economies in transition' is a case in point. This combines an appreciation of the economics of rent-seeking and the institutional or structural configurations of institutions and policies through which rent-seeking is rendered possible with an ideological component: the ideas and doctrines that underpin the 'legitimization and justification' of specific policies and institutions which naturalise the assumed ability of market-led development to deliver prosperity (Aligica and Tarko 2014: 156). In other interpretations, such as Galbraith's (2007) 'new industrial state', it is suggested that there has been a shift from a 'free-enterprise society' to a 'structured state' controlled by the largest companies which manage demand and manufacture consumer 'needs' through advertising. Multinational corporations represent the continuation of this power system on an international level according to Galbraith. This points to a frequent tension in advanced neoliberalism between the myth of a level and competitive playing field and the reality of monopoly capitalism especially in relation to the provision of services most citizens depend on such as energy, water and transport and which are the target of transition initiatives.

Before proceeding with an analysis and assessment of the role of the industrial state in sustainability transitions, we need firstly to historicise the industrial state: in particular, the historical character and nature of statehood organised around the defence and expansion of state territory through military means and the exploitation of natural resources in the pursuit of national economic development, understood as 'overriding imperatives of all states and constitutive of the state's very form' (Eckersley 2004: 19). Industrialism is characterised by a number of different traits, including, at the most general level, the use of sources of material power in production and the circulation of commodities, the mechanisation of production and prevalence of manufacturing production and the centralised organisation of human social relations. The centralisation of state power 'was the necessary condition of the formation of commodity money' (Giddens 1985: 154). More malignly, as Giddens (1985: 152) suggests regarding the incorporation of wage workers within regularised conditions of production, 'Without the centralisation of a coercive apparatus of law, it is doubtful that this process could have been accomplished, or that the rights of private property as capital could have become firmly embedded'. What is missing from this analysis is an account of the violence and dispossession associated with the enclosures, primitive accumulation (whereby capitalist accumulation results from the separation between the owners of the means of production and those who own nothing but their own labour-power) (Wood 2002) and 'accumulation by dispossession' (Harvey 2006). Critical accounts from Gramsci (1971) to Illich (2000 [1971]) also highlight the importance of the outer reaches of the state in institutions such as schools, media and churches in training citizens with the skills and shaping the attitudes and behaviour required for a role in a centralised, disciplined, consumerist industrial society.

Besides the problematic and arbitrary nature of sovereign borders from an ecological point of view, formed as they are through violence and political settlement (Tilly 1993), it is also the division of the world into sovereign entities which affords transnational capital in particular structural power over states keen to attract increasingly mobile capital to invest in their territories (Gill and Law 1988). As was noted earlier, states increasingly resemble 'competition states' more attuned to the needs of global investors than their own citizens (Cerny 1995). Cox (1995: 39) suggests: 'neoliberalism is transforming states from being protective buffers between external economic forces and the domestic economy into agencies for adapting domestic economies to the exigencies of the global economy'. It is, after all, states that sign trade and investment agreements that remove protection, that choose not to regulate finance and that issue licences to operate to companies to produce in ways which knowingly destroy the environment, exploit labour and displace communities. The reliance of states on capital for investment, jobs and tax has distorted the purpose and rationale of government, tilting the balance away from collective public protection and towards individual private accumulation, and can (but does not always) lead to competitive deregulation and lowering or freezing of standards of protection in some sectors and regions of the world. The overall effect of this and the evidence for a 'race to the bottom' is contested, but there is no question that policymakers take very seriously the threats of firms and business associations to relocate their operations in the face of proposals to tighten environmental regulations (Newell 2012). Such threats of capital flight have been invoked by major firms across all sectors of the economy which are globally integrated and where credible exit options exist. Hence the effect of environmental measures on anything from chemical or mining regulation to climate policy measures can be challenged with reference to 'leakage' (pollution will get displaced but reduced) and the prospect that other competitors will be lent a commercial advantage by the imposition of such measures.

'Disciplinary neoliberalism', where the granting of aid, investment or market access is offered or denied to countries according to their willingness to adopt neoliberal reforms, has a long history and has been applied to check progressive policy moves by states and to assert and enforce the preferences of a transnational capitalist class (Gill 1995). This has the effect of restricting the 'policy autonomy' and 'developmental space' of states to pursue their preferred development pathways. Globally, these expressions of power manifest themselves in the 'new constitutionalism' and are observable in provisions in regional and global trade and investment agreements, development cooperation and investor dispute tribunals that protect the rights of capital (Gill 2002; Glatzer et al. 2024). Major energy firms are now invoking provisions in investment treaties, such as the Energy Charter Treaty, to legally challenge government policies aimed at phasing out fossil fuels through Investor–State Dispute Settlement (ISDS) bodies. Amid the rising number of investment treaties, there is real concern that recent moves to bring cases by the energy company RWE against the Dutch government over its coal phase-out, or by Keystone over the cancellation of the Keystone XL oil pipeline in the US, for example, presage the use of a new weapon some corporations will use to slow the pace and ambition of climate action (Tienhaara et al. 2022). Fear of capital flight and investment strikes are among the strategies used to impede the introduction of higher social and environment standards.

There are of course countervailing pressures to these forms of lock-in from social movements, and 2022 saw a series of encouraging decisions by countries in Europe such as Germany, Italy, the Netherlands, Spain, the UK and Poland to leave the Energy Charter Treaty, making it likely that the EU will have to exit the treaty, suggesting scope for governments to extract themselves from such constraining obligations. This occurs alongside efforts to strengthen investor obligations, including regarding human rights protection. Remarkably, it was not until December 2016 that Morocco and Nigeria signed the first international investment agreement to contain a clause establishing that investors need to respect human rights. Argentina also claimed in a case against the water company Urbaser that the provider had violated the investor's 'commitments and its obligations under international law based on the human right to water', though the tribunal noted only that this 'entails an obligation of compliance on the part of the State, but it does not contain an obligation for performance on part of any company providing the contractually required service' (O'Neill 2005).

It is also important to acknowledge that even if globalised forms of capitalism intensify these challenges, extractivism and unsustainability and the political programmes which enable them are not exclusive to capitalism, as the toxic legacy of former Communist regimes makes clear (Economy 2019). Hence, from an ecological perspective, whomever owns the means of production, and to whomever they distribute the fruits of it, is, to some extent, secondary to the question of the model of extractivist growth upon which it is based (Porritt 1989). The state is not then a neutral actor with regard to the actors and processes which produce environmental harm (Paterson 2001; Saurin 2001). Indeed, building on accounts grounded in Marxism reviewed in Chapter 2, it is possible to question the very division of state and market. Vlachou (2004: 928) puts it the following way: 'state policies towards nature and the ecological changes initiated in capitalism are not "external or artificial" barriers to capital. They are the outcome of internal processes and also constitutive elements of capital as a social relation.' Political elites often have major interests in key economic sectors which exact significant environmental damage, including commercial logging, mineral and oil exploitation and plantation cropping (Dauvergne 1997; Evans et al. 2002). We find evidence here of Marx's contention that the capitalist state is 'based on the contradiction between public and private life, on the contradiction between general interests and private interests' (1975: 46) noted in Chapter 2. Its role is to maintain market discipline and mediate between the contradictions of general and particular interests within capital, such that competing fractions of capital seek to present their interests as consistent with those of capital-in-general in environmental as in other issue areas (Newell and Paterson 1998).

Indeed, states assume many of the key functions of coercion, regulation and enforcement required to reproduce the conditions for the expansion of capital, public and private. Legal rules cannot be divorced from the material conditions in which they are produced and seek to preserve (Cutler 2002), often violently.

Violent acts of dispossession have characterised capitalism since its birth (Wood 2002) and occur alongside efforts to construct laws which protect and safeguard the interests of businesses and discipline citizen protest and labour agitation as well as interventions in social and cultural spheres aimed at legitimising and reinforcing state power and visions of 'development'. Hence the complicity of the industrial state in ecological destruction, even in ways which undermine the ability of the economy to reproduce itself: what James O'Connor (1991) refers to as the 'second contradiction of capitalism'. This amounts to what Ulrich Beck (1999) referred to as 'organised ecological irresponsibility' which results from an inability to reconcile these contradictions, moving problems around rather than resolving them. For Dryzek (1992), however, it is the *combination* of capitalism, liberal democracy and the administrative state that compound ecological problems where the former 'imprisons' the state by constraining policy freedom and applying punishments to those states that step out of line.

This goes to the heart of tensions around the role the state, cast simultaneously as promoter and regulator of industries, with all the tensions and contradictions that flow from this (Newell 2008a). As Levi-Faur (2005: 14) puts it, regulation is, or rather has become, 'both a constitutive element of capitalism (as the framework that enables markets) and the tool that moderates and socializes it'. The functions of *production* and *protection* are overseen by the same actors, often with close ties to those they are charged with regulating and often even with common material interests at stake, as with state-owned companies, for example, or where politicians have shares or hold directorships with private entities they are meant to oversee: the 'revolving door' that often operates between major firms and the state officials that are meant to regulate them. For example, the 'revolving door' between fossil fuel companies and government agencies has been documented in countries such as Australia, Poland, Spain, the US and the UK and provides a key means for obstructing more ambitious climate action (Lucas 2021; Reyes 2018; Szulecki 2018b). To take one example, the UK's Department for Energy and Net Zero has given ex-employees of Shell influential roles within the department overseeing energy market policy, hydrogen strategy and heat pump deployment, and ex-senior executives from BP have been given non-executive director roles (Daley et al. 2024).

As discussed in Chapter 2, some accounts of the state have been criticised for being too generalising, ascribing timeless, ahistorical and universal characteristics and immovable logics to states as reified structures involved in a treadmill of production and thus downplaying or undermining possibilities for their reform (Mol 2003). The question is how far these constraints upon the state constitute a structural imperative or rather reflect a prevailing, but changeable, consensus around the desirability and necessity of growth: acts of strategic selectivity

(Jessop 2016). This speaks to how the project of growth politically, and as a set of specific metrics which afford a way to measure growth, is a recent phenomenon when set in broader historical terms (Dale 2012). Moreover, the tension in capitalist states between accumulation and legitimation (Habermas 1975) creates contradictory pressures which create openings to delegitimise destructive accumulation strategies and question the social licence to operate (as is happening in relation to protests and shareholder activism targeted at oil companies, for example). This potentially creates space to separate 'the state' from a particular understanding and pursuit of growth grounded in industrialism, but which could potentially adopt a more post-industrial form in the future.

4.2 The Industrial State and Transitions

Historically speaking, transitions in technology, industry and finance have been driven by shifts in the global economy (Dicken 2007), dissatisfaction on the part of restless capital with the ability of existing regimes of accumulation to generate sufficient profit (Perez 2002) and, relatedly, the prospect of new economic opportunities that can only be brought about through 'creative destruction' (Schumpeter 1942). In such orthodox accounts, technological innovation is seen as the 'engine of growth' (Ashford and Hall 2011). Hence, as we saw in Chapter 3, though the distinction is often a fragile one in practice, since they overlap and coexist, there are more incremental and more radical types of innovation in industry where radical innovations are often more discontinuous and may disrupt and displace dominant and incumbent firms (Freeman 1992). For the sorts of transformational change envisaged in this book, however, our analytical focus needs to move beyond innovations aimed at improving performance within a particular technological and industrial trajectory to the more fundamental reform of the industrial state itself: the goals it pursues, who it serves and how.

The industrial state to be effective needs to stabilise and manage industrial relations and it does so through selective strategic interventions (Jessop 2008). As introduced earlier, a key function of the state is to mediate between competing fractions of capital, between capital and labour and between shifting social forces and coalitions of actors as it seeks to manage and reconcile contradictions between accumulation and legitimation, production and protection and growth and sustainability. Immense political work is required to build coalitions and alliances that will support and can then sustain and deliver transition projects, as well as contain and deflect social demands for more transformative and disruptive change to dominant power relations (Newell 2018). As Lockwood (2015a: 86) notes, 'successful transformations not only require instigation, but also have to be politically sustained for long periods. Coalitions need to be created around a number of different objectives, but they also have to be kept together and expanded over time', at least until the point at which they become (economically and politically) self-sustaining. Patterson and Paterson (2024: 1) conceptualise these dynamics in terms of an 'unfolding series of battle-settlement events whereby heated episodic political struggles over a certain policy object or issue play out and eventually settle in ways that structure future debates'.

Policy design is important to generating positive 'feedback effects' that distribute gains to key political constituencies that through material incentives are able and willing to sustain support for transition projects which helps to embed and lock them in. It can involve building new identities, issue and discourse coalitions or wider advocacy coalition frameworks (Sabatier 1988). Lockwood (2015a: 92) provides the example of state support to renewable industries in Germany, noting 'because renewables policy was linked to industrial policy ... employment in factories producing wind turbines and solar PV panels created a new constituency in favour of a strong renewables policy', thereby spreading the benefits across society. A similar story can be told in China regarding the use of state industrial policy to build a globally competitive wind energy industry simultaneously generating domestic employment and export earnings. By contrast, the renewables obligation in the UK 'created weak positive feedback effects and left the growth of renewables in the UK exposed to considerable negative feedback effects' (Lockwood 2015: 93). The preference – or refusal – to use policy mechanisms reflects broader policy paradigms regarding the role of state intervention in the economy reflective of the varieties of capitalism which prevail from Germany's 'ordoliberalism' social market approach (which employs a '*Rechtsstaat*' of general rules to limit concentrations of economic power, ensure competition and mobilise state power to compel compliance with the rules of the market (Gamble 2014)) to the UK's more laissez-faire neoliberal doctrine (Hall and Soskice 2001).

4.2.1 Developmental States

The concept of the 'developmental state' has been used to describe the exercise of state power to enhance industrial development. It has been applied particularly to East Asian development states (Weiss 1995; Chang 2006). For Leftwich (1995), the key features of a developmental state include: a 'determined developmental elite' committed to the modernisation project (an extension of the notion of an 'entrepreneurial elite' discussed in Chapter 3); 'relative autonomy' from major capitalist economic interests who are always keen to capture the state; 'a powerful, competent and insulated economic bureaucracy' that enjoys the highest possible political support but operates without too much political interference; a 'weak and subordinated civil society' which means there are no rival centres of alternative policy formation and development; the 'effective management of non-state economic interests' via formal structured compacts, incentives and penalties; and accessible and usable institutions of 'repression, legitimacy and performance'.

Put another way, for Weiss (2003a: 247), developmental states can be distinguished by 'their commitment to production enhancing, growth oriented priorities; their organisational arrangements (a relatively insulated pilot agency in charge of that transformative project); and institutionalised government-business cooperation (formal and informal links with organised economic actors privileging sectors or industry associations rather than simply individual firms) as the basis for policy input, negotiation and implementation'. It is not just about economic features, therefore, but where a political system 'supports a shared project of economic transformation, where there is elite cohesion over core national goals and where the economic bureaucracy is given sufficient scope to take initiatives and act effectively' (Weiss 2003a: 247). Underpinned by notions of autonomy and lack of political conflict and contestation, the idea of a developmental state clashes with visions of democratising transitions aimed at opening up different pathways to transformation through the state explored in Chapter 6. This combination of features also clearly better describes and lends itself more to some parts of the world and certain political economies than others. Describing the situation in South Africa, Swilling et al. (2016: 651) suggest that:

> [D]evelopmentally South Africa has not built a 'relatively autonomous' strong DS [development state] apparatus to pursue an employment creation-through-industrialization strategy (a la East Asia), preferring a non-developmental welfarism to address inequalities using fiscal policy, accommodating the mineral-energy complex (MEC) rather than promoting secondary industrialization and promoting financialization. And yet since 2006 a vast array of environmental and sustainability policies have emerged, fusing into what is referred to as the 'green economy' approach as one way of catalysing low-carbon growth. But for this to materialize into a sustainability transition, the self-same state capabilities that are needed to drive the structural transformations to promote 'developmental welfarism' are needed to drive a sustainability transition.

Key characteristics of developmental states then include an ability to promote sustained growth and development via aggressive industrialisation based on an 'ability to extract and deploy capital productively, generate and implement national and sectoral plans, and effect dynamic egalitarian and productivity-enhancing development programmes in land, education and training, small enterprise, infrastructure and housing sectors' (Swilling et al. 2016: 652). Exploring how state agencies, local entrepreneurs and transnational corporations shaped the development of key industries in Brazil, India and Korea during the 1970s and 1980s, Evans (2012) provides an explanation for variation in states organisation and embeddedness within society. He suggests: 'In some nations, like Zaire, the state is predatory, ruthlessly extracting and providing nothing of value in return. In others, like Korea, it is developmental, promoting industrial transformation. In still others, like Brazil and India, it is in between, sometimes helping, sometimes hindering.'

The question of autonomy from industrial interests is key, yet the distinctions are often blurred and fragile in reality. Writing about Brazil's oil strategy, Massi and Nem Singh (2018) show how the sector-specific industrial development strategy was the product of a tight relationship between the state, Petrobras and industrial elites which makes it harder to 'sustain institutional capacity to direct rents towards investment and innovation'. There is clearly then a diversity of configurations of industrial state from the chaebol in Korea to South Africa's minerals-energy complex (Fine and Rustomjee 1997; Baker et al. 2014), but most examples of the operations of industrial states in practice point to deep entanglements between industrial actors, finance capital and the states supporting and regulating them (Fine et al. 2015). The nature of those entanglements can change in the face of domestic reforms and international pressure. In China, for example, Pearson (1997: 1) notes that, in the transition from a planned to a market economy, 'Reflecting the central government's perception that it depends increasingly on members of the new business elite to promote industrialisation, it has granted members of this elite greater economic authority and control over economic resources'.

Rather like in the discussion of the entrepreneurial state in Chapter 3, there are industrial states, plural, which face different challenges and enjoy different degrees of autonomy and power over the industrial interests they are charged with managing and ostensibly steering towards sustainability. Path dependencies, feedback effects and institutional legacies conspire to open up or close down different pathways to change (Weiss 2003a). Attempts to import models of industrial policy from one setting to another have frequently enjoyed limited success. Sun (2007: 601) suggests, in this regard, 'the institutional framework of the Chinese state differs from its counterparts in Korea and Japan in some fundamental aspects. Among these, the fragmented and uncoordinated Chinese bureaucracy contributes significantly to the inefficacy of policy implementation', frustrating attempts to replicate the success of those economies.

But there are also some commonalities. Some states may be more 'predatory' than others, but all are engaged in projects of extractivism within and beyond their borders (Gudynas 2021). From a critical sustainability perspective, therefore, what different varieties of state capitalism have in common in terms of the dominant economic model they embrace is more important than subtle differences in the ways in which they embed capitalism institutionally at the national level. Globally unequal power relations shape why some countries have 'open veins' (Galeano 1977) for the export of resources, while others are able to build 'fortresses' around their assets and resources. Critical to facilitating extractivism are infrastructures.

Infused with power relations, infrastructures shape our worlds in all sorts of direct and indirect ways (Bridge et al 2018; Szabó and Fabok 2020). From transport networks that get us to and from places, pipes that carry our sewage, flood mitigation structures or 'green infrastructures' in cities to less tangible structures that shape economies, governance and representation, infrastructures mediate social-environmental interactions and establish knowledge structures. Within and between countries, colonial and internal colonial logics have often guided the location of pipelines, railways and ports, for example to minimise distances between key sites of extraction and key centres of capital accumulation (often capital cities and regional centres).

Despite these common characteristics, the industrial state is not a fixed entity, however. Berry et al. (2022) develop the notion of 'the substitutive state' to explore the changing character of state institutions and state action in the context of neoliberalisation in contrast to 'the regulatory state' and 'the competition state' explored earlier. 'Substitutive statism', they suggest, 'is aligned with a wider accumulation regime which state actors perceive as immutable; they are therefore willing to intervene to sustain this regime, irrespective of market signals' (Berry et al. 2022: 242). It is observable in 'interventionist mechanisms' enrolling the very private economic actors the intervention is designed to target or which are used 'to relieve the private sector from serving unprofitable market segments' (Berry et al. 2022: 242). Bailouts and furlough might be examples of such mechanisms at work, or the ways in which state actors bankroll private actors through maintaining basic infrastructures (such as railway tracks or water sanitation plants) while allowing private actors to reap the profits of running services: a form of predatory capitalism. This implies a privileging of specific actors and sectors, whether because of their political power and the constituencies they represent or because of the centrality of their fraction of capital to the growth objectives of the state as with major energy providers (Newell and Paterson 1998). The strategic issue then is whether those roles and functions are thought to be fixed and immutable or subject to reconfiguration and redefinition. There are important questions about which sectors of the economy are protected and privileged and afforded state power, protection and resources and those which are not – particularly in relation to energy which cuts across diverse state functions and mandates because of its centrality to questions of growth, security and militarism. Though the state may be captive to certain interests (Monbiot 2000), fractions of capital and sectoral interests lobby to secure strategic state support for their firms and sectors rather than leave it to chance by assuming state actors will adequately meet their needs without their direct input.

These structural imperatives and dependencies give rise to an ideological effect which shapes, constrains and disciplines transition pathways. Preferred futures are those which generate new sites of capital accumulation and investment as well as employment and which support technological innovation. Reproducing economic orthodoxy, Lehtonen and Kern (2009: 103) note how 'to justify a policy change politicians and civil servants often feel compelled to identify "market failures" which they will help to correct, or alternatively to explain why the "first-best" market based solution is not appropriate in a given situation'. Significant political work is, nevertheless, required to rationalise and normalise one pathway over the other within these ideological parameters. Newell and Phillips (2016), writing about neoliberal transitions in Kenya, show, for example, how donors pave the way for neoliberal reforms by attributing blame for failures in the energy system to systems of public ownership which then need to be unbundled into separate functions of generation, distribution and transmission. Likewise, water scarcity is often presented as a problem produced by inefficient state institutions and a failure to incentivise conservation by allocating property rights, such that privatisation becomes the obvious solution (Bakker 2010).

Others are more critical of accounts which emphasise the constraints imposed on national autonomy (and by extension the industrial state) by globalisation. Weiss (2003b: 245) suggests: 'Contrary to the idea of globalisation as a constraint, the global economy does not preclude a role for national governance but tends increasingly to demand it'; as increasing and deepening patterns of economic exchange require oversight and regulation, policy innovations may require state research, training and innovation capacity and raise distributional issues which need to be addressed. There are of course other drivers of conformity and convergence. The fact that industrial states require knowledge for industry gives rise to technocracies and epistemic communities and the production of hegemonic economic knowledge and modelling which is often pressed into the service of validating the policy preferences and preferred pathways of elites, whether through cost-benefit analysis or deliberate moulding of policy debate. For example, Franta (2022: 555) shows how an

> influential group of economic consultants hired by the petroleum industry from the 1990s to the 2010s to estimate the costs of various proposed climate policies … used models that inflated predicted costs while ignoring policy benefits, and their results were often portrayed to the public as independent rather than industry-sponsored. Their work played a key role in undermining numerous major climate policy initiatives in the US over a span of decades, including carbon pricing and participation in international climate agreements.

In transition debates, integrated assessment models (IAMs) are frequently used to assess and evaluate competing policy pathways. They seek to combine knowledge from multiple disciplines in formal integrated representations to inform policymaking, prioritise key uncertainties and advance knowledge of broad system linkages and feedbacks, particularly between socio-economic and biophysical processes. But they combine simplified representations of the socio-economic determinants of energy pathways, the atmosphere and impacts on human activities and ecosystems and potential policies and responses (Parson 1995). As Newell (2021a: 78) notes:

> Though modelling and forecasting have traditionally been thought of as neutral techniques (or technologies of governance) for guiding policy interventions in the energy domain, in reality these forecasts have often been used for partisan purposes to push through, or oppose, energy developments threatening to incumbent interests (Midttun and Baumgartner 1986). Sometimes the politicisation is subtle; at other times it is more explicit and overt. It can operate at the level of unconscious bias and neglecting to expose basic assumptions to critical discussion.

Rather than forecasting with all its in-built but rarely stated assumptions about growth and efficiency, Ashford and Hall (2011: 14) advocate for backcasting, which 'enables policymakers to look back from a desirable future to create strategies that will, it is hoped, enable the future visions to materialize'. Hence targets still have a role to play, but the state needs to resist incumbent control over them and how they are realised and to 'use its position as a trustee to represent the future generations and the future technologies to back cast what policies are necessary to produce the required technical, organisational and social transformations' (Ashford and Hall 2011: 14).

By contrast, the effect of dominant approaches to knowledge production for transition is to privilege some ways of knowing and pathways over others. For example, cost-benefit analysis 'remains the "gold standard" of economic appraisal in energy policy' (Lehtonen and Kern 2009: 108) and many other areas of sustainability policy besides. This 'elevates economic efficiency as the only rational aim and appropriate framing for certain policy questions' (Lehtonen and Kern 2009: 108). Willingness to pay, aggregating costs and benefits, discounting the future and using monetary valuation to make disparate impacts and values commensurate are all techniques deployed to legitimise the prior choices of state managers aimed at enhancing the power of the industrial state. Critiques of models used to promote the benefits of airport expansion or new nuclear power plants by groups such as the New Economics Foundation point to key areas of (deliberate) oversight in terms of neglected or undervalued impacts on health, community cohesion and the environment and both the exaggeration and inflation of economic benefits and the discounting and futuring of costs: passing them on to future generations or under-represented groups (Smythe and Pendelton 2018) in an effort to close the loop between accumulation and legitimation.

The political and self-fulfilling nature of modelling based on a premise of 'predict and provide' assumes that resource pathways and levels of consumption are locked in. For example, 'energy gap' analysis takes as given rising energy demand

and then looks at which energy sources and technologies need to be stacked up to meet the gap, a process that inevitably privileges large-scale centralised industrial provision of energy. The same holds true for road building where new roads are sold on the basis that they will help reduce congestion in spite of evidence that traffic expands to fit new capacity as new roads make driving a more desirable option (Pfleiderer and Dieterich 1995). In other words, models of the future, as well as attempts to understand the present, take as given an industrial growth-oriented society that will continually, often exponentially, increase production and consumption and, therefore, the throughput of resources. Hence, while the means of securing and expanding those objectives can be debated and improved, the goals themselves are apparently beyond question and critical interrogation. This is one of the discursive means by which 'plug-and-play' strategies to transition are normalised, ones which enable changes to technology and energy source, for example, but not modes of ownership, production or consumption. This is something scholars such as Keyßer and Lenzen (2022) have sought to challenge. They suggest that 'the integrated assessment modelling community and the IPCC have neglected to consider degrowth scenarios, where economic output declines due to stringent climate mitigation'. The result of this neglect is to build in a reliance on negative emissions technologies and speculative uptake of technologies such as carbon capture and storage (CCS). Instead, they propose 'degrowth scenarios minimize many key risks for feasibility and sustainability compared to technology-driven pathways, such as the reliance on high energy-GDP decoupling, large-scale carbon dioxide removal and large-scale and high-speed renewable energy transformation'.

4.3 Transforming the Industrial State

The very dynamism, uncertainty, volatility and ostensibly competitive nature of global capitalism which currently drives unsustainability can also lead to openings for transformation and revival, creative construction following destruction and the reconfiguring of alternatives. We saw in Chapter 3, how finance can be a disruptor of dominant regimes of innovation (Perez 2002) (as well as the limits of this): how it can build and destroy industries and transform whole sectors and societies.

At a political level, engaging with latent transformations means identifying cracks and fragilities and excavating beneath the outward manifestations of incumbent power: finding the 'cracks where the light gets in' as Leonard Cohen put it. Just as assemblages are stitched together through political practice, institutional work and discursive manoeuvres (Soto Hernandez and Newell 2022), so too at their seams they present opportunities and openings for intervention, disruption and recasting alliances. Even in Marxist analysis, where the openings for change within the capitalist state might be thought to be slight, fractions of capital compete for state attention and attempt to present their interests as those of capital in general (Newell and Paterson 1998). Given the rising costs that uncontrolled climate change imposes upon society, the traditional ability of fossil fuel companies to make such claims (by virtue of their provision of 'cheap' energy for all other sectors of the economy: a prerequisite for growth) may increasingly be in doubt as the costs of inaction on climate change rise for all sectors. Discourse or advocacy coalitions can be created (Hajer 1995; Sabatier 1998) to build consensus and carry forward new industrial visions. Current dominant framings of 'green economy' or a 'green new deal' on the Left are suggestive of how new visions of industrial landscapes can take hold and gain traction to build necessary political capital between trade unions, environmentalists and progressive business, for example, underneath a broad discursive umbrella. While such discursive projects undertake valuable political work, they mask key tensions and contradictions and reflect a strategy of 'passive revolution' which, for Jessop (2016: 178), involves 'a process of transformation, absorption, and incorporation that translates contentious politics into bureaucratic or technical questions'. In the case of the EU's agreement on a European Green Deal (EGD), Silvester and Fiske (2023: 8) argue that 'Even a cursory glance at its stated goals makes it clear that as a state project it reflects a somewhat contradictory compromise between environmentalist, capitalist, and welfarist interests'.

Such a project can be understood, nevertheless by scholars of varieties of capitalism as an attempt to develop a comparative institutional advantage supportive of a green economy. Some scholars, such as Drucker in his book *The Future of Industrial Man*, suggest the industrial state is at a key juncture where its legitimacy is waning and needs to be renewed (Drucker 1995). Rather than the polycrisis and deepening social and environmental woes forming the basis of its legitimacy crisis, for Drucker the central challenge is how to maintain individual freedom in an increasingly bureaucratised world and, implicitly it seems, how to preserve the freedom of capital.

A key issue then is how best to understand and engage with incumbent power and control over the industrial state in more progressive ways. As Stirling (2019: 2) suggests:

> [M]ainstream notions like 'the regime' can represent incumbency to be significantly more topologically confined and discrete than may often actually be the case. This is referred to as an 'eagle-eye view', since the incumbency-sustaining dynamics thereby highlighted appear to be monocongruent and singular – as if viewed from a lofty perspective that foreshortens appreciation of greater complexity, depth or scope. Since these kinds of reduction tend to favour incumbent interests, the point is made that it is perhaps not surprising that such simplifications are so prominent in academic and policy understandings of incumbency and associated possibilities for intervention.

Indeed, 'intensely romanticised ideas of elite agency can foster potentially seriously misleading "illusions of control"' (Stirling 2019: 7). Correspondingly, Stirling (2019: 2–3) suggests:

> [A] 'worm-eye view' offers to extend scope for understanding incumbency in many important ways – in particular highlighting necessities for counter-incumbency actions to take forms that cannot be achieved mainly by performance of vertical policy interventions choreographed from a notional governance '*cock-pit*'. What may often be required as well, in order to address the full depth and extent of incumbency, are more unruly, horizontal and mutualistic forms of political action. It is these kinds of engagements that can be restricted in more reformist efforts that over-rely on conventionally reified expert models, formal procedures and policy mixes. So, 'creative destruction' of incumbency is often better enabled not so much by specific policies – or even 'policy mixes' – as by more diverse general (and deeply political) processes of grassroots mobilisation, collective action, cultural expression and democratic struggle.

As noted here and in previous chapters, the achievement of an ecological or Green state implies a more fundamental transformation in the very *raison d'être* of the state in order to play a meaningful, effective and progressive role in sustainability transitions, one that might be articulated and promoted from within civil and political society in the first instance. This might improve the chances that, unconstrained by elite techno-imaginaries and unbound by structural imperatives, industrial expansion may no longer be viewed as an end in itself but rather a project of state renewal could be envisaged which uses the levers of state power to nurture a sustainable economy that might be smaller, more localised, more decentralised, more commonly owned. In the context of ecological limits and inequalities within and between societies, industrial expansion at any cost is no longer permissible. Marx talked about the 'abolition of industry' (*Abschaffung der Industrie*) and the 'liberation from industry' (*Befreiung von der Industrie*), in *The German Ideology* (Marx and Engels 1975: 52, 80, 205). This would require a state with greater autonomy from industrial interests that is willing to put down limits and nurture and deliver a vision of the common good the like of which we have yet to see on a large scale. It might be informed by visions of 'doughnut economics' or degrowth proposals (Raworth 2017; Kallis 2018). Ashford and Hall (2011), for example, propose a series of roles for a state in advancing a sustainable society that address some of the shortcomings in conventional approaches identified in this chapter. These include, for example, the state 'Moving beyond markets and acting as a trustee for minority interests, subsequent generations and new technologies by forcing and encouraging innovation through coordinated regulatory, industrial, employment and trade policy' (Ashford and Hall 2011: 12), a call which covers many aspects of state power covered in this book. Such propositions may sound naïve, and certainly it asks a lot of the democratic state (see Chapter 6) to bring about such a profound reorientation of who the state serves and how when stark power inequalities enable opponents of change to stall and delay such shifts. But struggle for control of key state institutions and functions has to feature centrally in discussions about transformations to sustainability for reasons of scale, speed and the nature of coordinated change in critical processes over which the state continues to exercise predominant control. In so far as states and corporations are the primary actors driving environmental degradation through conventional and extractivist visions of industrialism and corporations are only marginally and indirectly responsive to social pressure, states will remain key targets for mobilisation both because of their own role in financing destruction and because of the power they have, should they choose to use it, to rein in corporate power (Korten 1995). States are 'more amenable to democratization than corporations' Eckersley (2004: 8) reminds us.

It is also worth recalling that some states, in some places, at some times, have played proactive, interventionist leadership roles in driving progressive change in the functioning and purpose of the industrial state (Simms 2013). Drawing on these experiences can provide the basis of a strategy to accelerate action in the here and now, arguing that state action has brought about radical, progressive, rapid and disruptive change in the past and can do so again today. Think of the New Deal in post–Second World War America, a green version of which is now enjoying a revival in the US and Europe today, strategies of wholesale industrial conversion in the UK or state-led 'energy revolutions' in Cuba (Simms and Newell 2017). Ideologies and ideas of what states can and should do, the degree of policy autonomy and developmental space they have been able to enjoy, are not fixed, therefore. They are negotiated and contingent on the weight of historical forces at key moments. Hence, as noted, after decades of onslaught on the efficiency and effectiveness of the state, the prevailing orthodoxy today is that states need to and can play a proactive part in leading transitions to sustainability which will require a transformation in the industrial base of their economies. Indeed, in the UK after years of policy orthodoxy that the state should play only the most minimal role in the energy sector, the new Labour government has announced plans to create a new state company, GB Energy, while the neoliberal heartland of the US sought to enact a bold Keynesian vision in the form of the Inflation Reduction Act (IRA). The failings of market-led transitions are exposing once again the need for state-led interventions across regions and sectors of the economy even in its neoliberal heartlands.

Indeed, many environmentalists foresee a major role for national government in creating the framework within which a green economy can flourish. This should include the setting of suitable tax incentives and the control of industries which are contributing to environmental harm. Likewise, there are clear roles imagined for redistribution and planning. The tension is that, while many are in favour of an interventionist state in relation to regulation and taxation over other market-based mechanisms, for example, this assumes the existence of a powerful, well-resourced central state which many scholars and activists are understandably uncomfortable with. Many environmentalists are in favour of ecological taxation, taxing pollution rather than labour, and recognise that only the state has the power to rebalance the economy. Hence there is a desire to see the government take a stronger role in controlling corporations whose activities are destructive to the environment, including removing their licences to trade. And in contrast to more liberal and Marxist visions of the state and accounts of political economy which view industrialism as (eventually) leading to peace between either capitalist or socialist states (Giddens 1994), a more holistic approach to considering the state's relationship to sustainability would challenge the violence associated with the project of industrialism: something which links the industrial state as a site and project of organised extractivism with militarism and policing in various guises as we will see in Chapter 5. Though nineteenth-century thinkers sought to draw distinctions between 'industrial' and 'military' societies (Giddens 1985), in practice they are intertwined as we shall see in Chapter 5.

5

The Military State

> The nation-state is the prime vehicle of political organisation in the contemporary world, recognised as holding legitimate monopoly of the means of violence by its own subject population and by other nation-states. As the possessor of the means of waging industrialised war, in a global context of the continuing application of science to the advancement of military technology, the state participates in and furthers a generalised process of militarisation within the world system as a whole. (Giddens 1985: 254)

The relationship between states and their militaries has long been a subject of social enquiry, reflecting the fact that 'war and military organisation have been central to the development of the state system that still provides the basic organizing principle of human societies across the globe' (Dandeker 1994: 110). Most nation-states have their origins in war, formed and reformed by external conflict and civil wars (Tilly et al. 1985; Mann 1987). As Charles Tilly (1993) famously noted, 'war made the state and the state made war'. For this reason, Machiavelli observes, a prince should 'have no other aim or thought, nor take up any other thing for his study, but war and its order and discipline, for that is the only art that is necessary to one who commands' (Machiavelli 2020: 61). Classic understandings of the state often refer to 'the monopoly of the legitimate use of physical force within a given territory' (Weber 1948: 78). What counts as a legitimate use of force, as well as how to put limits on the exercise of force beyond a 'given territory', is a key concern for states around 'humanitarian intervention' and the 'responsibility to protect', for example.

But the centrality of security as the *raison d'être* of the nation-state, combined with the political nature of security itself, has led some to conclude that modern politics itself is a 'security project' (Dillon 1996: 12) given that the provision of security is central to legitimacy in all forms of political community. One of the main functions of a state, or one which it assumes for itself, is the protection of citizens through exercising a monopoly on the use of violence. Bourdieu (2014) famously modified Weber's (1978) emphasis on the monopoly on the use of force in a given territory as a core state function and privilege by expanding it to a monopoly of legitimate physical *and* symbolic violence, where the latter is the condition for the possession and exercise of the former. He suggests: 'The state can be reduced neither to an apparatus of power in the service of dominant groups nor to a neutral site where conflicting interests are played out: rather it constitutes the collective belief that structures the whole of social life.' Resort to physical violence can be avoided because 'symbolic capital' can be mobilised to make 'people see the world in a specific way, which, if this power is sufficiently strong, appears as the only possible, universal and natural way' (Buch-Hansen et al. 2024: 77). 'The "collective fiction" of the state, a fiction with very real effects, is at the same time the product of all struggles between different interests, what is at stake in these struggles and their very foundation' (Bourdieu 2014: 1). While its collective properties may at times appear fictional, the forms of power that flow from this performative legitimation and representational credibility nevertheless make themselves felt in everyday acts of violence and oppression (of some) and acts of protection (for others) within and beyond its borders as we will see throughout this chapter.

Indeed, the military aspects of state power are intimately tied to all other aspects of state power as we have seen already in relation to its industrial and entrepreneurial roles and will see later in relation to its democratic and global dimensions. For example, the application of techniques of industrial production to weaponry is key to the 'industrialisation of war' (Giddens 1985). Indeed, transitions in key sectors like transport are prerequisites for the conduct of mass warfare. Gidden's (1985: 224) notes, 'More than any other single technological innovation, the railway made possible mass warfare', just as railways were in large part constructed to meet the requirements of the military (the rapid mobilisation of troops and weaponry) and, I would add, the industrial state: for the purposes of extractivism through the 'open veins' that transport links laid bare (Galeano 1997) which allowed colonising powers to extract resources and commodities for their own benefit. The arms industry and the innovators working for it are great beneficiaries of the drive for permanent war and generate significant business from state contracts, just as the armed forces 'depend upon the productive apparatus of industrialism, harnessed through the sovereign authority of the territorial state' (Giddens 1985: 228). As Giddens (1985: 226) reflects, 'the meshing of industrial production and military strength is of prime importance among the influences that have shaped the modern world … Industrial capitalism provided the means for the industrialisation of war, but the activities and involvements of nation-states are at the origin of the phenomena.' The most visible and grotesque illustration of this mutual dependency and the mass slaughter that ensued perhaps is the First World War, which Giddens (1985: 235) suggests 'could not have happened without the long prior development of industrialism and the conjoining of industrial production to the means of violence', though numerous episodes of colonial violence combine the same dynamics (Tharoor 2018).

Nevertheless, Liberal accounts of the peace doctrine (Doyle 2011) are underpinned by the notion that democratic institutions committed to rule of law, when combined with growing international interdependencies through the market, will oversee the demise of war and military establishments which fuel it (Durkheim 1957; Spencer 1967) or most ambitiously a 'warless society' where economic competition replaces military conflict (Moskos 1994). For Marxists, on the other hand, military power is exercised domestically in order to quell industrial disputes and class conflicts and internationally in the pursuit of imperial ventures between competing capitalist powers (Lenin 1927). Growing attention to colonialism also posits state violence as central to the subjection of peoples in Asia, Africa and Latin America (Rodney 2018; Tharoor 2018) and the systemic exploitation of their resources through extractivism (Galeano 1997). Those writing within a more neo-Machiavellian or Hobbesian tradition, however, argue for the inevitably of war as inherent to human social relations whichever way and by whomever they are organised (Hobbes 1914 [1651]). The role of the state then is to manage those impulses (or direct them towards the defence of the sovereign realm). Realist International Relations is informed by similar premises about the inevitability of war and conflict in an international system characterised by anarchy and the absence of an overarching authority (Morgenthau 1948; Waltz 1959) and doctrines of war propagated by Machiavelli (as noted earlier in the chapter) and Clausewitz (2003).

In different ways and to differing degrees, these diverse insights about state violence, militarism and its intimate relationship to extractivism can usefully inform our understanding of this vital dimension of state power and its implications for sustainability.

5.1 Introducing the Military State

'War signifies the arrival of catastrophe. The proliferation of martial metaphors in this historical moment is a deplorable but apt reflection of how things stand', Andreas Malm writes in a book about 'war communism' reflecting on the experience of the Covid pandemic and what responses to climate change would look like if states treated it as a 'chronic emergency' (Malm 2020: 155). Debates about the pros and cons of framing responses to sustainability challenges in security terms have a long history (Deudney 1990; Homer-Dixon and Levy 1995), with discussions around the securitization of climate change and the 'state of exception' that responses to it might justify representing a new terrain of debate (Nyman and Zeng 2016). While, for activists, war metaphors might be attractive as mobilising devices and ways of conveying the severity of the issues (with fossil fuels being called 'weapons of mass destruction', for example), others are cautious about both the relevance of the parallels and the desirability of the politics they invite which may be counterproductive to collective, inclusive and peaceful responses to a multifaceted challenge that cannot adequately be addressed, and may well be exacerbated, by military mindsets (Patterson et al. 2021).

5.1.1 The Military-Industrial Complex

As noted, the military functions and characteristics of the state are intimately interwoven and connected to its role in reproducing industrialism. As we can see in Figure 5.1, it is no coincidence that the world's two largest economies and rival powers spend the most amount of money on their militaries. The protection, policing and expansion of extractivist growth and maintenance of (neo)colonial relations of uneven exchange necessitate a spectrum of active, passive and 'slow violence' (Nixon 2011) from military interventions to policing of infrastructures and the resistance to them through to forms of everyday economic and physical violence suffered by people living in close proximity to resource frontiers and pollution corridors.Though the notion of a military-industrial complex (MIC) is a product of a particular (Cold War) history, its constitution and reconfiguration exhibit contemporary manifestations. Clearly it reflects the historical moment in which it was conceived at the height of the Cold War. However, the mechanisms, dependencies and networks of power it describes to some extent persist and live on in dominant petro-military imaginaries. Upon leaving office, President Dwight D. Eisenhower gave this famous warning in 1961:

> [The] conjunction of an immense military establishment and a large arms industry is new in the American experience … [W]e must guard against the acquisition of unwarranted influence, whether sought or unsought, by the military-industrial complex. The potential for the disastrous rise of misplaced power exists and will persist. We must never let the weight of this combination endanger our liberties or democratic processes. (Eisenhower 1961)

What he was referencing was the 'large, permanent defense establishment, which had been created to fight World War II and then expanded because of the Cold War, and the open-endedness of its potential effects' (Fallows 2002: 46). Despite raising issues of liberty and democracy, Eisenhower's concern was also purportedly fiscal: the way in which 'the military itself, its allied contractors, and

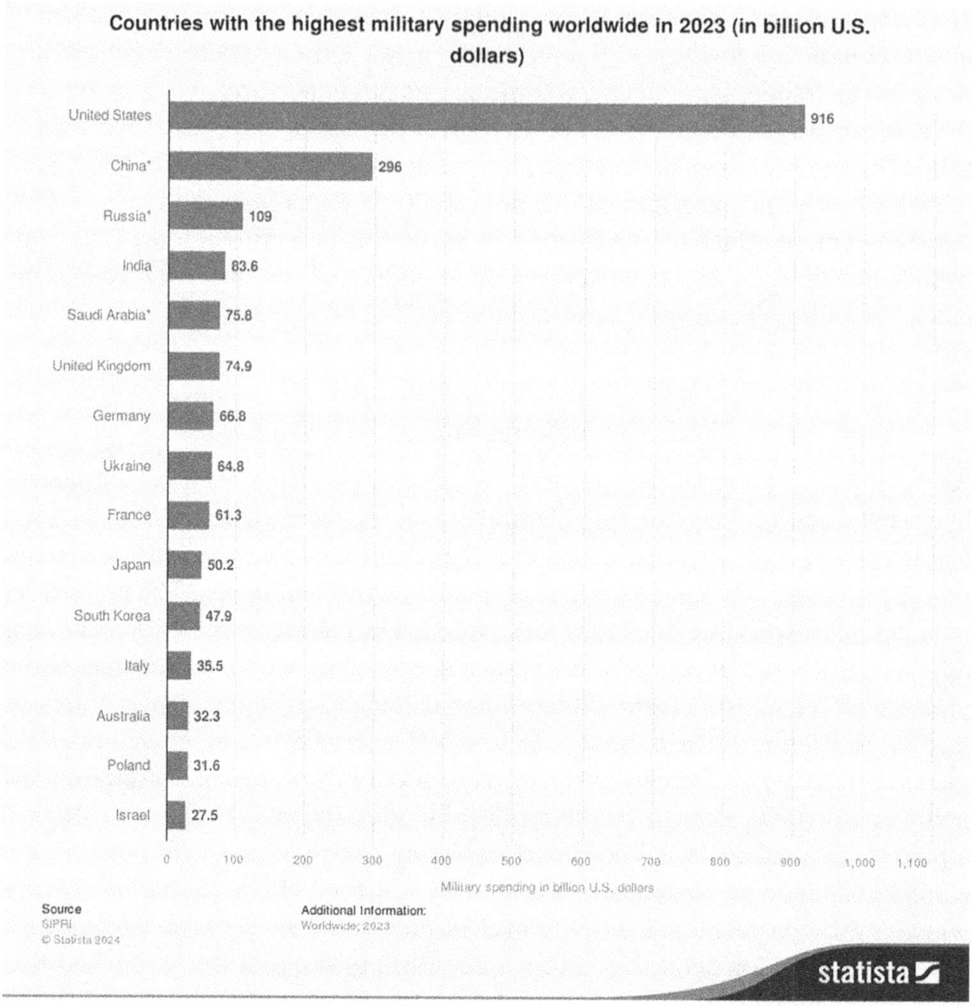

Figure 5.1 Military spending worldwide in 2022. Source: Statista 2023.

the appropriators in Congress all shared an interest in trumpeting potential perils and then building weapons to offset them' (Fallows 2002: 46). What is important in this regard is not whether weapons are ultimately used but that they are bought. As C. Wright Mills (1956) wrote in his influential book *The Power Elite*, 'As members of a professional officer corps, some military men develop a vested interest – personal, institutional, ideological – in the enlargement of all things military' (Wright Mills 1956: 200). Accounting for the operations of the military elite inevitably extends into the discussion of the global state in Chapter 8. As Wright Mills (1956: 205–206) comments, 'No area of decision has been more influenced by the warlords and by their military metaphysics than that of foreign policy and international relations'. The existence, weight and power of the MIC is often judged through metrics such as ratio of defence to other spending. For Giddens (1985: 247):

> If a military industrial complex can be said to dominate the economy, it has to be the case that there are sharply defined links of interdependence between military production and other areas of production; and that modern economies are so reliant upon the maintenance of those ties that those holding political office find themselves compelled to acquiesce in such production needs.

Indeed, military expenditure often constitutes one of the largest demands on state finances, systematically trumping other potential uses, and the often symbiotic relationship between energy and military regimes and complexes has led many scholars to propose the ongoing existence of an MIC (Koistinen 1980). Allocations of military funding can also be used to reinforce and pay off incumbents as part of a political appeasement strategy to manage this fear. Pentagon budget analyst Franklin Chuck Spinney uses the term 'political engineering' to describe the parcelling out of defence subcontracts to the districts of influential members of Congress (Fallows 2002: 47), what one Republican senator even described as 'blank checks to the military-industrial complex' (quoted in Dunlap 2011: 136).

The power of the MIC depends, in part, on the successful projection of new threats and the mobilisation of state resources to address them. Some accounts suggest the MIC, at least in the US, is in decline as a result of a confluence of factors, 'emasculating America's military-industrial complex' (Dunlap 2011: 140). Dunlap (2011: 135) suggests that 'as the manpower-centric strategies in Afghanistan and Iraq replaced technology-centric operations; as complicated defense acquisitions laws deterred companies from obtaining contracts; and as the economic downturn and rising national deficit have strained budgets, the defense industry has become less robust than it was in the Cold War era'. Such accounts point to the 'perils of a declining military-industrial enterprise' (Dunlap 2011: 137) such that 'a near-conspiratorial alignment of military leaders and their analogues in the arms industry ... does not exist' (Dunlap 2011: 142).

One key shift that has taken place is associated with the internationalisation of the arms industry (Buzan 1994; Dunlap 2011) and a key site where this co-dependency has been consolidated is of course science, technology and innovation policy, or what Wright Mills (1956: 217) calls 'the militarization of science'. Reflecting on the historical constitution of this relationship, Wright Mills (1956: 216–217) notes:

> Scientific and technological development, once seated in the economy, has increasingly become part of the military order which is now the largest single supporter and director of scientific research ... Since World War II, the general direction of pure scientific research

> has been set by military considerations, its major finances are from military funds, and very few of those engaged in basic scientific research are not working under military direction … Some universities, in fact, are financial branches of the military establishment, receiving three or four times as much money from the military as from all other sources combined.

The networks of funding and patronage that bind together universities and industry, technology providers and the military, which provide the basis of a more granular account of the MIC, require a more relational and networked understanding of the role and autonomy of the state (Johnstone and Newell 2018). Troath (2023) describes what holds Australia's military-industrial-academic complex together in the following terms: 'each of the three groups is actively seeking closer relationships with the other, driven by a patchwork of competing economic and strategic motivations, and powered by ideals of innovation and the entrepreneurial spirit. Each needs the other – for military advantage, for profits, and for survival.' Military actors play a critical, yet often under-acknowledged, role in setting the direction and pace of sustainability transitions. Cox et al. (2016) illustrate how the military and civilian sustain one another in relation to the nuclear industry in the UK, for example, highlighting the relevance of the notion of a 'deep state' discussed later. They reveal how the importance of maintaining the civilian infrastructure for nuclear weapons capability is a key, if obscured, factor shaping UK civilian energy policy, signalling the militarisation of energy policy and challenging the sanctity of the civilian–military firewall that serves as a bedrock of the international nuclear order (Stavrianakis and Stern 2018). The existence of an MIC is also manifest in secret state security services, the use of 'industrial espionage', spying and the 'surveillance state' whose presence became particularly apparent during the Cold War and whose impacts are clearly felt beyond sovereign borders and whose legacies still define politics in countries where they were present (Nehring 2022).

Military actors also seek to define new roles for themselves beyond the traditional 'theatres of war' and modalities of warfare. Militarisation has been used to secure environmental objectives, including 'war by conservation' (Duffy 2016) and the 'war for biodiversity' (Duffy 2014; Büscher 2018) where poaching, global security and the need for greater levels of surveillance, counter-insurgency, intervention and enforcement become intertwined. These links are forged in practice through efforts, for example, to label the trade in rhino horn as the 'white gold of jihad' alleging (based on very thin evidence) that terrorist groups such as Al-Shabaab used ivory to fund its operations (Duffy 2016). Here, it is the global state interfering in the affairs of other countries rather than direct action (albeit often complicity) from the state as the dominant means by which this violence unfolds. Elsewhere, 'green wars' in Guatemala have resulted in the 'racialized dispossession' of Indigenous groups such as the Q'eqchis in the Maya forest in pursuit of conservation objectives with the complicity of the state (Ybarra 2017).

Some scholars extend the definition of the MIC to include the 'military-industrial-prison complex' to incorporate the 'carceral state' into this analysis and to balance outward threat projection and militarisation with the, often deeply racialised, imprisonment of dissident and 'disruptive' individuals at home (Weaver and Lerman 2010). Just as imperial states 'recruited' heavily from their colonies to fill the ranks of their armies so too domestically citizenship rights are often linked to miliary service to ensure a continual flow of recruits to the military, such as in the US where military service is offered as a test of loyalty and a way to identify and reward 'good' immigrants with citizenship (Diaz-Strong et al. 2009).

5.1.2 Ecological Impacts of Militarism

Militarism's legacies are reflected in lock-in to particular transition trajectories as well as direct impacts which hinder efforts to transition away from fossil fuels, for example. Whether through military training, weapon production, storage, disposal or, above all, armed conflict (but perhaps especially nuclear, chemical and biological testing and warfare), militarism has proved to be a major cause of the most serious ecological degradation of the last century (Eckersely 2004). This includes the deliberate use of environmental damage as a tool of war through ecocide in Indochina (such as the use of Agent Orange to destroy forest cover and food crops in the Vietnam War), the burning of oil wells (in Kuwait 1990–1991) and the deliberate contamination of waterways (Elliott 2004). This critique of the environmental impact of militarism extends not just to the social and environmental devastation reaped by war and conflict but also to the everyday environmental impact (or 'bootprint') (Belcher et al. 2020) and use of resources by the military, including chemical use and the vast amount of fossil fuels militaries consume. The US military alone uses more oil than any other institution in the world (Belcher et al. 2019). Every year US armed forces consume more than 100 million barrels of oil to power ships, vehicles, aircraft and ground operations (Union of Concerned Scientists 2017). Indeed, the US military consumes more liquid fuels and emits more GHGs than most medium-sized countries. If it were a country, its fuel usage alone would make it the 47th largest emitter of GHGs in the world, sitting between Peru and Portugal (Crawford 2019). Militaries are also both primary beneficiaries of fossil fuel subsidies and secondary ones, given that in several countries the military owns companies involved in fossil fuel production and distribution (Johnstone and Newell 2018). By these means, militarism generates both longer-term security threats and 'everyday insecurity'.

Attention to the direct environmental impacts of the organisation, and conduct of the military, while hugely important, has tended to neglect the impact of militarism on transitions to sustainability. As Stavrianakis and Stern (2018: 3) suggest, 'While attention to security has grown exponentially over the last few decades, militarism – the preparation for and normalization and legitimation of war – has not received the widespread and sustained focus it warrants in mainstream or critical circles'. They argue: 'The prevalent emphasis on security has taken precedence over the study of the ways in which war and militarism continue to permeate societies the world over, in different forms and to different degrees' (Stavrianakis and Stern 2018: 4). Militarism is defined by Stavrianakis and Selby (2013: 1) as 'the social and international relations of the preparation for, and conduct of, organized political violence, an abiding and defining characteristic of world politics'. In a similar fashion, Mann (1987: 35) suggests militarism is 'a set of attitudes and social practices which regards war and the preparation for war as a normal and desirable social activity'. Unsurprisingly, therefore, it takes a variety of forms (Mabee and Vucetic 2018), all of which have implications for the pursuit of sustainability.

5.2 The Military State and Transitions

The military state is embroiled in the politics of sustainability transitions in a number of direct and indirect ways: from direct ecological impacts, to the diversion of financial resources and distortion of priorities for research and technological development, and the enactment and enforcement of geopolitics which transform the 'landscape' of transition politics around the world. But it also extends to the shaping of techno-imaginaries of alternative futures and the everyday enforcement of the exclusions, dispossessions and violence required by an industrial economy organised around extractivism.

Some scholars refer to the state's role in perpetuating 'a treadmill of destruction', a play on eco-Marxist concerns with the 'treadmill of production' (Buttel 2004). Building on Wright Mills' inclusion of militarism as one of the three pillars of the power elite (2000 [1956]), Hooks and Smith (2005: 19) argue, however, that there exists a treadmill of destruction that 'maintains a distinct logic relating to geopolitics and arms races that cannot be reduced to capitalism. The 20th century has witnessed unprecedented growth in the research, testing, storage, and employment of both conventional weaponry and weapons of mass destruction. In focusing on this development, the distinctive role the state plays in creating a treadmill of destruction is stressed.' Yet the relationship goes the other way too: capitalism (and industrialism more broadly I would add) is the essential foundation of modern armies and wealth accumulation always precedes the possibility of engaging in war, as the discussion earlier elaborated. Hence, just as 'The development of modern armed forces formed the administrative backbone of the modern state as an organization exercising sovereignty over territory and as an actor in the international system' (Dandeker 1994: 110), so too 'Through the technological, financial and demographic resources released by the industrial and democratic revolutions, the modern state was able to build disciplined, bureaucratically organised, armed forces' (Dandeker 1994: 110).

Externally, military power is called upon to secure access to energy resources: to acquire oil (such as when oil companies like BP were threatened by the Iranian Revolution), to protect supplies (in Kuwait and Iraq in the Gulf Wars) or to protect infrastructures (such as the Suez Canal or oil pipelines in Afghanistan) and key corridors (Rees 2001). The securitisation of energy at once fuels and reinforces the power of the MIC, consolidating the material capacity to secure and extract more energy. In this sense, as Huber (2008: 105) notes, 'the ecological politics of climate change and the anti-war politics of Iraq both converge on a similar object of disdain – oil'. Moving beyond carbon means unsettling a politico-military order that both consumes and secures vast amounts of fossil fuels. Yet states continue to fulfil their growing energy needs through a range of geopolitical strategies, from diplomacy and multilateralism to violence and war. This makes energy, in particular, an issue of high politics. As Moran and Russell (2009: 2) note:

> It is in the energy sector that strategic planners now find it easiest to imagine major states reconsidering their reluctance to use force against each other. 'Energy security' is now deemed so central to 'national security' that threats to the former are liable to be reflectively interpreted as threats to the latter. In a world in which territorial disputes, ideological competition, ethnic irredentism and even nuclear proliferation all seem capable of being normalized in ways that constrain the actual use of military force, a crisis in the global energy supply stands out as the last all-weather casus belli when the moment comes to hypothesize worst case scenarios.

The current war in Ukraine provides a timely and alarming insight into that very dynamic, recasting regional and global energy geopolitics and military alliances and raising the spectre of nuclear conflict. The Russian invasion in 2022 has recast the politics of gas in critical ways and been used both to call for greater energy independence from fossil-fuelled superpowers by accelerating a switch to renewable energy pathways, on the one hand, and, on the other, to justify domestic fossil fuel extraction (such as in the UK) under the pretext of helping achieve 'energy sovereignty' and to heighten pressure on African countries with reserves of gas to export them to Europe. The militarisation of energy resource management necessarily permeates the politics of competing energy transition pathways and responses to climate crises around securing borders, disaster risk management and policing migrant flows, where the spaces and infrastructures of the rich are secured from the poor and dispossessed in conditions of accelerated climate disruption. In this sense, militarism is often mobilised to protect the 'secure' and their assets and not the dispossessed, who in their role as migrants and refugees are constructed as threats to security. In their book *The Secure and the Dispossessed*, Buxton and Hayes (2016: 1) show 'how the military and corporations plan to maintain control in a world reshaped by climate change. With one eye on the scientific evidence and the other on their global assets, dystopian preparations by the powerful are already fuelling militarised responses to the unfolding climate crises.' This is unlikely to form the basis of a progressive or effective response to global climate change or other related sustainability challenges. Consistent with strategies employed by the MIC, dominant framings come from actors with a stake in protecting or expanding expenditure in their sector and who benefit from threat proliferation which justifies their existence and, indeed, growth. The pitch to policymakers is around adaptation, boosting resilience and their ability to secure assets and infrastructures and to protect borders.

Energy, in particular, has a unique relationship with the military state. Oil wars (Kaldor et al. 2007; Colgan 2013) and conflicts over Suez or in Iran to prevent nationalisations of industries show the lengths powerful states will go to in order to guarantee abundant supplies of natural resources, employing force where necessary and revealing the blurring and permeability of public and private interests (Rees 2001). Put most bluntly and polemically, having access to 'cheap' energy requires states to be willing to fight wars where supplies of those resources are threatened with interruption. This is the violent cost of protecting and preserving industrial society and the state it serves, particularly in the core of the global economy, from its ecological contradictions. Energy is heavily implicated in violent politics (Watts 2008), imperialism (Bromley 1991) and changing balances of power, for example, brought about by the shift in power in the world oil regime that occurred as producing and exporting nations took control over the supply and price of oil through collective action (Odell 1981). The protection afforded by states also means that, in exchange, demands can be made of companies in the pursuit of foreign policy goals such that oil companies were asked not to charge for the oil they sold to what was then Western Europe as part of the Marshall Plan.

In considering the geopolitics of energy transitions, it is important to consider, of course, the military as a driver of shifts in consumption and demand for energy (Yergin 1991). Ediger and Bowlus (2018), for example, show how geopolitics, military decision-making and energy security hastened the transition from oil to coal prior to the First World War. They demonstrate how Britain, Germany and the US sought to transition their naval fleets from coal to oil to gain a military advantage at sea which created, for the first time, the problem of oil-supply security. Through government-led initiatives to address oil-supply security, vast new supplies of oil came online and prices fell, the ideal environment for oil to eclipse coal as the dominant source in the global energy system (Ediger and Bowlus 2018: 1). Revealing how a state-led transition in the military sector paved the way for oil to become dominant in the commercial market, they suggest: 'Geopolitics drove governments to enact the transition from coal to oil in the naval sector' (Ediger and Bowlus 2018: 5).

The preparation and conduct of war have implications for transitions in sectors other than energy of course. Examples include the production of consumer durables and the industrialisation of food production, accelerating new methods of 'fast food' and mass food production that could be stored and conserved for longer periods of time (such as packet and tinned food), fundamentally shifting dietary patterns and modes of consumption. As noted in Chapter 3 on the entrepreneurial state, many key epoch-defining technological innovations have their origins in war, from civilian aviation to telecommunications and IT (Giddens 1985).

As well as affecting the pace of transitions, at times slowing or at other times accelerating them, state violence is also mobilised to police them. It is important to recognise that state violence is exercised just as often not to repel external enemies but against citizens and forms of social mobilisation defined as dissident, criminal or subversive or somehow standing in the way of a desired pathway or infrastructure project. Within the state, this takes the form of disciplining and criminalising dissent and 'policing ecocide' (Dunlap and Brock 2022) through surveillance of 'disruptive' and unruly elements in society (protestors) and imprisoning them where necessary if they continue to attack state interests or impede the accumulation of capital, resonating with the discussion of the 'carceral state' earlier.

This reflects the reality that for large swathes of the world's population the primary threat comes from their own state and not an enemy one (Booth 1991). This is especially the case for environmental defenders whose lives are often threatened by the fact they live in resource frontiers lined up for new waves of extractivism (IEN 2021; Menton and LeBillon 2021). Some scholars invoke the term 'social warfare' in this regard. Social war is a 'colonial theory' that helps to illustrate the 'indispensability of political concessions and political military "hold" techniques for maintaining internal stability' (Dunlap and Correa Arce 2021). Building on Foucault's notion of 'politics as a continuation of war by other means' (Foucault 2003: 15), it views the 'colonial/state apparatus and its politics, economy, divisions of labor and hierarchical orderings as a complex apparatus of subjugation' (Dunlap and Correa Arce 2021: 7). In other words, 'social warfare dissects the "hard" coercion and "soft" social technologies of pacification emblematic of counterinsurgency' (Dunlap and Correa Arce 2021: 8).

Beyond its military expressions, others refer to the 'deep state'. Energy of course is deeply intertwined with the politics of the deep state as preserving access to and control over energy sources is fundamental to the ability of elites to govern, whomever is in power. For some, this manifests itself in the power and influence of 'big oil' and its subversion of democracy (Scott 2017). But the deep state takes different forms depending on from whence the claims are made. For those on the libertarian right, it is based on claims of 'invisible bureaucrats working for the vast web of agencies that actually dictate our foreign policy, defense posture, and security decisions' (Lofgren 2016: back cover). It is suggested that 'Actual power lies in the Deep State, Washington's shadowy power elite, in the pockets of corporate interests and dependent on the moguls of Silicon Valley, whose data-collecting systems enable the U.S. government to spy on our every move, swipe, and click' (Lofgren 2016: back cover). Interestingly, populist leaders such as US President Trump invoke the concept to describe what they perceive to be civil service resistance to their reform programmes in a manner that subverts the 'will of the people', the 'shadowy network of unelected bureaucrats that illegitimately holds the levers of real power' (Horwitz 2021: 473). This is the notion that the will of the people is the 'supreme authority in the state': that there is no authority above the people (Beckman 2021). The sense in which non-appointed actors, networks and institutions subvert democratic processes extends, in some analysis, to the role of the monarchy, with some studies showing how democratic procedures have been bypassed by interventions by royal families to exempt themselves from environmental policy requirements, including the use of courts as 'a surrogate king for purposes of its own self-interested hegemonic preservation' (Mérieau 2016: 445).

Hence though the state may seek to steer and align military forces, full control is often not exercised and power and dependency run in multiple directions, with many governments acutely aware of the power of militaries and their willingness to exercise it to oust them from power as they have done so repeatedly throughout history. Indeed, the historical record underscores the ways in which states depend on militaries for their survival in a literal sense but also seek to maintain their support for fear of military coups, the like of which we have seen throughout history and continue to see around the world today, most recently in Venezuela and Myanmar, but whose intervention is called upon even in advanced contemporary democracies such as Brazil by supporters of the far-right ex-president Jair Bolsonaro.

Regarding the industrial component of the complex, militarism is a function of and intrinsically linked to the capitalist industrial society of which it is part, whose project it polices and whose strictures it is called upon to enforce 'at home' and 'abroad' in the service of the industrial state and its growth imperatives (Newell 2019). Militarism was always thus. Mann (1987: 38) notes that, even in the 'age of the theorist–generals and diplomats' – of Clausewitz and von Moltke, of Metternich and Bismarck – 'militarism became military science, harnessed to the logic of geo-political strategy, partaking in the scientific and technological developments of industrial capitalism'. Militaries and militarism provide, therefore, a key means by which states resource their economic expansion and growth and thereby maintain and lock in unsustainable pathways. There is the internal everyday violence that industrialism requires and generates in its wake, discussed in Chapter 4. This results from its extractivist orientation and growth obsession which demands what Harvey (2004) refers to as 'accumulation by dispossession'. The extraction of resources such as oil and minerals, often against the wishes of host communities who rarely benefit from the revenues from it, necessitates acts of dispossession against excluded groups such as Indigenous peoples and other environmental defenders (Menton and LeBillon 2021). It produces a deliberate neglect or blindness towards the 'slow violence' (Nixon 2011) and everyday environmental injustices visited upon poor groups in society by wealthier groups with the state's endorsement, complicity or active involvement. In this regard, the state is viewed by social ecologists as a vehicle for mobilising violence for the preservation of hierarchies and social order based on extracting wealth from rich to poor, South to North and rural to urban areas (Bookchin 1982; Pineault 2023).

That this is so should perhaps be unsurprising given the intertwined nature of the rise of the industrial and military state. Wright Mills (1956: 215) writes, for example, 'Within the span of one generation, America has become the leading industrial society of the world and at the same time one of the leading military states'. He notes:

> What the main drift of the twentieth century has revealed is that as the economy has become concentrated and incorporated into great hierarchies, the military has become enlarged and decisive to the shape of the entire economic structure; and moreover, the economic and military have become structurally and deeply interrelated as the economy has become a seemingly permanent war economy; and military men and policies have increasingly penetrated the corporate economy. (Wright Mills 1956: 215)

This proximity and entanglement with state power shapes worldviews, opening up some while closing down other pathways and 'techno-imaginaries' (Jasanoff and Kim 2013), and in Mill's account leads to the 'subordination' of 'all other ways of life' to militarism (Wright Mills 1956: 223). The effect of this closing down, as Wright Mills (1956: 221) observes, is 'that there is no free and wide debate of military policy or of policies of military relevance'. The systematic refusal to subject military emissions to scrutiny and oversight in the context of the UN climate change negotiations offers a case in point of deliberate *un*-governance at work. As Wright Mills (1956: 220) notes: 'The content of this great effort reveals its fundamental purpose: to define the reality of international relations in a military way, to portray the armed forces in a manner attractive to civilians and thus to emphasise the need for the expansion of military facilities.'

For Wright Mills, this constitutes 'the very highest form of propaganda warfare', constructing a 'reality within which only certain limited viewpoints are possible' (Wright Mills 1956: 222). One of the ways in which this is achieved is by embedding militarism in everyday life. Hence the critique of prevailing approaches to security encompasses not only institutionalised violence and its embodiment in the state but the social and systemic sources of violence. The latter is taken to refer to everyday insecurity brought about by domination, patriarchy, masculinist culture (Mellor 1992; Plumwood 1993), competition, disaffection and alienation, fragmented communities and social disenfranchisement (Boyle and Simms 2009). This means 'Paying attention to *how* people, institutions, practices, processes, and so on are militarized or rendered the subjects of security or securitized' (Stavrianakis and Stern 2018: 12; emphasis in original), including by the state itself. This is the constant preparation for war as an enterprise in itself, 'the dominance of means over ends for the purpose of heightening the prestige and increasing the power of the military' (Wright Mills 1956: 222). Attention to the social and cultural politics of militarism necessarily blurs the boundaries between the domestic and the foreign, the civilian and the military, the public and the private and war and peace.

The systematic state bias towards the ideology and practice of militarism, reflected in policy priorities and institutional access which results from these closely knit relations of power, points to another area of critique: the (mis)allocation of state resources for destructive rather than sustainable ends. Globally, arms expenditure runs at around $1.7 trillion a year (SIPRI 2018). Andrew Smith asks:

> What would happen if the government put peace and social justice ahead of militarism and war? What would happen if the level of resources currently being put into promoting military might were used to make the world a better place? This year alone, the UK will spend £37 billion on arms and the military. What if a similar figure was invested in promoting social and environmental justice and creating jobs in the renewable sector? There is a severe skills shortage in science, technology, engineering and maths (STEM) and a greater emphasis could see the UK as a global leader. However, at present the government spends 25 times more on research and development (R&D) for the military (£1.4 billion) as it does on R&D for renewable energy (£58 million). Every year, taxpayers subsidise arms companies to the tune of hundreds of millions of pounds to export their wares into war zones and to arm oppressive regimes. One estimate, from the Stockholm International Peace Research Institute puts the level of UK arms export subsidies at £700 million a year. These weapons don't just provide military support, they provide political support too, and give a sign of UK support for atrocities taking place across the world. (Smith 2016)

So, these are the histories, relations and practices which have configured the actually existing military state today, adapting to as well as shaping geopolitics, accommodating threats to its legitimacy while preserving and extending incumbent power, including through the pursuit of techno-managerial industrial military strategies of control. So, how might they be challenged and changed?

5.3 Transforming the Military State

The dismantling of many aspects of the military state will be a prerequisite for more radical notions of sustainability. This is so for a number of reasons. Firstly, the direct impacts of military operations, both every day and in the conduct of war, are a major driver of unsustainability, as we saw earlier in the chapter. How will the military state adapt to a low- or zero-carbon world, or one in which degrowth becomes a valid social goal and way of organising the economy, when every facet of its operations depends on a model of vast consumption of resources, especially fossil fuels but also water, land and forests, and the construction and maintenance of energy-intensive infrastructures often combined with the exercise of violence?

Secondly, military actors and establishments are not neutral with respect to sustainability pathways. As we saw in the discussion of the MIC, they often depend upon and advocate for technological fixes, R&D for military ends and the committal of vast amounts of state resources (written into the modus operandi of NATO membership, for example, where a fixed percentage of a country's growth should be committed to military expenditure) to military rather than other social and ecological programmes. Contrary to the myth of the 'apolitical military' that is excluded from the formal conduct of politics, in reality it forms 'an influential corporate group in all states' (Dandeker 1994: 110).

In many ways, then, more radical transformations towards a sustainable society require nothing less than a wholesale dismantling of the military state: a severing of the intimate and duplicitous relationship between state rulers and their militaries. This is not to suggest an armed force of some description would not need to be maintained even in more radical visions of a sustainable society. As Eckersley (2004: 25) suggests, 'it would be naïve for greens to believe that states can function without military and police forces. Once this is acknowledged, then from a democratic green perspective, everything should turn on whether those forces are deployed in legitimate ways to further legitimate ends.' But the scale of resources, infrastructure, technological development, innovation and training dedicated to the preparation and conduct of war would need to be radically curtailed. Given the gravity and significance of other threats facing the world, resources need to be redirected elsewhere as well as arms control accelerated given the imminent and real threat that nuclear weapons continue to present in the world. It is also the case that military personnel will increasingly need to be redeployed instead as civilian forces dealing with climate-induced disasters and their social consequences, from evacuations and mass migration to civic violence and social unrest.

5.3.1 Towards Ecological Security

At the heart of transforming the military state is the need to rethink the very notion of security. Advocates of 'planet politics' pose the challenge to traditional ideas and thinking about security in the following way:

> Security comes from being more connected, not less. Gone are the days of billiard ball states and national security based on keeping the Other out or deterred. The Other is always already inside, so bound up with us in a common process that it no longer makes sense to speak of inside and outside. We cannot survive without accepting the cosmopolitan and enmeshed nature of this world. We are an array of bodies connected and interconnected in complex ways that have little to do with nationality. States will wither in the coming heat, freeze in the prolonged winters, and be lost under the rising oceans. We will not survive without the biggest and most complex system we know: the biosphere. (Burke et al. 2016: 502)

Ecologically, 'Concepts of violence, harm and (in)security that focus only on humans ignore at their peril the destruction and severance of worlds, which undermines the conditions of plurality that enables life on Earth to thrive' (Burke et al. 2016: 518). Indeed, writers such as Dennis Pirages noted more than two decades ago that 'The greatest challenges to human well-being in the next century are more likely to come directly from nature than from the malignant designs of malevolent dictators' (Pirages 1997: 55). This requires collective security for a collective fate. In pursuit of this broad, ambitious and quite radical normative vision, a range of strategies might be considered.

These might include both greening traditional security agendas or seeking to recast the meaning and pursuit of security in some of the ways proposed in this chapter. In the case of the former, it is a question of attracting the attention of military strategists, a plan that brings its own risks and dilemmas (Deudney 1990). Indeed, it is precisely the interest on the part of the military establishment that makes many both suspicious and critical of linking these issues. State diplomatic power and foreign policy influence could be directed to arms control but often are not. It might be possible to repurpose the MIC for productive civilian and sustainable uses, such as the production of low-carbon energy, but control would still rest with incumbent actors. Dramatic shifts from civilian to military use and back again have historical precedents, however (Simms and Newell 2017). Such shifts would include worker-led proposals for reconversions of production, such as the Lucas Plan in 1970s Britain (Smith 2016). The deeper shift, however, would need to be in the goals of security and that which is to be secured: from populations thought to be in competition and latent conflict with one another to the biosphere as the lifeforce which sustains all life on earth (McDonald 2021). That implies deeper, cultural and moral shifts which might first be debated, nurtured and negotiated through the democratic state to which we turn our attention next.

In conjunction with efforts to embed more ecological thinking in relation to security, a prerequisite for such a shift might be a revisioning of the goal and purpose of the economy, at least in richer countries in the first instance. If endless waves of extractivist growth no longer serve as the goal and means of securing human and planetary well-being, the violence which goes hand in hand with such a model of economic development would become less necessary. If policing the 'open veins' of uneven ecological exchange and economic development abroad and supressing protests against resource grabs and new commodity frontiers is no longer required, there is a space to reduce the power of the military state. A world in which mutual dependencies existed more in the political and cultural realms than the largely economic would require a very different, probably much smaller and less globally organised military establishment even if multilateral peacekeeping and humanitarian forces would be needed, perhaps increasingly so as conflicts intensify over dwindling natural resources, exacerbated by the impacts of global environmental change.

6

The Democratic State

6.1 Introducing the Democratic State

The relationship between democracy and sustainability is a contentious one. It centres on the role of the state in protecting and deepening the former in order to achieve the latter. Definitions of democracy vary, but according to democratic theorists, it embodies in essence a notion of 'polyarchy': rule by the many and the 'continuing responsiveness of the government to the preferences of its citizens considered as political equals' (Dahl 2008: 1–2). While lack of democratic oversight of political and economic systems is often taken to be a reason for the hold incumbent actors have over societal pathways, controversially, others point to the scale of the polycrisis (of which the climate and biodiversity crisis is just one component) and the need for accelerated action as a basis for suspending certain forms of democratic politics as usual. For some, then, questions are raised about the 'suitability' of democracy for dealing with environmental problems: 'whether, or how far, it is feasible or desirable for responses to environmental problems to be decided democratically' (Holden 2002: 5), while for others democratic struggle over future pathways is vital to them being inclusive, progressive and effective (Stirling 2014).

Indeed, if the state is to play a more supportive role in enabling and accelerating transformative change, it will need to garner the sort of far-reaching legitimacy required 'to interfere with deep socio-economic structures, consumer choice and individual liberties in order to meet the sustainability challenges of our age' (Hammond and Hausknost 2021: 4). Given the intrinsic uncertainties and contingencies which characterise collective attempts to wrestle with such profound socio-ecological and economic challenges, ensuring ownership, engagement and support mean deliberation and contestation over pathways will have to be a permanent feature of either the transition state or a state seeking to support transformational change: a function few states have shown themselves willing to perform to date. It may also be the case that the future democratic state will face greater challenges in the form of both elite and popular backlash against interventions which aim to reset the economy and society since they inevitably produce losers in the short term and often very powerful ones. This is partly a function of the fact modern democratic systems have co-evolved with and been sustained by a period of resource abundance and dependence on ‘cheap’ (for some) fossil fuels in particular from the post–Second World War ‘great acceleration’ onwards (Mitchell 2011; Hammond and Hausknost 2021). Likewise, Mitchell (2011) shows how the materiality of specific energy sources such as coal and oil played a large part in shaping democratic politics as some forms of extraction and exchange could be blocked and disrupted more easily, leading to concessions to labour demands for welfare, for example. Cultures of contentment and informal social contracts often rest on rising material wealth as a quid pro quo for public acquiescence and acceptance of political order, state control and tolerance of social and economic inequalities (Galbraith 2017). Such tacit social settlements might well fray in an era in which mass production and consumption, especially in the ‘core’ of the global economy, have to be controlled to live more ecologically.

Layered upon these tensions between legitimacy, speed, equity and inclusion is the disturbing fact that large parts of the world are governed by authoritarian or totalitarian regimes where citizens have little to no say in their collective fate (ICNL 2020) (see Figure 6.1 on the composition of political regimes around the world and Figure 6.2 on the state of democracy). Additionally problematic from the point of view of sustainability transitions, many of those non-democratic regimes, such as China, Russia and Saudi Arabia, are also major contributors to key environmental problems such as biodiversity loss and climate change and home to ‘carbon bombs’ which, if ‘diffused’, will blow global carbon budgets (Kühne et al. 2022), and in so far as they are home to environmentalism, it takes an authoritarian form such as in China (Beeson 2010). But the threat to democracy is a generic one and is not just a function of regime type. As a recent report noted, ‘Across the world, a broad and well-evidenced consensus now exists that civic space is under attack and shrinking. This long-running trend over at least the past fifteen years is observed not only in non-OECD settings but also in countries of the global north’ (Newell et al. 2022: 10). The adoption of new and wide-ranging policing and criminal justice provisions in countries like the UK provides a case in point, explicitly invoking the need to deter environmental protestors following moves to overturn bans on fracking and expand oil exploration in the UK, which have both been the target of significant grassroots activism from groups such as Just Stop Oil whose activists have been handed down lengthy prison sentences. In times of crisis, democratic institutions and basic rights are often particularly vulnerable to being eroded or suspended, a fact which cautions against the generic deployment of emergency framings by activists (Patterson et al. 2021).

Figure 6.1 The world by political regime type in 2022. Source: Our World in Data.

Additional threats to democracy come from the rise of populism, 'fake news' and obscure funding for orchestrated 'citizen' backlash against sustainability initiatives. Firstly, regarding populism, the growing list of authoritarian leaders who have recently won or consolidated power, often by deploying or harnessing some variant of populism, appears to threaten democratic liberalism and populist movements often form around the goal of excluding racialised, migrant and 'foreign' minorities. This phenomenon can be understood as a widespread protest against decades-long neglect of working classes and rural populations that has resulted in stark economic inequalities that restructuring associated with sustainability transitions, unless managed well, has the potential to exacerbate. The recent case of redundancies associated with the Port Talbot steelworks in Wales in the UK illustrates this dynamic: an area in terminal industrial decline where the owner Tata

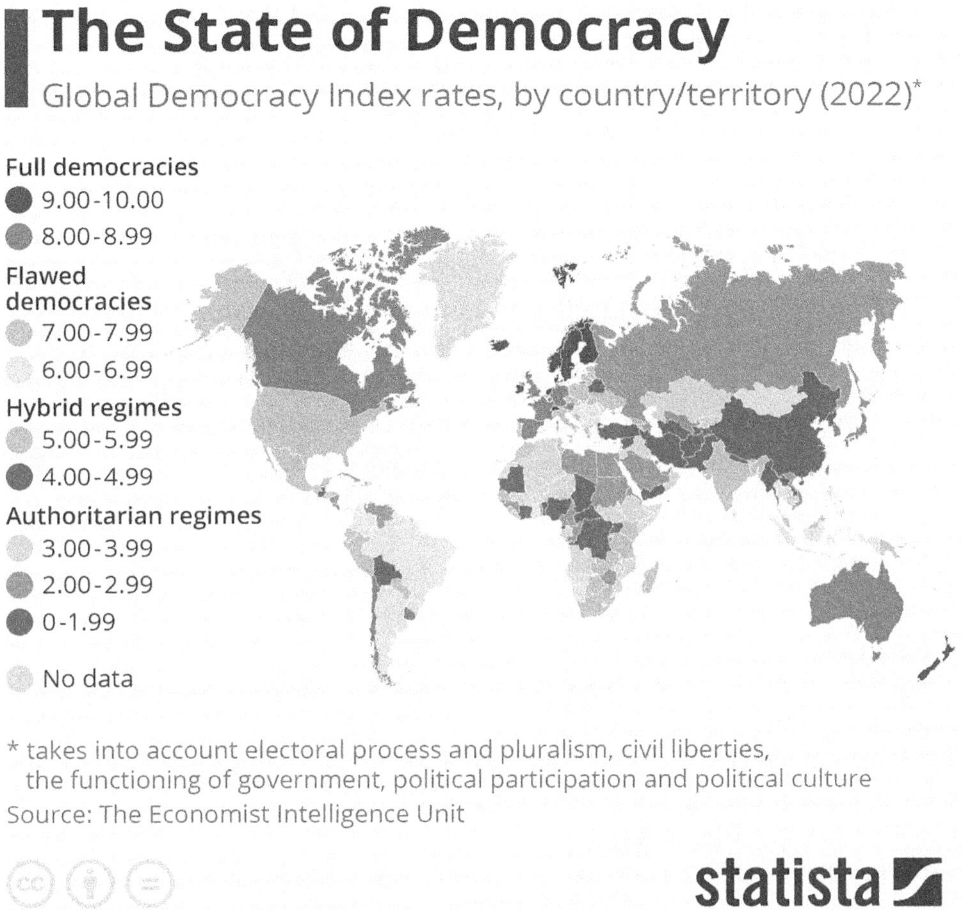

Figure 6.2 The state of democracy. Source: Statista.

Steel claims it was losing £1 million per day, but the job losses were blamed by opponents of net zero on the drive for electric furnaces for steel (rather than coal-fired furnaces). In this attack on then Labour shadow climate and energy minister Ed Miliband, the news presenter Darren Grimes seethed, ‘This is the same man responsible for the Climate Change Act and the Greta Thunberg disciple who has said we must go harder and faster on Net Zero. THIS man is responsible for speeding up these crippling job losses!’ (Sharp 2024). Likewise, moves towards low-traffic neighbourhoods and congestion charges in places like London have been toxified by right-wing activists presenting these initiatives as a threat to liberty by an overbearing ‘nanny’ state (a framing that has resonated with anti-vax movements) in order to mobilise their opposition to traffic-calming measures.

Whether populist resentments channel into progressive, inclusive and democratic disruptive politics remains an open empirical question, therefore. As

McCarthy (2019) notes, right-wing authoritarian populist regimes share common features, one of which is promises of strong direct action to respond effectively to threats. In this vein, crises can present opportunities for regressive military interventions (Buxton and Hayes 2016) and 'shock doctrine' strategies in which people turn to political actors that proclaim to have decisive solutions to 'fix' the crisis. This happened, for example, with the rapid rollout of neoliberal development projects in the wake of the violent aftermath of the Indian Ocean tsunami in 2004 and Hurricane Katrina in 2005 (Klein 2007). The point is that populism and authoritarianism can actively undermine sustainability transitions and the track records of former and current populist leaders on the right and libertarian end of the political spectrum such as Trump (US), Bolsonaro (Brazil), Orbán (Hungary) and Milei (Argentina) certainly give grounds for concern given their demonstrated willingness to weaponise sustainability and blame environmental measures for working-class economic insecurity. For Trump, this has taken the form of 'cancelling' the Paris Agreement on climate change combined with calls to 'drill baby drill', while Bolsonaro used his presidency to roll back protections of Indigenous land which he claimed were inhibiting Brazil's development and accelerate destruction of the Amazon Rainforest.

Secondly, there is orchestrated 'citizen' backlash against sustainability measures. Often front groups claiming to represent 'ordinary citizens' such as Net Zero Watch in the UK, a group formed from the climate sceptic Global Warming Policy Foundation, successfully access mainstream media to create the impression of conflict and dissensus around environmental policy objectives: classic strategies from 'the play book' of corporate obstructionism (Jacquet 2022). These trends compound the barriers to an informed citizenry, underscoring the importance of the distinction Plato drew between 'knowledge' and 'opinion' (Plato 2007). Democracy can be further subverted by permissible but obscure patterns of party funding, privileged access, revolving doors between business elites and government officials, internships and other practices removed from public view which further tip the balance of power in favour of ruling and commercial elites and incumbent actors (Ford and Newell 2021), sometimes reinforced by techno-managerial 'post-politics' (Swyngedouw 2010) and deference to elites, fuelling claims about the 'failure of democracy' (Shearman and Smith 2007).

Indeed, incumbent-friendly transitions can directly undermine inclusive, fair and representative participation in decision-making. Since accelerating sustainability transitions requires financial, technical and organisational resources, policymakers inevitably have to work with major investors and incumbent firms whom they rely on for tax, investment and jobs. For example, incumbents have the technological capabilities and intellectual property needed for scaling low-carbon innovations like electric vehicles, heat pumps, offshore wind, nuclear reactors, hydrogen or carbon capture and storage (CCS). However, a tension arises from the fact that working with such incumbents to accelerate transitions may lead to transition pathways which are less attentive to social justice: privileging large-scale transition pathways while neglecting others which seek to advance 'just transitions' rather than scale up technologies as an end in itself. Likewise, the financial actors that are able to mobilise large sums of money (like state development banks, pension funds or commercial banks) prefer to invest in large-scale options (e.g., offshore wind parks) over which they (rather than local communities) have control and rarely embrace justice concerns over short-term returns on investment (Newell, Sovacool and Geels 2022).

On the one hand, then, greater participation and representation from civil society in the governance of socially just transitions has the *potential* to reinforce the distributional and procedural capacities of the state as well as the means to strengthen democratic practice against authoritarianism. At the same time, the state seeks to manage (and at times subdue) populations through biopower and surveillance and modes of governmentality that wield 'technopower' over everyday life. The implication for debates about sustainability transitions is to understand and then challenge dominant state practices of control: the coercion, domination, hierarchy and surveillance that states employ to manage and subjugate citizens. This requires a different, more granular, approach to the study of the state to understand and resist the deployment of these techniques of control.

Against this background of the tension between opening up and closing down spaces for citizen engagement with sustainability transitions, there has been significant academic interest in 'ecological democracy' and its relationship to, as well as differences with, liberal democracy over the past four decades. Questions of democracy have been the focus of a spectrum of environmental thinking in the 1980s and 1990s (Dryzek 1992; Goodin 1992; Doherty and de Geus 1996; Eckersley 2004). More recently, the advent of the Anthropocene epoch has reposed the question of whether the concept and practice of ecological democracy needs to be recast on a planetary scale (Pedersen et al. 2022).

The term 'social contract' is often used to describe the democratic duties and obligations that exist between the state and citizens concerning issues of protection, welfare and basic rights which are central to discussions about sustainability. While the term can be traced back to the seventeenth century, its modern incarnation is representative democracy where, in ideal circumstances at least, citizens vote to determine their government periodically according to manifesto promises and election pledges. Under such a system, citizens can vote the government out if they feel the social contract has been broken by the state's inability to protect them or improve their well-being, for instance: a phenomenon we might anticipate as ever more likely as the ecological crisis deepens. Hence the obligations and responsibilities of state and citizens flow both ways. The climate and ecological crisis, with its increasingly frequent and severe disruption of all aspects of social and economic life, places the social contract under renewed pressure. Put simply, the role of the state is to keep its citizens safe, but the climate and ecological crisis is limiting its ability to do that, and governments' own (in)actions in driving that crisis are undermining their capacity to protect citizens. Indeed, this has been the basis of recent legal challenges by civil society groups regarding the consistency of government policies with their climate obligations (Mayer and Van Asselt 2023) including the ongoing case involving the UK government regarding the Rosebank oilfield on the grounds that it is not compatible with the government's plans to meet legally binding climate targets.

But the law is just one expression of this social contract. Often the relationship between the state and citizens centres on the question of citizenship and the respective rights and duties that apply to states and those over whom they govern (Dobson 2003). We see concrete expressions of this around discussions of 'energy citizenship' or the 'right to energy' (Hossain et al. 2021) or the right to food, water and land. The current energy crisis has brought these issues into stark relief with citizens demanding state intervention to secure affordable energy in the face of an unstable geopolitical environment exacerbated by the war in Ukraine. In a world of interdependent markets, and often only partial state control over the energy sector, the scope to intervene in such ways to protect citizens is often limited where provision is held in private hands (McDonald 2009). In other contexts, conflicts have arisen between rights to water expressed in constitutions in states such as South Africa and the means of enforcing those rights when the responsibility for the provision of water has been outsourced to the private sector as part of a programme of privatisation (Newell and Wheeler 2006).

The emphasis on citizen engagement implies a more active conception of citizenship. It relates to discussions about the difference between passive participation and active citizenship, or what Cornwall and Gaventa (2001) describe as the difference between 'users and choosers' (consumers) and 'makers and shapers' (citizens). Mathie and Gaventa (2015: 5) identify two types of active citizenship: active citizenship as a *horizontal phenomenon*, where citizens engage with one another in their own community motivated by civic duty and a shared sense of responsibility, and active citizenship as a *vertical phenomenon*, where citizen action is aimed at claiming rights and decisions from the state. Both are relevant to discussions about community-led food, energy or water systems in the case of the former and to strategies for holding states to account in the latter.

But there are very uneven geographies of participation, including closing civic space in many parts of the world as previously noted. This means that assumptions which circulate in global debates in relation to procedural justice and inclusion (albeit often not explicitly articulated) include tripartite bargaining between the state, private sector and labour, with a key role for trade unions; an engaged and responsive private sector; a cohesive and engaged civil society, underpinned by high levels of democratic space; and state capacity as well as willingness to act. While this may be an appropriate description of civic spaces for discussions of just transition in wealthy countries with consolidated democracies (though not always in those contexts either), it poorly describes many settings around the world. It is worth noting that participation and deliberation from citizens is often harder around issues such as energy because of its high political status and (deliberately) increased political barriers to participation by non-specialists (Newell et al. 2024) but also in relation to contentious land politics and decisions about access to water where movements struggle to make their voices heard.

Yet transformative systemic change, the like of which has been called for by the IPCC (2018), will not be achieved without widespread social buy-in because of the changes to production, consumption, modes of governance and lifestyles that it implies. There is a lot at stake and resistance to change is deep-seated as many forms of wealth creation in the current global economy depend upon the large-scale use of fossil fuels, the majority of which now need to be left in the ground if we are to meet the goals of the Paris Agreement (SEI et al. 2021; Trout et al. 2022). Tipping the balance of power in favour of the beneficiaries of sustainability transitions means overcoming resistance to change and bringing new stakeholders into policy design and implementation, including those most affected (poorer and racially marginalised and Indigenous communities) and those not yet represented (younger people and future generations). Citizen engagement, through a variety of means and strategies, is one way to achieve this. 'Disruptions and interventions from state and corporate actors around policy, financing or the development of new technologies are often prefigured by years of campaigning, resistance and building alternatives from below which create pressure and prepare the ground for interventions by elite actors' (Newell 2021a: 170).

This brings with it several challenges, especially as in many parts of the world spaces of civic engagement are being closed down. The world is a risky place for environmental defenders, tens of thousands of whom sacrifice their lives each year defending the environment (Global Witness 2021; Menton and Le Billon 2021). The challenges of deepening citizen engagement are not of course unique to environmental issues. For example, the technical nature of the topic and the difficulty in communicating it is a challenge for citizen engagement in trade and investment policy too (Newell 2007) and powerful status quo actors exist in most sectors of the global economy. What makes citizen engagement on sustainability issues so difficult is the combination and simultaneous interplay of these factors: the dispersed beneficiaries of action within and between societies; the fact that some of the greatest beneficiaries are not yet born, yet the costs of action have to be paid now; the scale, enormity and complexity of the challenge; the paucity of levers of change over which citizens seemingly have direct control; the still low salience of sustainability issues compared to other issues which dominate mainstream and social media; and the strength of opposition to transformative action. Blühdorn (2021: 28) describes the 'eco-political dysfunctionality of democracy' which now functions as 'a tool for the politics of unsustainability' because of the ways in which citizen expectations of prosperity and consumer choice function as a 'glass ceiling' on more ambitious and transformative approaches to sustainability, presaging the end of the 'love affair with democracy' (Shearman and Smith 2007: 121).

6.2 The Democratic State and Transitions

The need to radically increase the ambition of moves towards a sustainable economy poses challenges for all political systems. Diverse groups of citizens need to be engaged in the design and implementation of policies and actions across all scales and sectors for them to succeed and be socially acceptable. But how? From protest and mobilisation to participation in policy and the creation of new spaces of citizen engagement through climate assemblies, citizen juries on genetically modified (GM) crops and scenario work on food futures, many governments, businesses, cities and civil society actors are grappling with the challenge of how best to engage citizens in addressing a series of threats to global sustainability.

It is often noted that if transitions are to be deepened and accelerated and regarded as legitimate and just, they need to bring 'the public' with them. Questions of social acceptance feature frequently in literatures on socio-technical transitions (Barry et al. 2008; Roddis et al. 2018). As well as democratic rationales for public engagement and the mobilisation of consent, it is also often claimed that decision-making is improved and made more robust by citizen input into exploring and assessing different pathways, 'adjudicating rival knowledge claims' through discursive democracy (Holden 2002: 48) and identifying challenges and ways forward (Stirling 2014). Democratic engagement can also serve as a check on the short-termism of elected representatives. Dryzek (1992: 44) notes 'an outcome is legitimate to the extent that its production has involved authentic deliberation on the part of the people subject to it'. On the flip side, failures to consult and engage affected publics often result in backlash over fuel prices, for example, or rising energy costs in the wake of subsidy removals (Lockwood 2015a; Hossain et al. 2021) as well as resistance and 'blockadia' by environmental defenders (IEN 2021).

Pickering et al. (2022) explore the role of democratic practices in accelerating or obstructing five key dimensions of sustainability transformations – institutional, social, economic, technological and epistemic – finding 'substantial evidence that democratic practices can foster transformations towards sustainability'. Nicely identifying the spectrum of opinion regarding the, at times, fraught relationship between democracy and transformations to sustainability, they note:

> Proponents of environmental democracy envisage democratic states as best suited to governing sustainability transformations. However, far-reaching sustainability transformation may conflict with the inherent incrementalism of decision-making and reform in democratic states. Accordingly, some scholars argue that even reformist states will eventually hit the 'glass ceiling' of socio-ecological transformation rather than challenging the traditional sources of their legitimacy (e.g. ongoing pursuit of economic growth). Proponents of ecological democracy claim that a radical reconfiguration of the state and/or a shift away from the state towards decentralised, citizen-centred governance is needed, while advocates of eco-authoritarianism argue that only centrally controlled states are capable of implementing the wide-ranging reforms necessary for transformation. (Pickering et al. 2022: 5)

'Authoritarian statism' (Poulantzas 1978) or 'eco-authoritarianism' in China is of course a case in point, where a centralised state in a command-and-control economy is able to drive change throughout the economy and society, albeit not always as successfully as assumed and often at the expense of social and environmental justice (Lo 2020). Likewise, looking at the military bureaucratic state in South Korea, Hellmann (2018: 67) provides a more nuanced account, arguing 'whether non-democratic rulers can harness the infrastructural power of the state to implement strategies of regime stabilization depends on three crucial factors: the state's social embedding, the international context, and the extent of elite cohesion'. While scholars have attempted more general comparisons of the performance of different types of democratic systems (i.e., those based on proportional representation and corporatist modes of interest group representation), a lot of attention focusses on particular sites and democratic practices (Pickering et al. 2022). Proposed innovations to both check incumbent power and pluralise decision-making have focussed on rebalancing representation of excluded and unrepresented groups (such as future generations) and lowering the voting age to increase representation of publics most affected by environmental (in)action, as well as disrupting and untangling the tightly knit social and financial ties which bind private and public elites together in ways which corrupt democratic politics (Newell and Martin 2020).

But it is public participation that has attracted most attention as one core component of the democratic state. The notion that public participation in environmental decision-making is vital to policy success has been underscored in numerous international legal and policy instruments, including Principle 10 of the Rio Declaration, which declares:

> Environmental issues are best handled with the participation of all concerned citizens, at the relevant level. At the national level each individual shall have appropriate access to information concerning the environment … and the opportunity to participate in decision-making processes. States shall facilitate and encourage public awareness and participation by making information widely available. Effective access to judicial and administrative proceedings, including redress and remedy, shall be provided.

Similarly, Article 1 of the Aårhus Convention of 1998 on *Access to Information, Public Participation in Decision-Making and Access to Justice in Environmental Matters* states that 'each party shall guarantee the rights of access to information, public participation in decision-making and access to justice in environmental matters in accordance with the provisions of this Convention'. The convention contains provisions on access to information, access to justice and public participation in decision-making. Many treaties, including the United Nations Framework Convention on Climate Change (UNFCCC), also underline the importance of public participation and education, noting, 'While public awareness strategies are grounded on efforts to share information as widely as possible, they also enable diverse voices to contribute to global and local discussions. Public awareness is a core element of Article 6 of the convention because it has the power to create critical mass engagement for one of the greatest challenges that we face.'[1]

A number of claims are advanced about the value of citizen engagement in sustainability transitions. Firstly, the fact that it can improve policy. By trialling and piloting policies and soliciting feedback through commissions and citizens' assemblies for example, citizen engagement can bring lay and experiential knowledge to bear on proposed policy solutions. Such engagements can act as a 'temperature check' on the public acceptability of policy proposals across social divides such as class, race and gender, for example. In many cases, more extended and deeper forms of citizen engagement highlight the appetite for more radical and transformative policy, emphasising the multiple pathways available to communities in varied contexts as the experience of climate assemblies bears out (Elstub et al. 2021). More participatory governance emphasises that hierarchical steering characterised by a government-led, expert-centred approach can lead to poor policymaking, as well as being disempowering for citizens themselves (Stirling 2005). In many least developed country settings this is exacerbated by limited regulatory capacity, reflecting human resource and financial constraints, as well as a dearth of reflexive governance mechanisms.

Participatory processes offer the potential for a more comprehensive and inclusive evidence base by including local knowledge about the unanticipated potential social and environmental impacts of infrastructural developments or proposed policies. Social acceptance literature also suggests that public participation has contributed to public acceptance of renewable energy projects in countries including

Germany, Denmark, Canada, South Africa and Malaysia, amongst many others (Renn et al. 2014; Jarbandhan et al. 2018; Wan Abdullah et al. 2020). Involvement of local citizens and actors in the funding and governance of sustainable energy transitions helps to reposition citizens from consumers of the transition plans of others to more active proponents for transition (Rüdinger 2019).

Secondly, public participation can build social acceptance and reduce opposition, improving the potential longevity and 'political sustainability' and buy-in for projects and policies by building a constituency of support to sustain policy interventions. Demands for citizen engagement are often expressed in the first instance as a concern over potential public resistance and the need to gain societal 'acceptance' for urgent yet difficult policy decisions and technological changes (Roddis et al. 2018). Conversely, if there is widespread awareness of a policy and measure and its multiple benefits, positive citizen engagement and sustained public support is far more likely. This is particularly important for interventions that require behaviour change on the part of individual citizens around carbon reduction, water use or waste reduction strategies, for example.

Thirdly, public participation can strengthen legitimacy. There will always be opposition to policies. But if it can be shown that extensive efforts have been made to engage citizens across society, and policy addresses their concerns, governments and other actors can claim they have a legitimate democratic mandate to act. Citizen engagement can also help to counter the tendency for policy decisions to be based on 'imagined publics': where representations and assumptions about abilities, knowledges, identities, behaviours and responsibilities (Rodhouse et al. 2021) mean that some publics are recognised, involved and acknowledged while others are not (Chilvers et al. 2018).

The depth and the progressive nature of this move towards participatory governance has, nevertheless, been questioned by some amid claims about the incompatibility of neoliberalising programmes led by states and their experiments with participatory governance (Abram 2007, 2008). The concern is that participatory or inclusive governance may be hijacked, deflecting local resistance through 'talking shops' rather than offering effective democratic and inclusive governance. Other studies have shown how many invited spaces delimit scope to question underlying preferences and assumptions about the benefits of particular economic or technological pathways, around genetic modification, for example (Newell 2010). Opening up opportunities for greater inclusion and genuinely democratic practices to address sustainability challenges requires symbolically and affectively linking disparate interests in a shared struggle (Laclau 2005). This, in turn, requires experimentation with many different forms of democratic participation bolstering direct forms of democratic participation with deliberative institutions and processes.

6.2.1 Citizen Action in Practice

Chilvers et al. (2021: 256) capture well the nature and scale of the challenge of deepening citizen engagement with sustainability pathways:

> As the world moves into a low-carbon era, urgent policy and technological developments are placing increasing strain on established relations between science, politics and society. Under these conditions the governance of low-carbon transitions needs to be responsible, inclusive of and responsive to societal values, public concerns and human needs. This is about more than public acceptance and behaviour change. It is crucial to renewing the social contract between citizens and governing institutions and accounting for 'the public interest' in ways that address human needs and ensure more equitable energy transitions. Mainstream approaches to eliciting public views, such as surveys and deliberative processes, are of undoubted value, but underplay and can exclude an ever-growing multiplicity of public engagements with energy and climate change, fuelled by the digital revolution, the rise of social media, citizen-led mobilizations, moves to more distributed energy systems and so on.

As this passage illustrates, the nature and scale of required transitions both intensify and amplify existing challenges for democracies while also bringing new ones. Despite (or perhaps because of) the very many challenges that confront deeper and more meaningful forms of citizen engagement aimed at propelling sustainability transitions, a bewildering diversity of forms of citizen engagement have taken hold around the world. Some have been taken up in recent years as an appreciation of the scale and gravity of the climate and ecological crisis has become clearer, combined with frustration and alarm at the lack of leadership from governments and corporations, while others have been part of the repertoire of citizen engagement and civil society action for decades (Newell et al. 2024).

Firstly, a range of strategies have been used to raise the ambition of government action and strengthen the social mandate of governments to accelerate action. Activists have sought to provide a new mandate to local councils to intensify efforts to address the climate crisis including popular drives to get councils to declare 'climate emergencies' with potentially direct implications for local energy pathways and trajectories, as well as large infrastructure projects. Many local authorities in the UK and elsewhere have started declaring 'climate emergencies' and committed to plans genuinely in line with meeting legally binding climate targets. Following in the wake of the Welsh market town of Machynlleth declaring a 'climate emergency' in late 2018, within just three months, 40 had signed the pledge – representing more than 17 million people between them across the UK and more than 34 million in the US, Australia, Canada and Switzerland. Signatories committed to a climate emergency pledge to reduce CO_2 emissions by at least 40 per cent by 2030.

Climate or citizens' assemblies provide one citizen-led way of shaping climate action that has become prominent in recent years. A comparative case study of two processes that ran in the UK in 2019 (the Leeds Climate Change Citizens' Jury and the Oxford Citizens' Assembly on Climate Change) found that the impact of these processes is not uniform across different contexts. They have an indirect impact on policymaking by creating momentum around climate action and supporting the introduction of pre-planned or pre-existing policies, rather than a direct impact by being a truly citizen-centred policymaking process conducive to new climate policy (Wells et al. 2021). In France, the approach was characterised by sustained interactions between citizens and the steering board, a significant input from technical and legal experts and a strong emphasis on creating consensus. This resulted in the citizens approving 149 measures, 146 of which President Macron committed to follow up on. Yet, as implementation is now under discussion, 'the promise that measures would pass "unfiltered" appears increasingly questioned' (Giraudet et al. 2021: 1). In Ireland, the Irish Citizens' Assembly and Joint Oireachtas Committee on Climate Action (JOCCA) deliberations on climate action have also attracted attention. Harris (2021: 677) analysed the extent to which children, young people and future generations were included in the process by analysing the membership of both institutions, the public submissions to them and the invited expertise presented. Harris (2021: 677) found that the Irish Citizens' Assembly was 'too tightly coupled' on this issue and notes that 'this may have been beneficial in terms of impact, but it came at the expense of input legitimacy and potentially intergenerational justice'.

Secondly, there are strong levels of citizen engagement in policy and planning at all levels of government. This is true across the realms of housing to energy and transport policy. Research has shown that self-organised citizen participation can be a major driver of innovation in urban planning. For example, a study on the Chilean city of Santiago found that organised citizens reinforced pro-change trends across diverse scales and that they generated more transparent processes favouring sustainability and democratisation (Sagaris 2014). It started as a social movement opposing the country's first major highway concession but ended up challenging and changing urban planning paradigms by founding a citizen institution, Living City (Ciudad Viva), which became a prize-winning 'citizen-led planning institution' (Sagaris 2014: 74). A key conclusion based on this experience was that 'thinking about citizens as planners in their own right, rather than as mere participants at specific points in a planning process', opens the way to more effective strategies for innovating responses to the climate crisis (Sagaris 2014: 74).

At the national level, there are interesting examples of innovative practice in state engagement with citizens. Costa Rica's Citizen's Climate Change Advisory Council suggests one model of how to engage citizens directly in policy. The Citizens' Advisory Council on Climate Change, also known as 5C, was created in 2018 by the Costa Rican Ministry of the Environment and Energy in fulfilment of one of its commitments under the Paris Agreement. The council is made up of representatives of a cross-section of civil society, Indigenous, business and trade union groups that are engaged with the climate issue and serves as a deliberative space that advises the Ministry of Environment and Energy on issues related to climate change. In turn, the Ministry, along with other government entities, may submit to the council consultations on the design, implementation and evaluation of their climate policies, programmes and metrics. The council then monitors the implementation of the National Determined Contribution presented by Costa Rica to the COP and the UN Sustainable Development Goals (SDGs). The council meets regularly and provides a form of 'co-governance' generating 'non-binding decisions'.[2]

Thirdly, as a pre-emptive or restorative strategy of engagement with a different arm of the state (the courts), legal activism provides another important channel of citizen engagement with transitions that can be used to hold governments and corporations to account for existing commitments, to challenge discrepancies between rhetoric and reality or to compel more ambitious action. Much of this activism has thus far focussed on national courts: either judicial decisions enforcing existing commitments, highlighting procedural obligations that could strengthen climate action or challenging the consistency of other policies with national climate change strategies. Regarding the successful case brought by the group Urgenda against the oil giant Shell in the Netherlands, the Dutch court ruled that Shell must cut its emissions by 45 per cent by 2030 (Mayer and van Asselt 2023). Legal actions also open up other avenues of resistance and accountability.

In terms of using the law to challenge infrastructures, the case of the proposed expansion of London's Heathrow airport offers another pertinent example. Plans for a third runway at Heathrow airport have been ruled illegal by the court of appeal because ministers did not adequately take into account the government's commitments to tackle the climate crisis (Carrington 2020). The case sets a potentially critical precedent that new infrastructure projects must demonstrate compatibility with the goals and ambitions of the Paris Agreement, to which the UK government is a signatory: a precedent successfully tested by a legal challenge against the UK's governments approval of a new coal mine in Cumbria brought by the local community group South Lakeland Action on Climate Change and Friends of the Earth. One of the grounds on which the case was successful was the fact 'The Secretary of State failed to have regard to evidence and submissions on the impact of a decision to grant planning permission for the coal mine on the ability of the United Kingdom to perform its leadership role in promoting international action to address climate change'.[3] Elsewhere, after years of resistance, in June 2019 a Kenyan tribunal cancelled a developer's licence to build a new coal plant at Lamu, a stunning coastal UNESCO World Heritage Site. And in a historic victory, after a long campaign, the state of Paraná in Brazil passed a law to permanently ban fracking and Santa Catarina state followed weeks later, meaning that Latin America's largest shale reserves will go untapped. Despite the challenges of making effective use of the law as a strategy for securing environmental justice (Newell 2001), victories can be won, though it is notable that authoritarian and less democratic regimes which are often also major polluters (such as China, Russia and Saudi Arabia) are more insulated from the trend towards using litigation for climate ends (Mayer and van Asselt 2023).

6.2.2 *Just Inclusive Transitions*

As well as improving the inclusiveness and effectiveness of policy, citizen engagement also has the potential to ensure greater attention to issues of justice without guaranteeing equitable outcomes from policy. Regarding industrial conversion and the emergence of new markets, engaging citizens regarding their livelihoods, job security, skills and training, and the future direction that their respective industries might take in the near future is vital to the success of just transitions (Newell et al. 2023). There is some evidence that many workers in heavy polluting or fossil fuel industries support the idea of transitioning to more sustainable jobs when provided with support and skills and training (Oczkowska and Pellerin-Carlin 2019). But resistance from the Gilets Jaunes in France, from farmers in Germany and the Netherlands over controls on the use of fertilisers, and in the UK over fuel tax rises in the early 2000s illustrates the need for policies to be debated, alternatives presented and equity and fairness in terms of 'ask' and 'offer' to be clear.

Interventions imposed from above where social implications are ill-considered often result in backlash. Examples from the politics of fossil fuel subsidy reform (Lockwood 2015b) suggest the need for equity and sequencing so that poorer consumers are not hit hardest first by companies just passing costs straight on to consumers. At the same time, engaging publics is a time-consuming and costly process and may not result in consensual outcomes (Newell et al. 2022). Involving publics may give rise to scepticism rather than enhancing trust when the participants express doubts or challenge the equity and sincerity of the participatory processes and outcomes. This occurs when participants perceive that those participatory approaches are used as a means of deflecting protest, inhibiting actions or 'rubber-stamping' a predetermined decision or when prior commitments to act on citizens' recommendations are subsequently diluted (as with the earlier example from the French climate assembly).

Scope to address these procedural deficits depends very much on context, especially as noted in the context of closing civic space in many parts of the world. There is some emerging positive practice, nevertheless. In Spain, for example,

Ana Belén Sánchez of the Instituto para la Transición Justa describes how the government has helped oversee 15 just transition agreements through a participatory process of diagnoses of employment and other impacts, tripartite social dialogues and plans for alternatives. Tools to address these include grants to small businesses, local infrastructural projects including social housing, job banks, training for 'green' jobs and efforts to address gender inequities given the male-dominated nature of work in coal plants and nuclear installations, for example.[4] There is also a long and rich history of contentious resource politics which has involved attempts to open up spaces for meaningful citizen engagement from which lessons can be drawn for more inclusive just transitions from experiments in participatory budgeting and auditing to foresight panels and standing commissions through to more 'claimed spaces' of people's development plans that propose alternatives to state visions and permanent people's tribunals on the performance of private actors in key sectors such as water (Newell et al. 2024).

6.2.3 The Limits of the Democratic State

Notwithstanding some progress in implementing democratic innovations for environmental protection (Mol 2003), prospects for ecological democracy have become mired in broader concerns about whether democratic institutions can be sustained in the face of populism and authoritarianism and the pressures on the conduct of political debate generated by the reach, immediacy and popularity of social media campaigns which fill the political vacuum, encouraging short-term reactive gestures above deliberation over long-term issues. At the same time, increasingly dense networks of activism, supported by social media and the possibility of instant polling, information sharing and launching petitions to trigger parliamentary debates, for example, can change the dynamics of participation and representation. In the UK, for example, if enough people sign a petition demanding a parliamentary discussion on an issue, the government is obliged to host one.

But these openings coexist with the reality that civic spaces in many parts of the world are being closed down by governments fearful of dissent and seeking to control media and freedom of speech and to protect incumbent interests. Enhanced citizen engagement is not a one-way street. Recent developments in India where the assets of major environmental NGOs such as Greenpeace have been seized and offices threatened with closure show what is possible even in the world's most vibrant democracies with a vast and active civil society. As one report put it:

> The rise of a global climate movement has been accompanied by a crackdown on civic space for climate activists worldwide. As climate strikes, protests, and mass mobilization become more widespread, many governments have teamed up with private actors to quell climate activism. This suppression has taken many forms, from laws criminalizing

legitimate expression and assembly, to attempts to paint activists as 'eco-terrorists,' to civil lawsuits and physical persecution. (ICNL 2020: 1)

It is also the case that sustainability transitions have become weaponised in public debates and embroiled in the culture wars whereby environmental action is portrayed as 'woke', an infringement on civil liberties and evidence of the overbearing state. Hence it needs to be acknowledged that there is a great deal of citizen engagement *against* environmental action and aimed at stalling transitions, albeit sometimes orchestrated by incumbent actors. Indeed, it is often the case that the more ambitious action on sustainability appears to be, the stronger the resistance. There is engagement from (un)civil society using violence and intimidation against those advocating for bolder action as well as organised resistance in the form of localised opposition to low-carbon projects such as wind energy farms (Dunlap 2018), sometimes also referred to dismissively as NIMBYism (Not-In-My-Backyard-ism) and the formation of 'astro-turf' groups that appear to raise citizen concerns about environmental action but are funded by industry groups seeking to stall action (Rowell 1996; Beder 1997). This can take the form of front groups such as the Information Council for the Environment or in a more recent manifestation the rebranding of climate sceptic groups as 'watchdog' NGOs. An example of the latter is Net Zero Watch, referred to earlier, which could easily be mistaken for an activist group monitoring the integrity of net zero commitments but is in fact a vehicle for pushing back against net zero policies wherein one of the key strategies is providing a platform for 'concerned citizens' about the effect of government climate policies on their well-being (Taylor and Horton 2022). More spontaneously, albeit coordinated and mobilised behind the scenes, this takes the form of affected groups (such as taxi drivers) self-organising against policies such as congestion charges and low-traffic neighbourhoods (in London, for example).

These pressures intensify strains and constraints that states already face which have been the focus of scholarly critique. The first area of critique is of the administrative state, one that is incapable of systematically responding to the challenge of sustainability because of the concentration of political power and distance from the everyday lives of citizens. As Eckersley (2004: 86) puts it, the 'coercive, highly centralized and bureaucratic centres of power with a set of security, disciplinary, surveillance and/or administrative imperatives … are fundamentally at odds with the green vision of participatory democracy and the ideal of the green public sphere'. For some, the state is regarded as an embodiment and crystallisation of hierarchies and social exclusions along multiple social axes and not just of dominant alignments of social forces as explored previously. Barry (1999: 80) cites the social ecologist Kossoff as saying, 'The state consolidates and protects the family of hierarchies [class, gender, race, age, mind-body] becoming a hierarchy in its own right', embodying dominant social relations.

Generic concerns with whom the state serves are often combined with a concern that liberal democracy performs particularly poorly in protecting long-range public environmental interests. This is especially the case with regard to safeguarding the interests of future generations where today's decision-makers often engage in 'intergenerational discounting', passing costs and risks of today's decisions on to generations yet unborn. The temporal limitations of the democratic state in adequately addressing the intergenerational nature of ecological crises result from a preoccupation with short-term election cycles, ties to interest groups such as corporations or trade unions with a stake in sustaining an unsustainable economy, and the existence of multiple veto points and political opportunity structures which systematically allow for privileged access for well-resourced groups to the exclusion of the majority of citizens. The potential for elite capture in such systems is high because of a combination of party funding by wealthy interest groups, concentrations of ownership in the media and narrow class dominance of institutions of the state, judiciary, police and military (Jones 2014; Poulantzas 2014).

Beyond the desire to protect incumbent and class power (as discussed in Chapter 2), large bodies of work on resource curses also show that states heavily reliant on revenues from resources such as oil are less responsive to the needs of their citizens because the social contract, based on 'no representation without taxation', breaks down (Watts 2008; Ross 2012). Governments less reliant on taxation, which is dwarfed by the revenues they receive from oil exploitation, for example, are harder to hold to account for their (inactions) since citizens cannot claim that it is 'their' money that the state is misallocating. Autonomy and isolation confer upon elites the power to continue consuming above ecologically sustainable levels long after crisis has struck poorer members of society. What results in practice are 'low-intensity democracies' (Gills and Rocamora 1992) where fragile institutional constructs are bypassed and undermined by patronage and clientelist networks. In part, the lack of space for meaningful public engagement and representation is a function of the fact that some social goals and strategies for acquiring them are non-negotiable, and so many fundamental questions about political visions for the achievement of the 'good life' are placed off limits by prior commitments to industrialism and growth at all costs. As Torgerson (1999: 145) suggests, 'modernity appears flawed and incomplete because by its own standard of rationality the irresistible momentum of progress rules out rational deliberation over its purpose and direction'.

Indeed, decision-making is loaded in favour of industrial interests at the expense of communities affected by the impacts of industrialism by the privileging of growth as a meta-goal of policy of the industrial state (see Chapter 4), combined with channels of representation that are more accessible to those with wealth and elite social connections: the power elite (Wright Mills 1956). Literature on environmental justice struggles shows how procedural injustices leave those most affected excluded from consultation and decision-making and, therefore, most exposed to uneven and unjust distributional outcomes (Cole and Foster 2001; Bullard 2005). Barriers to citizen participation, high requirements for legal and scientific expertise and the resolution of conflicts in arenas in which powerful actors dominate further load the dice in favour of corporate actors (Newell 2001). Moreover, states often intervene to override local decisions which oppose environmentally destructive initiatives – such as fracking in Lancashire in the UK where the local council had voted to oppose a proposed fracking development but had this decision overturned by central government.

For some on the left, the challenge is then to wrest the state away from incumbent actors while recognising the division between the state and incumbent actors is fragile and porous at best where the two are either deeply entwined or are actually the same actor (as with state-owned enterprises). Andreas Malm proposes eco-Leninism or 'ecological war communism' as necessary to rein in the power of fossil capital (Malm 2020), a project which 'leaps at any opportunity to wrest the state in this direction, break with business-as-usual as sharply as required and subject the regions of the economy working towards catastrophe to direct public control. It would mean that "one part of the population imposes its will upon the other part", to speak with Engels ... But what state?' (Malm 2020: 151). As noted earlier, the capitalist state is structurally constrained from taking these steps, 'yet there is no other form of state on offer' (Malm 2020: 151). Indeed, 'all we have to work with is the dreary bourgeois state, tethered to the circuits of capital as always. There would have to be popular pressure brought to bear on it, shifting the balance of forces condensed in it, forcing apparatuses to cut the tethers and begin to move' (Malm 2020: 151). He suggests:

> Clearly it would be the state that would have to do this. No mutual aid group in Bristol could even hypothetically initiate a programme of this kind. Note the word 'draconian'. Progressives of all stripes might shudder at it, but they should return to the chapter on the working day in the first volume of *Capital* – the ten hours' day being the original victory of the proletariat, realised when enforcement finally became a little harsh, after all the laxities and prevarication of the early factory legislation. One doesn't curb capitalist exploitation by carrots. (Malm 2020: 131)

Malm starts to articulate what this might look like in practice: the nationalisation of all private companies extracting, processing and distributing fossil fuels, either through acquisition or 'confiscation without recompense' (Malm 2020: 139). He suggests: 'It means learning to live without fossil fuels in no time, breaking the resistance of dominant classes, transforming the economy for the duration ... organising the transitional period of restoration' (Malm 2020: 139). Yet, as he later acknowledges, 'The journey from war communism to tyranny was short to non-existent' (Malm 2020: 165). Statements such as this feed concerns that the cure may be worse than the disease (Kester and Sovacool 2017). The dilemma for Malm is 'how to execute control measures in an emergency without trampling on democratic rights but rather by securing, building on and drawing force from them' (Malm 2020: 165). It remains under-specified what concrete form such an approach would take.

Struggles over the state, won through alliances with labour, are seen to provide the way forward for writers such as Matthew Huber (2022) who argue that only the state has the authority and ability to coordinate action at the scale and speed now required, pointing to ambitious state-led projects of transformation of infrastructures and the delivery of electricity for all, for example. Daniela Gabor (2021a) similarly invokes the idea of a 'big green state'. What is sometimes missing from such accounts is a critical reflection, also informed by Marx's own analysis, of the dependence of labourers on capitalists (including fossil capitalists) for their livelihoods, a fact which ties their fate to the very actors driving the climate crisis. Severing these dependencies to form alliances with environmentalists and other social movements to tackle the climate emergency in opposition to fossil capital will not be done easily. There are certainly opportunities for some labourers to do the work of green transformation, but there are many potential losers too, as the discussion about just transitions makes clear. As Huber (2022) also concedes, Indigenous people's and other resistance to pipelines and other fossil fuel infrastructures posits climate justice activists at times in opposition to labouring classes. This is also leaving aside the tensions associated with the assumption that a socialist industrialist state would be more sustainable given its equally strong commitment to extractivist growth as its capitalist enemy (Porritt 1989).

At the same time as state power can be mobilised to obfuscate the nature of the crisis, the urgency of tackling the ecological crisis can also be invoked for anti-democratic ends and pursued through non-democratic means. Responding to calls for 'eco-Leninism', this is perhaps a case of being careful what you wish for. The demand for accelerated action can give rise to claims about the need to suspend democratic politics as usual (Patterson et al. 2021). This can take the form of overriding planning decisions (such as that of Lancashire Council in the UK around fracking noted earlier) or speeding them up (to accelerate the adoption of nuclear invoking the urgency of transitioning to a low-carbon economy, for example) given the need to accelerate the adoption of technologies labelled 'low-carbon' by policy elites (not by an allegedly progressive Left vanguard). Urgency can be used to trump and supersede political conflict, what has been referred to as 'post-politics' (Swyngedouw 2010), and accelerate the diffusion of controversial technologies (such as geoengineering, genetic engineering and negative emissions technologies) or to suspend forms of political engagement that are incompatible with business-as-usual politics and economics on the basis that we have to 'go with the grain' of existing actors and institutions. As Stirling (2015) puts it: 'urgency compels obedience. Democracy is increasingly dubbed a "failure" or a "luxury" that cannot be afforded – or even queried as an "enemy of nature".'

Mann and Wainwright (2018: 15) contend meanwhile that 'the drive to defend capitalist social relations will push the world toward "Climate Leviathan", namely, adaptation projects to allow capitalist elites to stabilise their position amid planetary crises', something which presages the emergence of 'planetary sovereignty' defended as an 'exception proclaimed in the name of preserving life on earth' (Mann and Wainwright 2018: 15) able to wield extensive powers to bring about the social and economic transformations required to address the climate and ecological emergency. States theories reviewed in Chapter 2 assume that exceptional states often arise from crises of hegemony which 'suspend the rule of law to facilitate constitutional and administrative changes allegedly required to help solve the hegemonic crisis' (Jessop 2008: 130). Calls for stronger forms of (top-down) Earth systems governance (Biermann 2014) and planet politics (Burke et al. 2016) have been critiqued on these grounds (Chandler et al. 2017), described by some as a form of 'cockpit-ism' whereby a self-appointed planetary elite steers the world onto a safer ecological footing (Hajer et al. 2015). Barry (1999: 195) notes 'Ophuls' justification of his anti-democratic stance [being] basically the traditional argument of "the ship of the state" requiring the best pilots and the dangers of "rule by the ignorant" when faced with such a complex and complicated issue as socio-environmental dilemmas'. This was the basis of his call to place power 'in the hands of the few who know how to run the ship' (Ophuls 1977: 159).

This underscores the danger that an emphasis on urgency and, by definition, crisis management frames responses in terms of top-down interventions from elite actors, that is, those with the power, resources and control over finance, production and infrastructures thought to be necessary to respond to crises or that can call upon the coercive powers of the state. This diminishes scope for more plural, bottom-up, inclusive and deliberative pathways to sustainability where transformations are cultured and follow an ethic of 'care' rather than 'control' (Stirling 2011, 2014), further hollowing out the democratic state. 'The paths taken by scientific and technological progress are far from inevitable. Deliberately or blindly, the direction of progress is inherently a matter of social choice. A move towards plural, conditional advice would help avoid erroneous "one-track", "race to the future" visions of progress', Stirling (2011) suggests. This relates closely to concerns with techno-managerial solutions to social and political crises as well as 'scientisation' and deference to the expertise of epistemic communities and the pursuit of incumbent-dominated visions of what a more sustainable future should look like. For Machin (2021: 164), disagreements over competing futures can be 'a source and resource of politics, as engendering a motion towards futures that must remain inevitably opaque and always uncertain'. At the same time, Blühdorn (2021: 43) cautions, the 'democratisation of science … also politicised the authority of scientific diagnoses, relativised the validity of ecological imperatives and propelled the proliferation of eco-political uncertainty' paving the way for populist renditions of common sense based on 'alternative facts' and backlash against elite science manifest in both climate scepticism and vaccine scepticism, for example. There is a difficult tightrope to walk here between pluralising knowledge for transition and unintentionally creating the means for any opinions to discredit the evidence base for action.

The concern with expanding state power for ecological ends comes not just from democratic theorists or more anarchist traditions, however, but also of course from market liberals and those on the political Right who prefer 'market rule' to any notion in which the state determines the public interest. The freedom of the consumer to choose is often invoked by market liberals in arguing against measures that environmentalists might be in favour of such as moratoria (on GMOs) and bans on certain goods and products (factory-farmed meat or diesel cars) aimed at exnovation (see Chapter 3) and reference is often made, correctly, to liberal trading rules enforced by the World Trade Organization (WTO) which prohibit interventions in the market considered to be incompatible with the rules which the global trade body espouses. The primacy of consumer choice – to purchase products, however destructive in social or environmental terms they might be – amounts to a significant barrier to progress towards a sustainable society. The pushback from the liberal state would be equally strong in defence of the primacy of civil liberties and individual freedoms. Marcel Wissenburg (1998) in the book *Green Liberalism: The Free and Green Society* argues that liberal democracy is incompatible with any legal restrictions that seek to alter or dictate or restrict people's preferences, whether around birth control, consumption choices or lifestyle. The preference is always for softer modes of information sharing among notionally free agents in a liberal market through education, labelling and the like.

This reveals a tension in radical environmental thinking between anti-statism and an appreciation of the deeply embedded nature of the state in ecologically destructive social and economic relations on the one hand and rejection of liberal insistence on laissez-faire approach combined with frequent calls for a more interventionist and protectionist 'transition' state on the other. In the latter regard, it might be possible to countenance restrictions on freedom of investment, production, consumption and property such that the task of 'laying down sustainability parameters' is one that should fall to the state (Eckersley 2004: 95). This type of sustainability politics is 'post-' not 'anti-liberal'. Important in this regard is separating free market capitalism as the dominant political mode of organising the economy from liberalism as representative democratic governance in the creation of a sustainable society. These critiques should not lead to a rejection of democracy but rather of the corrupted form which prevails in many parts of the world today where the state is often captive to corporate interests (Monbiot 2000).

6.3 Transforming the Democratic State

We have entered a crucial decade to rapidly reverse the drivers of the climate change and biodiversity crisis, to adapt to the impacts that are already locked in and to realise the ambitious goal of achieving the SDGs by 2030. The urgency of action and the scale and breadth of change now required mean that citizens must be more seriously engaged in efforts to build a more sustainable society as no part of the economy or society will remain untouched either by the effects of ecological change or by society-wide measures to address it.

It is often claimed that bolder transitions will not be possible until citizens have demonstrated 'demand' for it, as politicians fear adopting unpopular measures and not bringing voters with them (Willis 2020). Though frequently invoked to justify inaction, or delay further action, such claims need to be treated with extreme caution since most people are rarely asked about the level, pace or nature of the change they would like to see, or which of the costs associated with inaction they would be willing to bear. An international survey of 1.2 million people, across 50 countries, found that two-thirds of people believe climate change is a 'global emergency' (UNDP 2021). In the UK, Sweden, and China too, nearly half of people polled are 'extremely' or 'very worried' about climate change and nearly 60 per cent want to see urgent action to address it (CAST 2021). As Moberg et al. (2019: 508) argue: 'the door for stronger government intervention is already "half-open". Governments already intervene with command-and-control measures in several high mitigation potential areas, so one may assume that this means there is already public acceptance for such intervention … Respondents specifically call for stronger government intervention in the high mitigation potential areas as of yet receiving minor policy focus.'

In terms of shaping future policy, citizen engagement can also articulate alternatives. Moving from what is to 'what if?' (Hopkins 2019) demonstrates the possibility of change through action. One live experiment in this vein is the 'Which way Nigeria?' exercise involving 35 civil society organisations selected according to criteria of diversity, regional and sectoral presentation to iteratively build scenarios for the future of the country. Surprisingly to those leading the process, including the Nigerian NGO Spaces for Change, energy and climate issues featured highly as people sought to imagine 'life after oil' in Nigeria. An important feature of this example is that environmental issues are related to other areas of citizen concern around the economy, security and well-being rather than handled separately which provides a sounder basis for acting upon the multiple interconnections between SDGs. A key challenge in such exercises is ensuring government buy-in, especially when a parallel government-led envisioning process is underway. As well as articulating and envisioning alternatives, building positive alternatives demonstrates their viability. Whether it is food and energy cooperatives, transport sharing or repair workshops or solidarity economies and experiments in communal living, 'nowtopians' are not waiting for others to deliver structural change, nor willing to assume that it will take a form consistent with their values; they are doing it for themselves, building concrete utopias in the present (Carlsson 2015).

6.3.1 Accountability

Deepening accountability for action and inaction by the state and other actors with the power to act is vital to transforming the democratic state. Accountability is often described as being composed of *answerability* and *enforceability* (Schedler et al. 1999). Answerability assumes both the right of citizens to accountability and the right to a justification for (in)action from the actor exercising power in a given situation. Enforceability refers to there being consequences and sanctions when actors, such as a government, fail to deliver on their obligations. In other words, it furnishes the means to secure accountability.

There is a wealth of real-world examples of measures implemented around the world for strengthening accountability, in terms of both *answerability* and *enforceability*. One such example is the creation of independent bodies or committees whose sole purpose is to collate evidence and provide policy guidance on matters of climate mitigation and adaptation. The UK's Climate Change Committee (CCC), created through the 2008 Climate Change Act, does just this. The CCC provides the UK government with updated carbon budgets every five years, as well as policy advice on matters ranging from coastal erosion to industrial decarbonisation. The CCC has made significant progress in creating and implementing effective climate policies with mechanisms for accountability and transparency (Lysack 2020).

Other measures to foster and strengthen accountability include the installation of ombudspeople for future generations, which have been introduced in Hungary, Australia, Israel and Wales, for example. The role of these ombudspeople is to increase the influence of younger generations over government decision-making and, in turn, improve accountability. Unlike the traditional role of an ombudsperson, who often focusses on maladministration, individual complaints and the failure of government procedures, an ombudsperson for future generations represents a collection of interests from people not directly represented through democratic process and policy decision-making (Andersen 2018). While there are clear benefits for accountability in creating such posts, there is a very real risk that the stability and effectiveness of such independent institutions will be vulnerable to changes in government, electoral cycles and constitutional changes.

Another measure that can foster accountability, as well as expanding modes of deliberation beyond matters of policy, is the use of citizen audits of finance and participatory budgeting building on the experience of citizen innovations in this area in places like Porto Alegre, Brazil. Participatory budgeting could be an impactful way of engaging citizens and stimulating action on sustainability. Inspired by Porto Alegre's example, in 2019 the Portuguese city of Lisbon introduced a 'green participatory budget' that sought to galvanise support for mitigation and adaptation projects. Once empowered and resourced, citizens allocated public funds towards cycle lanes, tree planting schemes to reduce urban heating and water capture and storage initiatives. This participatory scheme has also ensured consistent annual investments into Lisbon's low-carbon transition, while raising the awareness of citizens of the benefits mitigation and adaptation policy can bring to their everyday lives, from cleaner air to more child-friendly streets. While participatory budgeting has the potential to be introduced in cities around the world, participatory budgeting projects often need to go hand in hand with efforts to secure greater devolution from central governments. There is significant scope to include citizens in decision-making over funding allocations for sustainability transitions to ensure resources are targeted to the most pressing needs in the most inclusive way.

New approaches need to recognise the need to expand and deepen citizen engagement across all aspects of the transitions that need to take place: from innovation and the design of technology and production systems to finance and governance. This needs not just to be restricted to arenas traditionally thought of as spaces of environmental policy but applies equally to decision-making arenas within and beyond the state that relate to the everyday drivers of unsustainability around trade, energy, transport, investment and agriculture. This means revisiting key assumptions then about who participates in which spaces and who gets to decide this if more transformational approaches are to take hold. Returning to the theme introduced at the start of the chapter, this speaks to the need for a new social contract in which the functions of protection, regulation and responsibility are rebalanced. This includes a move from more passive models of citizens as consumers to proactive forms of citizenship through prosumers and broader efforts to re-common and democratise control and ownership over systems of provision such as energy, food, water, housing and transport.

Citizen engagement is not a panacea, especially when conceived of in narrower institutional terms. The main reason we now face a climate and ecological emergency is not for a lack of citizen engagement. Incumbent power, intensive lobbying from corporate interests, institutional inertia and poorly functioning markets are among a myriad of reasons why we have failed to bend the emissions curve (Stoddard et al. 2021) and are overshooting planetary boundaries. In theory, much more ambitious action could be forthcoming without an increase in citizen engagement should state and corporate leaders show the leadership and vision now required of them. But history shows that the key drivers of change often come from below and transitions that are just and equitable are often articulated first within civil society (Stirling 2015).

Challenging incumbency through greater citizen engagement, controls on party funding, changes to corporate governance, independent climate committees, votes for 16-year-olds and ombudspeople for future generations may be among the democratic and participatory innovations that prepare the ground for transformation. As a first step, some of this might require greater attention to the innocuous sounding 'good governance': an effort to ensure greater transparency and accountability and scrutiny over decisions about future pathways. It would also need to shine a bright light, however, on the economic and political ties between incumbent actors, severing ties between incumbent business and state. This could imply having clearer party financing rules, registries of politicians' interests, boards of companies they sit on and corresponding restrictions on which committees they sit on and policymaking processes they are part of when there are obvious conflicts of interest. For example, nearly 90 per cent of people leaving the UK's Department of Energy and Climate Change (now known as the Department for Energy Security and Net Zero) took up jobs in the energy sector, including six former energy ministers. But the door swings both ways. In 2010, Lord Browne, former CEO of BP, was appointed by David Cameron to be the 'lead nonexecutive director' at the Cabinet Office. He was also the chair of the fracking company Cuadrilla at the time and pledged to do 'whatever it takes' to promote shale gas. Charles Hendry, meanwhile, when Minister of State for Energy, secured £3,333 a day as a consultant for Vitol, the world's biggest oil trader handling 270 million tonnes of oil in 2016 (Cato 2018).

Such an approach to transforming the democratic state needs to go beyond isolated sites of engagement such as citizens' assemblies, important though they are, and independent oversight committees, such as the committees on climate change, to incorporate areas of state decision-making that are traditionally protected from democratic scrutiny and oversight and forms of citizen engagement. This includes policy domains of 'high politics' concerned with industrial policy, energy and trade policy, for example. These are decision-making sites where incumbent power is strongest and which exercise most power over the direction, speed and nature of transitions and who therefore benefits from them. This would break down the division between more open and participatory spaces for 'softer' issues and closed and expert-only venues for discussion of 'harder' or 'high political' issues of security and economy.

More ambitiously still, sustainability transitions require extending the boundaries of accountability to new communities of the affected beyond state borders, into the future and including more-than-human species through conferring rights upon ecosystems such as rivers and exercises in listening to animals, for example, and various forms of indirect representation. As Eckersley (2004: 111) puts it, 'all those potentially affected by a risk should have some meaningful opportunity to participate or otherwise be represented in the making of the policies or decisions that generate the risk'.

6.3.2 Towards Ecological Democracy

Deepening democracy would then extend to democratic control over the economy for the common good. Eckersley (2004: 242) suggests: 'Ecological democracy would differ from liberal democracy in enabling more concerted political questioning of traditional boundaries between what is public and private, domestic and international, intrinsically valuable and instrumentally valuable.' It would imply a range of constitutional innovations and charters that deal with issues such as rights, responsibilities, participation and consultation, but combined with liability and redress. Together these would amount to a fundamental reframing of the purpose of the state.

Strategies for democratising the state and improving downward accountability include the decentralisation of power towards regional and local decision-making bodies, consistent with principles around subsidiarity. This requires 'a reconceptualization of the demos as no longer fixed in terms of people and territory' (Eckersley 2004: 113) where those not necessarily capable of reciprocal recognition are included. In practice, this could be pursued through ideas about addressing environmental harm through corporate accountability measures in international law, transnational environmental litigation and the like to avoid the unfair distribution and concentration of burden and risk on poorer communities, often in the Global South (Newell 2001; Mason 2005). In terms of temporal and intergenerational justice, there is scope to adopt some forms of proxy representation for future generations and non-human species described earlier, as well as tribunes for non-citizens and an independent environmental defenders office (Dobson 1996; Eckersley 2004). These could play a key role in preventing the discounting of costs and risks of decisions taken today that will be predominantly borne by future generations. Representation would obviously and necessarily be indirect and would require a degree of internalising and projecting what the interests of groups without voice and direct participation would be. This is, in many ways, a second-best solution but, as Goodin (1996) argues, this is preferable to their interests not being considered at all. As well as facilitating a degree of intergenerational empathy and justice, decision-making informed by such an approach requires current decision-makers not to close off alternative pathways and options by pursuing policies that are non-reversible, or which are characterised by high degrees of lock-in which deny choices to future generations. Reversibility and reflexivity in this way help to pluralise decision-making in the here and now with the requirement to avoid mutually exclusive pathways.

Democracy would be deepened through deliberation moving beyond 'power trading among self-interested actors' and in favour of 'unconstrained egalitarian deliberation over questions of value and common purpose in the public sphere' (Eckersley 2004: 115). Optimistically, this is conceived of as the means and process by which we learn and can act upon an appreciation of mutual dependence and dependence upon the environment enabling better collective decision-making about longer-range problems (Baber and Bartlett 2005; Bäckstrand et al. 2010). There may be limits to the notion that the 'force of the better argument' wins through amid stark social and resource, and therefore power, inequalities, as well as the deeply engrained belief systems around growth and progress that are intrinsic to industrialism but which need to be challenged. An assumed openness to change opinions perhaps also implies that participants do not have a (material) stake in the outcome, or indeed in preserving the status quo, such that privileging general over private and vested interests is easier called for than enacted. This is the basis of critiques of deliberation – for its assumptions about the possibility of dispassionate and rational exchange as well as being very Eurocentric in the models from which it draws inspiration. Moreover, as Owens (2000: 1145) notes, 'at times it seems as if the restless search for new procedures has become a substitute for confronting the failure of existing institutions'.

The challenge then is to expand, extend and deepen democratic arenas of decision-making, while being alert to the power dynamics which may frustrate the ambitions and practice of deliberative democracy. Hence it is the processes by which decision-making is organised and institutionalised, the extent to which law and science are the mediums of exchange and the means by which competing claims are evaluated, for example, as well as the question of who is represented, that matter. A democratised and decentralised state is seen as a necessary institution to promote the common good of sustainability and a sense of justice and connection between past, present and future generations (Read 2012).

The challenge can also not just be reduced to the state of course. As Pickering et al. (2022: 10) note, 'deep democratisation of the state is an important pathway for the broader democratisation of sustainability transformations', yet 'it is increasingly clear that democratising the state is insufficient, given that a shift towards more sustainable practices is required at all levels of governance. This underscores the need for a polycentric and transnational approach to both sustainability and democratic transformations', an issue we return to in Chapter 8 on the global state. It is also the case that many of the strategies, innovations and democratic practices discussed here are, as Pickering et al. (2022: 10) note, 'intrinsically valuable for other reasons (e.g., political equality) irrespective of their instrumental effects on sustainability'.

As with many other aspects of state power and authority explored in the book, the issue of democracy cannot be reduced to a matter of institutional reconfiguration and design, for it also describes power and the need to shift it. It extends to the economy and ideas about economic democracy and citizen engagement with the everyday conduct of political and economic life. For the state, meanwhile, it is central to strategies of legitimation which it requires to sustain and expand dominant strategies of accumulation. A key strategy question is whether, how and at what point the ecocidal pursuit of the latter undermines state legitimacy.

7

The Welfare State

7.1 Introducing the Welfare State

What is the welfare state? Centring on key state functions of protection and the promotion of the economic and social well-being of citizens, it describes a range of functions 'related to state intervention aimed at reducing the risk of market failure, ensuring a decent living standard and a certain degree of equality and intergenerational distribution. The welfare state thus often plays a central role in relation to essential issues of people's daily lives such as housing, employment, income security, health and education' (Greve 2015: 31). For Bourdieu (2014), the welfare state is part of the 'left hand' of the state: that side of the state concerned with welfare, health, education and employment which is often in conflict with the 'right hand' of the state which enforces fiscal and budgetary discipline and penal sanctions.

Though the connections are infrequently made, it is increasingly clear that the ability of the state to continue to adequately perform these roles, reconcile these (at times competing) functions and safeguard the protection of its citizens is likely to be overwhelmed and diminished by the scale and depth of disruption associated with the climate and ecological crisis. This is so not only because of the financial and resource demands that will be placed on states to deal with growing social, economic and ecological stresses but also because of the direct impact of these stresses on people's health, security and livelihoods. These are already observable in increasing incidences of floods, droughts, extreme weather events, disruption of livelihoods and disease outbreaks associated with global heating. Working Group II of the IPCC notes, 'Human-induced climate change, including more frequent and intense extreme events, has caused widespread adverse impacts and related losses and damages to nature and people, beyond natural climate variability. Some development and adaptation efforts have reduced vulnerability … Across sectors and regions the most vulnerable people and systems are observed to be disproportionately affected' (IPCC 2022: 9).

The welfare state has been referred to as the 'distributive state' (Weiss 1995), sometimes rolled into a general account of the 'good state' (mainly applied to Scandinavian countries such as Sweden) where high levels of domestic welfare are combined with ethical internationalism and duties of care to the citizens of other states (Lawler 2013). While all states are expected to safeguard to the best of their ability the welfare of their citizens, far fewer of them have well-resourced welfare states as a key means to realise that ambition (Gough 2016). Hence, the extent to which states are able to guarantee decent standards of living, provide a degree of equality or redistribute resources differs widely across international society.

Adopting a more critical perspective, political economy accounts point to the role of the welfare state in managing the excesses of capitalism and staving off labour unrest in order to shore up the status quo (Gough 1979). Habermas' (1975) analysis of the legitimation crisis facing the capitalist state took as its point of departure the erosion of the welfare state which he saw as central to democratic support for modern capitalism and without which capitalism would struggle to survive. Streeck (2014) made a similar argument more than 30 years later, suggesting that the stability of capitalism is founded on 'non-capitalist foundations' which it depletes through processes of extraction and alienation. His focus was labour, but the same can be said of ecological extractivism. The former implies making sufficient concessions to popular demands and doing the minimum to maintain an educated and healthy workforce as a perquisite to production while denying financial independence and control over the means of production such that people have to sell their labour to the owners of capital. Drawing on Offe (1984), Koch (2021: 118) argues a 'general state role is the maintenance of a minimum of social cohesion and, at the same time, the legitimisation of remaining inequalities'.

In this regard, the emergence of the modern welfare state in post–Second World War Europe is not a coincidence. Reflecting on this historical period in which social protection was restored, Felli (2021: 11) (drawing on a Polanyi) notes, 'The "Trente Glorieuses" or Golden Age that followed 1945 … doubtless constituted a moment of *re*-regulation of capitalism, restraining capital's freedom of action and socialising a growing part of social reproduction'. A key driver of welfare reforms was a fear of communism taking hold amid widespread social discontent and high levels of unemployment in post-war Europe, especially in the wake of both the Russian Revolution, the encroaching Cold War and popular communist parties in Italy and France, and with the Spanish Civil War still fresh in the minds of policy elites. In some critical accounts, therefore, welfare provision is a key safety valve for releasing pressure for more systemic and structural change in the allocation of power and resources between classes (Therborn 1984). Jessop (2002: 141) proposes moreover that 'welfare regimes may help to secure some of the key conditions for capital accumulation' by guiding market forces and correcting market outcomes and failures, operating as a key 'interface between the economic and extra-economic conditions for capital accumulation' and seeking to manage 'the contradictory functions of the welfare state' (Jessop 2002: 169).

In most accounts, therefore, welfare states are viewed as the product of a new social compact forged in the wake of the Second World War. In many European contexts, what Gough (2017: 10) refers to as 'a new social settlement or class compromise' contained commitments to full employment, access to free or affordable health and education and regulation of key industries. Affording basic levels of social protection is seen as a quid pro quo for workers abiding by the rules of capitalism and selling their labour on the 'free market': the basis of an often unarticulated social contract. Indeed, welfare states are more embedded in political economies characterised by corporatism and the type of tripartite bargaining more associated with coordinated market economies that make such a contract possible (Hall and Sokiscke 2001). As Figure 7.1 on social spending as a share of GDP illustrates, more laissez-faire 'liberal' market economies such as the US, Canada and UK fall some way behind countries pursuing the 'European social model' such as France, Finland, Belgium, Spain, Germany and Italy in terms of social spending as a percentage of the GNP.[1] As Jessop (2002) notes, however, overemphasis on variation in forms of welfare state sometimes obscures key areas of congruence among them.

Historically, in so far as it is understood more broadly as social policy, mediating between the private sphere of the market economy and the public sphere of the government, the welfare state has a much longer history (Kaufmann 2001). There are many earlier instances of welfare provision aimed at pacifying social revolt over exploitative working conditions going back, for example, to the German social insurance legislation of the 1880s, beginning with the Health Insurance Act of 1883. Others have argued that the decisive period for the crystallisation of the core features of the welfare state was the 1960s and 1970s when strong worker protection and labour market regulation emerged (Epsing-Andersen 1999, 1990) reflecting a balance of social forces in favour of organised labour (Jessop 2002). Peter Flora and Arnold Heidenheimer are worth quoting at length on the context of the origins of the welfare state to help historicise its formation and evolution:

> What is the essence of the welfare state? The concept of the welfare state cannot be defined by relating its meaning too closely to the specific reform-minded spirit of Britain in the 1940s, which was characterized by an unusual situation of war and austerity creating a high degree of solidarity among its citizens. Nor should the concept be defined, without regard to historical context, by a mere designation of policy boundaries and their underlying principles. Rather, the concept is defined by interpreting the welfare state as an answer to basic and long-term development processes and the problems created by them. From the perspective of a theory of political development, it is interpreted as an answer to increasing demands for socio-economic equality in the context of the evolution of mass democracies. The theory of modernization or structural differentiations on the other hand, leads

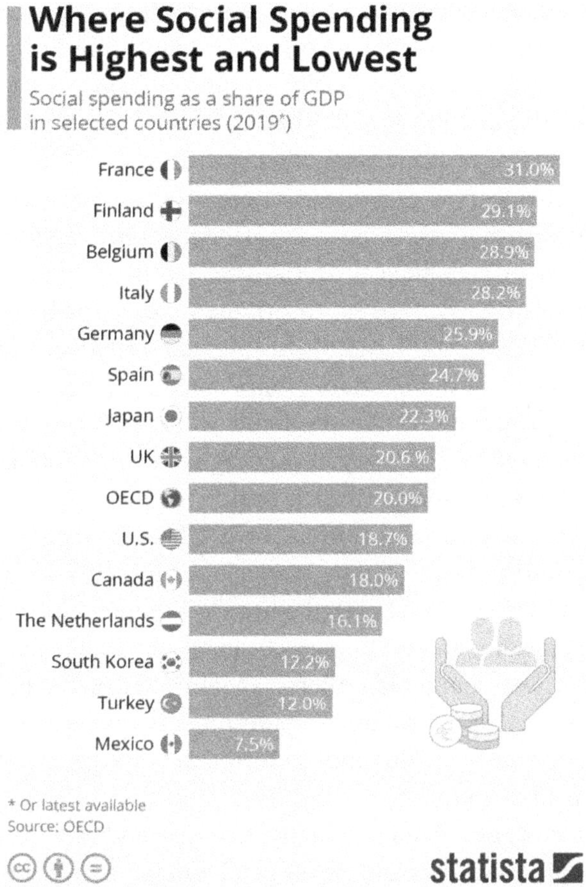

Figure 7.1 Social spending as a share of GDP. Source: Statista.

us to understand the welfare state as an answer to the growing needs and demands for socio-economic security in the context of an increasing division of labour, the expansion of markets, and the loss of 'security functions' by families and other communities. In this sense, the basic goals and legitimizing principles of socio-economic security and equality are interpreted as the core of the welfare state. (Flora and Heidenheimer 1981: 8–9)

Over time, alongside the evolution of the welfare state, has developed the rise of what Jessop (2002: 148) calls 'welfare for capital' or corporate welfare: a reference both to the increasingly private provision of what were once welfare services provided by the state around health, education and pensions provisions and to state subsidies for the private sector through private finance initiatives and contracting for infrastructure provision, for example (Whitfield 2001). This shift is interpreted as a function of the growing entrenchment of neoliberalism from the late 1970s and throughout the 1980s involving the rollback of state support for key services in many settings and a rebalancing of power away from labour (and welfare for labour) to capital and from public to private (notwithstanding the permeability of this divide in practice) (Harvey 2005). Robinson (2004: 106) refers to this as the 'dissolution of the welfarist or Keynesian class compromise' in the face of the heightened power of transnational capital over labour. These shifting power relations manifest themselves in patterns of corporate capture of key elements of service provision and what others have described as the 'captive state' (Monbiot 2000) observable in private finance initiatives, public–private partnerships and other attempts to sell off state assets to private enterprises as part of the 'Wall Street Consensus' (Gabor 2021). Means-testing, surveillance, withdrawal of benefits and the installation of deliberately complicated systems to access them have been the flip side of withdrawing non-profitable welfare. Where gaps and shortfalls emerge, other actors, out of necessity or ideological impulsion, have sought to fill the void through the 'big society' of civil society or the 'participation society' in the Netherlands (Frantzeskaki and Wittmayer 2019) in the form of community and citizen-led attempts to provide welfare provision. Moments of crisis, such as the Covid pandemic, however, reveal both the limits of mutual aid and ongoing (albeit often latent) state capacity and willingness to intervene in the economy when necessary to avoid broader economic collapse (Malm 2020). Examples of the latter include a willingness of some wealthier governments to convert industries, effect changes to work patterns, provide funds to furlough workers and reprioritise social protection over profit at any cost.

The welfare state is not a fixed and bounded entity and therefore not immune to shifting geopolitical landscapes and ideological winds. It is, as Jessop (2002: 140) suggests, 'by no means an irreversible evolutionary achievement'. It rather functions as a set of state agencies, actors, initiatives and institutions that fuse public and private funding and authority to promote the welfare needs of a demographically shifting population and in the face of major demands on its resources from different dimensions of the polycrisis, including conflict, migration, health and environmental crises. The imbalance in the ratio of economically active contributors through taxation to a swelling ageing population of beneficiaries is of particular concern. These demands and the ability of states to meet them are subject to constant change and evolution often in the face of critiques of their effectiveness and role in society from the right and the left of the political spectrum. This fluidity can, nevertheless, be an opportunity to advance just transitions through the welfare state as I explore in Section 7.3.

The fate of welfare states and their ability to survive repeated shocks is a function of the wider institutional setting in which they are embedded. Contrary to popular generic narratives about the erosion and rollback of the welfare state as a result of globalisation (apparent in some of the claims cited earlier in the chapter), erosion, reconfiguration and resilience take different forms in diverse contexts (Rhodes 2005). Swank (2003: 58) suggests that 'globalisation has not led to a significant welfare entrenchment in coordinated market economies; coordinated market institutions shape the interests, strategic choices and capacities of labour, capital and the state in ways favourable to the maintenance of social protection. Alternatively, globalisation has contributed to welfare state retrenchment in uncoordinated market economies.' This reflects scope for national coordination through economy-wide collective bargaining and more centralised employer and trade union associations which enhance the prospect of more stable and long-term employer–employee relations in countries such as Germany and Sweden as compared with more (neo)liberal economies such as the UK, for example, where rollbacks in social protection around pensions, income support and health and social services were a feature of neoliberal reforms under Prime Minister Margaret Thatcher and maintained and expanded by many of her successors.

Framed more broadly, the question of welfare and social protection as it is affected by, or contributes towards, sustainability transitions has to extend beyond the welfare state since, as noted, it is an institutional model that has effectively been applied and maintained in relatively few states in the global economy. For many, struggles for welfare and their intersection with the pursuit of sustainability transitions around issues of employment, security and health take a range of forms across different sites even if the state remains a central point of reference for calls for protection based on explicit and often implicit understandings of citizenship and the rights and duties this confers through a social contract between states and citizens (Rhodes 2016). It is notable, for example, that at election times in democratic contexts questions of state spending on health and education move centre stage as citizens seek commitments from political parties about how they will enhance their welfare.

7.2 The Welfare State and Transitions

So, what does the welfare state have to do with sustainability transitions? At the most basic level, systems of provisioning (such as food, energy, transport and housing) and their associated socio-technical configurations that are the subject of transition scholarship and practice have to take into account welfare impacts if they are to be effective, let alone socially just. Access to those services to meet those needs is a function of social differentiation (along class, racial and gender lines and ability) and so shifts in systems of provision need to be cognisant of those inequalities and the diversity of ways in which people engage with socio-technical systems. This is vital for reasons of social acceptance of transitions as well for considerations of equity, as discussed in Chapter 6.

Nevertheless, despite some initial explorations of the relevance of perspectives grounded in sustainability transitions for understanding processes of change and innovation in welfare states (Frantzeskaki and Wittmayer 2019), the question of welfare remains a neglected area in transition studies and, until recently, in environmental studies more broadly. The neglect is mutual, with Gough (2017: 2) observing 'with a few exceptions the study of social policy has (blindly or wilfully) ignored the environment and planetary limits within which the pursuit of human needs and wellbeing must necessarily take place'. Yet, just as citizen engagement and social acceptance are key to the fate of transitions as we saw in Chapter 6, so is an ability to protect welfare as part of a just transition.

Social policy is required to address issues of inequality and social exclusion. Understood in its broadest meaning, it refers to 'the mobilisation of collective action and state power to improve human well-being' (Gough 2017: 2) and we might add, ecological well-being, on which human and more-than-human well-being depends. At the very least, social policy has to help ensure that transitions are not undertaken at the expense of the poorest and most marginalised in society who have contributed least to causing the problems which sustainability transitions (ostensibly at least) set out to address, 'making sure no one is left behind' as some just transition policies put it, adopting the language of the Sustainable Development Goals (SDGs).[2] At the their best, such policies serve as a buffer against efforts by elites (incumbent actors, polluter elites and ruling classes) to pass the costs of adjustment on to the poor. As an example of a failure to do this in the UK, the former government of Liz Truss sought to fund an energy price freeze through borrowing recovered over time from consumers themselves, rather than through a windfall tax on energy generators that have profited spectacularly from the rising costs of energy, to the tune of more than £170 billion in one quarter, more than the state needed to borrow to fund this energy price bailout (Wickham and Gillespie 2022).

Inequalities and exclusions have regional, geographical as well as gendered, racial, class and other dimensions. A report commissioned (and then cancelled because of the controversy it generated) by the UK government on *Gender, Race and Social Inclusion – Net Zero Transitions* (Hooper et al. 2021: 7) which is worth quoting at length argues:

> Social differences and resulting experiences are multifaceted. They often intersect and change over time producing different, and sometimes deeper challenges to engaging with the net zero transition. Inclusions and exclusions from decision-making about energy and low carbon futures are frequently produced on the grounds of socioeconomic differences, socio-cultural differences such as gender, race, class, and other natural differences determined by user physiology. These differences can intersect with physical factors, such as physical isolation or informational factors associated with digital exclusion, potentially

exacerbating challenges. These factors can exclude groups from accessing technologies, energy services and information, and can shape their experiences of these challenges through the adoption of different coping mechanisms. They can limit users in their choices and decisions around low carbon technologies and behaviours. Whether, and how users engage with the low carbon transition will depend on their capacity and flexibility to act. Net zero policies and technologies that are unresponsive to these differentiated needs and capacities risk exacerbating or creating new social inequalities.

Given the gross imbalances in the use and consumption of resources, it is vital to address the redistribution of access and entitlements between social groups within (and between) countries as part of a sustainability transition to address the inevitable (in)justices that it might generate. As well as dealing with the social fallout from the managed decline of polluting industries and the restructuring of the industrial base of the economy, there is also a clear and obvious need to tackle uneven consumption within countries. Across Europe, analysis reveals that the carbon emissions reductions achieved since 1990 have predominantly come from lifestyle changes and the reduced consumption of lower- and middle-income EU citizens, while the total emissions of the richest 10 per cent have grown. Over the period of 1990 to 2015, the richest 10 per cent of EU citizens were responsible for 27 per cent of the EU's total cumulative carbon emissions – the same level of emissions as the poorest half of the EU population combined (Gore and Alestig 2020). We can see then the divergent nature of consumption among different income groups, with the richest sections of society even increasing their consumption-related emissions, while the sharpest contractions in emissions have taken place among the middle- and lower-income groups. Gore and Alestig (2020) note that, between 1990 and 2015, consumption emissions from the poorest 50 per cent of the EU population fell by 24 per cent and emissions from the 40 per cent of 'middle-income' Europeans fell by 13 per cent. Emissions from the most affluent 10 per cent of European citizens, however, grew by 3 per cent and those from the wealthiest 1 per cent – the super-rich – rose by 5 per cent. These figures clearly demonstrate the need for a differentiated approach to transitions which aims to promote behaviour change, as well as how the responsibility for emissions reductions and the capacity to reduce them is not shared equally across society. For example, to meet a 1.5°C consistent emissions pathway by 2030, the richest 1 per cent of humanity needs to reduce their emissions by a factor of at least 30, while the poorest 50 per cent could increase their emissions by around three times the current level (Gore and Alestig 2020). These inequalities given lie to the anodyne narrative about citizen action on sustainability that 'we are all in it together'.

Levels of inequality within society are important here not only in terms of responsibility, or because they determine who bears the cost of action, but because they drive competitive consumption (Schor 2015). As Dorling (2017) highlights, 'in more unequal societies, there is a proliferation of products that are designed not to last, so as to allow greater profits to be made. Producing endless must-have new versions exploits the higher levels of emotional insecurity that living with great inequality generates'. Soper (2020: 64) puts it more bluntly still, noting that 'people are exhorted to define and value themselves in terms of what they can afford to acquire even if this means borrowing to do so'.

7.2.1 Financing the Welfare State

Taxation is a key means by which the 'tax state' raises revenue not just for war – what Goldscheid regarded as the 'moving motor of the whole development of public finance' (cited in Giddens 1985: 159) – but also to fund welfare programmes and other state spending, including for transition projects of building new energy and transport infrastructures or providing financial aid to niche actors domestically and through aid and loans to other states. Less benignly, tax is also a mode of state control and surveillance. Giddens (1985: 157) notes:

> Taxation in the modern state is a means of underwriting the state's expenses, since productive enterprise is largely carried on outside the scope of its direct control. But taxation also becomes closely bound up with the surveillance operations of the state. Tax policies come to be used both to monitor and to regulate the distribution and activities of the population.

For economic liberals, objections to the 'tax state' are that public spending is parasitic on the private sector which is constructed as the source of wealth generation in society (Gamble 2014). Yet, for Habermas (1975), tax is central to the pact between the state and capital whereby the former protects the latter in exchange for expanding tax revenues. This also relates to the discussion about the democratic state in Chapter 6 against the background of claims about 'no taxation without representation', a slogan that emerged at the time of the American Revolution. Conversely, governments able to sustain themselves on abundant resource revenues – what is often referred to as the 'resource curse' (Ross 1999) – are often less reliant on taxation and more insulated from citizen demands for more just transitions and a fairer division of resource revenue.

Yet many governments are denied the means of collecting taxes, outmanoeuvred by transnational corporations engaging in tax evasion and avoidance (Jenkins and Newell 2013). Tax loopholes and tax havens not only inhibit the means of redistribution but also facilitate the concentration of wealth and political power which is closely correlated with much higher emissions by the 'polluter elite' (Kenner 2019) as we saw earlier. As Green (2021: 372) observes, 'When corporations avoid taxes, they amass wealth which can be used to influence elections and regulations, and advocate for deregulation. They contribute to growing inequality, which fuels climate change.' She continues, 'If states choose not to intervene to perform the basic function of taxation, it is not likely that they will intervene at the scale necessary to aggressively decarbonize. In other words, correcting tax evasion is a necessary but not sufficient condition for ambitious climate policy' (Green 2021: 375) and, it might be added, policies to address a whole range of sustainability issues. Tax reform would not only repatriate billions of dollars in missing capital from these havens and loopholes; it also helps to create the political conditions for meaningful action on decarbonisation (Green 2021). Tax havens are estimated to shelter $12 trillion or $13 trillion in private deposits, collectively costing governments between $500 billion and $600 billion a year in lost corporate tax revenue, depending on the estimate (Cobham and Janský 2018), of which low-income economies account for some $200 billion (IMF 2019). Moreover, they are being used by the 'carbon majors' to boost their profits and reinvest in fossil fuels, further exacerbating the climate crisis. Oil and gas companies including Shell, BP, Chevron and Exxon are shifting their profits to tax havens to avoid hundreds of millions of dollars in taxes using affiliate insurance and financial organisations in the Bahamas, Bermuda, Switzerland and the UK Channel Islands to park profits, where tax rates are low to non-existent (Bergin and Bousso 2020). Additionally, transfer pricing causes developing countries to lose $160 billion in tax revenues every year (Jenkins and Newell 2013). Adequately financing the future welfare state, which will face even greater demands to address the health, poverty and other impacts of accelerated environmental change, and heightened needs for new forms of education and training in what governments hope will be a greener economy, will mean addressing the tax base of their societies to ensure fiscal sustainability.

7.2.2 Just Transitions: The State and Global Welfare

Questions of work, employment and labour are intimately connected to questions of welfare and the welfare state. Indeed, one of the key functions of a welfare state is to support the unemployed. The welfare state can be used to both enable and hardwire social protection into transitions to protect 'stranded workers' and has a key role to play and will be heavily impacted by the social costs and adjustments brought about by the disruptions and dislocations that transitions inevitably bring in their wake. In the words of the UN Secretary-General Guterres, 'a just transition is absolutely critical. We must recognize the human costs of the energy shift. Social protection, temporary basic income, re-skilling and upskilling can support workers and ease the changes caused by decarbonization' (UNFCCC 2020), and of course responses to a whole range of sustainability challenges. There is now a large literature on just transitions which ranges from typologies of its dimensions (Swilling and Annecke 2012; Newell and Mulvaney 2013; Morena et al. 2019) to case studies of just transitions in practice. But the specific role of the state in welfare provision as part of that process is often neglected.

Yet, as well as anticipating, managing and reducing future inequalities associated with the transition, the state has a key role in dealing with these issues within current regimes and dominant socio-technical configurations. One key challenge for the state is the provision of protection: addressing social inequalities and environmental injustices that result from existing patterns of resource use. For example, the production of energy, in particular, has often formed the frontline of emblematic environmental justice struggles in Louisiana's 'cancer alley' (Allen 2003) or Indigenous resistance to oil extraction in Ecuador (Kimmerling 1996), for example. In the latter case, the national referendum on the future of the Yasuní Park in August 2023 was an attempt to involve citizens in a major decision about future energy pathways. In light of the victory for the campaign to protect the reserve and keep the oil in the ground (which received 58 per cent of the vote), the struggle now is to ensure that the state honours that popular mandate, something it is threatening not to do in the face of pressure from incumbent oil interests. The state is expected and often called upon to play a central role in enabling and enforcing procedural and distributive justice. Yet critical literatures on environmental justice also point to the limits of the law as a vehicle and remedy for environmental injustices for excluded and often racially marginalised groups (Cole and Foster 2001; Newell 2001). They also point to the ways in which the costs of resource extraction fall unevenly and often disproportionately on communities of colour, women, children and Indigenous groups (Bullard 2005), such as nuclear waste being sited on Indigenous lands (Brook 1998).

The marginalisation and discrimination that these examples point to highlight the critical question of who speaks for whom in transition debates. Though promoting themselves as the rightful and most representative voice of labour nationally and internationally through organisations such as the International Labour Organization (ILO), trade unions have at times played uneven, inconsistent and sometimes obstructionist roles in transition debates (Obach 2004). As a key element of the triangle of tripartite bargaining (alongside the state and capital), they can help with coordination, anticipating sectoral impacts and representing worker concerns about transition plans while lobbying for new job opportunities, retraining and compensation. This is a role they have played productively in Spain's transition dialogues overseen by the Instituto para la Transición Justa. Drawing on a case study in Germany, other scholars have identified positive roles for trade unions, including tipping 'the scales in energy transition politics towards continuity or change' using 'political access' and 'internal homogeneity of interests' as bargaining resources (Prinz and Pegels 2018: 210).

Yet, in the UK, the UNITE union has backed airport expansion, fracking and nuclear energy pathways to the despair of environmentalists and GMB has been critical of proposals to leave reserves of oil and gas in the North Sea untapped, calling for 'plans not bans' (GMB 2023) and vetoing mention of the need to transition away from fossil fuels in conference resolutions, while the National Union of Mineworkers (NUM) in South Africa solidly backs coal (Baker et al. 2014) and Brazilian trade unions adopt an agnostic stance on wind power (Hochstetler 2021). Immediate concerns with jobs for their members often trump a broader and longer-term view of the impact on the rest of society and the environment. Hochstetler (2021: 110) notes of the NUM in South Africa: 'The whole union has a clear self-interest in the historic models of electricity generation in South Africa dominated by coal and Eskom.' Often the concerns around working conditions in the renewable energy sector are legitimate. Hochstetler (2021: 103) cites the Brazilian trade union activist Daniel Gaio objecting to wind and solar power being built 'by large transnational conglomerates where labour is subcontracted and precarious, making workplace organisation difficult', while workers in the oil and gas sector in the UK also bemoan the lack of equivalent job security in the wind industry.[3] And, of course, working conditions and localised impacts of renewable extractivism have come in for fire (Sovacool 2019; Soto Hernandez and Newell 2022).

The role of the state in managing distributional costs is perhaps especially pertinent in the case of rapid transitions where accelerated change might bring more disruption in its wake. The Dutch government decided in December 1965 to abandon all coal mining in the Limburg province within a decade, doing away with some 75,000 mining-related jobs, impacting more than 200,000 people. What made the transition successful was that the government strategically steered it, implementing countermeasures such as subsidies for new businesses, the relocation of government industries from the capital to regions of the country hardest hit by the mine closures, retraining programmes for miners and offering shares in Groningen to Staatsmijnen (the state mining company) (Sovacool 2016). This illustrates the potential for the state-led managed decline of some sectors and to actively discontinue some pathways.

In a similar vein, in 2003, the government of Ontario committed to retiring all coal-fired electricity generation by 2007, something it did accomplish, albeit a few years behind schedule. To achieve this transition, Ontario invested more than $21 billion in cleaner sources of energy, including wind, hydroelectricity, solar and nuclear power, as well as $11 billion in transmission and distribution upgrades and other investments in energy efficiency (Sovacool 2016: 210). Critically, beyond the climate change benefits, the 'coal switch' was estimated to save $4.4 billion per year in health, environmental and financial damages along with $95 million in displaced operating and maintenance costs, highlighting a series of social co-benefits of such a move. Recent studies of coal transitions around the world also demonstrate the central role of the state in managing social dislocation that can be produced by rapid shifts away from particular energy regimes (Caldecott et al. 2017). For example, in the 1990s, in Gelsenkirchen, Germany, a city that was a renowned industrial hub for coal, steel and glass industries until the relocation of heavy industry, local officials decided to regenerate land abandoned by the industry and set up an energy technology park. Supported by the EU, the federal government and the utility RWE, solar technology became the new focus of development. In 2001, the city took on a voluntary carbon reduction target aimed at transforming it from a city of a thousand furnaces to 'a city of a thousand suns' (Newell et al. 2011).

Policies can generate both co-benefits and adverse side effects and can compound or lessen inequalities depending on contextual factors, policy design and policy implementation. The risk of negative outcomes is greater in contexts characterised by high levels of poverty, corruption and economic and social inequalities, and where limited action is taken to identify and mitigate potentially adverse side effects. The impacts of climate policies in exacerbating inequalities can be mitigated (and possibly even prevented), but this requires conscious effort, careful planning and multi-stakeholder engagement. Seemingly, the best results can be achieved when potential inequality impacts are taken into consideration in all stages of policymaking, including policy planning, development and implementation (Markkanen and Anger-Kraavi 2019). This centres active citizen engagement as vital to the prospects of the state adequately attending to these justice elements of a transition (Newell et al. 2024). Historical examples from the coal sector demonstrate that transitions have been accompanied by large, persistent and painful social dislocation in some cases, for instance in the UK coal mining regions in the 1980s (Glyn and Machin 1997; Tomaney 2003); but also that more consensual and participatory programmes can work such as the 'Structural Vision Randstad 2014' in the Netherlands, where more anticipatory policy was able to ensure the implementation of a timely and generous policy to accompany coal sector transition, or the Hard Coal Financing Law in Germany, which sought to manage the decline of one set of industries while supporting the emergence of others, sparking the development of several economically and ecologically sustainable initiatives (Schulz and Schwartzkopf 2016).

Which approach is taken appears to be, at least in part, a function of political economy and ideology. For example, as Spencer et al. (2018) note, in liberal market economies such as the US and UK, the historical tendency has been to let losses suffered by workers and firms lie where they fall, albeit supplemented by a mix of ad hoc support to workers and, in the US case, coal firms. By contrast, in countries whose political economy (in general or at least in the coal sector) is characterised by greater coordination between government, unions and industry groups, such as Spain, Poland and the Czech Republic, policies to phase down coal have tended to be accompanied by high levels of compensatory assistance to workers and firms.

Rapid transitions need to be accompanied by a mix of policies designed with sustainability objectives in mind, and broader social, labour market, fiscal or regional development policies intended to smooth the political economy of transition. This means minimising impacts on the poor, who may be disproportionately hit by the transition. For example, dampening the impacts of fossil fuel decline on workers and communities can be enacted by using a mix of safety nets, vouchers and cash transfers. This implies developing and negotiating explicit social contracts for sustainability transitions with losers as well as winners, including compensation and severance packages, as has occurred in Poland, or (re)training assistance, which is currently a contested terrain in China in the face of closures of coal plants. In the case of Poland, significant help is sought from the EU since the government does not have at its disposal the billions of euros that Germany spent on compensating workers.

As a further means of enacting a 'just transition', some governments have sought to impose social obligations on investors through, for example, Black Economic Empowerment (BEE) criteria in South Africa's Renewable Energy Independent Power Producer Procurement Programme (REIPPPP) (Baker et al. 2014) to ensure job losses in the coal sector are compensated by jobs for poorer black workers in renewable energy, or by developing regional economic development programmes to manage transitions away from fossil fuels in more equitable ways (Lenferna 2018). The German case study suggests linking policies for phasing out incumbent technologies to accompanying measures for managing structural change in affected regions may facilitate compromise (Leipprand and Flachsland 2018: 190). In March 2015, the Federal Ministry for Economic Affairs (BMWi) proposed the 'climate contribution' (*Klimabeitrag*) targeted at emissions of power plants beyond a certain free amount. Affected actors such as utilities, labour unions and the governments of federal states with coal mining regions lobbied heavily against the climate contribution proposal. A 'lignite emergency standby reserve' was adopted in November 2015 and passed by parliament in June 2016. This allows plants which no longer produce electricity to be kept on hold for reactivation in extreme cases, for instance, of long-duration weather extremes (or now because of gas shortages produced by the war in Ukraine). Plant operators receive a financial compensation equivalent to the revenues they would otherwise have achieved from the electricity market during this period. The measure is expected to save between 11 million and 12.5 million tonnes of CO_2 in 2020 and to cost around €230 million annually for seven years.

Common themes emerge from country case studies of policies to accelerate and manage the decline of coal. For instance, many case studies highlight the deceptive attractiveness but limited effectiveness, even of relatively generous 'golden handshakes', for former workers. The limited effectiveness of some retraining policies – typically because of a mismatch between trained competences and local employment demand – is another common theme (Caldecott et al. 2017). At the same time, the evidence on employment in English and Welsh coalfields suggests that the number of jobs in the coal industry fell by 225,000 between 1981 and 2008 but that the number of male jobs in other sectors in the same places increased by 180,000, suggesting the possibility of a successful economic regeneration. The case of coal's decline in the UK highlights, nevertheless, the importance of financial aid for regional regeneration (Hudson and Sadler 1987) as well as coherent and well-integrated regeneration policies, backed up by sustained long-term funding (Waddington and Parry 2003). Comparing across Europe, Waddington and Parry (2003) suggest regeneration activity in the UK has been piecemeal and lacking the regional coherence of corresponding initiatives in Germany and to a lesser extent in Belgium.

This is not just about government intervention, though. The stance of the company is also crucial. An interesting example in this regard is given by the Belgian Limburg case study, where the government essentially promised to give a job to any former mining worker who wanted it and the company agreed not only to retrain but also to keep a large share (approximately one-third) of the workforce to employ in new jobs in the company. This meant that, in contrast to the UK or Polish cases, most workers were never separated from the workforce and thus the risk that they would fall into long-term unemployment was limited (Caldecott et al. 2017). In Germany, early retirement and on-the-job retraining schemes, as well as policies allowing the extensive transfer of miners between pits, have further enabled restructuring to occur 'without undue drama and confrontation' (Waddington and Parry 2003: 52). Crucial to the absence of conflict in this context was the existence of a federation of union, employer and government representatives, which is generally consulted over any plans for restructuring the industry or regenerating local economies. This even included a local coal producer (RAG) diversifying its activities into land reclamation and waste and product recycling, which have been the focal point of 'production clusters' made up of firms and institutions active in the environmental protection industry. Municipalities and local authorities have also played a larger role in managing the transition in Germany compared with the UK, for example, where the process is more centralised.

Funding just transitions may also mean hypothecating funds for regional economic restructuring and worker transition, by putting in place new taxes on mining activities to pay for transition, for example. This occurred in the Dutch case for instance, where a royalty on new gas sales was used to pay for the transition. The Nigerian government is also currently considering a carbon tax to fund economic diversification, though its effect may be offset by ongoing tax incentives to extract more oil and gas.[4] Sometimes combinations of incentivising new or existing businesses in the areas impacted have worked through tax reliefs, grants or concessional loans and 'managed retreat' – when workers and their families are encouraged to relocate to areas with greater economic opportunities. This is in recognition of the prohibitive costs of sustaining or developing new sectors in situ and the reliance on large subsidies.

Adopting this broader regional perspective is crucial in the case of coal for, as Spencer et al. (2018) point out, the main challenge of moving to a 1.5°C trajectory is not stranded assets but rather 'stranded regions' where workers, regional governments and the regional economy more broadly are dependent on the coal sector. Managing decline means being attentive to questions of justice. It means attending to key questions around what role communities and workers in regions that bore the brunt of the economic 'losses' involved in the long march away from fossil economies will play in seizing the gains of new green industrial policy centred around low-carbon technological futures. As Johnstone and Hierschl (2017: 460) suggest, 'it is imperative … that as coal phase out is rightfully given increasing policy attention, those regions and communities that have already incurred significant impacts and potential neglect through the transition away from coal economies, are not further alienated by the phasing out of coal fired power stations'. A briefing for the UN concluded:

> It is not a given that workers will be able to access net job gains, nor that the new jobs will be decent ones, so decision-makers must explore a range of practical, targeted tools for establishing social protection and long-term economic security. Potential mechanisms include targeted pension and job guarantees, cash transfers, income support, retraining and education, relocation packages and community grants. (Jenkins 2019: 12)

7.2.3 Global Just Transitions

The state clearly has a key role to play in distributing and managing the gains and losses from sustainability transitions to ensure that the welfare of the poorest groups in society is not compromised. States' ability to do this is constrained, however, by shifting global production dynamics, or what Jessop refers to as post-Fordist rescaling of the sites, scales and modalities of state welfare functions. He describes a 'Schumpeterian workfare post national regime' (Jessop 2002) where interventions and regulation at the regional and international level have an increasing bearing on 'domestic' labour, working conditions and welfare through trade and investment rules and everyday production eroding state capacity to control these things. I explore this further in Chapter 8 on the global state.

The dynamic runs the other way too. Though most discussions focus on how states do this within their own borders, there are also issues of a global duty of care and responsibilities which extend to those affected by decisions made by the state and those (such as corporations) located within its jurisdiction with operations overseas. The nature and extent of those duties and liabilities, morally and legally, is nevertheless contested by states, activists and corporations in the absence of a global welfare state. More critical political economy accounts would also point to the relational nature of welfare gains in an uneven global political economy, such that increases in welfare in the Global North and among global elites are likely to be secured at the expense of excluded classes, rendering the achievement of a globally just transition for all a distant prospect (Brand and Wissen 2021).

Beyond the distributional challenges, there are also immense procedural complexities. In relation to a globally just energy transition, for example, given historical inequities in contribution to the problem and contemporary inequities in access, responsibility and respective capacity to transition, how do we fairly decide who gets to extract the last fossil fuels in a carbon-constrained world? Lenferna (2018) asks: 'Can we equitably manage the end of the fossil fuel era?' It is a good question and a very difficult one to answer. More specifically, Lenferna (2018: 217) argues that 'equitably managing the end of the fossil fuel era is complicated by how economic efficiency or the interests of frontline communities might at times diverge from global distributive justice'. Initial steps towards trying to reconcile these criteria point to the need to identify areas where they converge. Various proposals have been put forward to define a 'safe and just operating space for humanity' (Raworth 2017) or to calculate fair carbon budgets, taking into account historical responsibility, current levels of poverty and uneven capacity such as the greenhouse development rights framework or the proposal for 'contraction and convergence' from the Global Commons Institute, though none have yet been adopted by governments (GCI 2018; GDR 2018).

Beyond these distributive criteria, establishing who speaks for whom in representing the interests of particular groups in different future sustainability pathways itself presents a huge challenge for procedural justice, particularly within global decision-making processes that are not amenable to the forms of extensive citizen engagement we explored in Chapter 6. The welfare state enters this domain as the vehicle by which intra-societal inequities can be addressed, while, as we will see in Chapter 8, the global state might be involved in multilateral efforts to ensure a fair phase-down of fossil fuels through initiatives like the Fossil Fuel Non-Proliferation Treaty, complete with mechanisms such as a Global Transition Fund to support alternative lower-carbon pathways in poorer fossil fuel dependent economies (Newell and Simms 2020).

Welfare concerns need to guide such efforts. For example, Collier and Venables (2015) make a strong argument for targeting coal in the first instance as part of a global phase-out because of the array of costs its burning imposes on society, the relatively low numbers of workers and communities directly affected and their concentrated nature, which makes targeted regional redevelopment, compensation and retraining packages easier to effectively target (notwithstanding the challenges noted earlier). This comes down to discussions of 'fair shares' of remaining carbon budgets, as well as the respective capabilities of countries and communities to diversify. Levels of dependence on fossil fuels need to be looked at alongside other opportunities for economic diversification and what amount of revenue is actually derived from them. For example, Iraq and Norway have similar levels of dependence on oil but very different levels of development and needs for the revenues generated from fossil fuels and cannot be meaningfully treated in the same way when employing equity criteria. Using the language of the UNFCCC, we can recognise both 'common but differentiated responsibility' for addressing these issues and 'respective capabilities' to do so. For communities, rich and poor, North and South, these are real and live issues that they have to confront as the required speed and scale of the decline in fossil fuel use is so sharp and steep that very few nations will be protected from its effects.

One high-profile initiative to address the issue of international compensation for leaving fossil fuels in the ground was Ecuador's Yasuní–ITT (Ishpingo Tambococha Tiputini) initiative. This proposal from the Ecuadorian state asked the international community for compensation for a percentage of the revenues the country could earn from exploiting the Ishpingo Tambococha Tiputini oilfields but which it was willing to forgo if adequate compensation was paid by the international community. The government asked for $3.6 billion, roughly half the value of the oilfields in order to prevent more than 400 million tonnes of potential CO_2 being released into the atmosphere, as well as protecting a biodiverse area of particular importance to Indigenous communities. The funds, had they been received, would have been used for social and environmental programmes aimed at supporting Ecuador's transition to a post-oil future. In the end, the project collected only $13 million of the requested $3.6 billion and so was called off in 2013 (Lenferna 2018). As Sovacool and Scarpaci (2016: 169) put it, 'the proposal essentially asked the world: Who wants to pay for stranded assets? The deafening answer [appeared] to be nobody.' The apparent failure of this initiative does not foreclose future attempts to compensate poorer communities for their contributions towards global climate action, and in August 2023 Ecuadorians were offered a national referendum on the issue of whether to drill for oil beneath the Yasuní national reserve which resulted in a positive vote of 59 per cent in favour of protecting the reserve indefinitely and leaving the oil in the ground. There are also many other proposals from efforts to link debt relief to commitments to leave fossil fuels in the ground to climate bailouts, bonds and an array of other financing mechanisms which seek to redirect finance away from fossil fuels and towards renewable energy as part of a global just transition (Newell 2024).

The challenges of deepening and accelerating sustainability heighten and intensify some of the tensions and contradictions facing the welfare state, and the provision of welfare and social protection more broadly, as it faces rising demands on its resources and difficulties in generating the resources for redistribution through taxation and state expenditure. How far and in what ways responsibilities to protect extend beyond borders complicates still further the simultaneous pursuit of welfare and sustainability goals. Running beneath all of these discussions is the need for a fundamental reassessment of the relationship between growth, prosperity, well-being and welfare.

7.3 Transforming the Welfare State

What might 'sustainable welfare' look like? For Koch and Mont (2016), it is essentially about meeting basic human needs within planetary boundaries, a notion informed by Raworth's (2017) conception of a safe and just operating space for humanity. In global terms, as discussed in relation to a globally just transition, this implies a significant contraction in levels of production and consumption in large parts of the Global North and among Southern elites and convergence towards agreed minimum levels of sustainable production and consumption for many people in the majority world (GCI 2018) but impoverished classes the world over. Indeed, proponents of degrowth envisage radical redistribution and decommodification with 'floors' and 'ceilings' for income and wealth which would imply a key role for the state in setting and enforcing those parameters. The Dutch scholar Ingrid Robeyns (2024) invokes the idea of 'limitarianism' whereby the state would place an upper limit on wealth accumulation on the basis that 'extreme wealth undermines democracy, is incompatible with ecological urgency, is almost always undeserved, and harms the interests of everyone, the super-rich included'.[5]

Given the intergenerational element intrinsic to the pursuit of sustainability and just transitions over time, the welfare of current and future generations is connected such that a key goal of policy and a core responsibility of states is, as the Brundtland Commission formulated it in *Our Common Future*: 'meeting the needs of current generations without compromising the ability of future generations to meet their own needs' (WCED 1987). As Koch (2021: 124) suggests, 'If environmental limits were to be respected, the distributive principles underlying existing welfare systems would be extended to include those living in other countries and in the future'. These demands stretch and place new pressures on traditional understandings of welfare: extending it to more-than-human species, extending into the future and across global society and severing its historically given association with both the state (as the main actor for delivering welfare) and economic growth (as the means of doing so). In this reading, welfare is not something that the state can provide for its own citizens or the environments in which they live, absent efforts by all other actors to secure a more sustainable future. Nor can it be achieved by an industrial and military state intent on extracting resources and concentrating and centralising power in competitive and exclusionary ways. This places great pressure on the global state as we will see in Chapters 8 and 9, to close the loop between where revenue for welfare is generated and where and by whom it is most needed and to collectively reorient the global economy in a managed way towards a viable and liveable future for all its inhabitants.

Where does this leave the state then? Is it possible that the changing nature of the welfare state in a competitive global economy faced with shifting global demands (socially, demographically, politically and ecologically) can create openings to fashion a welfare state that is able to support pathways to sustainability? Some governments, such as Finland, have announced they will deliver a carbon-neutral welfare society by 2035 (Saikkonen and Ilmakunnas 2023). Frantzeskaki and Wittmayer (2019: 136) suggest:

> [C]hanging welfare states also provide opportunities such as ecological modernization of food, agriculture, mobility, energy and healthcare systems, the integration of ICT technologies and infrastructure, the rise of grassroots movements, low carbon lifestyles, alternatives to capitalism, and the efficient utilisation and fast adoption of good practices and successful governance experiments focused on restructuring and innovating policy and governance of (infrastructure) systems.

For others, the challenge is less about how the welfare state can support ecological modernisation and more about how to rethink both welfare and the unsustainability of dominant economic systems. Buch-Hansen and Koch (2019) suggest, for example, that income and wealth caps can be used to embed a degrowth economy, while Büchs and Koch (2017, 2019) explore the relationship between postgrowth and well-being and the form that social policy would take without growth (Koch 2022). The idea of 'consumption corridors' follows a similar logic and shared purpose of redistributing wealth in sustainable ways (Fuchs et al. 2021). This is a moving target of course as consumption patterns themselves are in a process of transition and have evolved historically (Koch 2019). But, at the very least, it implies a reversal of what Brand and Wissen (2021) call the 'imperial mode of living' which rests on 'the worldwide exploitation of nature and wage and non-wage labour while simultaneously externalising the social and ecological consequences arising from it' (Brand and Wissen 2021: 4). In a way, as Koch and Mont (2016) suggest, a return to debates about needs (which, whose and how they are to be prioritised to live fairly and sustainably) is required and underpins contemporary concerns with rationing and carbon budgets, for example. They suggest, 'needs satisfiers do change over time and across space. The fact that they can take more or less sustainable forms makes the needs approach amenable to sustainability discourses, and especially where limits are concerned' (Koch and Hansen 2024: 418).

In rethinking welfare or embedding 'sustainable welfare' a number of challenges need to be confronted. The first key challenge is presented by what political economists refer to as a 'fiscal crisis of the state' (O'Connor 1973) which, in the context of climate change, would refer to how efforts to socialise the costs of production to underwrite private profits could cause a structural gap between expenditures and revenues as the costs of health impacts, extreme weather events and climate adaptation take a rising toll. Thus far, the provision of 'cheap energy' has been afforded greater political weight than social welfare. In this regard, regulation seeks to occupy the terrain between these (potentially) competing goals, such that regulation is a critical function for ensuring the continued accumulation of capital, performing as it does a delicate balancing act between accumulation and legitimation.

A second key challenge in many contexts is the dependence of welfare states for their financing on revenues from fossil fuels and other ecologically destructive activities: the internal growth dependencies of established social policies (Kongshøj 2023). Indeed, some of the most generous and well-funded welfare states rely heavily on either the use or the export of fossil fuels. For example, the Dutch welfare state is strongly linked to the production of gas, the income from which allowed it to invest amongst other things in infrastructure and innovation (Cuppen et al. 2019). Norway also relies heavily on oil revenues to support its generous welfare system and sovereign wealth fund, though it certainly has more scope to fund welfare from a more diversified economy than say Nigeria or Iran. For instance, revenue from oil and gas sources accounted for about 60 per cent of total federally collected revenue between 2010 and 2021 in Nigeria (ODI 2023). In the US, Resources for the Future (2022) note, 'Fossil fuels provide substantial revenue to the US federal government and many states, tribes, and localities – but changes to government tax policies can help replace declining revenue and help communities adapt', finding that, between 2015 and 2020, fossil fuels generated roughly $138 billion each year for US localities, states, tribes and the federal government. On the other hand, as Morris (2016: 1) argues, 'experience demonstrates mineral-related revenues are subject to wide swings resulting from fluctuations in energy markets. Currently, a number of states are facing significant budget shortfalls as a result of their fiscal dependence on fossil fuel production when just a few years ago they experienced a boom in revenue.' Shifting to revenue streams less subject to the whims of commodity cycles might provide greater long-term financial stability for both states and citizens dependent on the welfare state.

Currently, many people's pensions and welfare in retirement are tied to the fate of stocks and shares in fossil fuels invested on their behalf by pension funds. Looking at the global situation, the report *Beyond Fossil Fuels: Fiscal Transition in BRICS*, from the Global Subsidies Initiative (GSI) of the International Institute for Sustainable Development (IISD) and Leave it in the Ground Initiative (LINGO), estimated that, in 2017, taxes and other revenues from fossil fuel production and consumption amounted to 23.6 per cent of general government revenue in Russia, 17.8 per cent in India, 6.8 per cent in both Brazil and South Africa and 4.2 per cent in China (IISD et al. 2017). The challenge may be greater still in countries such as Nigeria, Mozambique, Angola and Colombia that are much poorer but heavily dependent on fossil fuel revenues, as noted earlier. In this sense, a key challenge is how to manage and sustain the fiscal transition away from fossil fuels.

In terms of mobilising new resources to finance shifts away from fossil fuels and to compensate and retrain workers dependent for their livelihoods on fossil fuels, we return to issues raised in the previous section: debt relief and taxation. Proposals to address tax include closing tax havens and loopholes and adopting common global measures for country-by-country reporting and collecting tax, as well as global asset registries to tackle evasion and avoidance (ICRICT 2019). Measures to address these issues could lever significant revenue when combined with 'Robin Hood' taxes on speculative finance and taxation on pollution. From the perspective of sustainability transitions, a key issue is whether pollution can be taxed through ecological taxation rather than taxing labour. Ecological taxation follows the logic of taxing more what you want less of (pollution) and taxing less what you want more of (labour). In many cases, this would imply higher levels of corporate taxation but also preferential tax rates for local businesses and social enterprises. Indeed, a range of progressive tax measures could be used to increase funds for action on climate mitigation and adaptation. Chancel et al. (2023) propose a '1.5 percent-for-1.5 degree' wealth tax. The tax on personal wealth would operate as follows: a global wealth tax on the centimillionaires (i.e., individuals owning more than $100 million net of debt) would raise substantial amounts of money, even when the tax rates are relatively low. This tax would apply to the 65,000 richest adult individuals, a group representing just a little more than 0.001 per cent of the global adult population. Chancel et al. (2023) suggest such a tax could raise about $300 billion every year. As they note, 'International transfers will not be sufficient to address climate inequalities, however. Profound transformations of international and national tax regimes will be necessary' (Chancel et al. 2023: 6). This is grounded in a recognition that 'global profits that are currently undertaxed could become a sustainable revenue source for LMICs [low- and middle-income countries]'. As chair of the G20, the Brazilian government has outlined its own plan for a 2 per cent wealth tax on billionaires, which would raise an estimated $250 billion annually from 3,000 individuals (Ayres 2024).

The challenge in making this a reality is that many countries still lack progressive capital income taxes, top inheritance taxes or progressive wealth taxes. Current discussions on the apportionment of multinationals profits, occurring under the auspices of the OECD, could lead to additional government revenues in the order of $110 billion to $160 billion (under so-called Pillars 1 and 2) for both high-income and low-income countries under a 15 per cent global minimum corporate tax rate. As UNCTAD (2019) have proposed, unitary taxation that recognises that the profits of multinational enterprises (MNEs) are generated collectively at the group level, combined with a global minimum effective corporate income tax rate on all MNE profits, could be set at around 20–25 per cent, which is the average of current nominal rates. There are clear, but perhaps not insurmountable, barriers to reforming the global tax regime. Subject to domestic pressure and advocacy work, OECD countries could support a new global tax environment that supports the ability of LMICs to recover and reinvest taxation and to properly integrate climate concerns in doing so. The aim is to conclude a new multilateral treaty: an international tax reform agreement to ensure MNEs pay a fair share of tax wherever they operate. Concerns remain, however, given its oversight by the OECD which represents the interests of richer countries where progress has been slowed by a combination of entrenched private sector lobbying, opposition from OECD members and the organisation's failure to provide a meaningful voice for lower-income countries. This has led some developing countries and tax justice activists to call for a UN treaty instead. A call to develop a UN Tax Convention was first put forward by the Africa Group at the UN in 2019, for example, a call that has been supported by the South Centre and many others since.

What this points to is the need for effective and just transitions to address questions of economic justice between nations and not only questions of welfare within them. For many social groups and countries in the Global South, this is the quid pro quo or global social contract for meaningfully engaging with global decarbonisation efforts and moves to leave fossil fuels in the ground. Entry points might include proposals for 'climate easements' (Synder and Ruyle 2020) or 'debt for climate swaps' given the fact that mounting debt pressures can lead developing nations to expand fossil fuel production (Price of Oil 2021). Debt for nature swaps have been used before to support conservation efforts and could be adapted to address the supply side. 'Debt for climate' swaps would provide debt relief to nations that choose to forgo extraction and keep reserves in the ground (Chamon et al. 2022). There is also scope to overlay this mechanism with global biodiversity hotspots so that the development of fossil fuel assets does not come at the cost of destroying the natural world.

7.3.1 Towards a Reset

Invoking deeper and more radical notions of transformational change, we might reflect on whether and how it might be possible to reconcile welfare provision and degrowth for example. Might it be the case, for instance, that there would be less demand for welfare in an economy where levels of social inequality and ecological depletion are lower, time more abundant and communities stronger? As Gough (2017: 14) puts it, 'An economy and society that can no longer rely on annual growth will require a radical redistribution of carbon, time and wealth'. This necessarily implies a more interventionist and coordinated economy than we have in most parts of the world today. At the same time, many states heavily reliant on fossil fuels such as petro-states in Africa, the Middle East and Latin America (think Nigeria, Saudi Arabia and Venezuela) have very weak systems of welfare provision showing that resource abundance and levels of welfare provision are poorly related. This often results from lack of democracy but also the 'resource curse' (Ross 1999) whereby the dependence of state elites on resource (normally oil) revenues means they are less reliant on taxation from their citizens which is a key means by which people hold governments to account.

There are opportunities to rethink the relationship between work, income and welfare. The need to reset work, income and consumption, rewiring the basics of the economy, offers scope for engaging with increasingly popular notions of prosperity that go beyond traditional notions of growth based on extractivism (Jackson 2011; Kallis 2018). Gough (2017), for example, argues for a shift from welfare states to 'climate mitigation states'. A key challenge in order to achieve deeper and more transformative change is not to think of the role of the state as financing and delivering welfare as a separate siloed activity to remedy the social impacts of capitalism as usual but rather to build an economy with well-being and prosperity at its heart. This would reduce the generation of the human and ecological costs of industrialism as usual in the first place. Redistribution will be vital to close the gap between the polluter elite (Kenner 2019) and a disenfranchised majority, one disproportionately affected by the impacts of environmental change. But distributional justice would also be required across generations such that 'basic needs of the future should take precedence over the extravagant luxury of the present' (Gough 2017: 174). Some see the development of Green states that could pursue such an agenda as similar in historical function to the emergence of welfare states at the end of the Second World War and as a corrective to the idea of a self-regulating market (Barry and Eckersley 2005; Duit 2016; Mol 2016).

Concrete interventions towards this end might then imagine bolder, more ambitious but also more politically contentious proposals such as upper income limits, job sharing, or a four-day working week to shift the drivers of overconsumption

(Schor 2011), including the better regulation of advertising. Changes to modes of working offer a powerful way of reducing pressure and stress in people's lives, as well as shifting patterns of consumption while improving welfare and the quality of life for the many and helping to address the 'care deficits' that characterise contemporary economies (Fraser 2022). As Simms et al. (2010: 3) argue, 'moving towards a much shorter working week would help break the habit of living to work, working to earn, and earning to consume'. Due to the need to radically curtail consumption in industrialised nations in particular, work time reduction has the potential for scaling sustainable behaviour change across regions and sectors. Research suggests that work time reduction could shift behaviours in more sustainable directions by decreasing the scale of economic output and the environmental intensity of consumption patterns (Rosnick and Weisbrot 2007; Knight et al. 2013), as well as improving life satisfaction and societal well-being (Borowy and Aillon 2017) and nurturing more intrinsic values (Kasser 2002). There is also a clear public health incentive for rethinking work, with long working hours contributing to more than 745,000 deaths globally in 2016, a 29 per cent increase since 2000 (Pega et al. 2021).

Despite its myriad benefits, work time reduction has stalled in countries over recent decades and has begun to reverse, with only some exceptions (Schor 2011; Burger 2015). In 2016, approximately 488 million people around the world were exposed to long working hours, with significant social and health impacts (Pega et al. 2021). Trends towards casualisation and zero-hour contracts heighten the precarity which drives unsustainable working patterns and the exhaustion of workers. Germany's *Kurzarbeit* part-time working policy, nevertheless, is an example, which allows business to pursue work time reduction during a period of structurally low aggregate demand (Contessi and Li 2013). The Spanish government too announced plans to pilot a four-day working week as a direct response to the economic challenges wrought by Covid-19 (Stone 2021). In the UK, a study of 50,000 businesses concluded that a carefully designed four-day week could be introduced immediately and be financially viable for most firms with more than 50 workers and be backed by national legislation to protect the rights of workers (Elliott 2020).

Alongside rethinking work and consumption, resetting the (political) economy also means tackling the uneven concentration of ownership and control over key systems of provision that need to be transitioned. Critical scholarship points to the need to bring more inclusive forms of ownership to the fore and, in the process, transform companies from vehicles for monopolising wealth extraction to economically coordinated, co-owned and regenerative entities (Lawrence et al. 2020). Many of the prospective policies to re-common private business, such as maximum pay ratios and a ban on share buybacks, would transform people's relationship to work, help address the inequalities between the polluter elite and the rest and ultimately repurpose the company towards more social ends. This, in turn, fuels demands to bring key systems of energy and transport provision, for example, back into public hands in the form of nationalisation or bottom-up attempts at community energy and food provision, as discussed in Chapter 6, guided by the need to meet human need rather than generate profit as an end in itself.

Rationing, consumption corridors, allowances and taxes (on highly polluting activities such as flying) are among the tools that have been proposed to rebalance consumption towards need over greed. Yet, building on insights from Chapter 6, resistance to these tools can be weaponised around claims of an overbearing state dictating how people live, devoid of a discussion of corresponding responsibilities on richer citizens to live differently so that others may simply live (as the activist slogan goes). Rationing of carbon has been proposed for a long time and energy rationing has made a return in the context of the war in Ukraine and the cost-of-living crisis created by rising gas prices. A key issue here then is the fact that redistribution is relational. As we have seen, well-resourced groups and polluter elites have disproportionate access to and influence over the state which provides them with multiple veto points and opportunities to resist actions threatening to their interests. Still, in terms of framing and building political support for measures which are explicitly distributive, making those connections can secure political capital. A concrete example would be the attempt by activists in the UK to link a windfall tax on the extraordinary profits of oil and gas companies to demands to finance a mass retrofit of housing to insulate the properties of poorer consumers whose fuel bills have risen exponentially.

Tackling the social and cultural drivers of overconsumption means addressing the sources of demand: advertising and the media's role in the normalisation and reification of high consumption behaviours. Regulation and 'choice-editing' have a role to play whereby governments, businesses and those with direct control over production restrict the availability of high-carbon products and services such as private jets and sports utility vehicles or use planning and building regulation to ensure better insulated homes (Newell et al. 2021). Such a shift would need to more fundamentally question cultural and social values around what it is to live a 'good life' informed by ideas of 'plentitude' (Schor 2011), prosperity and well-being (Jackson 2021), premised on the sharing of spaces, goods and facilities rather than the individualisation of ownership and use. This suggests the need for new indicators of progress, and new modes of organising economic relations, which focus on factors relating to sustainability and well-being, rather than economic output or labour productivity. Ideas around the Happy Planet Index or Gross National Happiness as adopted by the government of Bhutan suggest possible ways forward in that regard. In this first instance, such a strategy would need to disrupt and ultimately break the cycles of mass production and consumption established under the Fordist regime of accumulation where the role of the state is to 'integrate the circuits of the capital and consumer goods industries and by managing the conflicts between labour and capital over both the individual and social wage so that the virtuous circle of Fordist growth can be maintained' (Jessop 2002: 57). The constant deferral of the environmental (and social) costs of this Fordist model is coming home to roost, dependent as it was on ever intensifying and accelerating waves of extractivism to fuel unsustainable consumption.

Perspectives and strategies such as these challenge dominant perspectives grounded in welfare economics which is about the maximum satisfaction of individual consumer preferences. The rampant individualism associated with a perspective in which consumer sovereignty is primary and questions of what and how much can be consumed should be determined individually and expressed through the market poses a challenge to the notion that the state should play a role in 'choice-editing' and reducing consumerism and waste in line with ambitious sustainability goals. But it is a role the state must accept if it is to successfully address these challenges. This is so not just to protect and enhance the welfare of citizens within a state but to avoid the behaviour and consumption patterns of social elites within countries diminishing the life chances of citizens elsewhere. As we have seen throughout the book, transitions are relational and interconnected and duties and responsibilities (including around welfare) spill across borders and sovereign territories through the complex geographies of transition. This calls for a more disruptive politics that is only possible, in all likelihood, in the context of deepened and revitalised forms of democracy – including its ecological variant as discussed in Chapter 6. It inevitably implies deliberate shifts in power around the politics of participation and representation to broaden and deepen the terrain of issues that can be addressed. Radical innovations are required in the way we seek to identify, manage and meet diverse social and ecological welfare needs within and across societies, within and across generations and within and across species. The global state to which we now turn has a key role to play in supporting such innovations.

8

The Global State

8.1 Introducing the Global State

The state does not just seek to manage affairs within its borders. It exists within a competitive, uneven and unequal and highly fragmented international system. It shapes, and is shaped by, what other states do through processes of inter-state diplomacy and by being bound, to different degrees, by the norms, rules and procedures of regional and international institutions. States are also key nodal points and intersections in the flows of finance, goods, resources, people and technology that constitute the materiality of transitions and their quotidian organisation and assemblage through markets, supply chains and everyday practice. As Gramsci (1985: 181) argued, 'history is always "world history" such that particular histories exist only within the frame of world history'. Historical blocs extend beyond particular states based on a common superstructure and shared material interests on the part of dominant classes and social forces projected through dominant accumulation regimes such as Fordism and more recently a finance-led regime of accumulation. In this regard, Jessop (2002: 55) defines Atlantic Fordism as 'an accumulation regime based on a virtuous autocentric circle of mass production and mass consumption secured through a distinctive mode of regulation' materialised, as we saw in Chapter 7, in the form of the Keynesian welfare state. In a more contemporary context, shifts in the base of production have given rise to the sorts of geopolitical shifts we are seeing today anticipated by Gramsci, Marx and Poulantzas observable in the rise of China and India. Gramsci (1985: 196) wrote 'If China and India were to become modern nations with great volumes of industrial production, their consequent detachment from a dependency on Europe would in fact rupture the current equilibrium', as indeed it has.

As I will argue in this chapter, shifts among social forces within the state can give rise to, as well as on other occasions reflect and embody, global power shifts including hegemonic formations (Rupert 1995). This means 'technical-military expressions' modify international relations and the latter 'react both passively and actively on political relations' (Gramsci 1971: 176). For Gramsci, this means it is necessary 'to take into account the fact that international relations intertwine with these internal relations of nation-states, creating new, unique and historically concrete combinations' (Gramsci 1971: 182). This reflects the fact that in his view international relations follow fundamental social relations, rather than precede them.

States are deeply interconnected economically and politically as world systems and dependency theories have long shown through patterns of uneven but combined development, as well as ecologically, as accounts of ecologically uneven exchange have amply illustrated. Yet, while distinctions between domestic and international and internal/external are porous at best, the boundary is policed between internal and external because of its implications for state duties, responsibilities and maintenance of the realm (Walker 1993). Thinking about global aspects of state power as they relate to questions of transition cannot be reduced, therefore, to questions of foreign policy since there are global dimensions to, and implications of, the ostensibly domestic organisation of welfare, entrepreneurial, industrial, military and democratic states. Indeed, many key state functions in those critical areas only function because of global military alliances and arms trades, global networks of innovation and production and flows of finance and labour that sustain welfare states, for example, and often built upon 'cheap' labour and nature secured through contemporary and historical, particularly colonial, patterns of extractivism (Patel and Moore 2017). It is clearly the case that the nature and degree of insertion into global networks are a function of both the state in question and its power to project and enforce its preferences upon others and to resist the ability of rival states to do the same.

But is there a global state per se as some scholars claim? If so, what is global about the state? Is it that the globalisation of the economy is bringing into being a transnational state as some claim? For Robinson (2004), an emergent transnational state results from the activities of what Sklair (2002) calls a transnational capitalist class (TCC) constituted by 'hegemonic fractions of capital on a world scale' that have become 'transnationalized, increasingly detached from particular territories and from the old political and social projects of nation states' (Robinson 2004: 85). Their emergence reflects, in turn, the increasing transnationalisation of production. The transnational state, according to Robinson (2004: 99), 'is a particular constellation of class forces and relations bound up with capitalist globalization and the rise of the TCC embodied in a diverse set of political institutions. These institutions are transformed national states and diverse supranational institutions that serve to institutionalize the domination of this class as the hegemonic fraction of capital worldwide'. It is observable, he suggests, in 'an emerging network that comprises transformed and externally integrated national states, together with the supranational economic and political forums, and has not yet acquired any centralized institutional form' (Robinson 2004: 88). The relevant economic forums include the IMF, World Bank and WTO and political forums the G7, OECD and regional bodies such as the EU, ASEAN and NAFTA, each of which play important direct and indirect roles in the governance of transitions through shaping trade and investment rules (Van de Graaf 2013). This formation is significant in terms of advancing some forms of transition (those consistent and aligned with neoliberalism) and resisting (or accommodating) others which threaten to transform it (Newell 2018). This includes the role of global institutions in advancing fairly limited notions of what constitutes a 'just transition' to date (Newell et al. 2023): those compatible with a 'Wall Street Consensus' (Gabor 2021) focussing on de-risking investment for private capital and the liberalisation and privatisation of key systems of provision such as energy and water (McDonald 2009; Bakker 2010). For Ougaard (2018), it is less that there is an international state and more that there are 'state-like' features observable in this assemblage of global power. In understanding the basis of this configuration (whether understood as a global or transnational state or not), Brand et al. (2011: 162), drawing on Poulantzas' idea of the state as a 'condensation' of societal forces, suggest international institutions function as the 'condensation of the power relationship between competing "national interests" which are themselves shaped by domestic struggles and compromises'. Or, in Jessop's words, 'a form-determined condensation of the balance of political forces operating within and beyond the state' (Jessop 2002: 6).

What this points to is the use of global networks and institutions to project, institutionalise and enforce the preferences of particular elites, often ones based in richer states, traditionally (but not exclusively) in the global North, such that such global engagements afford a means of supplanting and extending some forms of state (commercial, military and soft) power. The fact that hegemonic states such as the US disproportionately fund key global economic institutions such as the IMF and World Bank and insist on having them located within their borders is not a coincidence or an exercise of benign good will. Global institutions, whether under imperial Britain or the hegemonic US (what Cox (1987) calls 'pax Britannica' and 'pax Americana' respectively) have always provided a means of maintaining a global order which benefits and consolidates the global power of states in the core of the economy. Increasingly, they will be called upon to manage geopolitical tensions produced by sustainability transitions, most particularly, perhaps, competition over critical minerals and market access for lower-carbon technologies, but also incumbent resistance to change and the competitive advantages this confers upon 'pollution havens' or those seeking to free-ride on global efforts to tackle environmental problems. It is no coincidence in this regard that the US and

EU have been at the forefront of the Just Energy Transition Partnerships (JETPs) being rolled out in numerous countries around the world (including South Africa, Vietnam, Indonesia and Senegal, for example). The rising number of trade conflicts over transition policies that have come before the WTO over the use of state aid and subsidies, the development of Carbon-Border Adjustment Mechanisms (CBAMs) to counter unfair competition on environmental grounds, resorts to investment tribunals such as the Investor–State Dispute Settlement (ISDS) mechanisms and conflicts over labour rights at new frontiers of extraction are illustrative of this new landscape which global institutions face.

Scholarship on hegemony, grounded in this neo-Gramscian tradition, has produced case studies of how this power is expressed through bodies such as the Trilateral Commission, Bilderberg and the World Economic Forum (Gill 1991) showing how disciplinary neoliberalism rewards states adopting neoliberal reforms and punishes those which deviate from what is expected of them through the provision of aid, loans and investment in the case of the former and withdrawal of aid, capital flight and reduced credit rating in the case of the latter (Sinclair 1994). This disciplining is performed through rankings and scorecards of countries depending on their performance in creating what are deemed to be key conditions for growth. Non-compliance has consequences. Glatzer et al. (2024) explore the example of the sudden termination in October 2019 by the US Millennium Challenge Corporation (MCC) of the concession agreement with the Ghanaian government by way of punishment for not privatising the Electric Company Ghana, 'effectively denying the Ghanaian government US $190 million in previously agreed development funds' (Glatzer et al. 2024: 463).

This locks in and constrains policy space at the national level with global institutions often serving as transmission belts for the interests of transnational capital and states in the core of the global economy (Cox 1987). Glatzer et al. (2024) show how, even after formal independence, many postcolonial states remain 'open to external forces able to intervene and reconstruct economic or juridical spheres using soft power or else disciplinary forces' (Glatzer et al. 2024: 467). The significant steering roles of these globally connected boards of directors and investors warrants further attention in transition debates to connect with discussions of incumbency and regime stabilisation which are often contained with the state. For example, the Atlas Network has played a coordinating and leading role in pushing for the rollback of environmental measures and tougher punishments for environmental defenders in its support for populist leaders around the world, unsurprising given its funding ties to the Koch brothers and oil and coal companies known for supporting obstructionism, crushing climate policy initiatives in the US and financing climate sceptics. As Monbiot (2024) suggests, 'We might describe certain policies as being Milei's or Bolsonaro's, or Truss's or Johnson's or Sunak's, but they're all variations on the same themes, hatched and honed by junktanks belonging to the same network. Those presidents and prime ministers are just the faces the programme wears.' This is a programme the right-wing neoliberal think tanks the Institute of Economic Affairs and the Heritage Foundation play a leading role in articulating, centred on 'destroying regulations that protect workers, vulnerable people and the living world' (Monbiot 2024). At the regional and national level, activist and academic scholarship has shown how business elites have played a key part in securing their preferred model of capitalist market integration over social (and environmental) objectives (Van Appeldoorn and de Graaff 2015; Ryner and Cafruny 2016) or how states have become 'captive' to private actors (Korten 1995; Monbiot 2000).

Different states (and indeed different parts of the state) interact differently and unevenly with global regimes including the regime complexes around energy and food central to the global governance of transitions in those domains (Colgan et al. 2012; Newell and Taylor 2018). This means that 'globalising state bureaucrats' (Sklair 1995) and some parts of the state are more internationalised than others and, therefore, have a greater bearing over the direction of the global politics of transition, particularly ministries of finance and foreign affairs whose concerns with investment, security and geopolitics often crowd out concerns with sustainability and the justice elements of sustainability for which ministries of the environment and labour have greater responsibility. International law affords a key means of globalising and enshrining elite preferences. Conceptually, Gill (1995) argues that law, in the form of the 'new constitutionalism', serves to expand the private sphere of capital accumulation while constraining potentially democratizing influences. In this regard, 'new constitutional agreements tend to provide hard or binding rights for corporations and investors but only require soft or voluntary responsibilities of them' (Gill 2014: 13). This is unsurprising in so far as Cutler (2002: 231) suggests: 'The law globalises rules that facilitate transnational patterns of capital accumulation, attenuating certain regulatory practices while advancing others. Thus, the ability of states to regulate production, trade and finance for national policy purposes is subordinated to the need for states to act as market participants or "competition states" in the search for expanding market opportunities.' In this way, in Gramscian terms, globalised law 'advances the interests of a transnational class whose members function as the "organic intellectuals" for the globalization of capitalism' (Cutler 2002: 231). There are many examples of the way in which trade and investment law is being used to constrain policy space: from provisions in trade treaties such as NAFTA which allow companies to sue governments, to the Energy Charter Treaty that has been used by companies to challenge the ambitions of governments' energy transitions plans, to global trade restrictions on the use of policy tools such as infant industry protection, local content requirements and subsidies that governments may need to use to support niche actors in the renewable energy space, for example (Newell 2007; Tienhaara et al. 2022).

Partly as a result of these shifts, there is also attention to the way in which the state form as a whole is undergoing a transformation as core state functions are shifting in relation to global imperatives, with the 'competition state' on the ascendance (Cerny 1995). Hence, while the basic structure of the state system has endured since the seventeenth century and the Treaty of Westphalia, nation-states are not universal in character, nor are the organising principles of that system static as it co-evolves with the development dynamics of capitalism (Wallerstein 1979). This challenges the Weberian (1978) notion of a separation of the economic and political spheres of the state, such that globalisation cannot be seen as an external logic as much as a function and extension of social relations intrinsic to the state and rooted most profoundly in the relationship between the state and capital. Here the state is not 'suspended in mid-air', as Marx famously observed (1978: 607), but rather gives political form to economic institutions and production relations.

The scale and nature of the ecological crises may, nevertheless, present new organisational and scalar challenges to the state and the forms of organising the economy that it supports; in addition to the threats to state legitimacy and critique of dominant models of wealth creation that they imply. This has invoked calls for 'planet politics': a new global politics and ethics and reinvigorated efforts to construct new global institutions (Burke et al. 2016) around the pursuit of 'planetary justice' (Biermann and Kalfagianni 2020). The question remains whether any such notion is fanciful in the face of the ongoing hegemonic power of the US to shape the global order despite accounts of its alleged demise as a hegemonic power (Panitch and Gindin 2012). In relation to energy specifically, McGowan (2009) refers to as the 'paradox of sovereignty', whereby states have less control over energy policy due to the globalisation and interdependence of energy markets but nevertheless remain reluctant to act jointly, cooperate or strengthen multilateral organisations with responsibilities for governing energy, reflected in the weakness of global energy governance (Florini and Sovacool 2009). These competing tendencies and pressures underscore again the deeper patterns of continuity and change noted throughout the book which shape and circumscribe the politics of sustainability transitions, including its global dimensions.

In some ways, such debates about the shifting functions and powers of the state within the global economy can be seen as a series of reactions and counter-reactions. The perceived neglect of the state led to calls to bring the state back in (Evans et al. 1985). Likewise, the lack of attention to the way in which globalisation was reconfiguring, and some argued eroding, state authority led to claims about the 'retreat of the state' (Strange 1996) or the existence of a 'borderless world' (Ohmae 1990). This, in turn, led to other scholars calling out what they called 'the myth of the powerless state' (Weiss 1995) and the 'follies of globalisation theory' (Rosenberg 2003), leading to attempts to develop more inflected and nuanced accounts of which aspects of state power and authority were rising and falling, where and why (Paul et al. 2003). Critically, however, the issue is not just a zero-sum transfer of power from state to market, public to private, or between states and international institutions given the blurring of these actors and distinctions in practice, but also the processes and strategies by which transition policies diffuse, are enforced or otherwise travel across the global economy in ways which spatially, economically and ecologically connect one transition to another. The issue then is the globally connected and mediated simultaneous co-construction of transitions in different parts of the world which produces their uneven and unequal nature.

Clearly the power of states to shape and police the international system and enforce the rules that regulate it is unevenly distributed. The ways in which states behave in this regard reflect, in part, the resources they have at their disposal to project and enforce their geopolitical and other preferences, often using their financial, political and at times military power (as we saw in Chapter 5) to secure spatial and temporal fixes to the transition dilemmas and contradictions they face by pushing costs into the future or onto other populations (Newell 2021). For example, Arcand and Meadowcroft (2024: 15) suggest 'a nation's power is likely to determine the importance of the geopolitical and economic elements of their industrial strategies'.

Nevertheless, what these distributions of power mean for the prospects of progressive politics is contested. In Liberal versions, the focus is on global governance and global cosmopolitanism (Held 1995) as the basis for supporting global democracy (Scholte 2011) and the extension of a duty of care to global citizens through an expanded notion of political community and global rights protection (Linklater 1998). Such projects are guided by an aspiration and normative desire for a post-Westphalian order made up of elections to global parliaments through direct representation, some ability to collect and redistribute global taxes and enhanced capacity to provide global public goods (Kaul et al. 1999). These visions are clearly threatened by a series of challenges to liberalism (Jahn 2018) and the liberal international order, including the role of multilateralism within it in the current political climate but also by the geopolitical manoeuvres of 'contender states' such as Russia and China (Van der Pijl 1998) and the rise of what Coker (2019) calls the 'civilisational state' which he also uses to describe the globalising ambitions of theological states such as Iran. Such an analysis of course also forms the point of departure for the much cited and much criticised 'clash of civilisations' hypothesis of Samuel Huntingdon (1993). Though interesting in and of themselves, such discussions (for our purposes here at least) need to be taken down several levels to relate to the concrete question of what they mean for sustainability transitions.

8.2 The Global State and Transitions

At minimum, an understanding of the role of the state in supporting or frustrating transitions needs to be placed in a global (and regional) context as sovereignty, finance, authority and of course resources are (unevenly) exchanged across scales and sites of decision-making. This requires, as van der Vleuten and Högselius (2012) note, a 'transnational perspective' on transitions and on regime dynamics in particular. This sheds light on 'landscape-regime interactions as a site for negotiating transnational regime stability and change' (van der Vleuten and Högselius 2012: 75). The authors contrast this approach with transitions research which 'seems to tacitly and uncritically reproduce the nation-state as its presupposed core of analysis. Such a priori nation-centred analysis includes nation-nation comparisons and nation-nation transfer studies which equally frame transition dynamics in fundamental national boxes' (van der Vleuten and Högselius 2012: 78). This reflects a tendency to view niches and regimes in national terms and to mainly focus on niche–regime interactions, such that 'International dynamics tend to be analytically "exogenised" to the macro-level of landscape developments; the international dimension of regime and niche organisation fades from view' (van der Vleuten and Högselius 2012: 79). Moving beyond dominant forms of methodological nationalism, and this 'cascade' view of governance (Bulkeley 2005), whereby decisions and resources are assumed to flow from one level to the next in a linear and downward fashion, allows us to explore entanglements, enmeshments and assemblages of actors and networks which traverse these scales and the ways in which they impact upon regime stability and change. For example, as van der Vleuten and Högselius (2012: 79) suggest: 'Cross border entanglements and interdependencies in terms of technological infrastructure, system operation … financial investments, exchange contracts or organisational structures may counteract any power company or national government attempt to achieve radical change in isolation. And vice versa … such transnational entanglements may constitute an avenue for a radical chain reaction.' The idea of assemblages has been used to get a handle on these entanglements which, in a more critical vein, enable and enforce extractivism (Soto Hernandez and Newell 2022).

But it is the multi-directionality of power that is key here, reflecting a more Foucauldian view of the capillaries of power that connect actors and institutions (Foucault 2019) while acknowledging their grounding in material relations characterised by sharp inequalities. This means not reducing geopolitics to a set of landscape pressures bearing down on a regime. Think of the conflict in Ukraine and its impact on national gas regimes; but also how those regimes' strategies of engagement or withdrawal help to sustain or disrupt the war: the ways in which gas infrastructures and the national policies of particular states create, reproduce or disrupt regional and global geopolitics (van der Vleuten and

Högselius 2012). Hence, 'international gas relations (international pipelines and bilateral long term contracts in particular) [are] dominant as by far most countries are gas importers' such that 'regime stability and change … are not driven by companies or governance in isolation: companies, sector international organisations, national legislators and bilateral negotiations and treaties were entangled in one and the same transnational space where regime dynamics played out' (van der Vleuten and Högselius 2012: 99). This invites a broader and less state-centric understanding of the geopolitics of transition as proposed in Chapter 2.

It remains the case, however, that states can weaponise economic interdependence (Farrell and Newman, 2019) by manipulating commercial ties, imposing sanctions and blocking rival investments. Examples include the use of Gazprom by the Russian state to secure its geopolitical objectives (Wigell and Vihma 2016) or the extension of Beijing's power and influence in the global economy through Chinese state-owned enterprises (Norris 2016). Attempts to fracture these close configurations of public and private power include the sanctions imposed by European countries on Russian private and state-owned enterprises after the invasion of Ukraine on the basis of those companies' close ties to the Kremlin and their support for Russia's war effort. Within International Relations, the evolving relationship between the state and economic actors in the foreign policy realm is accounted for by the 'statecraft' and 'fragmented state' approaches. The statecraft approach is based on a general presumption of state control over economic actors. It asserts that political leadership has sufficient leverage to rein in economic actors and employ them in an instrumental manner for foreign policy purposes (Balzacq and Krebs 2021). From this perspective, economic activities, in particular those of state-owned enterprises, constitute part of a political 'grand strategy' (Early and Preble 2021; Narizny 2021). Hence, a state deploys mergers, acquisitions, loans and investments in a strategic manner in order to increase its power and influence while fuelling other states' dependence. Concepts such as 'geoeconomics' and 'authoritarian state capitalism' dominate the debates within this approach.

The fragmented state approach, on the other hand, recognises that states are complex entities rather than unitary actors and that economic actors have the capacity to bargain with the state. The outcomes of this interaction for foreign policy vary from case to case (Hameiri and Jones 2016; Hameiri et al. 2019). While the state and economic players often share compatible goals, it is by no means a unidirectional relationship. Economic players often lead, rather than merely follow, state action; they mobilise the state to protect their own parochial interests and can frustrate the implementation of political leadership's grand designs (Jones and Hameiri 2021). As a consequence, foreign policy results from bargaining between the state, individual state institutions and economic actors, what Stopford et al. (1991) referred to as 'triangular diplomacy' between rival states and rival firms.

8.2.1 The Geopolitics of Transition

Capturing the scales and sites and networks through which geopolitics operate has to be underpinned by a recognition of the way in which they are often entwined with the use of violence by state and private actors. Giddens (1985: 252) proposes that there are three key 'institutional dimensions of the world military order today: super-power hegemony; the arms trade; and systems of military alliance', which are interrelated by virtue of the fact superpowers also tend to dominate the arms trade and take the lead in constructing global alliances such as NATO (North Atlantic Treaty Organization). Such alliances and the constitution of spheres of influence which combine the expansion and spread of industrialism with that of the nation-system have resulted in most states having arsenals of arms that exceed those even of traditional empires (Giddens 1985), globalising the military state. As we have seen already in Chapter 5, the military state is closely enmeshed with the industrial and entrepreneurial state. Historically, power – in a literal and figurative sense – was crucial to the exercise of hegemony in reshaping world orders. As Selby (2022: 338) notes:

> [F]ossil fuels have always been central to patterns of hegemony, empire and geopolitical power. Britain's industrialisation and rise to global pre-eminence had many causes – but … would not have been feasible without coal. Coal-powered steamships and railways were, perhaps more than any other innovations, what made the 19th century age of European imperialism and partition of Africa possible, enabling colonists to penetrate deep into continental interiors.

Likewise, 'Coal, together with steel, also underpinned Germany's late 19th-century rise and 20th-century descent into militarism and total war – hence the necessity of creating an institution to regulate these sectors, the European Coal and Steel Community, in post-1945 Europe' (Selby 2022: 338). Similarly, 'Oil became the lynchpin of both the US-dominated post-war financial order, and the adjustments to it following the collapse of the Bretton Woods system and 1970s oil crisis. Control of oil as a strategic commodity became key to US hegemony more broadly' (Selby 2022: 338). 'Even today', Selby continues, 'the two main fossil fuel producers in the world are the two pre-eminent military powers, the US and Russia' (2022: 339) and regional powers in the Middle East (Saudi Arabia and Iran) and Africa (South Africa) are major fossil fuel producers. In recognition of the intimate relationship between control over energy sources and expressions of geopolitical power, there has been growing attention to the geopolitics of energy (Goldthau et al. 2019; Blondeel et al. 2021), especially pertinent in the context of the Ukraine crisis and the 'new cold war' and its geopolitics of gas, as well as to the geopolitical implications of the contemporary growth of renewable energy (IRENA 2019). This latest wave of interest is predated by scholarship on oil hegemony (Bromley 1991) but also how energy diplomacy over gas and nuclear played a key role in the original Cold War as part of Willy Brandt's Ostpolitik (Bösch 2014), for example.

In a narrower sense, scholars have also focussed on 'commercial diplomacy' as a particular sub-field of foreign policy. Commercial diplomacy has been defined as 'political support for foreign-investing businesses' and applied to cases such as the EU (Stoddard 2017: 1048). Development cooperation, for example, is a key vehicle for exporting and transnationalising the economic bloc's policy preferences. In this regard, scholars have shown how 'the existing tools of EU energy and climate diplomacy create governance structures: bilateral partnerships, trade agreements, regional and multilateral orders are per se instruments to govern the underlying relationship between the EU, its member states and third countries' (Barra and Svec 2018: 245). Energy diplomacy has a key role to play in an age of energy transition in mobilising finance, sharing technology, securing market access and building consensus about respective responsibilities and capabilities for accelerating transitions. Griffiths (2019) shows not only how 'A global, low-carbon energy transition impacts the geopolitics of energy' but also how 'Bilateral energy diplomacy is a key foreign policy tool to manage geopolitical consequences of low-carbon energy transition'. In this regard, Huda (2024) suggests 'renewable energy diplomacy' has two aims: to address the geopolitical challenges associated with energy transitions and to enhance bilateral and multilateral cooperation on cleaner energy.

A 'mini-lateral' approach, meanwhile, underpins the rollout of so-called Just Energy Transition Partnerships (JETPs) supported by the US, EU, UK and Japan, for example in countries such as South Africa, Vietnam, Indonesia and Senegal, mainly coal-dependent countries of strategic interest to major powers. Concerns have been expressed by trade unions and civil society organisations about the model of transition being promoted with a strong emphasis on concessional loans (which might increase indebtedness) and de-risking private finance (with public finance covering only half of the promised $20 billion package) for Indonesia's JETP, for example, and lack of transparency and public participation in the process of setting priorities and how to distribute the finance (UNRISD 2023). These dimensions and conditions around unbundling and privatisation underscore a sense in which JETPs provide a(nother) 'trojan horse' for exporting and embedding neoliberal transitions under the guise of addressing climate change and in this case supporting 'just transitions'.

Scholars have also explored the role of 'rising powers' in supporting and frustrating transitions, most especially energy transitions in other parts of the world (Power et al. 2016). This has included analysis of the role of Russia, China (Wang 2019) and Brazil (Santos Vieira de Jesus 2013) in general and in relation to specific countries like Iran (Wu 2015). For example, China's nuclear energy diplomacy in the Middle East is said to be driven by the desire to 'expand the market share of its nuclear-power enterprises in the Middle East, elevate its image as a rising nuclear-energy power, and advance nuclear-energy cooperation between China and Saudi Arabia, the UAE, Iran, Algeria, Turkey, Egypt, Jordan, and Sudan through multi-lateral or bilateral mechanisms' (Sun et al. 2022: 41). Attempts have been made to categorise and interpret strategies as 'resource neo-mercantilism' or the exercise of 'great power politics' (Gueldry and Liang 2016). This is alongside studies on the energy diplomacy of powers such as Australia (Downie 2019) and in specific regions and over certain resources (such as oil in the Arctic) (Pincus and Ali 2015). Through such means, states globalise, export and at times impose their energy transition pathways on other states. This includes the important work of coordinating efforts by multilateral institutions around specific aspects of transitions such as their justice dimensions which continue to be sidelined by preoccupations with trade, investment and technology for transition (Newell et al 2023). A global perspective then becomes critical to understanding how the sustainability (or otherwise) of particular pathways is contingent on transition policies elsewhere through international modes of exchange and extraction and the extent to which dominant global actors endorse and are willing to finance them.

In terms of understanding the historical foundations and resourcing of the transition state, a global and historical perspective is also key, however. The wealth of many richer countries is a product first of looting and then the entrenchment and ongoing enactment of colonial relations of dependency and the institutions set up to oversee and preserve it (Rodney 2018 [1972]). There are historical links to imperial and colonial power (Newell 2021b; Bhambra and Newell 2022) as fossil capital was globalised, extracted and imported (Malm 2016) and the 'Plantationocene' expanded (Murphy and Schroering 2020). These are forms of historical 'lock-in', to use a favoured phrase in the transitions community (Unruh 2000), that need to be foregrounded in order to appreciate the current constitution of the global economy: *how* and *for whom* exchange is organised, who sets and enforces the rules of the game around trade and industrial policy and who gets punished for their violation of them. For example, discussions about how to decarbonise energy systems in the global South and support the adoption of supply-side policies have to start with a recognition that what drives the need to exploit and expand fossil fuel reserves is high levels of indebtedness, such that primary questions of economic justice have to be addressed in transition debates, as we saw in Chapter 7 on the welfare state. Being cognisant of these dynamics enables an appreciation of why debates about aid, technology transfer and capacity building for systems in the global South (with all their attendant presumptions about what can learned and emulated from the global North) often ring hollow in the absence of discussions about historical responsibility, ecological debts or even reparations. What this points to is the need to take seriously the uneven and combined development of transitions: not just their international relations but the global circulations of trade, production and finance between and across regions and classes which bind them together, historically and in the contemporary context.

This historicisation is central to an understanding of the development of the modern state. But the social and economic relations it describes also account for the maintenance of extractivism and inequality which underpin the development pathways of richer countries in the contemporary world. Countries on the periphery of the world economy, on the other hand, often lack a strong state able to exert preferences and exercise global power in the same way. As Wallerstein (1979: 133–134) notes:

> [O]nce capitalism was consolidated as a system and there was no turnback, the internal logic of its functioning, the search for maximum profit, forced it to continually expand – extensively to cover the globe, and intensively via the constant (if not steady) accumulation of capital, the pressure to mechanise work in order to make possible still further expansion of production, the tendency to facilitate and optimise rapid response to the permutations of the world market by the proletarianization of labour and the commercialisation of land.

From the get-go, the nation-state was unable to constrain the ambitions of global capital. 'Capitalism was from the beginning an affair of the world economy and not of nation states … capital has never allowed its aspirations to be determined by national boundaries in a capitalist world economy' (Wallerstein 1979: 19). On the contrary, the division of the world into competing sovereign states affords capital a source of structural power (Gill and Law 1988).

8.2.2 Global States and Policy Space

These forms of diplomatic practice and geopolitical manoeuvring are also observable within the multilateral system where global governance over key areas of sustainability transitions from food (Newell et al. 2017) to energy (Van de Graaf and Sovacool 2020) and water (Gupta and Pahl-Wostl 2013) impacts upon questions of access and the nature and directionality of transition pathways, reflective of who sets the rules for whom and on whose behalf, or whose rules rule (Newell and MacKenzie 2004).

Powerful states use their influence within multilateral institutions and banks to lever open new markets for energy investments by their companies through trade agreements, as a condition of structural adjustment, or through power sector reform programmes (Tellam 2000) and the construction of 'governance states' (Harrison 2004), extending and consolidating their power globally. This is an additional way in which states use and project their influence to the benefit of domestic capital to create new outlets for surplus production and new sites for accumulation overseas; whether it is the Brazilian state using commercial diplomacy to build a global production model for biofuels (Power et al. 2016), the British state promoting geothermal in Kenya (Newell and Phillips 2016), the Danish state promoting wind energy in South Africa (Baker et al. 2014) or the Chinese state creating new sites of accumulation for Chinese solar PV firms in the face of diminishing returns in domestic markets (Shen and Power 2017). For Hammarlund (1976: 168) in this regard, 'the state's principal mission is to promote favourable conditions for growth by reducing vulnerabilities and lowering the costs of national adaptation to the changing global energy situation'. Indeed, states have often faced criticism for using state aid money or export credits to support their energy industries overseas, even in ways which contradict their own climate change ambitions. The UK's decision to ban fracking at home while supporting the 'Vaca Muerta' fracking project in Argentina is a case in point (Ambrose 2019).

Shifting geopolitical conditions can quickly change states' preferences, however. Hence, Russia's invasion of Ukraine saw many European countries move from persuading many African countries to move away from fossil fuels to negotiating deals with them to export their gas to the region to replace lost access to Russian gas. Even at the climate COP27 summit in Egypt, while the climate talks debated language on phasing down fossil fuels, gas deals were being struck on the side lines of the negotiations. Egypt signed a memorandum of understanding with Germany to expand liquefied natural gas (LNG) export capacity by 2050, Tanzania committed to a $40 billion LNG deal with Equinor and Shell, while Germany and the US agreed to finance Egyptian renewables to 'free up' gas for export and Italy struck gas deals with Angola, Algeria and the Republic of Congo (Levantesi and Cooke 2022).

There are also clear differences among states in terms of resource endowments, autonomy and capacity to chart their own resource pathways (Power et al. 2016; Newell 2018). Silvester and Fiske (2023: 4) note: 'State projects straying too far from the norms promoted and defended through global organisations such as the United Nations, the International Monetary Fund, and the World Bank, and regional bodies such as the EU, tend to become excluded through economic and diplomatic sanctions, trade embargoes and so forth.' There are different ways of conceptualising these historical and contemporary relationships. Newell and Phillips (2016) draw on Gill's (1995) notion of 'disciplinary neoliberalism' to understand how key development agencies and multilateral development banks (MDBs) constrain the policy autonomy and 'developmental space' of poorer countries over whom they exercise control through their lending practices (Gallagher 2005). They suggest that this has occurred through a first wave of power sector reforms and then a second wave of interventions aimed at trying to address energy poverty (produced in part by the first wave of reforms) and the challenge of decarbonisation simultaneously: a dynamic usefully understood through the lens of 'governance states' (Harrison 2004). Harrison (2004: v) uses this term to describe the World Bank's attempts at 'reconciling a global political economy with its own designs and a specific set of challenges posed by the African region'. McDonald (2009), meanwhile, illustrates two key moments in neoliberal reform processes. One that dismantles the ideological and institutional vestiges of the previous Fordist-Keynesian regimes of accumulation and a second that creates new and revised modes of neoliberalism that respond to the failures and contradictions of the first wave of reforms. What follows is what we have seen in the energy sector: a belated recognition by the World Bank and other actors of the importance of the state and the limits of market-based approaches alone in the face of resistance and failed initiatives (World Bank 2010). The popularity of public–private partnerships, state-led development corporations and efforts to de-risk finance are examples of this partial recognition of the need to combine public and private power and resources. The projects remain the same, however. As Brenner and Theodore (2002: 362) put it, it is 'the creation of new infrastructure for market-oriented economic growth, commodification and the rule of capital'. Ironically, this rollout phase often implies a strengthening rather than a weakening of the state (Peck and Tickell 2002).

In states characterised by high levels of aid dependence and a high level of external influence, whereby actors such as the World Bank are intimately involved in policymaking, any clear distinction between the Bank and an autonomous state becomes difficult to discern. Energy pathways are narrowed or opened up by the presence and interests of global actors and their interactions with state elites (Sovacool and Brisbois 2019). In the case of the US Millennium Challenge Corporation's energy treaty with Ghana, the text of the compact gives the US donor the power 'to terminate the compact if Ghana were to substitute fossil fuels with environment-friendly options' (Glatzer et al. 2024: 477). This raises key questions about what instruments states have available to them to address the challenges of building sustainable economies in a socially just manner when many have ceded, and been placed under pressure to cede, direct control over key systems of provision such as energy, water and transport.

As well as looking at the organisation and political nature of the state, it is important to recognise the power that a range of public and private transnational actors bring to bear on seemingly state-based sustainability pathways. As with the organisation and political nature of the state, such global political economy dynamics are material to shaping the procedural and distributional effects of sustainability interventions. Issues of policy autonomy and 'developmental space' are important here: the ways in which the scope governments have to independently chart and follow their own policy pathways is affected by levels of aid dependence, trade ties and their status as importers or exporters and how much scope they have to impose conditions on investors around employment, local content requirements and so on (Power et al. 2016; Newell 2018). If poorer countries are to be enabled to pursue just transitions, they need to be allowed to deploy some of the policy tools that richer countries used to gain competitive advantage, nurture niche industries and generate both employment and revenue. These include support to infant industry, tax measures that support local procurement and training of workers, conditions on sourcing of local materials, preferential tariffs for local producers and more sustainable forms of production and looser forms of IPR protection (UNCTAD 2022). Strategies adopted by richer countries which appear to 'kick away the ladder' (Chang 2002) by constraining the policy space through multilateral and bilateral trade and investment rules that restrict the use of the policy tools described here will disincentivise transitions in many areas of the global South (Mulugetta et al. 2022).

Of course, it is not just global economic institutions that shape transition pathways. The climate regime itself is a significant 'landscape' actor. Newell and Bulkeley (2016: 650) suggest that considering how the climate regime can best support the embryonic transitions that are slowly taking form around the world 'requires a more nuanced understanding of the role of the state in governing these transitions beyond the notion of a cohesive state serving as rule-enforcer and transition manager'. They further suggest:

> Over the past two decades, international climate policy has emphasized a state-led, finance-driven model of technology deployment, where it is assumed establishing the appropriate costs of carbon and making these costs visible together with providing specific support for alternative energy sources (and other industrial processes) can induce a market-led transition to a new low-carbon economy (OECD, 2013; World Bank, 2012). Yet this model has been troubled both by the empirical realities of how, where and by whom low-carbon transitions are emerging, but also by critiques of their underlying assumptions … experience suggests, at the very least, that policy design and delivery in this area has not adequately accounted for the relationship between establishing market mechanisms and the political economies and practices of decarbonization. (Newell and Bulkeley 2016: 654)

Under the auspices of the United Nations Framework Convention on Climate Change (UNFCCC), states are the key actors that are expected to negotiate and implement international agreements. Likewise, as we saw in Chapter 2, according to transition theory, they are expected to perform key steering and convening functions among disparate social actors with competing interests in order to achieve transformative change (Meadowcroft 2009). However, in practice, state-led models of climate policy and energy transitions have been unfolding alongside an ever more significant role of transnational forms of climate governance and a multiplicity of actors and forms of authority involved in governing climate change at different scales (Bulkeley et al. 2014). Moreover, in many settings it is clear the state is not in a position to perform key roles in relation to innovation, lacks convening power and resources to deliver targets and goals and often also has only limited autonomy to assert policy preferences that diverge from those of transnational businesses, donors and other powerful states. Especially where they are heavily aid-dependent or through processes of power sector reform have relinquished a degree of control over the energy system to private providers (Tellam 2000), many states find it hard to set the terms of energy sector reforms aimed at decarbonisation – even if they have the political will to undertake them. In the case of Kenya, for example, donors funded and coordinated the conclusion of the country's National Action Plan on Climate Change (Newell et al. 2014).

The key point is not that states in such settings are powerless, as they still control large parts of systems of electricity generation and transmission. It is rather that state capacity and autonomy to chart and pursue lower-carbon pathways is shaped by relations with various other actors and is unevenly distributed. With regard to renewable investments, powerful countries such as South Africa can induce investors through its Renewable Energy Independent Power Producer Procurement Programme (REIPPPP). But in most cases investments result from commercial and geopolitical interest in new energy resources rather than because of state-led climate policy, responding to the saturation of domestic markets or attempts to build up global supply chains – as is the case with the high levels of interest shown by Chinese solar firms in investing in Sub-Saharan Africa (SSA) (Shen and Power 2017).

Rather than it being a matter of a national energy regime subject to singular transition pathways coordinated by the nation state, multiple forms of energy transition are being orchestrated by a range of actors within and beyond the nation state. What we see in practice are competing energy pathways being supported and financed by different combinations of business actors, nongovernmental organisations (NGOs), donors and parts of the state. The transnational governance of transitions, therefore, requires attention (Truffer 2012) together with a more nuanced, realistic and desegregated understanding of which states are able to deliver which types of transition. This will need to be informed by the degree of policy autonomy the state has from investors and donors, as well as consideration of the uneven capacity within the state to advance transitions in the face of powerful incumbent interests.

This suggests the need to engage in multilevel analysis to understand how power dynamics operate across scales, not in linear and uniform ways but mediated by the nature of institutions and material and discursive practices of power. States and actors within states navigate complexity in different ways since, as van de Graaf and Sovacool (2020: 200) note, 'There is no single, overarching global institution for governing energy. Instead, energy is governed by a Byzantine architecture of nested, parallel and overlapping regimes.' Insights from global political ecology are useful in understanding the macro–micro power dynamics linking global environmental politics to local outcomes (Peet et al. 2011; Newell and Bumpus 2012). Methodologically and analytically, this helps to understand and trace up and down the consequences of decision-making for particular regions and groups of people, or following finance or decisions through the assemblages which organise them. Rather than leave analysis at the international level, the challenge is to read and locate the global locally, and vice versa, through the relations of power which connect the two. Following the transition in this way also provides a more contextualised and nuanced account of how and why countries take up global initiatives, of which features of their institutions and political economies make them more likely to do so and more or less vulnerable to pressure from global governance actors.

8.3 Transforming the Global State

Given current trends in foreign policy, conflictual geopolitics and the systematic downplaying of sustainability priorities when they conflict with economic or high political priorities such as security and economic growth, and the comparably weak nature of multilateral institutions concerned with environmental issues, what are the entry points for transformation in the form of a realignment and rebalancing of politics and priorities in the global state?

Contemporary global economic institutions, in particular, operate as the vanguards of a 'petro-market civilisation' (Di Muzio 2015) by enabling, funding and protecting extractivist strategies in a fossil fuel dependent era. As we have seen, across global governance arenas from trade and investment, to food and agriculture, and energy and climate change, enormous political work is required to protect the current model of global extractivism from facing up to its contradictions. It is vital for its beneficiaries to accommodate threats to its everyday functioning and legitimacy from a range of environmental, labour, human rights activists and Indigenous social movements through discursive shifts and accommodations, and from limited participation in invited spaces and co-option through to the token allocation of funding for 'sustainable' projects alongside major extractivist ones.

Key shifts would be required to bring the mandates and powers of institutions in line with the imperatives of addressing sustainability. For example, the WTO could take on a stronger mandate to pursue sustainable development, allowing exemptions from normal trading rules for policies and measures aimed at tackling climate change or a range of other environmental threats, or be redesigned along the lines of a body on International Trade and Sustainable Development (LeQuesne 1996). Fundamental reform of the IMF and World Bank would also be required, if not the disbandment of those institutions, given the narrow ideologies and policy proscriptions they advocate that are incompatible with designing economies for a more sustainable world and, as noted, the policy and developmental space they deny to states to pursue autonomous pathways to sustainability. If fundamentally reformed, these institutions that have invested so heavily in fossil fuel infrastructures and agro-industrial complexes to date could play a central role in financing the transition to a more sustainable economy through taxes on fossil fuels, unsustainable meat production, illegal timber and the redistribution of fossil fuel subsidies through mechanisms such as a Global Transition Fund (Newell and Simms 2020). These institutions are alert to the need to reinvent and revalidate themselves in the face of sustainability challenges (as well as other aspects of the polycrisis) and to both accommodate threats to their legitimacy and position themselves to access and oversee new funding flows. For example, there are growing calls for a 'new Bretton Woods' and moves to position the World Bank as a global climate bank, 'the perfect climate change lender' according to *The Economist* that will somehow 'turn billions into trillions' by 'unlocking private finance' (The Economist 2023: 78), a goal that has evaded all endeavours to date.

As well as shifting mandates and institutional configurations, a clearer role might also be envisaged for the UN Security Council in condemning and coordinating action against state actions that violate environmental norms, boundaries and targets. There is growing interest in the use of international law and the international authority of the UN and its institutions as vehicles for promoting a safer and more sustainable world. Whether it is calls for a Fossil Fuel Non-Proliferation Treaty organised along the lines of existing nuclear non-proliferation treaties (Simms and Newell 2018; Newell and Simms 2019; Newell et al. 2022) or for international laws and tribunals on 'ecocide' and the rights of nature (Higgins 2010), international law and diplomacy provides one more set of tools in the struggle for a sustainable society. There have also been calls for a 'world constitution for environmental and ecological justice', including a World Environment Council and a World Environment Court (Eckersley 2004). *Planet Politics* advocates propose the creation of an 'Earth System Council' much like the current UN Security Council that would operate on the basis of majority voting with representation from Earth system scientists, major ecosystems, species groups and states (Burke 2016: 516). There is a clear commitment in many quarters, therefore, to an enhanced and bolder multilateralism to pursue security, social justice and sustainability as part of a broader vision of planetary justice.

Alongside this, there is also a need for the articulation of clear principles of transnational harm and liability for environmental negligence beyond state borders (Eckersley 2004; Mason 2005), including strengthened corporate liability regimes, such as Foreign Direct Liability, in order to hold companies to account for common and universal social, human rights and environmental responsibilities when operating abroad (Newell 2001; Ward 2002). Indeed, the push to democratise global governance extends to consciously delimiting the powers of global institutions, including overhauling or abandoning agreements such as the Energy Charter Treaty which are being used to undermine state action on energy transitions (Tienhaara et al. 2022). But it would also include preventing incursions on resources by global institutions under the guise of trade and investment treaties which aim to open up new resource frontiers for exploitation. Efforts to conserve and expand the space for national control over resources and protecting policy space for poorer countries can align with efforts to reclaim control over land, water and energy and key sectors of the economy such as health and education as part of a defence of the commons. Building on the discussion in this chapter, perhaps what this points to is the need for greater coordination and alignment across multi-level systems of governance but guided by the principle of subsidiarity which gives preference to local decision-making wherever possible.

Given the lack of substantive progress to date in respecting planetary boundaries while meeting the goals of the UN SDGs, an almost permanent crisis mode can be expected to become the norm for the institutions of global governance. As governments face increasing demands on their resources and tests of their legitimacy and ability to protect their citizens as a result, it is far from guaranteed that responses will be guided by a new ethic of humanitarianism, as opposed to a lifeboat ethic where richer populations protect themselves at the expense of others (Hardin 1968). Following on from normative commitments to enhance procedural justice in global governance, some activists and academics have sought to identify and promote greater direct and indirect representation of citizens in global decision-making through citizens' assemblies and the like (Stevenson and Dryzek 2014). In terms of the questions of voice and representation, there have been calls for an ombudsperson for future generations (Read 2012) following moves to create representatives for future generations in parliaments as diverse as Wales, Israel and Hungary. Burke et al. (2016: 516), meanwhile, propose that 'It is time to consider whether major ecosystems – such as the Amazon basin, the Arctic and Antarctic, and the Pacific Ocean – should be given the status of nations in the UN General Assembly and other bodies, or new organisations established with the sole purpose of preserving their ecological integrity.' How to balance the simultaneous desires to 'ecologise' and 'democratise' global governance and determine which objective takes precedence, where questions of urgency and the perceived desirability of top-down solutions might be allowed to trump the preference to deepen democracy across all spheres of global politics, will define the terrain of discussion about desirable and feasible strategies for aligning the existing system of global governance with the imperatives of sustainability for many years to come.

Renewed internationalism might be driven by the leadership of 'good states' (Lawler 2013) exercising normative power globally. Explicitly normative projects often invite scepticism and ridicule where they seek to reconcile power and principle in international politics. As Lawler (2013: 19) suggests, 'Overt declarations of morality in a state's foreign policy pronouncements are to be treated largely as masks for self-regarding conduct, a moralism aimed primarily at a domestic audience or simply a waste of breath.' Despite this, he notes: 'long-standing Scandinavian social democratic internationalist sentiment in which the State would not only strive to be a dutiful member of a community of states, but also would endeavour to enhance and extend that sense of community beyond the confines of the West through policies of solidarity, with the developing world' (Lawler 2013: 20). This chimes with Woodrow Wilson's 14 Points and earlier efforts to construct a liberal international order. Global solidarities expressed through notions such as 'responsibility to protect' and humanitarian intervention and their limits are well known, in particular the 'moral cover' they can provide for military moves by any other name. In the end, of course, it is critical not to fetishise the state as intrinsically good or bad but rather to contextualise state–society complexes that give rise to and sustain more ethical conduct domestically and internationally. Lawler (2013: 34) reflects:

> States – Good States – may be the necessary agents of its expression and concrete realisation, but outside of a fascistic statism, the Good State only makes moral sense in relation to peoples, be they within or outside of its nominal boundary. Determining who those people are and what precisely their relationship is to the State, especially in the fluid complexities of the contemporary global order, must remain a matter of constant scrutiny and debate. Context is everything. Equally, the State, good or otherwise, can make no claim to exclusive or permanent agency, even if present circumstances suggest that States are likely to remain key enactors or inhibitors of change for the foreseeable future.

Global principles articulated in climate treaties around the 'just transition', 'common but differentiated responsibilities and respective capabilities' recognise uneven historical responsibilities and contemporary capacity for addressing the imperatives of sustainability transitions and the need to compensate the 'loss and damage' already caused by inaction. As such, they recognise the interconnected nature of transition processes, replete with calls for technology transfer and capacity building and funding mechanisms, and provide entry points for future international cooperation aimed at the managed and fair decline of fossil fuels (Van Asselt and Newell 2022). But they actively avoid scrutiny and accountability for the reasons why that finance, technology and capacity are required in the first place, let alone the nature of the historical accumulation of wealth that lies beneath them. Just transitions, to deal with their interplay and the potential for burdens and opportunities to be captured by some and passed on to others, will need international law and institutional oversight to manage the international relations of transition (Muttitt and Kartha 2020). The global governance of just transitions would require a shared duty of care to prevent the use of spatial and temporal fixes to pass on the costs of transition to others.

For this to happen globally, and across a highly uneven international system, global institutions have a potentially vital role to play in supporting and implementing just transitions that align with principles regarding the procedural, distributional, intergenerational and recognition-based aspects of justice, as well as help to address the temporal and spatial aspects of transitions (Heffron and McCauley 2018). Global institutions active in areas as diverse as trade, investment, labour, industrial policy, environment and human rights will need to play an active part in shaping and implementing just transitions, as well as mediating the different interpretations of justice at various scales of governance (Fraser 2009). Combined with the SDGs which, though full of tensions and contradictions, provide the sort of multi-sectoral universal perspective on the need for transformation, there may be grounds for hope about the progressive global governance of transitions. This is notwithstanding the need to confront questions of power and politics expressed in the formulation of *whose* and *which* transition.

9

Reimagining the State

This final chapter of the book pulls together key strands of analysis and insights from the preceding chapters and explores future potential for moving from an environmental or even a transition state (one that effectively manages key transitions in critical sectors of the economy without questioning dominant rationales and modes of statehood) to a state which plays a key critical convening, orchestrating and enabling role in supporting transformation of the drivers of unsustainability and where sustainability is at the centre of state practice.

The discussion in this book has made very clear that if the social, democratic and ecological dimensions of disruption and acceleration associated with the transformations required to move the world onto a more sustainable pathway are to be adequately attended to, we have to centre the state in our analysis. Only the state has the powers of convening, regulating, distributing and enforcing in legitimate, transparent and inclusive ways that will be called on to accelerate just transitions. As we have seen throughout the book, of course, often those roles are not performed in ways that many would class as legitimate, transparent and inclusive. And yet we abandon the project of state reform at our peril in a context in which short-term and large-scale change is urgently required and attention to the critical task of how to bridge the two takes centre stage.

Precisely because of the compromised, inadequate and often problematic exercise of state power in sustainability transitions, there are many other actors attempting to fill, incompletely and inadequately, but necessarily, key governance gaps around (grassroots) innovation, (patient) finance, (sustainable) welfare, (civil) regulation, (public) participation and (deepening) democracy and so on. In some cases, this takes the form of scaling up and supporting transition initiatives that originate in businesses, among cities or from community-based organisations. Some states are also clearly better placed and more able to perform those roles than others, suggesting the limits of overly generic prescriptions for the role of the state in sustainability transitions when in reality what is possible is shaped by very diverse contexts. As we have seen throughout the book, the state is not a monolithic entity and there are opportunities and spaces within and beyond the state to forge new alliances for progressive change, while recognising that such spaces are both limited and shrinking in some parts of the world. There are also opportunities (as well as challenges) presented by the devolution of state power and the democratisation of decision-making and control over systems of provision such as food and energy at the community level. In federal systems, this can magnify battles over authority between the state and federal states over who captures the rent from procuring and managing resources.

There is a danger here that responsibility gets pushed back and forth between different arenas of power. We can observe this in current discussions about the formation of citizens' assemblies on climate change where local councils are keen to emphasise how little power and authority they have over decision-making on transport, energy and housing policy, for example, to deflect citizen demands for more ambitious action up to the national level; while national governments claim many decisions over service provision are best taken locally. As well as more 'top-down' interventions, the state also needs to harness more bottom-up, alternative innovations, allow space for them to flourish and commit resources to them, while at the same time address the pressing need to roll back state support to incumbents as part of a deliberate rebalancing of forces aligned in favour of efforts to accelerate progressive transformations. The state then exercises power through inaction too: tolerating, allowing alternatives to flourish or at the very least not crushing or repressing them. By emphasising the importance of democracy throughout the book, the point is not to romanticise bottom-up change and grassroots mobilisation as the only way to deliver rapid and progressive transitions. Indeed, it is important to challenge the idea that rapid change is always necessarily top-down and regressive or market-led, when many rapid and progressive transitions have been state-led, often backed by progressive social forces such as labour and Indigenous people's movements (Newell and Simms 2020). But it is to say that there is both need and significant scope to open up the entrepreneurial, industrial, military, welfare, democratic and global state to greater citizen engagement and democratic scrutiny, a political shift that may well be a prerequisite for transitions to sustainability being both effective and just.

9.1 From the Transition State to States of Transformation?

How might we move from a transition state, where the governance and management of transitions aimed at reconciling them with the imperatives of the dominant economic system becomes an overarching state task, to states of transformation where the state plays an active and enabling role in addressing the multiple sources of unsustainability in economic, political and social systems as part of a broader project of transformation? What might such a project of repurposing and refashioning the state at this historical conjuncture look like?

Firstly, we have to start with an acknowledgement that there are no states that, by design, have policies aligned with the scale or degree of shifts in levels of production and consumption to make them sustainable or that operate within planetary boundaries. This is the case even if the Happy Planet Index shows that some states are far more sustainable than others, or states such as China claim to be engaged in a project of building an ecological civilisation. On one level, this makes it a normative and speculative discussion. But there is a growing recognition of scope for the greening of the state (Eckersley 2004; Barry and Eckersley 2005; Hausknost and Hammond 2021), exploring the types of legal, constitutional and institutional innovations we might expect to see in a greening state or in a fully fledged 'green state' (Barry and Eckersley 2005; Barry 2008) capable of supporting a more transformative vision.

Optimistically, accounts of the 'environmental' state show how there has been a growing entrenchment and institutionalisation of environmental policy as a key rationale and component of state policy and regulatory authority (Meadowcroft 2004). Assuming a broader range of responsibilities for resource management, protection and conservation and steering transitions, this argument finds strong resonance in claims of ecological modernisation, for example, regarding the ability of states to adapt their core functions to ecological imperatives (Mol 2003) suggesting the potential of a 'transition state'. On this basis perhaps, 'it is too hasty to assume that the social structures of international anarchy, global capitalism and the liberal democratic state are necessarily anti-ecological and mutually reinforcing or that they foreclose the possibility of any progressive transformations of states as governance structures' (Eckersley 2004: 14).

Nevertheless, in more normative visions of a state transformed, such as a 'Green state', Eckersley (2004: 83) reminds us, 'securing private capital accumulation would no longer be the defining feature or primary raison d'être of the state. The state would be more reflexive and market activity would be disciplined, and in some cases curtailed, by social and ecological norms.' This implies a reinvention of the state is in order: a broadening and deepening of the notion of ecological stewardship and the boundaries of the political community which the state serves and can be held accountable to. Hence the 'new' role of the state would be as 'ecological steward and facilitator of transboundary democracy' (Eckersley 2004: 3) grounded in new forms of ecological citizenship. In this reading, 'the anti-ecological behavioural dynamics that are generated by the social structures of international anarchy, global capitalism and administrative hierarchy can be reversed' (Eckersley 2004: 15). They can be reversed in her view through a combination of more ambitious environmental multilateralism, ecological modernisation and (transnational) environmental advocacy. In the case of the former, this builds on the development of principles of precaution and 'polluter pays', 'common heritage' and 'common but differentiated responsibilities' which appear in treaties covering issues such as climate change, acid rain and protection of Antarctica as well as Principle 21 of the Stockholm Declaration, for example, which places upon states 'the responsibility to ensure that activities within their jurisdiction or control do not cause damage to the environment of other States or of areas beyond the limits of national jurisdiction'.

The challenge is that despite each of these strategies being adopted over the last 50 years, trends towards environmental collapse deepen and accelerate. Critiques of ecological modernisation (Bailey et al. 2011), of the limits of even accelerated forms of earth systems governance (Stirling 2015) and of environmental advocacy (Dauvergne 2016) point to the limits of these strategies. It is also the case that for every progressive environmental principle in international law, commercial trade and investment law, which is frequently afforded greater protection and enforcement powers, provides a counterweight and often exercises a decisive influence, as discussed in Chapter 8. Hence, the mere expansion in the growth, volume and reach of environmental legislation should not be taken as a proxy for a broader greening of the state given significant non-implementation and non-enforcement and the undermining effect of business-as-usual and anti-environmental policy in areas such as trade, energy and industrial policy. This underscores the argument of the book about the need to engage with all aspects of state power and not just those which the 'environmental state' has sought to attend to so far.

Clear criteria about what constitutes a Green state capable of overseeing transformative change are elusive, therefore, and there is a slippage between the 'environmental state' embodying the notion of the ecological modernisation of the economy and a 'Green state': a more normative re-envisioning of the state on ecological grounds, one which is more likely to support states of transformation. For many, principles of post-sovereign governance, deepening democracy and non-militarism would have to be at the heart of configuring a Green state, principles which underpin some of the more transformative proposals reviewed in each of the chapters in the book. At the most general level, a Green state might be expected to use state power domestically and globally in defence of the environment or the pursuit of transitions to sustainability. For Christoff (2005: 41), 'Green states, were they to exist, would be characterized by the predominance of types of state activity aimed at strong ecological modernization' or where ecological considerations are at the core of state activities (Meadowcroft 2004). In this regard, Eckersley (2004) argues that Scandinavian and Nordic states most closely resemble the Green state, while others (Dryzek et al. 2003) suggest Germany is most likely to fulfil this potential. These examples raise questions about the ways in which wealth is accumulated in unsustainable ways to finance the activities of the 'green state' (oil wealth in Norway or destruction of forests in Sweden, for example), or of 'outsourcing' transitions: undertaking them by importing required food, water and energy from neighbouring states (such as, in the case of Germany, banning nuclear energy at home but importing electricity from nuclear and coal from other countries). This underscores the need to always keep in mind the relationality and interdependence of transitions, combined with a recognition of the accumulated ecological debts and privileged disposition of post-industrial states built on histories of environmental destruction at home and abroad (Acción Ecológica 1999). But it is also notable that these examples of 'green states' are also more in line with a 'transition state' than states leading transformative change.

Green states need to be resourced. As raised in Chapter 7 on the welfare state, a key outstanding question is how the state would sustain itself in a post-growth economy consistent with a more transformative project. From where will the wealth come that will be taxed and redistributed? It is certainly the case that some drains on public expenditure might fall away. Fewer resources would be required to support the military if the more transformative visions of the military state described in Chapter 5 were to be pursued. There would be fewer health and social costs for a welfare state to bear if the industrial state is transformed in the ways described in Chapter 4. Some might advocate for 'progressive austerity' in this regard where the curtailing of some areas of state expenditure can be a positive thing if combined with policies and programmes that tackle the root causes of ill health and economic insecurity, for example, rather than merely their symptoms. This relates to Dobson's (1990) telescope analogy whereby some areas of state power might be extended while others are contracted in pursuit of a sustainable society.

Also, in more normative iterations of the Green state, there have been attempts to reimagine the state as 'public ecological trustee', the embodiment of the collective will and protector of the public good, as well as good ecological citizen globally (Eckersley 2004). Important here is the notion of a Green 'public sphere' which rests on 'deepening the democratic accountability and responsiveness of states to their citizens' environmental concerns, while also extending democratic accountability to the environmental concerns of transnational civil society, international organizations and the society of states in general' (Eckersley 2004: 14–15). This resonates with calls to extend and deepen notions of transnational environmental harm for which states and other transnational actors can be held to account (Mason 2005). This would be accompanied by the promotion and embedding of deeper forms of ecological citizenship as part of a new social and ecological contract between states and their citizens (Dobson 2003). A new 'ecological social contract' would require citizens gaining increased decision-making power over the design and shape of the economy, society and politics, but within (ecological) limits set by the state and perhaps enshrined in a constitution (Dobson 2014). In other words, 'Ecological freedom for all can only be realised under a form of governance that enables and enforces ecological responsibility' (Eckersley 2004: 107).

For Barry (2008: 4), 'green constitutionalism' offers a way of 'conjoining a green commitment to human rights, procedural democratic rights and rights of participation, community right to know laws with protection of the environment and the political regulation of the economy for social and environmental and not just economic objectives such as profit-making'. Constitutionalism potentially provides the means to institutionalise environmental rights and confer legal standing upon more-than-human interests (such as rights for nature) and the institutionalisation of the precautionary principle. Importantly, constitutional-level political changes can alter and redistribute political and economic power within and between societies, especially with regard to 'setting and changing the terms on which the economy and its agents operates' (Barry 2008: 5). This is vital, since for this ecological re-embedding to be achieved, the economy must be politically re-embedded within society and social norms and attuned to non-economic institutions and objectives (Polanyi 1980 [1944]). This would imply constitutional and legal regulation of the economy 'to ensure that it does not grow and develop in a manner which undermines its own ecological foundations' (Barry 2008: 8).

Many question whether the liberal democratic state is up to the task of steering the economy and society along a genuinely ecologically sustainable path given the challenges it now faces, discussed in Chapter 6: compromised and constrained both by capital incumbents and by workers and their trade union representatives dependent on an extractivist economy for their livelihoods. There are grounds to fear both the omnipotence of the state and control over the lives of its citizens but also its seeming impotence in the face of the scale and complexity of the ecological problems and polycrises it confronts. This points again to the need in discussions of strategy to be precise about which state, which type of state and which state functions need to be changed and how. Hence, while only the state has the power, resources and legitimacy to deliver change at the speed and scale now required, there is plentiful evidence that even if states have the ability to deliver such change, their willingness to so is often lacking. But this is where the struggle for a different state, for a different society and world ecology, starts from: the work of reclaiming, reimagining and democratising the state.

Viewed this way, decentralising control and power over key systems around energy, food, water and transport provision is critical but more fundamentally is about extending democratic control over the economy and military establishment. Democratising elite control and the devolution of power serves to shift some of the discussion about desirable, achievable pathways to sustainability away from those actors that benefit most from unsustainability and the pursuit of business-as-usual and conventional 'plug-and-play' transition strategies of pricing, innovation and incremental reform. This would displace the narrower discussion of which combinations of big technologies and infrastructures can meet rising demand for ever greater production and consumption without first attending to the possibility of reducing demand and questioning patterns of consumption and production through changes to work, welfare and taxation, for example. Such shifts allow us to pose (and engage with) the more difficult questions of who and what transitions are for, who sets their terms and the overall direction of change. Who frames the issue of who and what is to be transitioned, towards what end and over which time frame will affect who is entitled to be involved and which pathways are pursued. These are first and foremost questions of democratic struggle.

For this reason, transformations of the state will most likely start in civil and political society in what Polanyi (1980 [1944]) described as 'moves' which might over time spawn movements, even counter-hegemonic ones (Gramsci 1971), gaining footholds, extracting concessions all the while building the foundations of alternative visions of a more ecological society. This is the political work that Jessop (2012: 215) describes 'to connect particular local struggles, generalize them and link them to a universal project of socio-ecological transformation'. For the military state to be repurposed and its power reduced, countervailing efforts to contest and reverse the hold that militarism exerts over the collective imagination about the means and ends of security and sense of power and place in the world will need to be mobilised. An entrepreneurial state would not operate untethered from the pursuit of pressing social and environmental priorities under the illusion that by bringing technology and innovations to market broader collective welfare will inevitably be enhanced. But again, this requires collective demands for a different type of entrepreneurial state encouraging social enterprise, community resource provision, solidarity economies and mutual aid based on more convivial and less individualised and market-centred values and ways of living. The same goes for an industrial state guided by a different vision for the economy that would have to emerge and take hold in civil society in the first instance, as is starting to happen with regard to the increasing penetration of ideas of post- and degrowth in even mainstream fora where once they were completely ridiculed and sidelined. For a global state to exercise responsible and benign leadership for the collective good, not just of its own citizens but of all global citizens, a strong backlash against nationalistic, parochial, ethnicist and xenophobic politics needs to take hold grounded in a recognition of the fact that we all share one planet whose destiny affects each and every one of us is the ultimate expression of the (often abused) notion that 'we are in it together'.

This implies new imagines or pluriverses that are able to break through the 'democratic glass ceiling' discussed in Chapter 6 which operates to restrict a politics grounded in different values and visions of the good life because of the material dependence many people have for their labour and livelihoods upon an ecocidal economic system, tying their fate to the reproduction and expansion of that system in spite of the costs it imposes on our well-being. Such an alternative vision would need to have at its core a new notion of prosperity grounded in a fundamental reset of the economy around its core pillars of work (and income), production and consumption. Pursuing such a vison, in turn, requires the sorts of power shifts discussed throughout the book between the state and capital, capital and labour, the state and citizens, as well as between states in the global political economy, which are only achievable through struggles and contestation across each of these axes. Returning to the Poulantzian idea of the state as a 'condensation' of wider social relations, these relations can be reconfigured through resistance and mobilising in key windows of opportunity, often triggered in the first instance by crises where elite power is threatened, new social contracts and concessions negotiated and granted and the balance of social forces reconfigured. A key question from the point of view of sustainability transitions is whether such a move (in a Polanyian sense) or movement could take shape around a post-industrial and post-'productionist' worldview which questions the goals and orientation of the system and not just the division of the spoils from its operation.

9.2 Conclusion

What emerges from the analysis in this book is caution about the possibility of a generic one-size-fits-all account or set of prescriptions about the scope for change in the state. A more holistic and geographical account of state power suggests leverage points and openings for change and contestation exist within and across many of the sites where state power operates, albeit shaped by historical inequalities and constrained by continuing patterns of uneven development. Some states have the power (militarily, economically and politically) to impose their vision of transition on others, while weaker or more dependent states find they have less autonomy to chart their own preferred pathways towards a more sustainable future. But an intricate ecology of power links them which affords multiple sites of resistance through complex capillaries of power (Foucault 1980). Given the interconnected and global nature of the economy, it is also the case that change in one site can reverberate and trigger change elsewhere, consistent with the notion of an ecosystem of transformation.

Whatever the ultimate vision or preference for the role of the transition state or its more transformative green incarnation, its existence and continuation in the short term represent a reality we will have to deal with, either as a force for good, providing protection and regulation for the common good, or as a vehicle of oppression and the centralisation of control and resources. In reality, we will have to deal with both aspects of state power, benign and malign. Eckersley (2004: 5) puts it the following way:

> [O]ne can expect states to persist as major sites of social and political power for at least the foreseeable future and that any green transformations of the present order will, short of revolution, necessarily be state-dependent … And if states are so implicated in ecological destruction, then an inquiry into the potential for their transformation or even their modest reform into something that is at least more conducive to ecological sustainability would seem compelling.

We need to keep in mind here Hedley Bull's (1979: 112) caution about engaging in a 'counsel of despair' by demanding the abolition of the state as a prerequisite for building an alternative society, rather than building upon what is there. Whichever way we look at it, the state will play a crucial, albeit contradictory, role in the politics of green transformations (Mazzucato 2015; Newell 2015; Johnstone and Newell 2018). From law maker to law enforcer, as the bearer of the monopoly on the use of force, as broker and intermediary, convenor of key social and economic actors, as notional representative of the will of the people (in many contexts at least), the state is clearly vital to the prospects of a sustainable society.

The problem lies in the fact that states have failed to turn around the key trends towards overshooting planetary boundaries, such that short-lived victories for environmental campaigners, or even seemingly effective environmental treaties, may have bought us time but have yet to buck the march towards environmental ruin. Pockets of decoupling and gains in efficiencies are too often dwarfed and overwhelmed by overall increases in resource use, underscoring the need for more fundamental shifts to reduce levels of production and consumption. These might include processes of enabling and overseeing political decentralisation and a reorientation of the global economy towards meeting local needs which require active state policy and intervention including plans for national resilience. Key challenges include how to square the demand for an internationalist, developmental, interventionist and, in many ways, Keynesian state, able and willing to stand up to transnational capital and powerful financial actors, with visions of a smaller and less well-resourced post-growth state.

Alliances and solidarities with other (global) states and social movements will be key to realising any such vision. Indeed, historically, progressive state leadership has often come from governments with strong links to social movements. Examples include Indigenous groups in Bolivia supporting Evo Morales, Indigenous and environmental groups helping to secure protection for the rights of nature in the Ecuadorian state, labour unions in advancing Roosevelt's New Deal in the US, the UK Labour Party's creation of a free National Health Service for all, Lula's zero hunger pledge in Brazil and organisations of the Left in supporting the government of Petro in Colombia in his call to leave oil reserves in the ground. Feminist, LGBTQI, human rights and disability movements have played critical roles in shifting state policy, reversing discriminatory state policy and culturing shifts in social values.

An historicised and contextualised account of *what* states have transformed, *when* and *for whom* provides a useful analytical point of departure and political entry point for challenging dominant orthodoxies and imaginaries about what is possible at this political conjuncture. Finance has been mobilised for green new deals and the Inflation Reduction Act (IRA) and for furlough schemes during the Covid pandemic when we were told such finance did not exist. Critical infrastructures such as railways have been rolled out over short time frames which contradict claims about the necessarily slow pace of infrastructural change. Bold new state visions get adopted and new social compacts realised as we have been in Colombia, Brazil, Bolivia and elsewhere, but they have to be fought for in the face of intense incumbent resistance. Governments have voluntarily set aside reserves of lucrative fossil fuels to show leadership on climate change, forming alliances to move beyond oil and gas and to avoid stranded assets, confounding the expectations of economists that it would be irrational to do so. Hence, while extractivism is hardwired into the industrial state, bold moves can and do occur underpinned by social pressure from below for a different political mandate and approach to governing. Behaviours change, models of production can be radically overhauled and social values shift. The pandemic showed the potential of the former and rapidly evolving attitudes towards race and sexuality illustrate the latter.

State forms and functions expand and contract in light of shifting demands made of the state, reconfigurations of global power and social pressure. The welfare state did not exist. It had to be created through social demands and mobilisation and, as we saw in Chapter 7, emerged as part of a new social compact after the Second World War in many settings and served the political purpose of pacifying demands for more far-reaching forms of redistribution amid a fear of socialism. The global state waxes and wanes with different degrees of commitment to internationalism and multilateralism on the part of leading states and hegemons. Crisis in the form of war formed the backlog to the creation of the Bretton Woods institutions to reset economic relations between nations. Contemporary waves of nationalism and xenophobia on the other hand are seeing key powers disengage from global institutions and duties. We saw in the chapters on the entrepreneurial and industrial states that these state functions are garnering renewed attention with the return of industrial policy, 'moonshot' projects and vast Keynesian projects of infrastructural financing and development such as the Inflation Reduction Act (IRA) in the US and the Green Deal in Europe. The industrial state was greatly expanded by the East Asian Developmental states in the 1990s and Latin American countries experimented with import substitution industrialisation to strengthen their policy space and economic might, but these state functions have been eroded in the face of neoliberal reforms. Even the military state has been deliberately shrunk in an imposed way in post-war Germany and Japan, and by design in countries like Switzerland and Costa Rica, while elsewhere it expanded, fuelled by a military-industrial complex always on the lookout for new global military threats. These shifts are uneven across the world even when unfolding within the same macro geopolitical context. The democratic state is retracting and shrinking in many parts of the world and even within the same state, such as the UK where some forms of deliberative democracy are being expanded (through climate assemblies and the like) at the very same time as coercive policing bills are introduced to suffocate protest and dissent.

State legitimation relies on the use of spatial and temporal fixes, the granting of concessions to popular movements and successful coalition building to prop up dominant regimes and class interests. But there are limits to these strategies. As Jessop (2008: 8) suggests 'structural coherence and social cohesion is necessarily limited in so far as it depends on one or more spatio-temporal fixes to displace and/or defer the effects of certain contradictions and lines of conflict'. The need to acquire ever more land to offset growing emissions on the part of states and capital in the core of the global political economy cannot be sustained amid intensifying competition and claims on available land; likewise, the race to secure access to critical mineral frontiers. The escalating costs of funding a welfare state to deal with the growing health impacts of polluted populations or unemployed workers whose jobs have been made redundant by artificial intelligence (AI) are hard to sustain in a context of neoliberal cost-cutting. These pressures and contradictions put pressure on the fragile coalitions and social compacts carefully constructed to preserve hegemonic power and look set to lead to further transformations in the state if these ecological and social contradictions are not attended to. We know from historical experience, informed by regulation theory, that dominant regimes of accumulation, such as the Fordist one, come to an end, are displaced by restless capital (Perez 2002) and modes of regulation challenged and transformed through struggle. As Jessop (2008: 24) suggests, accumulation strategies provide only 'a provisional, partial and unstable "substantive unity" to the various interconnected formal manifestations of the capital relation'.

The state may be *primus inter pares* in many contexts, but some roles will be indirect and function at the level of orchestration and steering, consistent with polycentric models of governance and a recognition of the reality of shared and delegated authority over many of the key processes and drivers of unsustainability as a result of previous (often self-inflicted) waves of neoliberal reform of the state and the multiplicity of governance actors across all levels and spaces of decision-making. Ironically, precisely because of the historical failures of states and private actors to address the ecological crisis, the state will be called upon to deal with emergencies as environmental disasters continue to increase in frequency and magnitude. Depending on how it responds to these situations, the 'disaster state' may either enhance its power through the popular legitimacy it gains from acting decisively and effectively on behalf of its citizens or be the target of a blame for its failure to deal with a multitude of problems for which it will be held to account, but over which in many cases it may only wield indirect control and responsibility.

A state committed to positive transformative change might look very different. It might be a smaller state, if military functions are reduced and greater control passed to local authorities and regions as part of projects to deepen the democratic state. But there may be a scope for a more activist and interventionist state, not afraid to stand up to incumbent actors and interests, willing to construct visions and plans for a sustainable society, using key state levers of tax and industrial policy and support to sustainable innovation but held to account for them through stronger mechanisms of citizen engagement and oversight. A state willing to support socially useful and ecological sustainable forms of technology and investment in new infrastructures, to redistribute wealth through a basic income scheme and to tax corporations and pollution to redirect resources to where they are most needed to centre sustainable welfare as a core goal sounds like an attractive proposition. As Andrew Simms (2013) shows in his book *Cancel the Apocalypse*, though you will not find a single state adopting all of these progressive measures at the same time, you will find many of them in some combination being implemented, or that have been in the past, such that there is 'evidence-based hope' that states can and do bring about progressive social and environmental change.

Recognising and reconciling the disparate (and at times competing) functions that states play simultaneously will pose serious challenges. It will require a state whose functions and roles can expand in some areas where necessary but also shrink and retract in others where its presence is no longer desirable or required. Here the state can extend and contract depending on function: retract around surveillance, control and dispossession, and extend in terms of regulation and distribution. The concrete politics of building such a state require further thought: in particular, how to unsettle the relations of power which bind the state, military and industrial sectors together so closely, and which will be united in their resistance to attempts to take power away from them. This will need to be addressed by counter-movements whose explicit agenda is a very different type of politics and a transformed notion of the role of the state and whom it should serve. These examples suggest the scope to recast state functions again around a more transformative project. And despite the hardwired relationship between the state and extractivism, the formal preoccupation with economic growth is a relatively modern phenomenon, embedded from the Second World War onwards in systems of national accounting (Dale 2012). Divorced from its currently close relationship to ideas of development and progress, there may be scope through social struggle to redefine the latter in general and the state's role in supporting sustainable well-being in particular. Da Costa Vieira (2024) suggests: 'Ultimately … when it comes to governmental action, tackling the root causes of the issue means severing the link between the state and capitalism's accumulation imperative – only then can the state be truly greened.'

Social movements can widen cracks, exploit fragilities and vulnerabilities in the system and mobilise around contradictions within the state to advance their interests and build the case for alternative counter-hegemonic projects. As Jessop (2008: 8) suggests, 'There is no unconditional guarantee that the modern state will always (or ever) be essentially capitalist'. As we have seen in the book, the emergence of the environmental, welfare and democratic state emerged through protracted and non-linear processes of struggle between social forces articulating demands of the state and contradictory visions of the state, society and the environment. It seems likely that this will be the way in which more transformative ideas about the state and sustainability will take hold. Arguing that it is 'difficult to imagine how such transformations could ever come to enjoy the necessary momentum on a societal scale in the absence of comprehensive state involvement', Buch-Hansen et al. (2024: 81) propose key roles for a more transformational state in supporting degrowth from national action for 'sustainable welfare' through prescribed reductions in working hours, progressive taxation, basic income schemes and redistribution, taking control of key industries, as well as devolution of powers to the local state, through to transnational action aimed at reforming global institutions in the ways described in Chapter 9 and aimed, in part, to avoid capital flight by corporations seeking to play governments off against one another. How such change would come about would very much reflect the prevailing political, economic and social nature of diverse state–society complexes across the world: the degree to which economies are more liberal or coordinated and the extent to which civic space exists to articulate alternative visions and mobilise counter-movements.

But the polycrises we are currently living through create new forms of legitimation crises for states and those ruling elites governing the global economy (Helleiner 2024). The increasingly obvious inability of the dominant economic system to protect life on earth and enhance human and more-than-human well-being, apparent in an array of what Gramsci (1971) called 'morbid symptoms' associated with an order in decline, affords opportunities to advance alternatives. This leads, Babic (2020: 72) suggests, to a '"crisis of authority" that leaves an ideological void and thus the possibility for different crisis solutions'. Conceptualised as 'systemic chaos' (Arrighi 2010) by some, or a period of what Gramsci (1971) called an 'interregnum', in which inter-elite and class conflict intensifies over the formation of a new hegemonic bloc that can chart a new pathway for the global economy, there are openings for social and environmental activists to struggle for a very different state–society complex. As scholars and activists, this requires us to revisit and widen our theories of change and adopt a more plural understanding of possible sites and sources of change and transformation. As we saw in Chapter 2 on theories of the state and then applied throughout the book, state practice increasingly seems to represent an evolving attempt to manage and contain multiple contradictions. The contradiction between growth and sustainability is fast becoming one of the most central and irreconcilable which the state faces, expressed as an increasingly manifest inability to contain (let alone reverse) the ecological and social effects of the economic model which industrial states have produced and continually seek to reproduce. The discussion in the book about the need for states to square legitimation and accumulation, however, creates openings for transformative change. Quastel (2016: 347) suggests 'the state is not necessarily a growth state; it also deals with crises and contradictions that emerge within capitalist economies.' The need to be seen to act on environmental and health crises in recent years has created pressures to shift state practice and priorities in order to accommodate threats to state legitimacy in the form of the questioning of its ability to perform basic state functions of protection.

We need to engage then with the relational nature of the state and its embeddedness within society, the economy and ecology. Strategies have to reflect this basic reality and not treat the state as an aspatial and universal, homogeneous governance structure abstracted from social, economic and ecological relations. In reality, the messy and everyday politics of transformation will necessarily be a function of the interplay between competing pathways and their associated ideologies, visions, networks and institutions, between more state-led, citizen-led and market-led pathways (Scoones et al. 2015). How they interact and unfold will be a function of the nature and capacity of the state, the role of political culture and where countries are located in the global economy such that moving from a transition state to state-led transformation will be an uneven and globally differentiated process. Effective strategies will need to reflect this if they are to succeed. It is a process rather than a clear end point regarding the form and character of the state. It will be a protracted and conflictual struggle given the changing nature of demands on the state from human and non-human sources in the face of ever-shifting challenges.

A more disruptive politics of transformation requires us to acknowledge and then challenge and change the relations of power where the state sits at the centre. It invites us to take a wider view of politics and a deeper view of the state to understand its role in disruption and acceleration. This requires us to better understand the military, global, welfare, industrial, entrepreneurial and democratic functions of the state and how these may impinge on the possibilities of transformative trajectories. There is no one model of 'the state', and just as there are varieties of capitalism, so too there will be varieties of transition and transformation. But, in most cases, the state is at the centre of competing claim-making about the politics of different pathways and continues to be critical to attempts to build a more sustainable world for which all of us now need to strive.

Notes

1 Introduction

1. Lawrence et al. (2022: 2) suggest: 'A global polycrisis occurs when crises in multiple global systems become causally entangled in ways that significantly degrade humanity's prospects.' See also Lawrence et al. (2024).

3 The Entrepreneurial State

1. African Union Development Agency-NEPAD (AUDA-NEPAD), 'Agenda 2063: Launch of decade of acceleration' (online), www.nepad.org/programme/grow-africa.
2. United Nations Climate Change, 'Work of the climate high-level champions' (online), https://climatechampions.unfccc.int/system/breakthrough-agenda/.

6 The Democratic State

1. United Nations Climate Change, 'Public participation under action for climate empowerment' (online), https://unfccc.int/topics/education-and-outreach/workstreams/public-participation.
2. LATINNO, 'Citizens' Climate Change Advisory Council', dataset (online), https://latinno.net/en/case/6115/.
3. Cornerstone Barristers, 'Cumbria coal mine permission quashed on four grounds', 13 September 2024 (online), https://cornerstonebarristers.com/cumbria-coal-mine-permission-quashed-on-four-grounds/.
4. Ana Belén Sánchez of the Instituto para la Transición Justa, JETP webinar organised by UNRISD July 11th 2023.

7 The Welfare State

1. Some authors elaborate further typologies and taxonomies of the welfare state such to include market liberal, social democratic, conservative-corporatist, Mediterranean and Confucian (Jessop 2002).
2. European Commission, 'The Just Transition Mechanism: Making sure no one is left behind' (online), https://commission.europa.eu/strategy-and-policy/priorities-2019-2024/european-green-deal/finance-and-green-deal/just-transition-mechanism_en.
3. The Conversation, 'UK oil and gas workers risk becoming the "coal miners of our generation"' (online), 24 September 2024, https://theconversation.com/uk-oil-and-gas-workers-risk-becoming-the-coal-miners-of-our-generation-239262.
4. Ernst & Young (EY), 'Nigeria enacts tax incentives to encourage development in oil and gas sector', EY Tax News (online), 14 March 2024, https://taxnews.ey.com/news/2024-0606-nigeria-enacts-tax-incentives-to-encourage-development-in-oil-and-gas-sector.
5. Utrecht University, 'What is limitarianism? Professor Ingrid Robeyns explains', Press and Media (online), 6 December 2023, www.uu.nl/en/in-de-media/what-is-limitarianism-professor-ingrid-robeyns-explains.

References

Abram, S. (2007) 'Participatory depoliticisation: The bleeding heart of neoliberalism'. In C. Neveu (ed.), *Cultures et pratiques Participatives: Perspectives Comparatives*. Paris: l'Harmattan, pp. 113–133.

Abram, S. (2008) 'Public participation and the problem of exclusion'. In C. Garston and M. Lindh de Montoya (eds.), *Transparency in a New Global Order*. Cheltenham: Edward Elgar, pp. 201–222.

Abramsky, K. (2010) *Sparking a Worldwide Energy Revolution: Social Struggles in the Transition to a Post-Petrol World*. Edinburgh: AK Press.

Acción Ecológica (1999) 'No more plunder, they owe us the ecological debt!', *Bulletin of Acción Ecológica* 78 (October), Quito, Ecuador: Acción Ecológica.

Aglietta, M. (2000) *A Theory of Capitalist Regulation: The US Experience*. London: Verso Books.

Agyeman, J., Bullard, R. D., & Evans, B. (eds.) (2003) *Just Sustainabilities: Development in an Unequal World*. Cambridge, MA: MIT Press.

Akenji, L. (2014) 'Consumer scapegoatism and limits to green consumerism'. *Journal of Cleaner Production*, 63: 13–23.

Alami, I., Babic, M., Dixon, A. D., & Liu, I. T. (2022) 'Special issue introduction: What is the new state capitalism?'. *Contemporary Politics*, 28(3): 245–263.

Alami, I., Dixon, A. D., Gonzalez-Vicente, R., Babic, M., Lee, S., Medbyd, I. A., & de Graaff, N. (2022) 'Geopolitics and the "new" state capitalism'. *Geopolitics*, 27(3): 995–1023.

Albert, M. J. (2020) 'Capitalism and earth system governance: An ecological Marxist approach'. *Global Environmental Politics*, 20(2): 37–56.

Alcamo, J., Thompson, J., Alexander, A., Antoniades, A., Delabre, I., Dolley, J., … & Scharlemann, J. P. (2020) 'Analysing interactions among the sustainable development goals: Findings and emerging issues from local and global studies'. *Sustainability Science*, 15: 1561–1572.

Aligica, P. D. & Tarko, V. (2014) 'Crony capitalism: Rent seeking, institutions and ideology'. *Kyklos*, 67(2): 156–176.

Allan, B. B. & Nahm, J. (2024) 'Strategies of green industrial policy: How states position firms in global supply chains'. *American Political Science Review*, 1: 1–15.

Allen, B. L. (2003) *Uneasy Alchemy: Citizens and Experts in Louisiana's Chemical Corridor Disputes*. Cambridge, MA: MIT Press.

Altenburg, T. & Pegels, A. (2012) 'Sustainability oriented innovation systems: Managing the green transformation'. *Innovation and Development*, 2(1): 5–22.

Ambrose J. (2019) 'Government "funding fossil fuel-burning plants abroad"'. *The Guardian*, 10 June. www.theguardian.com/environment/2019/jun/10/governmentfunding-fossil-fuel-burning-plants-abroad?CMP=share_btn_lin.

Andersen, V. (2018) 'Protecting the interests of future generations'. CUSP, Working Paper No. 14. Guildford: University of Surrey. www.cusp.ac.uk/wp-content/uploads/Protecting-the-interests-of-future-generations.pdf.

Andrews-Speed, P. (2016) 'Applying institutional theory to the low-carbon energy transition'. *Energy Research & Social Science*, 13: 216–225.

Arcand, B. & Meadowcroft, J. (2024) 'Net zero by 2050: The case for green industrial policy'. *Environmental Politics*, https://doi.org/10.1080/09644016.2024.2375899.

Argyriou, I. & Barry, J. (2021) 'The political economy of socio-technical transitions: A relational view of the state and bus system decarbonization in the United Kingdom'. *Energy Research & Social Science*, 79: 102174.

Arrighi, G. (2010) *The Long Twentieth Century: Money, Power, and the Origins of Our Times*. London: Verso Books.

Ashford, N. & Hall, R. (2011) *Technology, Globalization and Sustainable Development*. New Haven: Yale University Press.

Åslund, A. (2019) *Russia's Crony Capitalism: The Path from Market Economy to Kleptocracy*. New Haven: Yale University Press.

Audretsch, D. B. & Fiedler, A. (2022) 'Does the entrepreneurial state crowd out entrepreneurship?' *Small Business Economics*, 60(2): 1–17.

Avelino, F. (2017) 'Power in sustainability transitions: Analysing power and (dis)empowerment in transformative change towards sustainability'. *Environmental Policy and Governance*, 27(6): 505–520.

Avelino, F. & Rotmans, J. (2009) 'Power in transition: An interdisciplinary framework to study power in relation to structural change'. *European Journal of Social Theory*, 12(4): 543–569.

Avelino, F. & Rotmans, J. (2011) 'A Dynamic conceptualization of power for sustainability research'. *Journal of Cleaner Production*, 19(8): 796–804.

Avelino, F. & Wittmayer, J. (2015) 'Shifting power relations in sustainability transitions: A multi-actor perspective'. *Journal of Environmental Policy and Planning*, 18(5): 1–22.

Avelino, F., Grin, J., Pel, B., & Jhagroe, S. (2016) 'The politics of sustainability transitions'. *Journal of Environmental Policy and Planning*, 18(5): 557–567.

Ayers, A. J. (2013) 'Beyond myths, lies and stereotypes: The political economy of a "New Scramble for Africa"'. *New Political Economy*, 18(2): 227–257.

Ayres, M. (2024) 'G20 agree to work on Brazil's "billionaire tax" idea, implementation seen difficult. Reuters, July 26. www.reuters.com/business/finance/brazils-billionaire-tax-idea-well-received-g20-seen-difficult-implement-2024-07-25/.

Baber, W. & Bartlett, R. (2005) *Deliberative Environmental Politics*. Cambridge, MA: MIT Press.

Babic, M. (2020) 'Let's talk about the interregnum: Gramsci and the crisis of the liberal world order'. *International Affairs*, 96(3): 767–787.

Bachrach, P. & Baratz, M. S. (1962) 'Two faces of power'. *American Political Science Review*, 56: 947–952.

Bäckstrand, K. & Kronsell, A. (eds.) (2015) *Rethinking the Green State. Environmental Governance towards Climate and Sustainability Transitions*. London: Earthscan from Routledge.

Bäckstrand, K., Khan, J., Kronsell, A., & Lövbrand, E. (eds.) (2010) *Environmental Politics and Deliberative Democracy: Examining the Promise of New Modes of Governance*. Cheltenham: Edward Elgar Publishing.

Bahro, R. (1986) *Building the Green Movement*. London: GMP Publishers.

Baide, B. & Birnbaum, P. (1979) *The Sociology of the State*. Chicago: University of Chicago Press.

Bailey, I., Gouldson, A., & Newell, A. P. (2011) 'Ecological modernisation and the governance of carbon: A critical analysis'. *Antipode*, 43(3): 682–703.
Baker, S. (2016) 'Mexican energy reform, climate change and energy justice in indigenous communities'. *Natural Resources Journal*, 56(2): 369–390.
Baker, L., Newell, P., & Phillips, J. (2014) 'The political economy of energy transitions: The case of South Africa'. *New Political Economy*, 19: 791–818.
Baker, L. & Sovacool, B. (2017) 'The political economy of technological capabilities and global production networks in South Africa's wind and solar Photovoltaic (PV) Industries'. *Political Geography*, 60: 1–12.
Bakker, K. (2010) *Privatising Water: Governance Failure and the World's Urban Water Crisis*. Ithaca, NY: Cornell University Press.
Balanyá, B., Bolwer-Ailloud, M., & Gelebart, K. (eds.) (2005) *Reclaiming Public Water: Achievements, Struggles and Visions from around the World*. Amsterdam: Transnational Institute and Corporate European Observatory.
Balzacq, T. & Krebs, R. R. (eds.) (2021) *The Oxford Handbook of Grand Strategy*. Oxford: Oxford University Press.
Barra, M. & Svec, M. (2018) 'Reinforcing energy governance under the EU energy diplomacy: A proposal for strengthening energy frameworks in Africa.' *European Journal of Risk Regulation*, 9(2): 245–267.
Barry, J. (1999) *Rethinking Green Politics*. London: SAGE Publications.
Barry, J. (2008) 'Towards a green republicanism: Constitutionalism, political economy, and the green state'. *The Good Society: A PEGS Journal*, 17(2): 1–12.
Barry, J. (2012) *The Politics of Actually Existing Unsustainability: Human Flourishing in a Climate Changed, Carbon Constrained World*. Oxford: Oxford University Press.
Barry, J. & Eckersley, R. (eds.) (2005) *The State and the Global Ecological Crisis*. Cambridge, MA: MIT Press.
Barry, J., Geraint, E., & Robinson, C. (2008) 'Cool rationalities and hot air: A rhetorical approach to understanding debates on renewable energy'. *Global Environmental Politics* 8(2): 67–98.
Bartleson, J. (1995) *A Genealogy of Sovereignty*. Cambridge: Cambridge University Press.
Bazilian, M., Bradshaw, M., Goldthau, A., & Westphal, K. (2019) 'Model and manage the changing geopolitics of energy'. *Nature Comment*, 1 May. www.nature.com/articles/d41586-019–01312-5
Beblawi, H. & Luciani, G. (eds.) (1987) *The Rentier State*. London: Routledge.
Beck, U. (1999) *World Risk Society*. Cambridge: Polity.
Beckman, L. (2021) 'Popular sovereignty facing the deep state. The rule of recognition and the powers of the people'. *Critical Review of International Social and Political Philosophy*, 24(7): 954–976.
Beder, S. (1997) *Global Spin: The Corporate Assault on Environmentalism*. White River Junction, VT: Chelsea Green Publishing.
Beeson, M. (2010) 'The coming of environmental authoritarianism'. *Environmental Politics*, 19(2): 276–294.
Belcher, O., Bigger, P., Neimark, B., & Kennelly, C. (2020) 'Hidden carbon costs of the "Everywhere War": Logistics, geopolitical ecology, and the carbon boot-print of the US military'. *Transactions of the Institute of British Geographers*, 45(1): 65–80.
Benney, T. (2019) 'Varieties of capitalism and renewable energy in emerging and developing economies'. *Journal of Economic Policy Reform*. https://doi.org/10.1080/17487870.2019.1637584.

Bergin, T. & Bousso, R. (2020) 'Special report: How oil majors shift billions in profits to island tax havens.' Reuters, 9 December. www.reuters.com/article/global-oil-tax-havens-idUSKBN28J1IK.

Bernstein, S. & Hoffmann, M. (2019) 'Climate politics, metaphors and the fractal carbon trap'. *Nature Climate Change*, 9: 919–925.

Berry, C. et al. (2022) 'The substitutive state? Neoliberal state interventionism across industrial, housing and private pensions policy in the UK.' *Competition & Change*, 26(2): 242–265.

Bhambra, G. K. (2021) 'Colonial global economy: Towards a theoretical reorientation of political economy'. *Review of International Political Economy*, 28(2): 307–322.

Bhambra, G. K. & Newell, P. (2022) 'More than a metaphor: "Climate colonialism" in perspective'. *Global Social Challenges Journal*, 1: 1–9.

Biermann, F. (2014) *Earth Systems Governance: World Politics in the Anthropocene*. Cambridge, MA: MIT Press.

Biermann, F. & Kalfagianni, A. (2020) 'Planetary justice: A research framework'. *Earth System Governance*, 6: 100049.

Blair, H. (2000) 'Participation and accountability at the periphery: Democratic local governance in six countries'. *World Development* 28(1): 21–39.

Block, F. (1977) 'The ruling class does not rule: Notes on the Marxist theory of the state'. *Socialist Revolution*, 33: 6–28.

Block, F. (1987) *Revising State Theory: Essays in Politics and Post Industrialism*. Philadelphia: Temple University Press.

Block, F. (2008) 'Swimming against the current: The rise of a hidden developmental state in the united states'. *Politics & Society*, 36(2): 169–206.

Blondeel, M., Bradshaw, M. J., Bridge, G., & Kuzemko, C. (2021) 'The geopolitics of energy system transformation: A review'. *Geography Compass*, e12580.

Blühdorn, I. (2020) 'The legitimation crisis of democracy: Emancipatory politics, the environmental state and the glass ceiling to socio-ecological transformation'. *Environmental Politics*, 29(1): 38–57.

Blühdorn, I. (2021) 'The legitimation crisis of democracy: Emancipatory politics, the environmental state and the glass ceiling to socio-ecological transformation'. In D. Hausknost and M. Hammond (eds.), *The Political Prospects of a Sustainability Transformation: Moving beyond the Environmental State*. Abingdon: Routledge, pp. 38–58.

Bookchin, M. (1980) *Toward an Ecological Society*. Montreal: Black Rose Books.

Bookchin, M. (1982) *The Ecology of Freedom: The Emergence and Dissolution of Hierarchy*. Palo Alto: Cheshire Books.

Booth, K. (1991) 'Security and emancipation'. *Review of International Studies*, 17(4): 313–326.

Borowy, I. & Aillon, J. (2017) 'Sustainable health and degrowth: Health, health care and society beyond the growth paradigm'. *Social Theory & Health*, 15(3): 346–368.

Bösch, F. (2014) 'Energy diplomacy: West Germany, the Soviet Union and the oil crises of the 1970s'. *Historical Social Research (Köln)*, 39(4): 165–185.

Bosman, R., Loorbach, D., Frantzeskaki, N., & Pistorius, T. (2014) 'Discursive regime dynamics in the Dutch energy transition'. *Environmental Innovation and Societal Transitions*, 13: 45–59.

Bourdieu, P. (2014) *On the State: Lectures at the College de France 1989–1992*. Cambridge: Polity Press.

Boyer, D. (2019) *Energopolitics: Wind and Power in the Anthropocene*. Durham, NC: Duke University Press.

Boyle, D. & Simms, A. (2009) *The New Economics: A Bigger Picture*. Abingdon: Earthscan.

Bracey, G. (2015) 'Toward a critical race theory of state'. *Critical Sociology*, 41(3): 553–572.
Brand, U., Gorg, C., & Wissen, M. (2011) 'Second order condensations of societal power relations: Environmental politics and internationalisation of the state from a neo-Poulantzian perspective'. *Antipode*, 43(1): 149–175.
Brand, U. & Wissen, M. (2021) *The Imperial Mode of Living: Everyday Life and the Ecological Crisis of Capitalism*. London: Verso Books.
Brenner, N. & Theodore, N. (2002) 'Cities and the Geographies of "Actually Existing Neoliberalism"'. *Antipode*, 34(3): 349–379.
Bridge, G. & Le Billon, P. (2013) *Oil*. Cambridge: Polity Press.
Bridge, G., Özkaynak, B., & Turhan, E. (2018) 'Energy infrastructure and the fate of the nation: Introduction to special issue'. *Energy Research & Social Science*, 41: 1–11.
Brock, A. & Dunlap, A. (2018) 'Normalising corporate counterinsurgency: Engineering consent, managing resistance and greening destruction around the Hambach coal mine and beyond'. *Political Geography*, 62: 33–47.
Brock, A., Huff, A., Verweijen, J., Selby, J., Ockwell, D., & Newell, P. (2018) 'Fracking democracy, criminalising dissent'. *The Ecologist*. https://theecologist.org/2018/oct/18/fracking-democracy-criminalising-dissent.
Bromley, S. (1991) *American Hegemony and World Oil*. Cambridge: Polity Press.
Bromley, S. (2005) 'The United States and the control of world oil'. *Government and Opposition*, 40(2): 225–255.
Brook, D. (1998) 'Environmental genocide: Native Americans and toxic waste'. *American Journal of Economics and Sociology*, 57(1): 105–113.
Brown, M. (ed.) (2009) *Informal Empire in Latin America: Culture, Commerce and Capital*. Hoboken: John Wiley & Sons.
Brown, J. C. & Purcell, M. (2005) 'There's nothing inherent about scale: Political ecology, the local trap, and the politics of development in the Brazilian Amazon'. *Geoforum*, 36(5): 607–624.
Brusseler, M. (2022) *The Political Economy of US Green Industrial Planning: Building State Capacity for Deep Decarbonization*. London: E3G. Briefing.
Bryant, R. L. (ed.) (2015) *The International Handbook of Political Ecology*. Cheltenham: Edward Elgar Publishing.
Bryant, P. & Stone, L. (2020) 'Climate assemblies and juries: A people-powered response to the climate emergency'. Shared Future/PCAN. https://sharedfuturecic.org.uk/wp-content/uploads/2020/08/Shared-Future-PCAN-Climate-Assemblies-and-Juries-web.pdf.
Büchs, M. & Koch, M. (2017) *Postgrowth and Wellbeing*. Cham: Springer International.
Büchs, M. & Koch, M. (2019) 'Challenges for the degrowth transition: The debate about wellbeing'. *Futures*, 105: 155–165.
Buch-Hansen, H. & Koch, M. (2019) 'Degrowth through income and wealth caps?'. *Ecological Economics*, 160: 264–271.
Buch-Hansen, H., Koch, M., & Nesterova, I. (2024) *Deep Transformations: A Theory of Degrowth*. Manchester: Manchester University Press.
Buck, H. J. (2021) *Ending Fossil Fuels: Why Net Zero Is Not Enough*. London: Verso Books.
Bulkeley, H. (2005) 'Reconfiguring environmental governance: Towards a politics of scales and networks'. *Political Geography*, 24(8): 875–902.
Bulkeley, H. (2016) *Accomplishing Climate Governance*. Cambridge: Cambridge University Press.
Bulkeley, H., Andonva, L., Betsill, M. M., Compagnon, D., Hale, T., Hoffmann, M., … & VanDeveer, S. (2014) *Transnational Climate Change Governance*. Cambridge: Cambridge University Press.

Bull, H. (1979) 'The state's positive role in world affairs'. *Daedalus*, 108: 111–123.

Bullard, R. D. (2005) *The Quest for Environmental Justice: Human Rights and the Politics of Pollution*. Berkeley: University of California Press.

Burawoy, M. (2003) 'For a sociological Marxism: The complementary convergence of Antonio Gramsci and Karl Polanyi'. *Politics & Society*, 31(2): 193–261.

Burger, A. (2015) 'Extreme working hours in Western Europe and North America: A new aspect of polarization'. LSE 'Europe in Question', Discussion Paper Series.

Bürer, M. J. & Wüstenhagen, R. (2009) 'Which renewable energy policy is a venture capitalist's best friend? Empirical evidence from a survey of international cleantech investors'. *Energy Policy*, 37(12): 4997–5006.

Burke, A. et al. (2016) 'Planet politics: A manifesto from the end of IR'. *Millennium: Journal of International Studies*, 44(3): 499–523.

Burke, M. & Stephens, J. C. (2017) 'Energy democracy: Goals and policy instruments for sociotechnical transitions'. *Energy Research & Social Science*, 33: 35–48.

Büscher, B. (2018) 'From biopower to ontopower? Violent responses to wildlife crime and the new geographies of conservation'. *Conservation and Society*, 16(2): 157–169.

Buttel, F. H. (2004) 'The treadmill of production: An appreciation, assessment, and agenda for research'. *Organization & Environment*, 17(3): 323–336. https://doi.org/10.1177/1086026604267938.

Buxton, N. & Hayes, B. (2016) *The Secure and the Dispossessed: How the Military and Corporations Are Shaping a Climate-Changed World*. London: Pluto Press.

Buzan, B. (1983) *Peoples, States and Fear*. London: Wheatsheaf.

Buzan, B. (1994) 'The interdependence of security and economic issues in the new world order'. In R. Stubbs and G. Underhill (eds.), *Political Economy and the Changing Global Order*. Basingstoke: MacMillan Press, pp. 89–103.

Caldecott, B., Sartor, O., & Spencer, T. (2017) *Lessons from Previous 'Coal Transitions': High-Level Summary for Decision-Makers*. Paris: IDDRI and Climate Strategies.

Caldecott, B. et al. (2017) 'Managing the political economy frictions of closing coal in China'. Discussion Paper, Smith School of Enterprise and the Environment, University of Oxford. www.smithschool.ox.ac.uk/research-programmes/stranded-assets/Managing-the-political-economy-frictions-of-closing-coal-in-China-SFP-Working-Paper.pdf.

Capstick, S., Whitmarsh, L., Nash, N., Haggar, P., & Lord, J. (2019) 'Compensatory and catalyzing beliefs: Their relationship to pro-environmental behavior and behavioral spillover in seven countries'. *Frontiers in Psychology*, 10: 963.

Cardoso, F. H. & Faletto, E. (1979) *Dependency and Development in Latin America*. Berkeley: University of California Press.

Carlsson, C. (2015) 'Nowtopians'. In G. D'Alisa, F. Demaria, and G. Kallis (eds.), *Degrowth: A Vocabulary for a New Era*. London: Routledge, pp. 182–184.

Carrell, S., Evans, R., Pegg, D., & Savarese, M. (2022) 'Revealed: Queen's sweeping immunity from more than 160 laws'. *The Guardian*, 14 July. www.theguardian.com/uk-news/2022/jul/14/queen-immunity-british-laws-private-property.

Carrington, D. (2020) 'Heathrow third runway ruled illegal over climate change'. *The Guardian*, 27 February. www.theguardian.com/environment/2020/feb/27/heathrowthird-runway-ruled-illegal-over-climate-change.

Carruthers, B. & Stinchcombe, A. (1999) 'The social structure of liquidity: Flexibility, markets, and states'. *Theory and Society*, 28(3): 353–382.

CAST (2021) 'Public perceptions of climate change and policy action in the UK, China, Sweden and Brazil'. CAST Briefing. https://cast.ac.uk/wp-content/uploads/2021/10/01112021-Briefing-10-final.pdf.

Cato, M. S. (n.d.) 'Response from green house, the environmental think tank'. Environmental Audit Committee Inquiry into the Green Economy. www.greenhousethinktank.org/responses.html.

Cato, M. S. (2018) 'Revealed: The revolving door between Westminster and the fossil fuel industry', *Left Foot Forward*, 8 May. leftfootforward.org/2018/05/the-revolving-door-between-westminster-and-the-fossil-fuel-industry/.

Cerny, P. (1995) 'Globalization and the changing logic of collective action'. *International Organization*, 49(4): 595–625.

Ćetković, S. & Buzogány, A. (2016) 'Varieties of capitalism and clean energy transitions in the European Union: When renewable energy hits different economic logics'. *Climate Policy*, 16(5): 642–657.

Chamon, M., Klok, E., Thakoor, V., & Zettelmeyer, J. (2022) 'Debt-for-climate swaps: Analysis, design, and implementation.' IMF Working Paper 2022/162, Washington, DC: International Monetary Fund.

Chancel, L., Bothe, P., & Voituriez, T. (2023) *Climate Inequality Report 2023*. World Inequality Lab Study 2023/1.

Chandler, D., Cudworth, E., & Hobden, S. (2017) 'Anthropocene, capitalocene and liberal cosmopolitan IR: A response to Burke et al.'s "Planet Politics"'. *Millennium: Journal of International Studies*, 6(2): 1–19.

Chang, H. J. (2002) *Kicking Away the Ladder: Development Strategy in Historical Perspective*. London: Anthem Press.

Chang, H. J. (2006) *The East Asian Development Experience: The Miracle, the Crisis and the Future*. London: Zed Books.

Chapman, A. (2018) *Community Energy in the UK*. October Green European Foundation.

Chilvers, J., Bellamy, R., Pallett, H., & Hargreaves, T. (2021) 'A systemic approach to mapping participation with low-carbon energy transitions'. *Nature Energy*, 6(3): 250–259.

Chilvers, J., Pallett, H., & Hargreaves, T. (2018) 'Ecologies of participation in socio-technical change: The case of energy system transitions'. *Energy Research & Social Science*, 42: 199–210.

Chipkin, I. & Swilling, M. (2017) *Shadow State: The Politics of State Capture*. Johannesburg: Wits University Press.

Chomsky, N. & Pollin, R. (2020) *The Climate Crisis and the Global Green New Deal*. London: Verso Books.

Christoff, P. (2005) 'Out of chaos, a shining star? Toward a typology of green states'. In J. Barry and R. Eckersley (eds.), *The State and the Global Ecological Crisis*. Cambridge, MA: MIT Press, pp. 25–53.

Clausewitz, C. (2003) *On War*. London: Penguin UK.

Cobham, A. & Jansky, P. (2018) 'Global distribution of revenue loss from corporate tax avoidance: Re-estimation and country results'. *Journal of International Development*, 30(2): 206–232.

Coker, C. (2019) *The Rise of the Civilisational State*. Cambridge: Polity Press.

Cole, C. & Gnanapragasam, A. (2017) *Community Repair: Enabling Repair as Part of the Movement Towards a Circular Economy*. Nottingham: Nottingham Trent University and The Restart Project. http://irep.ntu.ac.uk/id/eprint/30462/:4.

Cole, L. & Foster, S. (2001) *From the Ground Up: Environmental Racism and the Rise of the Environmental Justice Movement*. New York: New York University Press.

Colgan, J. (2013) *Petro-aggression: When Oil Causes War*. Cambridge: Cambridge University Press.

Colgan, J. D., Keohane, R. O., & Van de Graaf, T. (2012) 'Punctuated equilibrium in the energy regime complex'. *The Review of International Organizations*, 7: 117–143.

Coll, S. (2012) *Private Empire: ExxonMobil and American Power*. Harmondsworth: Penguin Books.

Collett-White, R. (2019) 'COP25: Over 40 Gulf state delegates are current or former employees of fossil fuel companies'. 13 December. desmog.co.uk/2019/12/13/cop25-over-40-gulf-state-delegates-are-current-or-former-employees-fossil-fuel-companies.

Collier, P. & Venables, A. J. (2015) 'Closing coal: Economic and moral incentives'. *Oxford Review of Economic Policy*, 30(3): 492–512.

Conca, K. (2005) 'Old states in new bottles? The hybridization of authority in global environmental governance'. In J. Barry and R. Eckersley (eds.), *The State and the Global Ecological Crisis*. Cambridge, MA: MIT Press, pp. 181–207.

Contessi, S. & Li, L. (2013) *Translating Kurzarbeit*. Economic Synopses. Federal Reserve Bank of St. Louis.

Cornwall, A. & Gaventa, J. (2001) 'Bridging the gap: Citizenship, participation and accountability'. *PLA Notes*, 40: 32–35.

Cox, R. (1987) *Production, Power and World Order*. New York: Columbia University Press.

Cox, R. (1995) 'Critical political economy'. In B. Hettne (ed.), *International Political Economy: Understanding Global Disorder*. Halifax: Fernwood Publishing, pp. 31–45.

Cox, E., Johnstone, P., & Stirling, A. (2016) 'Understanding the intensity of UK policy commitments to nuclear power'. SWPS 2016–16. http://dx.doi.org/10.2139/ssrn.2837691.

CPI (Climate Policy Initiative). (2023) 'Global landscape of climate finance 2023'. www.climatepolicyinitiative.org/publication/global-landscape-of-climate-finance-2023/.

Craig, M. (2020) 'Greening the state for a sustainable political economy'. *New Political Economy*, 25(1): 1–4.

Crawford, N. C. (2019) 'Pentagon fuel use, climate change, and the costs of war'. Working Paper, Watson Institute of International and Public Affairs, Brown University.

Cuppen, E., Pesch, U., Remmerswaal, S., & Taanman, M. (2019) 'Normative diversity, conflict and transition: Shale gas in the Netherlands'. *Technological Forecasting and Social Change*, 145: 165–175.

Cutler, C. (2002) 'Historical materialism, globalization and law'. In M. Rupert and H. Smith (eds.), *Historical Materialism and Globalization*. London: Routledge, pp. 230–256.

Da Costa Vieira, T. (2024) 'Beneath the insuperable barrier: Accumulation, state managers and climate policy in Britain'. *Environmental Politics*. https://doi.org/10.1080/09644016.2024.2351787.

Dahl, R. A. (2008) *Polyarchy*. New Haven: Yale University Press.

Dale, G. (2012) 'The growth paradigm: A critique'. *International Socialism*, 134. http://isj.org.uk/the-growth-paradigm-a-critique/.

Daley, F. & Lawrie, C. (2022) 'Fuelling failure'. https://fossilfueltreaty.org/fuelling-failure.

Daley, F., Newell, P., McKie, R. & Painter, J. (2024) 'Climate obstruction in the United Kingdom'. In R. J. Brulle, J. Timmons Roberts and M. C. Spencer (eds.), *Climate Obstruction across Europe*. Oxford: Oxford University Press, pp. 26–57.

Dalzell, R. (1987) *Enterprising Elite: The Boston Associates and the World They Made*. Cambridge, MA: Harvard University Press.

Dandeker, C. (1994) 'War and the military establishment'. In L. Freedman (ed.), *War*. Oxford: Oxford University Press, pp. 109–112.

Dauvergne, P. (1997) *Shadows in the Forest: Japan and the Political Economy of Deforestation in South East Asia*. Cambridge, MA: MIT Press.

Dauvergne, P. (2016) *The Environmentalism of the Rich*. Cambridge, MA: MIT Press.

David, M. (2017) 'Moving beyond the heuristic of creative destruction: Targeting exnovation with policy mixes for energy transitions'. *Energy Research & Social Science*, 33: 138–146.

Davidson, D. J. (2019) 'Exnovating for a renewable energy transition'. *Nature Energy*, 4(4): 254.

Death, C. (2016) *The Green State in Africa*. New Haven: Yale University Press.

de Coninck, H., Fischer, C., Newell, R., & Ueno, T. (2008) 'International technology-oriented agreements to address climate change'. *Energy Policy*, 36(1): 335–356.

de Graaff, N. (2020) 'China Inc. goes global: Transnational and national networks of China's globalising business elite'. *Review of International Political Economy*, 27(2): 208–233.

De Schutter, O. & Dedeurwaerdere, T. (2021) *Social Innovation in the Service of Social and Ecological Transformation: The Rise of the Enabling State*. Abingdon: Routledge.

Desai, R. (2013) *Geopolitical Economy: After US Hegemony, Globalization and Empire*. London: Pluto Press.

Deudney, D. (1990) 'The case against linking environmental degradation and national security'. *Millennium*, 19(3): 461–476.

Dewald, U. & Fromhold-Eisebith, M. (2015) 'Trajectories of sustainability transitions in scale-transcending innovation systems: The case of photovoltaics'. *Environmental Innovation and Societal Transitions*, 17: 110–125.

Diaz-Strong, D., Gómez, C., Luna-Duarte, M. E., Meiners, E. R., & Valentin, L. (2009) 'Commentary: Organizing tensions – from the prison to the military-industrial complex'. *Social Justice*, 36(2): 73–84.

Dicken, P. (2007) *Global Shift: Mapping the Changing Contours of the World Economy*. London: SAGE Publications.

Dillon, M. (1996) *Politics of Security*. London: Routledge.

Di Muzio, T. (2015) *Carbon Capitalism: Energy, Social Reproduction and World Order*. London: Rowman and Littlefield.

Dobson, A. (1990) *Green Political Thought*. London: Routledge.

Dobson, A. (1996) 'Representative democracy and the environment'. In W. Lafferty and J. Meadowcroft (eds.), *Democracy and the Environment: Problems and Prospects*. Cheltenham: Edward Elgar Publishing, pp. 124–219.

Dobson, A. (2003) *Citizenship and the Environment*. Oxford: Oxford University Press.

Dobson, A. (2014) *The Politics of Post-Growth*. Dorset: Green House.

Doherty, B. & de Geus, M. (eds.) (1996) *Democracy and Green Political Thought: Sustainability, Rights and Citizenship*. London: Routledge.

Domhoff, G. W. (1996) *State Autonomy or Class Dominance?: Case Studies on Policy Making in America*. Piscataway, NJ: Transaction Publishers.

Dorling, D. (2017) 'Is inequality bad for the environment?' *The Guardian*, 4 July. www.theguardian.com/inequality/2017/jul/04/is-inequality-bad-for-the-environment.

DoT (Department of Transport UK). (2022) *Jet Zero Strategy: Delivering Net Zero Aviation by 2050*. London: Department of Transport.

Downie, C. (2019) 'Australian energy diplomacy'. *Australian Journal of International Affairs*, 73(2): 119–125.

Doyle, M. (2011) *Liberal Peace: Selected Essays*. London: Routledge.

Drucker, P. (1995) *The Future of Industrial Man*. London: Routledge.

Dryzek, J. (1992) 'Ecology and discursive democracy: Beyond liberal capitalism and the administrative state'. *Capitalism, Nature, Socialism*, 3(2): 18–42.

Dryzek, J., Downies, D., Hunold, C., Schlosberg, D. & Hernes, H. (2003) *Green States and Social Movements: Environmentalism in the United States, United Kingdom, Germany and Norway*. Oxford: Oxford University Press.

Dubash, N. K. & Morgan, B. (2012) 'Understanding the rise of the regulatory state of the South'. *Regulation & Governance*, 6(3): 261–281.

Duckett, J. (1998) *The Entrepreneurial State in China*. London: Routledge.

Duffy, R. (2014) ‘Waging a war to save biodiversity: The rise of militarized conservation’. *International Affairs (London)*, 90(4): 819–834.

Duffy, R. (2016) ‘War, by conservation’. *Geoforum*, 69: 238–248.

Duit, A. (2016) ‘The four faces of the environmental state: Environmental governance regimes in 28 countries’. *Environmental Politics*, 25(1): 69–91.

Duit, A., Feindt, P. H., & Meadowcroft, J. (2016) ‘Greening leviathan: The rise of the environmental state?’. *Environmental Politics*, 25(1): 1–23.

Dunlap, A. (2018) ‘Counterinsurgency for wind energy: The Bíi Hioxo wind park in Juchitán, Mexico’. *The Journal of Peasant Studies*, 45(3): 630–652.

Dunlap, C. J. (2011) ‘The military-industrial complex’. *Daedalus*, 140(3): 135–147.

Dunlap, A. & Brock, A. (eds.) (2022) *Enforcing Ecocide: Power, Policing & Planetary Militarization*. London: Springer Nature.

Dunlap, A. & Correa Arce, M. (2021) ‘“Murderous energy” in Oaxaca, Mexico: Wind factories, territorial struggle and social warfare’. *The Journal of Peasant Studies*. https://doi.org/10.1080/03066150.2020.1862090.

Dunleavy, P. & O’Leary, B. (1987) *Theories of the State: The Politics of Liberal Democracy*. Basingstoke: MacMillan Press.

Durkheim, E. (1957) *Professional and Civic Morals*. London: Routledge and Kegan Paul.

Early, B. R. & Preble, K. (2021) ‘Grand strategy and the tools of economic statecraft’. In T. Balzacq & R. R. Krebs (eds.), *The Oxford Handbook of Grand Strategy*. Oxford: Oxford University Press, pp. 370–388.

Eckersley, R. (2004) *The Green State*. Cambridge, MA: MIT Press.

Eckersley, R. (2020) ‘The green state in transition’. *New Political Economy*, 25(1): 46–56.

Eckersley, R. (2021) ‘Greening states and societies: From transitions to great transformations’. *Environmental Politics*, 30(1–2): 245–265.

Economy, E. C. (2019) *The River Runs Black: The Environmental Challenge to China’s Future*. Ithaca, NY: Cornell University Press.

Ediger, V. & Bowlus, J. (2018) ‘A farewell to King Coal: Geopolitics, energy security and the transition to oil 1989–1917’. *Historical Journal*, 62(2): 1–23.

Eisenhower, D. (1961) ‘President Dwight D. Eisenhower’s Farewell Address’. US National Archives. www.archives.gov/milestone-documents/president-dwight-d-eisenhowers-farewell-address.

Elliott, L. (2004) *The Global Politics of the Environment*. Basingstoke: Macmillan.

Elliott, L. (2020). ‘Four-day week would be affordable for most UK firms, says think-tank’. *The Guardian*, 29 December. www.theguardian.com/business/2020/dec/29/four-day-week-would-be-affordable-for-most-uk-firms-says-thinktank.

Elsner, C., Neumann, M., Müller, F., & Claar, S. (2021) ‘Room for money or manoeuvre? How green financialization and de-risking shape Zambia’s renewable energy transition’. *Canadian Journal of Development Studies*, 0(0): 1–20. https://doi.org/10.1080/02255189.2021.1973971.

Elstub, S., Carrick, J., Farrell, D. M., & Mockler, P. (2021) ‘The scope of climate assemblies: Lessons from the climate assembly UK’. *Sustainability*, 13(20): 11272.

Epsing-Andersen, G. (1990) *The Three Worlds of Welfare Capitalism*. Cambridge: Cambridge University Press.

Epsing-Andersen, G. (1999) *The Social Foundations of Post-Industrial Economies*. Oxford: Oxford University Press.

Evans, G., Goodman, J., & Lansbury, N. (2002) *Moving Mountains: Communities Confront Mining and Globalization*. London: Zed Books.

Evans, P. & Heller, P. (2015) 'Human development, state transformation and the politics of the developmental state'. In S. Leibfried, E. Huber, M. Lange, J. D. Levy, and J. D. Stephens (eds.), *The Oxford Handbook of Transformations of the State*. Oxford: Oxford University Press, pp. 691–713.

Evans, P., Rueschemeyer, D., & Skocpol, T. (eds.) (1985) *Bringing the State Back In*. Cambridge: Cambridge University Press.

Evans, P. B. (2012 [1995]) *Embedded Autonomy: States and Industrial Transformation*. Princeton, NJ: Princeton University Press.

Evans, R., Carrell, S., & Pegg, D. (2021) 'Queen secretly lobbied Scottish ministers for climate law exemption'. *The Guardian*, 28 July. www.theguardian.com/uk-news/2021/jul/28/queen-secretly-lobbied-scottish-ministers-climate-law-exemption.

Fairhead, J., Leach, M., & Scoones, I. (2012) 'Green grabbing: A new appropriation of nature?'. *Journal of Peasant Studies*, 39(2): 285–307.

Falkner, R. (2008) *Business Power and Conflict in International Politics*. Basingstoke: Palgrave.

Falkner, R. & Buzan, B. (eds.) (2022) *Great Powers, Climate Change, and Global Environmental Responsibilities*. Oxford: Oxford University Press.

Fallows, J. (2002) 'The military-industrial complex'. *Foreign Policy*, 133: 46–48.

Farrell, H. & Newman, A. L. (2019) 'Weaponized interdependence: How global economic networks shape state coercion'. *International Security*, 44(1): 42–79.

Felli, R. (2021) *The Great Adaptation: Climate, Capitalism and Catastrophe*. London: Verso Books.

Fine, B. & Rustomjee, Z. (1997) *The Political Economy of South Africa: From Minerals-Energy Complex to Industrialisation*. London: C. Hurst & Co.

Fine, B., Saraswati, J., & Tavasci, D. (2015) *Beyond the Developmental State: Industrial Policy into the Twenty-First Century: Beyond the Developmental State*. London: Pluto Press.

Flora, P. & Heidenheimer, A. (eds.) (1981) *The Development of Welfare States in Europe and America*. Chicago: University of Chicago Press.

Florini, A. & Sovacool, B. K. (2009) 'Who governs energy? The challenges facing global energy governance'. *Energy Policy*, 37: 5239–5248.

Foray, D., Mowery, D. C., & Nelson, R. R. (2012) 'Public R&D and social challenges: What lessons from mission R&D programs?' *Research Policy*, 41(10): 1697–1702.

Ford, A. & Newell, P. (2021) 'Regime resistance and accommodation: Toward a neo-Gramscian perspective on energy transitions'. *Energy Research & Social Science*, 79: 102163.

Foucault, M. (1980) *Power/Knowledge: Selected Interviews and Other Writings 1972–1977*. Brighton: Harvester Press.

Foucault, M. (2003 [1997]) *Society Must Be Defended*. New York: Picador.

Foucault, M. (2019) *Power: The Essential Works of Michel Foucault 1954–1984*. London: Penguin Books.

Foxon, T. J., Gross, R., Chase, A., Howes, J., Arnall, A. & Anderson, D. (2005) 'UK innovation systems for new and renewable energy technologies: Drivers, barriers and systems failures'. *Energy Policy*, 33(16): 2123–2137.

Franta, B. (2022) 'Weaponizing economics: Big oil, economic consultants, and climate policy delay'. *Environmental Politics*, 31(4): 555–575.

Frantzeskaki, N. & Wittmayer, J. M. (2019) 'The next wave of sustainability transitions: Elucidating and invigorating transformations in the welfare state'. *Technological Forecasting and Social Change*, 145: 136–140.

Fraser, N. (2009) *Scales of Justice: Reimagining Political Space in a Globalizing World*. New York: Columbia University Press.

Fraser, N. (2022) *Cannibal Capitalism: How Our System Is Devouring Democracy, Care, and the Planet – And What We Can Do about It*. London: Verso Books.
Freeman, C. (1992) *The Economics of Hope*. London: Pinter.
Fressoz, J.-P. (2024) *More and More and More: The All-Consuming History of Energy*. London: Allen Lane.
Friedman, M. (2009) *Capitalism and Freedom, Fortieth Anniversary Edition*. Chicago: University of Chicago Press.
Fuchs, D., Sahakian, M., Gumbert, T., Di Giulio, A., Maniates, M., Lorek, S., & Graf, A. (2021) *Consumption Corridors: Living a Good Life within Sustainable Limits*. London: Routledge.
Gabor, D. (2021a) 'The wall street consensus'. *Development and Change*, 52: 429–459.
Gabor, D. (2021b) 'Private finance won't decarbonise our economies – but the "big green state" can'. *The Guardian*, 4 June. www.theguardian.com/commentisfree/2021/jun/04/private-finance-decarbonise-economies-green-state.
Gadinger, F. & Scholte, J. A. (eds.) (2023) *Polycentrism: How Governing Works Today*. Oxford: Oxford University Press.
Galbraith, J. K. (2007) *The New Industrial State*. Princeton, NJ: Princeton University Press.
Galbraith, J. K. (2017) *The Culture of Contentment*. Princeton, NJ: Princeton University Press.
Galeano, E. (1997) *Open Veins of Latin America: Five Centuries of the Pillage of a Continent*, anniversary ed. New York: Monthly Review Press.
Gallagher, K. (ed.) (2005) *Putting Development First: The Importance of Policy Space in the WTO and International Financial Institutions*. London: Zed Books.
Gamble, A. (2014) 'Ideologies of governance'. In A. Payne and N. Phillips (eds.), *Handbook of the International Political Economy of Governance*. Cheltenham: Edward Elgar Publishing, pp. 13–32.
Gates, B. (2021) *How to Avoid a Climate Catastrophe: The Solutions We Have and the Breakthroughs We Need*. London: Allen Lane.
GCI (Global Commons Institute). (2018). http://gci.org.uk/.
GDR (Greenhouse Development Rights). (2018) 'Greenhouse development rights'. http://gdrights.org/.
Geddes, A., Schmidt, T. S., & Steffen, B. (2018) 'The multiple roles of state investment banks in low-carbon energy finance: An analysis of Australia, the UK and Germany'. *Energy Policy*, 115: 158–170.
Geels, F. W. (2002) 'Technological transitions as evolutionary reconfiguration processes: A Multi-level Perspective and case study'. *Research Policy*, 31(8/9): 1257–1274.
Geels, F. W. (2014) 'Regime resistance against low-carbon transitions: Introducing politics and power into the multi-level perspectives'. *Theory, Culture & Society*, 31(5): 21–40.
Geels, F. W. (2024) *Advanced Introduction to Sustainability Transitions*. Cheltenham: Edward Elgar Publishing.
Geels, F. & Schot, J. (2007) 'Typology of sociotechnical transition pathways'. *Research Policy*, 36(3): 399–417.
Geldenhuys, D. (2009) *Contested States in World Politics*. Basingstoke: Palgrave.
Gereffi, G., Humphrey, J, & Sturgeon, T. (2005) 'The governance of global value chains'. *Review of International Political Economy*, 1: 78–104.
Giddens, A. (1985) *The Nation State and Violence*. London: Polity Press.
Giddens, A. (1994) 'States and military power in social theory'. In L. Freedman (ed.), *War*. Oxford: Oxford University Press, pp. 112–118.
Gilio-Whitaker, D. (2019) *As Long as Grass Grows: The Indigenous Fight for Environmental Justice, from Colonization to Standing Rock*. Boston: Beacon Press.
Gill, S. (1991) *American Hegemony and the Trilateral Commission*. Cambridge: Cambridge University Press.

Gill, S. (1995) 'Globalization, market civilisation and disciplinary neoliberalism'. *Millennium: Journal of International Studies*, 24(3): 399–423.

Gill, S. (2002) 'Constitutionalizing inequality and the clash of globalizations'. *International Studies Review*, 4(2): 47–65.

Gill, S. (2014) 'Market civilization, new constitutionalism and world order'. In S. Gill and A. C. Cutler (eds.), *New Constitutionalism and World Order*. Cambridge: Cambridge University Press, pp. 29–44.

Gill, S. & Law, D. (1988) *The Global Political Economy*. Hemel Hempstead: Harvester Wheatsheaf.

Gills, B. & Rocamora, J. (1992) 'Low intensity democracy'. *Third World Quarterly*, 13(3): 501–523.

Giraudet, L.-G., Apouey, B., Arab, H. et al. (2021) 'Deliberating on climate action: Insights from the French Citizens' Convention for Climate'. Hal Open Science. https://enpc.hal.science/hal-03119539v1.

Glatzer, N., Neumann, M., & Müller, F. (2024) 'New constitutionalism across the North-South divide – Neoliberalization through development cooperation agreements'. *Review of International Political Economy*, 31(2): 463–486.

Gledhill, J. (2000) *Power and Its Disguises: Anthropological Perspectives on Politics*. 2nd ed. London: Pluto Press.

Gliedt, T., Hoicka, C., & Jackson, N. (2018) 'Innovation intermediaries accelerating environmental sustainability transitions'. *Journal of Cleaner Production*, 174: 1247–1261.

Global Witness. (2021) *Defenders of the Earth*. London: Global Witness.

Glyn, A. & Machin, S. (1997) 'Colliery closures and the decline of the UK Coal Industry'. *British Journal of Industrial Relations*, 35(2): 197–214.

GMB. (2023) 'UK energy needs plans not bans', 6 June. www.gmb.org.uk/news/uk-energy-needs-plans-not-bans.

Godfrey-Wood, R. (2016) 'Political challenges of addressing climate change through the "Entrepreneurial State"'. *IDS Bulletin*, 47(2A): 1.

Goldstein, J. & Tyfield, D. (2018) 'Green Keynesianism: Bringing the entrepreneurial state back in (to question)?'. *Science as Culture*, 27(1): 74–97.

Goldthau, A., Westphal, K., Bazilian, M., & Bradshaw, M. (2019) 'How the energy transition will reshape geopolitics'. *Nature*, 569: 29–31.

Goodin, R. (1992) *Green Political Theory*. Cambridge: Polity Press.

Goodin, R. (1996) 'Enfranchising the earth, and its alternatives'. *Political Studies*, 44: 835–849.

Gore, C. (2017) *Electricity in Africa: The Politics of Transformation in Uganda*. London: James Currey.

Gore, T. (2020) *Confronting Carbon Inequality: Putting Climate Justice at the Heart of the COVID-19 Recovery*. Oxford: Oxfam Publishing.

Gore, T. & Alestig, M. (2020) *Confronting Carbon Inequality in the European Union: Why the European Green Deal Must Tackle Inequality while Cutting Emissions*. Oxford: Oxfam Publishing. www.oxfam.org/en/research/confronting-carbon-inequality-european-union.

Gough, I. (1979) *The Political Economy of the Welfare State*. Basingstoke: MacMillan Press.

Gough, I. (2016) 'Welfare states and environmental states: A comparative analysis'. *Environmental Politics*, 25(1): 24–47.

Gough, I. (2017) *Heat, Greed and Human Need: Climate Change, Capitalism and Sustainable Well-Being*. Cheltenham: Edward Elgar Publishing.

Gramsci, A. (1971) *Selections from the Prison Notebooks*, edited and translated by Q. Hoare and G. Nowell Smith. New York: International Publishers.

Gramsci, A. (1985) *Selections from Cultural Writings.* London: Lawrence and Wishart.
Green, J. (2021) 'Beyond carbon pricing: Tax reform is climate policy'. *Global Policy*, 12(3): 372–379.
Green, J., Hadden, J., Hale, T., & Mahdavi, P. (2021) 'Transition, hedge, or resist? Understanding political and economic behaviour toward decarbonization in the oil and gas industry'. *Review of International Political Economy.* https://doi.org/10.1080/09692290.2021.1946708.
Green New Deal Group. (2008) *A Green New Deal.* London: Green New Deal Group.
Greenberg, E. & Meyer, T. (1990) *Changes in the State: Causes and Consequences.* London: SAGE Publications.
Greene, S. & Carter, A. V. (2024) 'From national ban to global climate policy renewal: Denmark's path to leading on oil extraction phase out'. *International Environmental Agreements: Politics, Law and Economics*, 1–19.
Greve, B. (2015) *Welfare and the Welfare State: Present and Future.* New York: Routledge.
Griffiths, S. (2019) 'Energy diplomacy in a time of energy transition'. *Energy Strategy Reviews*, 26. 100386. https://doi.org/10.1016/j.esr.2019.100386.
Gudynas, E. (2021) *Extractivisms: Politics, Economy and Ecology.* Warwickshire: Practical Action Publishing.
Gueldry, M. & Liang, W. (2016) 'China's global energy diplomacy: Behavior normalization through economic interdependence or resource neo-mercantilism and power politics?'. *Chinese Journal of Political Science*, 21(2): 217–240.
Gupta, J. & Pahl-Wostl, C. (2013) 'Global water governance in the context of global and multilevel governance: Its need, form, and challenges'. *Ecology and Society*, 18(4): 1–10.
Haag, S. (2022) 'Old colonial power in new green financing instruments: Approaching financial subordination from the perspective of racial capitalism in renewable energy finance in Senegal'. *Geoforum.* https://doi.org/10.1016/j.geoforum.2022.09.018.
Haas, T. (2019) 'Struggles in European Union energy politics: A Gramscian perspective on power in energy transitions'. *Energy Research & Social Science*, 48: 66–74.
Habermas, J. (1975) *Legitimation Crisis.* Boston: Beacon Press.
Hajer, M. A. (1995) *The Politics of Environmental Discourse: Ecological Modernization and the Policy Process.* Oxford: Clarendon Press.
Hajer, M. et al. (2015) 'Beyond cockpit-ism: Four insights to enhance the transformative potential of the sustainable development goals'. *Sustainability*, 7: 1651–1660.
Hale, T. & Roger, C. (2014) 'Orchestration and transnational climate governance'. *Review of International Organizations*, 9: 59–82.
Hall, P. & Soskice, D. (2001) *Varieties of Capitalism: The Institutional Foundations of Comparative Advantage.* Oxford: Oxford University Press.
Hamilton, K. (2009) *Unlocking Finance for Clean Energy: The Need for 'Investment Grade' Policy.* Energy, Environment and Development Programme Paper 09/04, December. London: Chatham House.
Hameiri, S. & Jones, L. (2016) 'Rising powers and state transformation: The case of China'. *European Journal of International Relations*, 22(1): 72–98.
Hameiri, S, Jones, L., & Heathershaw, J. (2019) 'Reframing the rising powers debate: State transformation and foreign policy'. *Third World Quarterly*, 40(8): 1397–1414.
Hammarlund, J. (1976) 'The international implications'. In J. Hammarlund and L. Lindberg (eds.), *The Political Economy of Energy Policy: A Projection for Capitalist Society.* IES Report 70. University of Wisconsin-Madison: Institute for Environmental Studies, 154–198.
Hammarlund, J. R. & Lindberg, L. (eds.) (1976) *The Political Economy of Energy Policy: A Projection for Capitalist Society.* IES Report 70. University of Wisconsin-Madison: Institute for Environmental Studies.

Hardin, G. (1968) 'The tragedy of the commons'. *Science*, 162: 1243–1248.

Harris, C. (2021) 'Looking to the future? Including children, young people and future generations in deliberations on climate action: Ireland's citizens' assembly 2016–2018'. *Innovation: The European Journal of Social Science Research*, 34(5): 677–693.

Harrison, G. (2004) *The World Bank and Africa: The Construction of Governance States*. London: Routledge.

Harrison, A., Martin, L. A., & Nataraj, S. (2017) 'Green industrial policy in emerging markets'. *Annual Review of Resource Economics*, 9(1): 253–274.

Harvey, D. (1981) 'The spatial fix: Hegel, von Thünen and Marx'. *Antipode*, 13(3): 1–12.

Harvey, D. (2003) *The New Imperialism*. Oxford: Oxford University Press.

Harvey, D. (2004) 'The "New" imperialism: Accumulation by dispossession'. *Socialist Register*, 40: 63–87.

Harvey, D. (2005) *A Brief History of Neoliberalism*. Oxford: Oxford University Press.

Harvey, D. (2006) *Spaces of Global Capitalism: Towards a Theory of Uneven Geographical Development*. London: Verso Books.

Hatzisavvidou, S. (2020) 'Inventing the environmental state: Neoliberal common sense and the limits to transformation'. *Environmental Politics*, 29(1): 96–114.

Hausknost, D. (2020) 'The environmental state and the glass ceiling of transformation'. *Environmental Politics*, 29(1): 17–37.

Hausknost, D. & Hammond, M. (2020) 'Beyond the environmental state? The political prospects of a sustainability transformation'. *Environmental Politics*, 29(1): 1–16.

Hausknost, D. & Hammond, M. (eds.) (2021) *The Political Prospects of a Sustainability Transformation: Moving beyond the Environmental State*. Abingdon: Routledge.

Haynes, J. (1999) 'Power, politics and environmental movements in the third world'. In C. Rootes (ed.), *Environmental Movements: Local, National and Global*. London: Frank Cass, pp. 222–243.

Heffron, R. J. & McCauley, D. (2018) 'What is the "just transition"?' *Geoforum*, 88: 74–77.

Held, D. (1995) *Democracy and the Global Order*. Cambridge: Polity Press.

Helleiner, E. (2024) 'Economic globalization's polycrisis'. *International Studies Quarterly*, 68: 1–9.

Hellmann, O. (2018) 'High capacity, low resilience: The "developmental" state and military-bureaucratic authoritarianism in South Korea'. *International Political Science Review*, 39(1): 67–82.

Hess, D. (2014) 'Sustainability transitions: A political coalition perspective'. *Research Policy*, 43(2): 278–283.

Hess, D. (2019) 'Cooler coalitions for a warmer planet: A review of political strategies for accelerating energy transitions'. *Energy Research & Social Science*, 57: 101246.

Heyen, A, D., Hermwille, L., & Wehnert, T. (2017) 'Out of the comfort zone! Governing the exnovation of 763 unsustainable technologies and practices'. *GAIA-Ecological Perspectives for Science and Society*, 26(4): 326–331.

Hickel, J. (2020) *Less Is More: How Degrowth Will Save the World*. London: William Heinemann.

Hicken, A. (2011) 'Clientelism'. *Annual Review of Political Science*, 14: 289–310.

Higgins, P. (2010) *Eradicating Ecocide*. London: Shepheard-Walwyn.

Hildingsson, R., Kronsell, A., & Khan, J. (2019) 'The green state and industrial decarbonisation'. *Environmental Politics*, 28(5): 909–928.

Hill, F. (2004) *Energy Empire: Oil, Gas and Russia's Revival*. London: FPC.

Hiteva, R. & Sovacool, B. (2017) 'Harnessing social innovation for energy justice: A business model perspective'. *Energy Policy*, 107: 631–639.

Hobbes, T. (1914 [1651]) *Leviathan*. London: J. M. Dent and Sons.

Hochstetler, K. (2021) *Political Economies of Energy Transition: Wind and Solar in Brazil and South Africa.* Cambridge: Cambridge University Press.

Hockerts, K. & Wüstenhagen, R. (2010) 'Greening goliaths versus emerging Davids – Theorizing about the role of incumbents and new entrants in sustainable entrepreneurship'. *Journal of Business Venturing*, 25(5): 481–492.

Hoffman, J. (1995) *Beyond the State*. Cambridge: Polity Press.

Hoffmann, C. (2018) 'Beyond the resource curse and pipeline conspiracies: Energy as a social relation in the Middle East'. *Energy Research & Social Science*, 41: 39–47.

Holden, B. (2002) *Democracy and Global Warming*. London: Continuum.

Holloway, J. & Picciotto, S. (eds.) (1978) *State and Capital: A Marxist Debate*. London: Edward Arnold.

Homer-Dixon, T. F. & Levy, M. A. (1995) 'Environment and security'. *International Security*, 20(3): 189–198.

Hooks, G. & Smith, C. L. (2005) 'Treadmills of production and destruction: Threats to the environment posed by militarism'. *Organization & Environment* 18(1): 19–37.

Hooper, K., Fellingham, L., Clancy, J., Newell, P., & Petrova, S. (2021) *Gender, Race and Social Inclusion – Net Zero Transitions: A Review of the Literature*, Department of Business, Energy and Industrial Strategy, October 2021.

Hopkins, R. (2019) *From What Is to What If? Unleashing the Power of Imagination to Create the Future We Want.* London: Chelsea Green.

Hörisch, J. (2015) 'The role of sustainable entrepreneurship in sustainability transitions: A conceptual synthesis against the background of the multi-level perspective'. *Administrative Sciences*, 5(4): 286–300.

Hornborg, A. (1998) 'Towards an ecological theory of unequal exchange: Articulating world system theory and ecological economics'. *Ecological Economics*, 25(1): 127–136.

Horwitz, R. B. (2021) 'Trump and the "Deep State"'. *Policy Studies*, 42(5–6): 473–490.

Hossain, N., Agbonifo, J., Atela, M., Gaventa, J., Gonçalves, E., Javed, U., … & Shankland A. (2021) *Demanding Power: Do Protests Empower Citizens to Hold Governments Accountable over Energy?*. Brighton: Institute of Development Studies.

Huber, M. (2008) 'Energizing historical materialism: Fossil fuels, space and the capitalist mode of production'. *Geoforum*, 40: 105–115.

Huber, M. (2013) *Lifeblood: Oil, Freedom and the Forces of Capital.* Minnesota: University of Minnesota Press.

Huber, M. T. (2022) *Climate Change as Class War: Building Socialism on a Warming Planet.* London: Verso Books.

Huda, M. S. (2024) 'Renewable energy diplomacy and transitions: An environmental peacebuilding approach'. *Environmental Innovation and Societal Transitions*, 50: 100815.

Hudson, R. & Sadler, D. (1987) National policies and local economic initiatives: Evaluating the effectiveness of UK coal and steel closure area re-industrialisation measures. *Local Economy*, 2(2): 107–114.

Hulbert, M. & Rayner, J. (2018) 'Reconciling power, relations, and processes: The role of recognition in the achievement of energy justice for Aboriginal people'. *Applied Energy*, 228: 1320–1327.

Huntingdon, S. (1993) The clash of civilizations. *Foreign Affairs*, 72(3): 22–49.

Husu, H. M. (2022) 'Rethinking incumbency: Utilising Bourdieu's field, capital, and habitus to explain energy transitions'. *Energy Research & Social Science*, 93: 102825.

ICNL (Center for Not-for-Profit Law). (2020) *Closing Civic Space for Climate Activists* Briefer by International Center for Not-for-Profit Law and European Center for Not-for-Profit Law Published June 2020.

ICRICT (Independent Commission for the Reform of International Corporate Taxation). (2019) A roadmap for a global asset registry. https://bit.ly/2JpEEgd.

IEA (International Energy Agency). (2009) *World Energy Outlook 2009*. Paris: IEA/OECD.

IEA (International Energy Agency). (2019) *World Energy Outlook*. Paris: IEA/OECD.

IEN (Indigenous Environment Network) and OCI (Oil Change International). (2021) *Indigenous Resistance against Carbon*. Washington, DC: Oil Change International.

IISD (International Institute for Sustainable Development) & LINGO (Leave it in the Ground). (2017) 'Beyond fossil fuels: Fiscal transition in BRICS'. www.iisd.org/publications/beyond-fossil-fuels-brics.

Illich, I. (2000 [1971]) *De-schooling Society*. London: Marion Boyars Publishers.

Illich, I. (2009 [1973]) *Tools for Conviviality*. London: Marion Boyars Publishers.

IMF (International Monetary Fund). (2019) 'Tackling global tax havens'. www.imf.org/en/Publications/fandd/issues/2019/09/tackling-global-tax-havens-shaxon.

IMF (International Monetary Fund). (2021) 'Still not getting energy prices right: A global and country update of fossil fuel subsidies', IMF Working Paper, Washington: IMF.

IPCC (Intergovernmental Panel on Climate Change). (2018) *Global Warming of 1.5°C: An IPCC special report on the impacts of global warming of 1.5°C above pre-industrial levels and related global greenhouse gas emission pathways* IPCC.

IPCC (Intergovernmental Panel on Climate Change). (2022) Summary for Policymakers [H.-O. Pörtner, D. C. Roberts, E. S. Poloczanska, K. Mintenbeck, M. Tignor, A. Alegría, M. Craig, S. Langsdorf, S. Löschke, V. Möller, A. Okem (eds.)]. In: *Climate Change 2022: Impacts, Adaptation and Vulnerability*. Contribution of Working Group II to the Sixth Assessment Report of the Intergovernmental Panel on Climate Change [H.-O. Pörtner, D. C. Roberts, M. Tignor, E. S. Poloczanska, K. Mintenbeck, A. Alegría, M. Craig, S. Langsdorf, S. Löschke, V. Möller, A. Okem, B. Rama (eds.)]., Cambridge: Cambridge University Press, pp. 3–33

IRENA (International Renewable Energy Agency). (2018) *Global Energy Transformation: A Roadmap to 2050*. Masdar City: IRENA.

IRENA (International Renewable Energy Agency). (2019) *A New World: The Geopolitics of the Energy Transformation*. Abu Dhabi: IRENA.

Irwin, T. (2015) 'Transition design: A proposal for a new area of design practice, study, and research'. *Design and Culture*, 7(2): 229–246.

Jackson, T. (2011) *Prosperity without Growth: Economics for a Finite Planet*. London: Earthscan from Routledge.

Jackson, T. (2021) *Post-Growth: Life after Capitalism*. Cambridge: Polity Press.

Jacobs, M. & Mazzucato, M. (eds.) (2016) *Rethinking Capitalism: Economics and Policy for Sustainable and Inclusive Growth*. Cheltenham: John Wiley & Sons.

Jacquet, J. (2022) *The Playbook*. London: Allen Lane.

Jahn, B. (2018) 'Liberal internationalism: Historical trajectory and current prospects'. *International Affairs*, 94(1): 43–61.

Jarbandhan, V. D. B., Komendantova, N., Xavier, R., & Nkoana, E. (2018) 'Transformation of the South African energy system: Towards participatory governance'. In P. Mensah, D. Katerere, S. Hachigonta, and A. Roodt (eds.), *Systems Analysis Approach for Complex Global Challenges*. Cham: Springer.

Jasanoff, S. & Kim, S.-H. (2009) 'Containing the atom: Sociotechnical imaginaries and nuclear regulation in the U.S. and South Korea'. *Minerva*, 47(2): 119–146.

Jasanoff, S. & Kim, S.-H. (2013) 'Sociotechnical imaginaries and national energy policies'. *Science as Culture*, 22(2): 189–196.

Jenkins, K. (2019) *Implementing Just Transition after COP24*. London: Climate Strategies Briefing.

Jenkins, R. & Newell, P. (2013) 'CSR, tax and development'. *Third World Quarterly*, 33(3) 378–396.

Jessop, B. (1990) *State Theory: Putting Capitalist States in Their Place*. Cambridge: Polity Press.

Jessop, B. (2002) *The Future of the Capitalist State*. Cambridge: Polity Press.

Jessop, B. (2008) *State Power: A Strategic-Relational Approach*. Cambridge: Polity Press.

Jessop, B. (2012) 'Obstacles to a world state in the shadow of the world market'. *Cooperation and Conflict*, 47: 200–219.

Jessop, B. (2016) *The State: Past, Present and Future*. Cambridge: Polity Press.

Johnstone, P. & Hielscher, S. (2017) 'Phasing out coal, sustaining coal communities? Living with technological decline in sustainability pathways'. *Extractive Industries and Society*, 4: 457–461.

Johnstone, P. & Kivimaa, P. (2018) 'Multiple dimensions of disruption, energy transitions and industrial policy'. *Energy Research & Social Science*, 37: 260–265.

Johnstone, P. & Newell, P. (2018) 'Sustainability transitions and the state'. *Environmental Innovation and Societal Transitions*, 27: 72–82.

Johnstone, P. & Stirling, A. (2020) 'Comparing nuclear trajectories in Germany and the United Kingdom: From regimes to democracies in sociotechnical transitions and discontinuities'. *Energy Research & Social Science*, 59: 101245.

Jones, L. & Hameiri, S. (2021) *Fractured China*. Cambridge: Cambridge University Press.

Jones, O. (2014) *The Establishment: And How They Get Away with It*. London: Penguin Books.

Jungk, R. (1979) *The Nuclear State*. London: John Calder Publications.

Kaldor, M., Lynn Karl, T., & Said, Y. (eds.) (2007) *Oil Wars*. London: Pluto Press.

Kallis, G. (2018) *Degrowth*. Newcastle upon Tyne: Agenda Publishing.

Kanger, L. & Schot, J. (2018) 'Deep transitions: Theorizing the long-term patterns of socio-technical change'. *Environmental Innovation and Societal Transition*. https://doi.org/10.1016/j.eist.2018.07.006.

Karlson, N., Sandström, C., & Wennberg, K. (2020) 'Bureaucrats or markets in innovation policy? A critique of the entrepreneurial state.' *The Review of Austrian Economics*, 34(1): 81–95.

Kasser, T. (2002) *The High Price of Materialism*. Cambridge, MA: MIT Press.

Kaufmann, F. -X. (2001) 'Towards a theory of the welfare state'. In S. Leibfried (ed.), *Welfare State Futures*. Cambridge: Cambridge University Press, pp. 15–36.

Kaul, I., Grunberg, I., & Stern, M. (1999) *Global Public Goods*. New York: Oxford University Press.

Keller, W. (2004) 'International technology diffusion'. *Journal of Economic Literature*, 42(3): 752–782.

Kenner, D. (2019) *Carbon Inequality: The Role of the Richest in Climate Change*. Abingdon: Routledge.

Kern, K. (2012) 'The discursive politics of governing transitions towards sustainability: The UK carbon trust'. *International Journal of Sustainable Development*, 15(1–2): 90–106.

Kern, F. & Rogge, K. (2018) 'Harnessing theories of the policy process for analysing the politics of sustainability transitions: A critical survey'. *Environmental Innovation and Societal Transitions*, 27: 102–117.

Kester, J. & Sovacool, B. K. (2017) 'Torn between war and peace: Critiquing the use of war to mobilize peaceful climate action'. *Energy Policy*, 104, 50–55.

Keyßer, L. T. & Lenzen, M. (2022) '1.5 °C degrowth scenarios suggest the need for new mitigation pathways'. *Nature Communication*, 12 (2676). https://doi.org/10.1038/s41467-021-22884-9.

Khan, M. (2010) *Political Settlements and the Governance of Growth-Enhancing Institutions*. Research Paper Series on Governance for Growth. School of Oriental and African Studies, London.

Kimberly, J. R. (1981) 'Managerial innovation'. In P. C. Nystorm and W. H. Starbuck (eds.), *Handbook of Organizational Design*. Amsterdam: Elsevier, pp. 84–104.

Kimerling, J. R. (1996) 'Oil, lawlessness and indigenous struggles in Ecuador Oriente'. In H. Collinson (ed.), *Green Guerillas: Environmental Conflicts and Initiatives in Latin America and the Caribbean*. London: Latin America Bureau, pp. 61–74.

Kivimaa, P., Laakso, S., Lonkila, A., & Kaljonen, M. (2021) 'Moving beyond disruptive innovation: A review of disruption in sustainability transitions'. *Environmental Innovation and Societal Transitions*, 38: 110–126.

Klein, N. (2007) *The Shock Doctrine*. London: Penguin Books.

Klein, N. (2015) *This Changes Everything: Capitalism versus the Climate*. London: Penguin Books.

Klein, N. (2019) *On Fire: The (Burning) Case for a Green New Deal*. New York: Simon & Schuster.

Knight, K., Rosa, E., & Schor, J. (2013) 'Could working less reduce pressures on the environment? A cross-national panel analysis of OECD countries, 1970–2007'. *Global Environmental Change*, 23(4): 691–700.

Koch, M. (2019) *Growth Strategies and Consumption Patterns in Transition: From Fordism to Finance-Driven Capitalism*. Cheltenham: Edward Elgar Publishing.

Koch, M. (2021) 'The state in the transformation to a sustainable postgrowth economy'. In D. Hausknost and M. Hammond (eds.), *The Political Prospects of a Sustainability Transformation: Moving beyond the Environmental State*. Abingdon: Routledge, pp. 115–134.

Koch, M. (2022) 'Social policy without growth: Moving towards sustainable welfare states'. *Social Policy and Society*, 21(3): 447–459.

Koch, M. & Hansen, A. R. (2024) 'Welfare within planetary limits: Deep transformation requires holistic approaches'. *Consumption and Society*, 3(3): 416–425. https://doi.org/10.1332/TIZB1819.

Koch, M. & Mont, O. (eds.) (2016) *Sustainability and the Political Economy of Welfare*. New York: Routledge.

Koddenbrock, K., Kvangraven, I. H., & Sylla, N. S. (2022) 'Beyond financialisation: The longue of finance and production in the Global South'. *Cambridge Journal of Economics*, 46(4): 703–733.

Koistinen, P. (1980) *The Military-Industrial Complex: A Historical Perspective*. New York: Praeger.

Kongshøj, K. (2023) 'Social policy in a future of degrowth? Challenges for decommodification, commoning and public support'. *Humanities and Social Sciences Communications*, 10: 850.

Korten, D. C. (1995) *When Corporations Rule the World*. West Hartford, CT: Kumarian Press.

Kropotkin, P. (2022 [1955]) *Mutual Aid: A Factor of Evolution*. London: Penguin.

Kühne, K., Bartsch, N., Tate, R. D., Higson, J., & Habet, A. (2022) '"Carbon bombs"-Mapping key fossil fuel projects'. *Energy Policy*, 166: 112950.

Kuzemko, C., Lockwood, M., Mitchell, C., & Hoggett, R. (2016) 'Governing for sustainable energy system change: Politics, contexts and contingency'. *Energy Research & Social Science*, 12: 96–105.

Lachapelle, E., MacNeil, R., & Paterson, M. (2017) 'The political economy of decarbonisation: From green energy "race" to green "division of labour"'. *New Political Economy*, 22(3): 311–327.

Laclau, E. (2005) *On Populist Reason*. London: Verso Books.

Laird, F. N. (2003) 'Constructing the future: Advocating energy technologies in the cold war'. *Technology and Culture*, 44(1): 27–49.

Lane, K. & Lane, D. (1976) *The Socialist Industrial State*. London: Routledge.

Lawhon, M. & Murphy, J. T. (2012) 'Socio-technical regimes and sustainability transitions: Insights from political ecology'. *Progress in Human Geography*, 36(3): 354–378.

Lawler, P. (2013) 'The "Good State" debate in international relations'. *International Politics*, 50: 18–37.

Lawrence, M., Buller, A., Baines, J., & Hager, S. (2020) *Commoning the Company*. Common Wealth Report. www.common-wealth.co.uk/reports/commoning-the-company.

Lawrence, M., Homer-Dixon, T., & Janzwood, S. et al. (2024) 'Global polycrisis: The causal mechanisms of crisis entanglement'. *Global Sustainability*, 7: 1–16.

Lawrence, M., Janzwood, S., & Homer-Dixon, T. (2022) 'What is a global polycrisis?' Discussion Paper 2022–2024. Cascade Institute. https://cascadeinstitute.org/technical-paper/what-is-a-globalpolycrisis/.

Leftwich, A. (1995) 'Bringing politics back in: Towards a model of the developmental state'. *Journal of Development Studies*, 31(3): 400–427.

Leftwich, A. (2000) *States of Development: On the Primacy of Politics in Development*. Cambridge: Polity Press.

Lehtonen, M. & Kern, F. (2009) 'Deliberative socio-technical transitions'. In I. Scarse and G. MacKerron (eds.), *Energy for the Future: A New Agenda*. Basingstoke: Palgrave, pp. 103–123.

Leipprand, A. & Flachsland, C. (2018) 'Regime destabilization in energy transitions: The German debate on the future of coal'. *Energy Research & Social Science*, 40: 190–204.

Lenferna, G. (2018) 'Can we equitably manage the end of the fossil fuel era?'. *Energy Research and Social Science*, 35: 217–223.

Lenin, V. I. (1927) *Imperialism*. New York: Vanguard Press.

Lennon, M. (2017) 'Decolonizing energy: Black lives matter and technoscientific expertise amid solar transitions'. *Energy Research & Social Science*, 30: 18–27.

LeQuesne, C. (1996) *Reforming World Trade: The Social and Environmental Priorities*. Oxford: Oxfam Publishing.

Levantesi, S. & Cooke, P. (2022) '"Back off": African climate groups decry Europe's dash for gas at COP27' *DeSmog*, 15 November. http://bit.ly/43NDnpU.

Levi-Faur, D. (2005) 'The global diffusion of regulatory capitalism'. *Annals of the American Academy of Political and Social Science*, 598: 12–32.

Lewis, J. (2014) 'The rise of renewable energy protectionism: Emerging trade conflicts and implications for low carbon development'. *Global Environmental Politics*, 14(4): 10–35.

Linklater, A. (1998) *The Transformation of Political Community: Ethical Foundations of the Post-Westphalian Era*. Cambridge: Polity Press.

Lo, K. (2020) 'Ecological civilization, authoritarian environmentalism, and the eco-politics of extractive governance in China'. *The Extractive Industries and Society*, 7(3): 1029–1035.

Lockwood, M. (2015a) 'The political dynamics of green transformations: Feedback effects and institutional context'. In I. Scoones et al. (eds.), *The Politics of Green Transformations*. Abingdon: Routledge, pp. 86–102.

Lockwood, M. (2015b) 'Fossil fuel subsidy reform, rent management and political fragmentation in developing countries'. *New Political Economy*, 20(4): 475–494.

Lockwood, M., Kuzemko, C., Mitchell, C., & Hoggett, R. (2016) 'Historical institutionalism and the politics of sustainable energy transitions: A research agenda'. *Environment and Planning C: Government Policy*, 35(2): 312–333.

Lockwood, M., Kuzemko, C., Mitchell, C., & Hoggett, R. (2017) 'Historical institutionalism and the politics of sustainable energy transitions: A research agenda'. *Environment and Planning C: Politics and Space*, 35(2): 312–333.

Lofgren, M. (2016) *The Deep State: The Fall of the Constitution and the Rise of a Shadow Government*. New York: Penguin Books.

Loftus, A. (2020) 'Political ecology II: Whither the state?' *Progress in Human Geography*, 44(1): 139–149.

Loorbach, D., Frantzeskaki, N., & Lijnis Huffenreuter, R. (2015) 'Transition management: taking stock from governance experimentation'. *Journal of Corporate Citizenship*, 58: 48–66.

Lucas, A. (2021) 'Investigating networks of corporate influence on government decision-making: The case of Australia's climate change and energy policies'. *Energy Research & Social Science*, 81: 102271.

Lysack, M. (2020) 'Best practices in effective climate policy implementation, governance, and accountability: The UK Committee on Climate Change'. In M. Mišík and N. Kujundžić (eds.), *Energy Humanities: Current State and Future Directions*. Cham: Springer, pp. 89–108.

Mabee, B. & Vucetic, S. (2018) 'Varieties of militarism: Towards a typology'. *Security Dialogue*, 49(1–2): 96–108.

Mabey, N., Hall, S., Smith, C. & Gupta, S. (1997) *Argument in the Greenhouse: The International Economics of Controlling Global Warming*. Abingdon: Routledge.

Machiavelli, N. (2020 [1532]) *The Prince*. Oviedo: King Solomon.

Macgaffey, J. (1987) *Entrepreneurs and Parasites: The Struggle for Indigenous Capitalism in Zaire*. Cambridge: Cambridge University Press.

Majone, G. (1994) 'The rise of the regulatory state in Europe'. In W. Muller and V. Wright (eds.), *The State in Western Europe: Retreat or Redefinition*. London: Routledge, pp. 72–102.

Makki, F. (2015) 'Reframing development theory: The significance of the idea of uneven and combined development'. *Theory and Society*, 44(5): 471–497.

Malerba, F. & Brusoni, S. (eds.) (2007) *Perspectives on Innovation*. Cambridge: Cambridge University Press.

Malm, A. (2016) *Fossil Capital: The Rise of Steam Power and the Roots of Global Warming*. London: Verso Books.

Malm, A. (2020) *Corona, Climate, Chronic Emergency: War Communism in the Twenty-First Century*. London: Verso Books.

Manchin, A. (2021) 'Democracy, disagreement, disruption: Agonism and the environmental state'. In D. Hausknost and M. Hammond (eds.), *The Political Prospects of a Sustainability Transformation: Moving beyond the Environmental State*. Abingdon: Routledge, pp. 155–173.

Mann, M. (1986) *The Sources of Social Power, Vol. 1: A History of Power from the Beginning to AD 1760*. Cambridge: Cambridge University Press.

Mann, M. (1987) 'The roots and contradictions of modern militarism'. *New Left Review*, 162(2): 27–55.

Mann, G. & Wainwright, J. (2018) *Climate Leviathan: A Political Theory of Our Planetary Future*. London: Verso Books.

Marchi, A. (2021) 'Molecular transformations: Reading the Arab uprisings with and beyond Gramsci'. *Middle East Critique*, 30(1): 67–85.

Markard, J., Suter, M., & Ingold, K. (2016) 'Socio-technical transitions and policy change: Advocacy coalitions in Swiss energy policy'. *Environmental Innovation and Societal Transitions*, 18: 215–237.

Markkanen, S. & Anger-Kraavi, A. (2019) 'Social impacts of climate change mitigation policies and their implications for inequality'. *Climate Policy*. https://doi.org/10.1080/14693062.2019.1596873.

Martin, D. (2017) 'Moving beyond the heuristic of creative destruction: Targeting exnovation with policy mixes for energy transitions'. *Energy Research & Social Science*, 33: 138–146.

Marx, K. & Engels, F. (1975) *The German Ideology*, vol. 5. London: Lawrence and Wishart.

Marx, K. & Engels, F. (1998 [1848]) *The Communist Manifesto*. London: Verso Books.

Mason, M. (2005) *The New Accountability: Environmental Responsibility across Borders*. London: Earthscan from Routledge.

Massi, E. & Nem Singh, J. (2018) 'Industrial policy and state-making: Brazil's attempt at oil-based industrial development.' *Third World Quarterly*, 39(6): 1133–1150.

Mathie, A. & Gaventa, J. (eds.) (2015) *Citizen-Led Innovation for a New Economy*. Nova Scotia: Fernwood Publishing.

Mayer, B. & van Asselt, H. (2023) 'The rise of international climate litigation'. *Review of European, Comparative and International Environmental Law*, 32(2): 175–184.

Mazzucato, M. (2011) *The Entrepreneurial State*. London: Demos.

Mazzucato, M. (2015) 'The green entrepreneurial state'. In I. Scoones et al. (eds.), *The Politics of Green Transformations*. Abingdon: Routledge, pp. 134–153.

Mazzucato, M. (2022) 'Financing the green new deal'. *Nature Sustainability*, 5(2): 93–94.

McCarthy, J. (2019) 'Authoritarianism, populism, and the environment: Comparative experiences, insights, and perspectives'. *Annals of the American Association of Geographers*, 109(2): 301–313.

McDonald, D. (2009) *Electric Capitalism: Recolonising Africa on the Power Grid*. London: Earthscan from Routledge.

McDonald, M. (2021) *Ecological Security: Climate Change and the Construction of Security*. Cambridge: Cambridge University Press.

McGee, J. & Taplin, R. (2006) 'The Asia – Pacific partnership on clean development and climate: A complement or competitor to the Kyoto protocol?'. *Global Change, Peace & Security*, 18(3): 173–192.

McGowan, F. (2009) International regimes for energy: Finding the right level for policy. In I. Scarse and G. MacKerron (eds.), *Energy for the Future: A New Agenda*. London: Palgrave Macmillan UK, pp. 20–34.

Meadowcroft, J. (2004) 'From welfare state to ecostate'. In J. Barry and R. Eckersley (eds.), *The State and the Global Ecological Crisis*. Cambridge: MIT Press, pp. 63–87.

Meadowcroft, J. (2008) 'From welfare state to environmental state'. *Journal of European Social Policy*, 18(4): 325–344.

Meadowcroft, J. (2009) 'What about the politics? Sustainable development, transition management, and long term energy transitions'. *Policy Sciences*, 42(4): 323–340.

Meadowcroft, J. (2011) 'Engaging with the politics of sustainability transitions'. *Environmental Innovation and Societal Transitions*, 1(1): 70–75.

Meadows, D. (1999) *Leverage Points: Places to Intervene in a System*. Hartland: The Sustainability Institute.

Meckling, J. (2011) *Carbon Coalitions: Business, Climate Politics, and the Rise of Emissions Trading*. Cambridge, MA: MIT Press.

Mellor, M. (1992) *Breaking the Boundaries: Towards a Feminist Green Socialism*. London: Virago Press.

Menton, M. & Le Billon, P. (eds.) (2021) *Environmental Defenders: Deadly Struggles for Life and Territory*. Abindgon: Routledge.

Mérieau, E. (2016) 'Thailand's deep state, royal power and the constitutional court (1997–2015)'. *Journal of Contemporary Asia*, 46(3): 445–466.

Mhango, N. N. (2018) *How Africa Developed Europe*. Bamenda: Langa Research and Publishing Group.

Midttun, A. and Baumgartner, T. (1986) 'Negotiating energy futures: The politics of energy forecasting'. *Energy Policy* 14(3): 219–41.

Miliband, R. (1973) *The State in Capitalist Society*. London: Quartet Books.

Miller, H. & Moraw, P. (1996) 'Clerics and the state'. In W. Reinhard (ed.), *Power Elites and State-Building*. Oxford: Clarendon Press, pp. 173–188.

Milman, O. (2015) 'Zuckerberg, gates and other tech titans form clean energy investment coalition'. *The Guardian*, 30 November. www.theguardian.com/environment/2015/nov/30/bill-gates-breakthrough-energy-coalition-mark-zuckerberg-facebook-microsoft-amazon.

Mitchell, T. (2011) *Carbon Democracy: Political Power in the Age of Oil*. London: Verso Books.

Mittelstadt, J. (2015) *The Rise of the Military Welfare State*. Cambridge, MA: Harvard University Press.

Moberg, E., Allison, E. H., & Harl, H. K. et al. (2021) 'Combined innovations in public policy, the private sector and culture can drive sustainability transitions in food systems'. *Nature Food*, 2: 282–290.

Moberg, K. R., Aall, C., Dorner, F. et al. (2019) 'Mobility, food and housing: Responsibility, individual consumption and demand-side policies in European deep decarbonisation pathways'. *Energy Efficiency*, 12: 497–519.

Mol, A. P. J. (2003) *Globalization and Environmental Reform: The Ecological Modernization of the Global Economy*. Cambridge, MA: MIT Press.

Mol, A. P. J. (2016) 'The environmental nation state in decline'. *Environmental Politics*, 25(1): 48–68.

Mol, A. P. J., Sonnenfield, D. A., & Spaargaren, G. (eds.) (2010) *The Ecological Modernization Reader: Environmental Reform in Theory and Practice*. London: Routledge.

Monbiot, G. (2000) *Captive State: The Corporate Takeover of Britain*. London: Pan MacMillan.

Monbiot, G. (2024) 'What links Rishi Sunak, Javier Milei and Donald Trump? The shadowy network behind their policies'. *The Guardian*, 6 January. www.theguardian.com/commentisfree/2024/jan/06/rishi-sunak-javier-milei-donald-trump-atlas-network.

Moore, J. (2015) *Capitalism and the Web of Life: Ecology and the Accumulation of Capital*. London: Verso Books.

Moran, D. & Russell, J. (eds.) (2009) *Energy Security and Global Politics: The Militarization of Resource Management*. Abingdon: Routledge.

Moran, M. (2002) 'Understanding the regulatory state'. *British Journal of Political Science*, 32(2): 391–413.

Morena, E., Krause, D., & Stevis, D. (2019) *Just Transitions: Social Justice in the Shift Towards a Low-Carbon World*. London: Pluto Press.

Morgenthau, H. J. (1948) *Power among Nations: The Struggle for Power and Peace*. New York: Alfred Knopf.

Morris, A. (2016) 'The Challenge of State Reliance on revenue from fossil fuel production'. *Climate and Energy Economic Discussion Paper*, 9 August, 2016.

Moskos, C. (1994) 'Armed forces in a warless society'. In L. Freedman (ed.), *War*. Oxford: Oxford University Press, pp. 134–139.

Mulugetta, Y., Sokona, Y., & Trotter, P. A. et al. (2022) 'Africa needs context-relevant evidence to shape its clean energy future'. *Nature Energy*, 7: 1015–1022.

Murphy, M. W. & Schroering, C. (2020) 'Refiguring the plantationocene: Racial capitalism, world-systems analysis, and global socioecological transformation'. *Journal of World-Systems Research*, 26(2): 400–415.

Muttitt, G. & Kartha, S. (2020) 'Equity, climate justice and fossil fuel extraction: Principles for a managed phase out'. *Climate Policy*, 20(8): 1024–1042.

Narizny, K. (2021) 'Economic interests and grand strategy'. In T. Balzacq & R. R. Krebs (eds.), *The Oxford Handbook of Grand Strategy*. Oxford: Oxford University Press, pp. 256–270.

Nehring, C. (2022) 'Files, agents, "Deep State," and Russian influence: The legacy of the communist state security service in Bulgaria'. *International Journal of Intelligence and Counterintelligence*, 35(2): 318–338.

Nem Singh, J. T. (2024) *Business of the State: What State Ownership Matters for Resource Governance*. Oxford: Oxford University Press.

Nem Singh, J. & Chen, G. C. (2017) 'State-owned enterprises and the political economy of state – state relations in the developing world'. *Third World Quarterly*, 39(6): 1077–1097.

Newell, P. (2001) 'Managing multinationals: The governance of investment for the environment'. *Journal of International Development*, 13(7): 907–919.

Newell, P. (2005) 'Citizenship, accountability and community: The limits of the CSR agenda'. *International Affairs*, 81(3): 541–557.

Newell, P. (2007) 'Trade and environmental justice in Latin America'. *New Political Economy*, 12(2): 237–259.

Newell, P. (2008a) 'The political economy of global environmental governance'. *Review of International Studies*, 34: 507–529.

Newell, P. (2008b) 'Civil society, corporate accountability and the politics of climate change'. *Global Environmental Politics*, 8(3): 124–155.

Newell, P. (2008c) 'Lost in translation? Domesticating global policy on genetically modified organisms: Comparing India and China'. *Global Society*, 22(1): 115–136.

Newell, P. (2010a) *Climate Capitalism: Global Warming and the Transformation of the Global Economy*. Cambridge: Cambridge University Press.

Newell, P. (2010b) 'Democratising biotechnology? Deliberation, participation and social regulation in a neo-liberal world'. *Review of International Studies*, 36: 471–491.

Newell, P. (2012) *Globalization and the Environment: Capitalism, Ecology and Power*. Cambridge: Polity Press.

Newell, P. (2015) 'The politics of green transformations in capitalism'. In I. Scoones, M. Leach, and P. Newell (eds.), *The Politics of Green Transformations*. London: Routledge, pp. 68–86.

Newell, P. (2018) '*Trasformismo* or transformation? The global political economy of energy transitions'. *Review of International Political Economy*, 26(1): 25–48.

Newell, P. (2019) *Global Green Politics*. Cambridge: Cambridge University Press.

Newell, P. (2021a) *Power Shift: The Global Political Economy of Energy Transitions*. Cambridge: Cambridge University Press.

Newell, P. (2021b) 'Race and the politics of energy transitions'. *Energy Research & Social Science*, 71: 101839.

Newell, P. (2024a) 'Towards a more transformative approach to climate finance'. *Climate Policy*, 25(2): 257–268.

Newell, P. (2024b) 'Back from the dead: the ecology of IR'. *International Relations*, 0(0). https://doi.org/10.1177/00471178241269708.

Newell, P. & Bulkeley, H. (2017) 'Landscape for change? International climate policy and energy transitions: Evidence from sub-Saharan Africa'. *Climate Policy*, 17(5): 650–663.

Newell, P. & Bumpus, A. (2012) 'The global political ecology of the CDM'. *Global Environmental Politics*, 12: 49–67.
Newell, P. & Daley, F. (2022) 'Cooking up an electric revolution: The political economy of e-cooking'. *Energy Research and Social Science*, 91: 102730.
Newell, P., Daley, F., Mikheeva, O., & Pesa, I. (2023) 'Mind the gap: The global governance of just transitions'. *Global Policy*, 14(3): 425–437.
Newell, P., Daley, F., & Twena, M. (2022) *Changing Our Ways? Behaviour Change and the Climate Crisis*. The report of the Cambridge Sustainability Commission on Scaling Behaviour Change.
Newell, P. & Johnstone, P. (2018) 'The political economy of incumbency'. In J. Skovgaard and H. Van Asselt (eds.), *The Politics of Fossil Fuel Subsidies and Their Reform*. Cambridge: Cambridge University Press, pp. 66–80.
Newell, P. & MacKenzie, R. (2004) 'Whose rules rule? Development and the global governance of biotechnology'. *IDS Bulletin*, 35(1): 82–92.
Newell, P. & Martin, A. (2020) *The Role of the State in the Politics of Disruption and Acceleration*. London: EIT Climate KIC.
Newell, P. & Mulvaney, D. (2013) 'The political economy of the just transition'. *The Geographical Journal*, 197(2): 132–140.
Newell, P. & Paterson, M. (1998) 'A climate for business: Global warming, the state and capital'. *Review of International Political Economy*, 5(4): 679–703.
Newell, P. & Paterson, M. (2010) *Climate Capitalism: Global Warming and the Transformation of the Global Economy*. Cambridge: Cambridge University Press.
Newell, P. & Phillips, J. (2016) 'Neoliberal energy transitions in the South: Kenyan experiences'. *Geoforum*, 74: 39–48.
Newell, P., Phillips, J., & Mulvaney, D. (2011) *Pursuing clean energy equitably*. UNDP-HDRO Occasional Papers (2011/03).
Newell, P., Phillips, J., Pueyo, A., Kirumba, E., Ozor, N., & Urama, K. (2014) 'The political economy of low carbon energy in Kenya'. *IDS Working Papers*, 2014(445): 1–38.
Newell, P., Price, R., & Daley, F. (2024) Landscapes of (in) justice: Reflecting on voices, spaces and alliances for just transitions. *Energy Research & Social Science*, 116: 103701.
Newell, P. & Simms, A. (2019) 'Towards a fossil fuel non-proliferation treaty'. *Climate Policy*, 20(8): 1043–1054.
Newell, P. & Simms, A. (2020) 'How did we do that? Histories and political economies of rapid and just transitions'. *New Political Economy*, 26(6): 907–922.
Newell, P., Sovacool, B., & Geels, F. (2022) 'Navigating tensions between rapid and just low-carbon transitions'. *Environmental Research Letters*, 17: 041006.
Newell, P. & Taylor, O. (2018) 'Contested landscapes: The global political economy of climate smart agriculture'. *Journal of Peasant Studies*, 45(1–2): 108–130.
Newell, P., Taylor, O., & Touni, C. (2018) Governing food and agriculture in a warming world. *Global Environmental Politics*, 18(2): 53–71.
Newell, P., Taylor, O., Naess, L. O., Thompson, J., Mahmoud, H., Ndaki, P., ... & Teshome, A. (2019) Climate smart agriculture? Governing the sustainable development goals in Sub-Saharan Africa. *Frontiers in Sustainable Food Systems*, 3: 55.
Newell, P., Twena, M., & Daley, F. (2021) 'Scaling behaviour change for a 1.5-degree world: challenges and opportunities'. *Global Sustainability*, 4: e22.
Newell, P. & Wheeler, J. (eds.) (2006) *Rights, Resources and the Politics of Accountability*. London: Zed Books.
Newell, P., Shankland, A., Wemanya, A., Pereira, C., Gonçalves, E., Bashir, I., Gaventa, J., Adow, M., Nampoothiri, N., Scott-Villiers, P. & McGee, R. (2022) *Making Space for Dialogue on Just Transitions in Africa's Oil and Gas Producing Regions*. London: British Academy.

Nixon, R. (2011) *Slow Violence and the Environmentalism of the Poor*. Cambridge: Harvard University Press.

Normann, H. (2015) 'The role of politics in sustainable transitions: The rise and decline of offshore wind in Norway'. *Environmental Innovation and Societal Transitions*, 15: 180–193.

Normann, H. (2017) 'Policy networks in energy transitions: The cases of carbon capture and storage and offshore wind in Norway'. *Technological Forecasting and Social Change*, 118: 80–93.

Norris, W. J. (2016) *Chinese Economic Statecraft: Commercial Actors, Grand Strategy, and State Control*. Ithaca, NY: Cornell University Press.

Nyman, J. & Zeng, J. (2016) 'Securitization in Chinese climate and energy politics'. *Wiley Interdisciplinary Reviews: Climate Change*, 7(2): 301–313.

O'Boyle, M. (2018) 'Investment-grade policy: De-risking renewable energy projects'. Forbes, 12 November. www.forbes.com/sites/energyinnovation/2018/11/12/investment-grade-policy-de-risking-renewable-energy-projects/#55764f624e77.

O'Brien, K., Carmona, R., Gram-Hanssen, I., Hochachka, G., Sygna, L., & Rosenberg, M. (2023) 'Fractal approaches to scaling transformations to sustainability'. *Ambio*, 52: 1–14.

O'Connor, J. (1973) *The Fiscal Crisis of the State*. New York: St. Martin's Press.

O'Connor, J. (1991) 'On the two contradictions of capitalism'. *Capitalism, Nature, Socialism*, 2(3): 107–109.

O'Connor, J. (1998) *Natural Causes: Essays in Ecological Marxism*. London: Guildford Press.

Obach, B. K. (2004) *Labor and the Environmental Movement: The Quest for Common Ground*. Cambridge, MA: MIT Press.

Ockwell, D. & Byrne, R. (2017) *Sustainable Energy for All: Technology, Innovation and Pro-poor Green Transformations*. Abingdon: Taylor & Francis.

Ockwell, D. G, Watson, J., MacKerron, G., Pal, P., & Yamin, F. (2008) 'Key policy considerations for facilitating low carbon technology transfer to developing countries'. *Energy Policy*, 36(11): 4104–4115.

Oczkowska, M. & Pellerin-Carlin, T. (2019) 'Just energy transition: A reality test in Europe's coal regions'. Jacques Delors Energy Centre, Policy Paper. https://web.uniroma1.it/bibbarone/sites/default/files/energy.pdf

Odell, P. (1981) *Oil and World Power*. London: Penguin Books.

ODI (Overseas Development Institute). (2023) 'Five opportunities for Nigeria to lead a clean and just energy transition at COP27 and beyond'. https://odi.org/en/insights/five-opportunities-for-nigeria-to-lead-a-clean-and-just-energy-transition-at-cop27-and-beyond/.

OECD (Organisation for Economic Co-operation and Development). (2013) *Effective Carbon Prices*. Paris: OECD.

Offe, K. (1984) *Contradictions of the Welfare State*. London: Hutchinson.

Ohmae, K. (1990) *The Borderless World*. New York: Harper Business.

Okereke, C. & Sakona, Y. (2022) 'Africa has vast gas reserves – here's how to stop them adding to climate change'. *The Conversation*, 15 November. https://theconversation.com/africa-has-vast-gas-reserves-heres-how-to-stop-them-adding-to-climate-change-194473.

O'Neill, T. (2005) 'Water and freedom: The privatization of water and its implications for democracy and human rights in the developing world'. *Colorado Journal of International Environmental Law & Policy*, 17: 357.

Ophuls, W. (1973) 'Leviathan or Oblivion?' In H. Daly (ed.), *Toward a Steady State Economy*. San Francisco: Freeman.

Ophuls, W. (1977) *Ecology and the Politics of Scarcity*. New York: W. H. Freeman and Co.
O'Rourke, D. (2004) *Community-Driven Regulation: Balancing Development and the Environment in Vietnam*. Cambridge, MA: MIT Press.
Ostrom, E. (2010) 'Beyond markets and states: Polycentric governance of complex economic systems'. *American Economic Review*, 100(3): 641–672.
Otto, I. M., Donges, J. F., Cremades, R., Bhowmik, A., Hewitt, R. J., Lucht, W., … & Lenferna, A. (2020) 'Social tipping dynamics for stabilizing Earth's climate by 2050'. *Proceedings of the National Academy of Sciences*, 117(5): 2354–2365.
Ougaard, M. (2018) 'The transnational state and the infrastructure push'. *New Political Economy*, 23(1): 128–144.
Owens, S. (2000) '"Engaging the public": Information and deliberation in environmental policy'. *Environment and Planning A*, 32(7): 1141–1148.
Pacheco, P. & Klingler-Vidra, R. (2019) 'The entrepreneurial developmental state: What is the perceived impact of South Korea's creative economy action plan on entrepreneurial activity?'. *Asian Studies Review*, 43(2): 313–331.
Panitch, L. & Gindin, S. (2012) *The Making of Global Capitalism*. London: Verso Books.
Papanek, V. (1971) *Design for the Real World: Human Ecology and Social Change*. New York: Pantheon Books.
Parker, M. (1994) *The Politics of Coal's Decline: The Industry in Western Europe*. London: Royal Institute of Economic Affairs.
Parson, E. (1995) 'Integrated assessment and environmental policy making: In pursuit of usefulness'. *Energy Policy*, 23(4/5): 463–476.
Patel, R. & Moore, J. (2017) *A History of the World in Seven Cheap Things: A Guide to Capitalism, Nature and the Future of the Planet*. Berkeley: University of California Press.
Paterson, M. (2001) *Understanding Global Environmental Politics: Domination, Accumulation, Resistance*. Basingstoke: Palgrave.
Paterson, M. (2010) 'Legitimation and accumulation in climate change governance'. *New Political Economy*, 15(3): 345–368.
Patterson, W. (1984) *The Plutonium Business and the Spread of the Bomb*. London: Paladin Books Granada Publishing.
Patterson, J. & Paterson, M. (2024) 'Embracing the politics of transformation: Policy action as "battle-settlement events"'. *Review of Policy Research*, 1–25.
Patterson, J., Wyborn, C., & Westman, L. et al. (2021) 'The political effects of emergency frames in sustainability'. *Nature Sustainability*, 4: 841–850. https://doi.org/10.1038/s41893-021-00749-9.
Paul, T. V., Ikenberry, J., & Hall, J. (eds.) (2003) *The Nation-State in Question*. New York: Princeton University Press.
Pearson, M. (1997) *China's New Business Elite*. Berkeley: University of California Press.
Peck, J. & Tickell, A. (2002) 'Neoliberalizing Space'. *Antipode*, 34(3): 380–404.
Pedersen, S., Stevis, D., & Kalfagianni, A. (2022) 'The earth system, justice, and governance in a planetary age: Engaging a social turn'. *Environmental Philosophy*, 32(7). https://doi.org/10.1068/a3330
Peet, R., Robbins, P., & Watts, M. (eds.) (2011) *Global Political Ecology*. London: Routledge.
Pega, F., Nafradi, B., Momen, N. et al. (2021) 'Global, regional, and national burdens of ischemic heart disease and stroke attributable to exposure to long working hours for 194 countries, 2000–2016: A systematic analysis from the WHO/ILO joint estimates of the work-related burden of disease and injury'. *Environment International*, 106595.
Pegels, A. (ed.) (2014) *Green Industrial Policy in Emerging Countries*. London: Routledge.

Pegels, A. & Lütkenhorst, W. (2014) 'Is Germany's energy transition a case of successful green industrial policy? Contrasting wind and solar PV'. *Energy Policy*, 74: 522–534.

Pegels, A., Vidican-Auktor, G., Lütkenhorst, W., & Altenburg, T. (2018) 'Politics of green energy policy'. *Journal of Environment and Development*, 27(1): 26–45.

Pepper, D. (1995) *Eco-socialism: From Deep Ecology to Social Justice*, 2nd ed. London: Routledge.

Perez, C. (2002) *Technological Revolutions and Financial Capital: The Dynamics of Bubbles and Golden Ages*. Cheltenham: Edward Elgar Publishing.

Pettifor, A. (2019) *The Case for the Green New Deal*. London: Verso Books.

Pfleiderer, R. H. & Dieterich, M. (1995) 'New roads generate new traffic'. *World Transport Policy and Practice*, 1(1): 29–31.

Phillips, J. (2018) 'Who's in charge of Sino-African resource politics? situating African state agency in Ghana'. *African Affairs*, 118/470: 101–124.

Phillips, J., Hailwood, E., & Brooks, A. (2016) 'Sovereignty, the "resource curse" and the limits of good governance: A political economy of oil in Ghana'. *Review of African Political Economy*, 43(147): 26–42.

Phillips, J. & Newell, P. (2013) 'The governance of clean energy in India: The clean development mechanism (CDM) and domestic energy politics'. *Energy Policy* 59: 654–662.

Pickering, J., Hickmann, T., Bäckstrand, K., Kalfagianni, A., Bloomfield, M., Mert, A., Ransan-Cooper, H., & Lo, A. Y. (2022) 'Democratising sustainability transformations: Assessing the transformative potential of democratic practices in environmental governance'. *Earth System Governance*, 11: 100131.

Pildes, R. H. & Sunstein, C. R. (1995) 'Reinventing the regulatory state'. *The University of Chicago Law Review*, 62(1): 1–129.

Pimbert, M. P. & Wakeford, T. (2002) *Prajateerpu: A Citizens Jury/Scenario Workshop on Food and Farming Futures for Andhra Pradesh*. India. IIED, London and IDS, Sussex.

Pincus, R. H. & Ali, S. H. (eds.) (2015) *Diplomacy on Ice: Energy and the Environment in the Arctic and Antarctic*. New Haven: Yale University Press.

Pineault, E. (2023) *A Social Ecology of Capital*. London: Pluto Press.

Pirages, D. (1997) 'Ecological theory and international relations'. *Indiana Journal of Global Legal Studies*, 5(1): 53–63.

Plant, R. (2010) *The Neo-liberal State*. Oxford: Oxford University Press.

Plato. (2007) *The Republic*. London: Penguin Books.

Plumwood, V. (1993) *Feminism and the Mastery of Nature*. London: Routledge.

Polanyi, K. (1980 [1944]) *The Great Transformation*. Boston: Beacon Press.

Porritt, J. (1989) *Seeing Green: The Politics of Ecology Explained*. Oxford: Basil Blackwell.

Poulantzas, N. (2014 [1978]) *State, Power, Socialism*. London: Verso Books.

Powell, D. (2018) *Landscapes of Power: Politics of Energy in the Navajo Nation*. Durham, NC: Duke University Press.

Power, M., Newell, P., Baker, L., Bulkeley, H., Kirshner, J., & Smith, A. (2016) 'The political economy of energy transitions in Mozambique and South Africa: The role of the rising powers'. *Energy Research & Social Sciences*, 17: 10–19.

Prinz, L. & Pegels, A. (2018) 'The role of labour power in sustainability transitions: Insights from comparative political economy on Germany's electricity transition'. *Energy Research & Social Science*, 41: 210–219.

Prudham, S. & Morris, A. (2006) 'Making the market "safe" for GM foods: The case of the Canadian Biotechnology Advisory Committee'. *Studies in Political Economy*, 78(1): 145–175.

Quashie-Idun, S. & Howard, E. (2022) '"How are we going to live?" Families dispossessed of their land to make way for Total's Congo offsetting project'. Unearthed, 12 December. https://unearthed.greenpeace.org/2022/12/12/total-congo-offsetting-land-dispossessed/.

Quastel, N. (2016) 'Ecological political economy: Towards a strategic-relational approach'. *Review of Political Economy*, 28(3): 336–353.

Quinson, T. (2023) 'Banks need even bigger low-carbon pivot to avert climate crisis'. *Bloomberg*, 28 February. www.bloomberg.com/news/articles/2023-02-28/banks-need-even-bigger-low-carbon-pivot-to-avert-climate-crisis?leadSource=uverify%20wall.

Race, M. (2023) 'No bids for offshore wind in government auction'. 8 September. www.bbc.co.uk/news/business-66749344.

Raworth, K. (2017) *Doughnut Economics: Seven Ways to Think Like a 21st-Century Economist*. London: Random House Business Books.

Read, R. (2012) *Guardians of the Future: A Constitutional Case for Representing and Protecting Future People*, Greenhouse Report.

Rees, J. (ed.) (2001) *Imperialism: Globalisation, the State and War*. International Socialism.

Reinhard, W. (ed.) (1996) *Power Elites and State-Building*. Oxford: Clarendon Press.

Renn, O., Köck, W., Schweizer, P. J., Bovet, J., Benighaus, C., Scheel, O., & Schröter, R. (2014) 'Public participation for planning new facilities in the context of the German "Energiewende"'. *Policy Brief Edition*, 1.

Resources for the Future. (2022) 'US revenues from fossil fuels, responsible for $138 billion annually, expected to fall regardless of climate action', Press Release, 13 January. https://bit.ly/3DF395h.

Reyes, O. (2018) '*Revolving doors in Spanish climate and energy policy*', Greens/EFA Group in the European Parliament, May 2018. www.greens-efa.eu/files/assets/docs/report_of_revolving_doors_digital_-min.pdf.

Rhodes, M. (2005) '"Varieties of capitalism" and the political economy of European welfare states'. *New Political Economy*, 10(3): 363–370.

Rhodes, M. (2016) *The Future of European Welfare: A New Social Contract?* Springer.

Roberts, C. & Geels, F. (2019) 'Conditions for politically accelerated transitions: Historical institutionalism, the multi-level perspective, and two historical case studies in transport and agriculture'. *Technological Forecasting and Social Change*, 140: 221–240.

Roberts, C., Geels, F. W., Lockwood, M., Newell, P., Schmitz, H., Turnheim, B., & Jordan, A. (2018) 'The politics of accelerating low-carbon transitions: Towards a new research agenda'. *Energy Research & Social Science*, 44, 304–311.

Robertson, M. (2006) 'The nature that capital can see: Science, state, and market in the commodification of ecosystem services'. *Environment and Planning D: Society and Space*, 24: 367–387.

Robeyns, I. (2024) *Limitarianism: The Case against Extreme Wealth*. London: Allen Lane.

Robinson, W. I. (2004) *A Theory of Global Capitalism: Production, Class and State in a Transnational World*. Baltimore: Johns Hopkins University Press.

Rockström, J., Steffen, W., Noone, K., Persson, Å., Chapin, III, F. S., Lambin, E. F., … & Foley, J. A. (2009) 'A safe operating space for humanity'. *Nature*, 461: 472–475.

Roddis, P., Carver, S., Dallimer, M., Norman, P., & Ziv, G. (2018) 'The role of community acceptance in planning outcomes for onshore wind and solar farms: An energy justice analysis'. *Applied Energy*, 226: 353–364.

Rodhouse, T., Pesch, U., Cuppen, E., & Correljé, A. (2021) 'Public agency and responsibility in energy governance: A Q study on diverse imagined publics in the Dutch heat transition'. *Energy Research & Social Science*, 77: 102046. https://doi.org/10.1016/j.erss.2021.102046.

Rodney, W. (2018 [1972]) *How Europe Under-Developed Africa*. London: Verso Books.

Rodrik, D. (2007) 'Industrial policy for the twenty-first century'. In D. Rodrik (ed.), *One Economics, Many Recipes: Globalization, Institutions and Economic Growth*. Princeton, NJ: Princeton University Press, pp. 99–145.

Rosenberg, J. (2003) *The Follies of Globalisation Theory: Polemical Essays*. London: Verso Books.

Rosenberg, J. (2013) 'The "philosophical premises" of uneven and combined development'. *Review of International Studies*, 39(3): 569–597.

Rosnick, D. & Weisbrot, M. (2007) 'Are shorter work hours good for the environment? A comparison of US and European energy consumption'. *International Journal of Health Services*, 37(3): 405–417.

Ross, M. (1999) 'The political economy of the resource curse'. *World Politics*, 51(2): 297–322.

Ross, M. (2012) *The Oil Curse: How Petroleum Wealth Shapes the Development of Nations*. Princeton, NJ: Princeton University Press.

Rowell, A. (1996) *Green Backlash: Global Subversion of the Environment Movement*. London: Routledge.

RTA (Rapid Transition Alliance). (2018) 'The rise of Brazil's sugarcane cars', 2 December. www.rapidtransition.org/stories/the-rise-of-brazils-sugarcane-cars/.

RTA (Rapid Transition Alliance). (2019) 'Make do and mend: The rise of repair cafes', 25 February. www.rapidtransition.org/stories/make-do-and-mend-the-rise-of-repair-cafes/.

RTA (Rapid Transition Alliance). (2022) 'Solar power surges in Spain', 30 August. www.rapidtransition.org/stories/solar-power-surges-in-spain/.

Rüdinger, A. (2019) *Participatory and Citizen Renewable Energy Projects in France – State of Play and Recommendations*. Paris: IDDRI and Climate Strategies.

Rupert, M. (1995) *Producing Hegemony: The Politics of Mass Production and American Global Power*. Cambridge: Cambridge University Press.

Rupert, M. & Smith, H. (eds.) (2002) *Historical Materialism and Globalization*. London: Routledge.

Ryner, M. & Cafruny, A. (2016) *The European Union and Global Capitalism: Origins, Development, Crisis*. London: Bloomsbury Publishing.

Sabatier, P. A. (1988) 'An advocacy coalition framework of policy change and the role of policy-oriented learning therein'. *Policy Sciences*, 21(2–3): 129–168.

Sagaris, L. (2014) 'Citizen participation for sustainable transport: The case of "Living City" in Santiago, Chile (1997–2012)'. *Journal of Transport Geography*, 41: 74–83.

Saikkonen, P. & Ilmakunnas, I. (2023) 'Reconciling welfare policy and sustainability transition: A case study of the Finnish welfare state'. *Environmental Policy and Governance*, 1–12. https://doi.org/10.1002/eet.2055.

Salah Ovadia, J. (2018) 'State-led industrial development, structural transformation and elite-led plunder: Angola (2002–2013) as a developmental state'. *Development Policy Review*, 36(5): 587–606.

Santos Vieira de Jesus, D. (2013) 'Lighting the fire: Brazil's energy diplomacy, 2003–2010'. *Diplomacy and Statecraft*, 24(3): 499–515.

Saurin, J. (2001) 'Global environmental crisis as "disaster triumphant": The private capture of public goods'. *Environmental Politics*, 10(4): 63–84.

Saward, M. (1998) 'Green state/democratic state'. *Contemporary Politics*, 4: 345–356.

Schaltegger, S., Hansen, E. G., & Lüdeke-Freund, F. (2015) 'Business models for sustainability: Origins, present research, and future avenues'. *Organization & Environment*. https://doi.org/10.1177/1086026615599806.

Schedler, A., Diamond, L. J., & Plattner, M. F. (eds.) (1999) *The Self-Restraining State: Power and Accountability in New Democracies*. Boulder, CO: Lynne Rienner Publishers.

Schmitz, H. (2017) 'Who drives climate-relevant policies in the rising powers?'. *New Political Economy*, 22: 521–540.
Scholte, J. A. (ed.) (2011) *Building Global Democracy? Civil Society and Accountable Global Governance*. Cambridge: Cambridge University Press.
Schor, J. (2011) *True Wealth: How and Why Millions of Americans Are Creating a Time-Rich, Ecologically Light, Small-Scale, High-Satisfaction Economy*. New York: Penguin Books.
Schor, J. (2015) 'Climate, inequality, and the need for reframing climate policy'. *Review of Radical Political Economics*, 47(4): 525–536.
Schot, J. & Geels, F. W. (2008) 'Strategic niche management and sustainable innovation journeys: theory, findings, research agenda, and policy'. *Technology Analysis & Strategic Management*, 20(5): 537–554.
Schulz, S. & Schwartzkopf, J. (2016) 'Instruments for a managed coal phase-out: German and international experiences with structural change'. E3G Briefing paper, July.
Schumpeter, J. A. (2011 [1947]) *Capitalism, Socialism and Democracy*, 2nd ed. Floyd, VA: Impact Books.
Scoones, I. (2006) *Science, Agriculture and the Politics of Policy: The Case of Biotechnology in India*. Hyderabad: Orient Blackswan.
Scoones, I., Leach, M., & Newell, P. (eds.) (2015) *The Politics of Green Transformations*. London: Routledge.
Scott, J. C. (2020) *Seeing Like a State: How Certain Schemes to Improve the Human Condition Have Failed*. New Haven: Yale university Press.
Scott, P. D. (2017) *The American Deep State: Big Money, Big Oil, and the Struggle for U.S. Democracy*. Updated ed. Lanham, MD: Rowman and Littlefield.
Seabrooke, L. & Wigan, D. (2017) 'The governance of global wealth chains'. *Review of International Political Economy*, 24(1): 1–29.
SEI, IISD, ODI, Climate Analytics, CICERO, & UNEP. (2021) Production Gap Report. Stockholm: SEI.
Selby, J. (2022) 'International/inter-carbonic relations'. *International Relations*, 36(3): 329–357.
Selwyn, B. (2019) 'Poverty chains and global capitalism'. *Competition & Change*, 23(1): 71–97.
Sen, A. & Darbi, N. (2021) *Tightening the Net: The Implications of Net Zero Climate Targets for Land and Food Equity*. Oxford: Oxfam Publishing.
Seyfang, G. & Haxeltine, A. (2012) 'Growing grassroots innovations: Exploring the role of community-based initiatives in governing sustainable energy transitions'. *Environment and Planning C: Government and Policy*, 30: 381–400.
Shane, C. (2003) *A General Theory of Entrepreneurship: The Individual-Opportunity Nexus*. Cheltenham: Edward Elgar Publishing.
Sharp, C. (2024) 'Ed Miliband's hypocrisy over Tata Steel exposed: "Responsible for speeding up job losses"'. *Daily Express*, 31 January. www.express.co.uk/news/politics/1861698/ed-miliband-hypocrisy-tata-steel-job-losses.
Shaw, M. (2000) *Theory of the Global State: Globality as Unfinished Revolution*. Cambridge: Cambridge University Press.
Shearman, D. & Smith, J. W. (2007) *The Climate Change Challenge and the Failure of Democracy*. Westport, CT: Praeger.
Shen, W. & Power, M. (2017) 'Africa and the export of China's clean energy revolution'. *Third World Quarterly*, 38(3): 678–697.
Shiva, V. (1998) *Staying Alive: Women, Ecology and Development*. London: Zed Books.
Shove, E. (2012) 'The shadowy side of innovation: Unmaking and sustainability'. *Technology Analysis & Strategic Management*, 24(4): 363–375.

Siebert, J. (2021) 'The greening of uneven and combined development: IR, capitalism and the global ecological crisis'. *Cambridge Review of International Affairs*, 34(2): 164–185.

Silvester, B. R. & Fisker, J. K. (2023) 'A relational approach to the role of the state in societal transitions and transformations towards sustainability'. *Environmental Innovation and Societal Transitions*, 47: 100717.

Simms, A., Coote, A., & Franklin, J. (2010) *21 Hours: Why a Shorter Working Week Can Help Us All to Flourish in the 21st Century*. London: New Economics Foundation.

Simms, A. (2013) *Cancel the Apocalypse: New Pathways to Prosperity*. London: Little, Brown and Company.

Simms, A. & Murray, L. (2023) *Badvertising: Polluting Our Minds and Fuelling Climate Chaos*. London: Pluto Press.

Simms, A. & Newell, P. (2017) *How Did We Do That? The Possibility of Rapid Transitions*. Brighton: STEPS Centre.

Simms, A. & Newell, P. (2018) 'We need a fossil fuel non-proliferation treaty – and we need it now'. *The Guardian*, 23 October. www.theguardian.com/commentisfree/2018/oct/23/fossil-fuel-non-proliferation-treaty-climate-breakdown.

Sinclair, T. J. (1994) 'Passing judgement: Credit rating processes as regulatory mechanisms of governance in the emerging world order'. *Review of International Political Economy*, 133–159.

Singh, J. N. (2024) *Business of the State: Why State Ownership Matters for Resource Governance*. Oxford: Oxford University Press.

Singh, J. N. & Chen, G. C. (2018) 'State-owned enterprises and the political economy of state – state relations in the developing world'. *Third World Quarterly*, 39(6): 1077–1097.

SIPRI (Stockholm International Peace Research Institute). (2018) 'Global military spending remains high at $1.7 trillion'. www.sipri.org/media/press-release/2018/globalmilitary-spending-remains-high-17-trillion.

Sklair, L. (1995) *Sociology of the Global System*. Baltimore: Johns Hopkins University Press.

Sklair, L. (2002) 'The transnational capitalist class and global politics: Deconstructing the corporate-state connection'. *International Political Science Review*, 23(2): 159–174.

Smith, A. (1776 [2014]) *The Wealth of Nations*. London: Shine Classics.

Smith, A. (2014) 'Socially useful production'. STEPS Working Paper 58. Brighton: STEPS Centre.

Smith, A. (2016) 'From arms to renewables'. *GreenWorld* Magazine, 2 February.

Smith, N. (2010) *Uneven Development: Nature, Capital, and the Production of Space*. Georgia: University of Georgia Press.

Smith, A., Fressoli, M., Abrol, D., Around, E., & Ely, A. (2016) *Grassroots Innovation Movements*. Abingdon: Routledge.

Smith, A., Hargreaves, T., Hielscher, S., Martiskainen, M., & Seyfang, V. (2016) 'Making the most of community energies: Three perspectives on grassroots innovation'. *Environment and Planning A: Economy and Space*, 48(2): 407–432.

Smythe, E. & Pendelton, A. (2018) *Flying Low: The True Cost of Heathrow's Third Runway*. London: New Economics Foundation.

Snyder, B. F. & Ruyle, L. E. (2020) 'A just compensation for leaving it in the ground: Climate easements and oil development'. *Environmental Science & Policy*, 112: 181–188.

Soper, K. (2020) *Post-Growth Living: For an Alternative Hedonism*. London: Verso Books.

Soto Hernandez, D. & Newell, P. (2022) 'Oro blanco: Assembling extractivism in the lithium triangle'. *The Journal of Peasant Studies*, 49(5): 945–968.

Sovacool, B. (2016) 'How long will it take? Conceptualizing the temporal dynamics of energy transitions'. *Energy Research & Social Science*, 13: 202–215.

Sovacool, B. K. (2021) 'Who are the victims of low-carbon transitions? Towards a political ecology of climate change mitigation'. *Energy Research & Social Science*, 73, 101916.

Sovacool, B. K. & Brisbois, M. C. (2019) 'Elite power in low-carbon transitions: A critical and interdisciplinary review'. *Energy Research & Social Science*, 57: 101242.

Sovacool, B. K, Geels, F., & Newell, P. (2022) 'Navigating tensions between rapid and just low-carbon transitions'. *Environmental Research Letters*, 17: 041006.

Sovacool, B. K., Hook, A., Martiskainen, M., & Baker, L. (2019) 'The whole systems energy injustice of four European low-carbon transitions'. *Global Environmental Change*, 58: 101958.

Sovacool, B. K. & Scarpaci, J. (2016) 'Energy justice and the contested petroleum politics of stranded assets: Policy insights from the Yasuní-ITT initiative in ecuador'. *Energy Policy*, 95: 158–171.

Sovacool, B. K., Turnheim, B., Martiskainen, M., Brown, D. & Kivimaa, P. (2020) 'Guides or gatekeepers? Incumbent-oriented transition intermediaries in a low-carbon era'. *Energy Research & Social Science*, 66: 101490.

Spencer, T. H. (1967) *The Evolution of Society*. Chicago: Chicago University Press.

Spencer, T., Colombier, M., Sartor, O., Garg, A., Tiwari, V., Burton, J., Caetano, T., Green, F., Teng, F., & Wiseman, J. (2018) 'The 1.5°C target and coal sector transition: At the limits of societal feasibility'. *Climate Policy*, 18(3): 335–351.

Starr, H. (2009) *Dealing with Failed States: Crossing Analytic Boundaries*. London: Routledge.

Stavrianakis, A. & Selby, J. (eds.) (2013) *Militarism and International Relations: Political Economy, Security, Theory*. London: Routledge.

Stavrianakis, A. & Stern, M. (2018) 'Militarism and security: Dialogue, possibilities and limits' *Security Dialogue*, 49(1–2): 3–18.

Steckel, J. & M. Jakob (2018) 'The role of financing cost and de-risking strategies for clean energy investment'. *International Economics* 155: 19–28.

Stephan, B. & Lane, R. (eds.) (2015) *The Politics of Carbon Markets*. New York: Routledge.

Sterl, S., Hagemann, M., Fekete, H., Höhne, N., Cantzler, J., Ancygier, A., Beer, M., Hare, B., Wouters, K., Deng, Y., Blok, K., Cronin, C., Monteith, S., Plechaty, D., & Menon, S. (2017) *Faster and Cleaner 2: Kick-Starting Global Decarbonization: It Only Takes a Few Actors to Get the Ball Rolling*. www.climateworks.org/wp-content/uploads/2017/04/Faster-and-Cleaner-2-Full-Technical-Report.pdf.

Stern, N. (2006) *The Stern Review on the Economics of Climate Change*. London: HM Treasury.

Stevenson, H. & Dryzek, J. (2014) *Democratizing Global Climate Governance*. Cambridge: Cambridge University Press.

Stiglitz, J. E., Lin, J. Y., & Patel, E. (eds.). (2013). *The Industrial Policy Revolution I: The Role of Government beyond Ideology*. New York: Palgrave Macmillan.

Stirling, A. (2005) 'Opening up or closing down? Analysis, participation and power in the social appraisal of technology'. In M. Leach, I. Scoones, and B. Wynne (eds.), *Science and Citizens: Globalization and the Challenge of Engagement. Claiming Citizenship*. London: Zed Books, pp. 218–231.

Stirling, A. (2011) 'Pluralising progress: From integrative transitions to transformative diversity'. *Environmental Innovation and Societal Transitions*, 1(1): 82–88.

Stirling, A. (2014a) 'Emancipating transformations: From controlling "the transition" to culturing plural radical progress'. STEPS Working Paper 64, Brighton: STEPS Centre.

Stirling, A. (2014b) 'Transforming power: Social science and the politics of energy choices'. *Energy Research & Social Science*, 1: 83–95 https://doi.org/10.1016/j.erss.2014.02.001.
Stirling, A. (2015) 'Time to rei(g)n back the Anthropocene'. STEPS blog, 16 October. https://steps-centre.org/blog/time-to-reign-back-the-anthropocene/.
Stirling, A. (2019) 'How deep is incumbency? A "configuring fields" approach to redistributing and reorienting power in socio-material change'. *Energy Research & Social Science* 58: 101239.
Stoddard, E. (2017) 'Tough times, shifting roles: Examining the EU's commercial diplomacy in foreign energy markets'. *Journal of European Public Policy*, 24(7): 1048–1068.
Stoddard, I., Anderson, K., Capstick, S., Carton, W., Depledge, J., Facer, K., … & Williams, M. (2021) 'Three decades of climate mitigation: Why haven't we bent the global emissions curve?' *Annual Review of Environment and Resources*, 46(1): 653–689.
Stone, J. (2021) 'Spain set to pilot four-day week as response to coronavirus pandemic'. *The Independent*, 28 January. www.independent.co.uk/news/world/politics/spain-covid-four-dayweek-pilotb1794322.html.
Stopford, J. M., Strange, S., & Henley, J. S. (1991) *Rival States, Rival Firms: Competition for World Market Shares*. Cambridge: Cambridge University Press.
Strange, S. (1996) *The Retreat of the State*. Cambridge: Cambridge University Press.
Streeck, W. (2014) *Buying Time: The Delayed Crisis of Democratic Capitalism*. London: Verso Books.
Sultana, F. (2022) 'The unbearable heaviness of climate coloniality'. *Political Geography*, 99, 102638.
Sun, P. (2007) 'Is the state-led industrial restructuring effective in transition China? Evidence from the steel sector'. *Cambridge Journal of Economics*, 31(4): 601–624.
Sun, D., Xu, H., & Tu, Y. (2022) 'In with the new: China's nuclear-energy diplomacy in the Middle East'. *Middle East Policy*, 29(1): 41–60.
Sun, Z., Scherer, L., Tukker, A., Spawn-Lee, S. A., Bruckner, M., Gibbs, H. K., & Behrens, P. (2022) 'Dietary change in high-income nations alone can lead to substantial double climate dividend'. *Nature Food*, 3(1): 29–37.
Swank, D. (2003) 'Withering welfare? Globalisation, political economic institutions and contemporary welfare states'. In L. Weiss (ed.), *States in the Global Economy: Bringing Domestic Institutions Back In*. Cambridge: Cambridge University Press, pp. 58–83.
Swilling, M. & Annecke, E. (2012) *Just Transitions: Explorations of Sustainability in an Unfair World*. South Africa: UCT Press.
Swilling, M., Musango, J., & Wakeford, J. (2016) 'Developmental states and sustainability transitions: Prospects of a just transition in South Africa'. *Journal of Environmental Policy & Planning*, 18(5): 650–672.
Swyngedouw, E. (2010) 'Apocalypse forever? Post-political populism and the spectre of climate change'. *Theory, Culture and Society*, 27(2–3): 213–232.
Szabó, J. & Fabok, M. (2020) 'Infrastructures and state-building: Comparing the energy politics of the European Commission with the governments of Hungary and Poland'. *Energy Policy*, 138: 111253.
Szabó, J. & Newell, P. (2024) 'Driving towards a just transition? The case of the European car industry'. *Energy Research & Social Science*, 115: 103649.
Szulecki, K. (2018a) 'Conceptualizing energy democracy'. *Environmental Politics*, 27(1): 21–41.
Szulecki, K. (2018b) *The Revolving Door between Politics and Dirty Energy in Poland: A Governmental-Industrial Complex*, Greens/EFA Group in the European Parliament, Report, May 2018. www.greens-efa.eu/files/assets/docs/report_of_revolving_doors_digital_-min.pdf.

Taylor, M. & Horton, H. (2022) 'Tories fighting net zero plans are dragging climate into new culture war, experts say.' *The Guardian*, 8 February. www.theguardian.com/politics/2022/feb/08/tories-fighting-net-zero-plans-are-dragging-climate-into-new-culture-war-experts-say

Tatchell, P. (1985) *Democratic Defence: A Non-nuclear Alternative*. London: GMP Publishers.

Teschke, B. (2003) *The Myth of 1648: Class, Geopolitics and the Making of Modern International Relations*. London: Verso Books.

The Economist (2023) 'A new Bretton Woods'. 25 February, p. 78.

Tellam, I. (ed.) (2000) *Fuel for Change: World Bank Energy Policy – Rhetoric and Reality*. London: Zed Books.

Tharoor, S. (2018) *Inglorious Empire: What the British Did to India*. London: Penguin UK.

Therborn, G. (1984) 'Classes and states welfare state developments, 1881–1981'. *Studies in Political Economy*, 14(1): 7–41.

Thompson, H. (2022) 'The geopolitics of fossil fuels and renewables reshape the world'. *Nature*, 11 March. www.nature.com/articles/d41586-022-00713-3.

Tienhaara, K., Thrasherb, R., Simmons, A., & Gallagher, K. (2022) 'Investor-state disputes threaten the global green energy transition'. *Science*, 376 (6594): 701–703.

Tilly, C. (1993) *Coercion, Capital, and European States, AD 990–1990*. Oxford: Wiley Blackwell.

Tilly, C., Evans, P., Rueschemeyer, D., & Skocpol, T. (1985) 'War making and state making as organized crime'. *Violence: A Reader*, 35–60.

Tomaney, J. (2003) 'Politics, institutions and the decline of coal mining in North East England'. *Mining Technology*, 112(1): 40–46.

Torgerson, D. (1999) *The Promise of Green Politics: Environmentalism and the Public Sphere*. Durham, NC: Duke University Press.

Trencher, G., Rinscheid, A., Rosenbloom, D., Koppenborg, F., Truong, N., & Temocin, P. (2023) 'The evolution of "phase-out" as a bridging concept for sustainability: From pollution to climate change'. *One Earth*, 6(7): 854–871.

Troath, S. (2023) 'The political economy of Australian, militarism: On the emergent military – industrial – academic complex'. *Journal of Global Security Studies*, 8(4). https://doi.org/10.1093/jogss/ogad018.

Trotsky, L. (2019 [1942]) *In Defence of Marxism*. London: Wellred Books.

Trout, K., Muttitt, G., Lafleur, D., Van De Graaf, T., Mendelevitch, R., Mei, L., & Meinshausen, M. (2022) 'Existing fossil fuel extraction would warm the world beyond 1.5°C'. *Environmental Research Letters*, 17(6): 064010. https://doi.org/10.1088/1748-9326/ac6228.

Truffer, B. (2012) 'The need for a global perspective on sustainability transitions'. *Environmental Development*, 3: 182–183.

Tuathail, G. O., Dalby, S., & Routledge, P. (eds.) (1998) *The Geopolitics Reader*. London: Routledge.

Turnheim, B. & Geels, F. (2012) 'Regime stabilisation as the flipside of energy transitions: Lessons from the history of the British coal industry (1913–1997)'. *Energy Policy*, 50: 35–49.

UNCTAD (United Nations Trade and Development). (2019) *Financing a Global Green New Deal*. Trade and Development report Geneva: UNCTAD.

UNCTAD (United Nations Trade and Development). (2022) Financing for development: Mobilizing sustainable development finance beyond COVID-19 Trade and Development Board Intergovernmental Group of Experts on Financing for Development Fifth session Geneva, 21–23 March 2022.

UNDP (United Nations Development Programme). (2021) *The Peoples' Climate Vote*. UNDP Report. www.undp.org/publications/peoples-climate-vote#modal-publication-download.

UNFCCC (United Nations Framework Convention on Climate Change). (2020) 'UN Secretary-General: "Making peace with nature is the defining task of the 21st century"'. December 2. https://unfccc.int/news/un-secretary-general-making-peace-with-nature-is-the-defining-task-of-the-21st-century

Union of Concerned Scientists. (2017) 'The US military and oil'. www.ucsusa.org/clean_vehicles/smart-transportation-solutions/us-military-oil-use.html#.WLAzTstv.i.

UNRISD (United Nations Research Institute for Social Development). (2023) 'Just energy transition partnerships toward a collective assessment'. Research and Policy Brief No. 41 Geneva: UNRISD.

Unruh, G. C. (2000) 'Understanding carbon lock-in'. *Energy Policy* 28: 817–830.

Urpelainen, J. & Van de Graaf, T. (2013) 'The international renewable energy agency: A success story in institutional innovation?' *International Environmental Agreements: Politics, Law and Economics*, 15(2): 159–177.

USAID (United States Agency for International Development). (2022) 'Climatescope'. www.usaid.gov/energy/toolkits.

Van Appeldoorn, B. & de Graaff, N. (2015) *American Grand Strategy and Corporate Elite Networks: The Open Door and Its Variations since the End of the Cold War*. London: Routledge.

Van Asselt, H. & Newell, P. (2022) Pathways to an international agreement to leave fossil fuels in the ground. *Global Environmental Politics*, 22(4): 28–47.

Van de Graaf, T. (2013) *The Politics and Institutions of Global Energy Governance*. Basingstoke: Palgrave.

Van de Graaf, T., Overland, I., Scholten, D., & Westphal, K. (2020) 'The new oil? The geopolitics and international governance of hydrogen'. *Energy Research & Social Science*, 70: 101667.

Van de Graaf, T. & Sovacool, B. K. (2020) *Global Energy Politics*. Cambridge: Polity Press.

Van der Pijl, K. (1998) *Transnational Classes and International Relations*. London: Routledge.

Van der Vleuten, E. & Högselius, P. (2012) 'Resisting change?: The transnational dynamics of European energy regimes'. In G. Verbong and D. Loorback (eds.), *Governing the Energy Transition*. Abingdon: Routledge, pp. 75–100.

Verbong, G. & Loorbach, D. (eds.) (2012) *Governing the Energy Transition: Reality, Illusion or Necessity?* Abingdon: Routledge.

Vinsel, L. & Russell, A. (2020) *The Innovation Delusion*. New York: Currency.

Vlachou, A. (2004) 'Capitalism and ecological sustainability: The shaping of environmental policies'. *Review of International Political Economy*, 11(5): 926–952.

Vogel, S. K. (2018) *Marketcraft: How Governments Make Markets Work*. New York: Oxford University Press.

Waddington, D. & Parry, D. (2003) 'Managing industrial decline: The lessons of a decade of research on industrial contraction and regeneration in Britain and other EU coal producing countries'. *Mining Technology*, 112(1): 47–56.

Wade, R. H. (2003) 'What strategies are viable for developing countries today? The World Trade Organization and the shrinking of "development space"'. *Review of International Political Economy*, 10(4): 621–644.

Walker, R. B. J. (1993) *Inside/Outside: International Relations as Political Theory*. Cambridge: Cambridge University Press.

Wallerstein, I. (2007 [1979]) *World-Systems Analysis: An Introduction*, 5th ed. Durham, NC: Duke University Press.

Wallerstein, I. (2014) *Historical Capitalism*. London: Verso Books.

Waltz, K. (1959) *Man, the State and War: A Theoretical Analysis*. New York: Columbia University Press.

Wan Abdullah, W., Zainudin, W., Mohamad Ishak, W., Sulong, F. & Zia Ul Haq, H. (2020) 'Public Participation of Renewable Energy (PPRED) model in Malaysia: An instrument development'. *International Journal of Renewable Energy Development*, 10(1): 119–137.

Wang, X. (2019) 'Leadership-building dilemmas in emerging powers' economic diplomacy: Russia's energy diplomacy and China's OBOR'. *Asia Europe Journal*, 18(1): 117–138.

Ward, H. (2002) 'Corporate accountability in search of a treaty? Some insights from foreign direct liability'. Briefing Paper No. 4, Chatham House. London: RIIA.

Watt, H. (2017) 'Hinkley point: The "dreadful deal" behind the world's most expensive power plant'. *The Guardian*, 21 December. www.theguardian.com/news/2017/dec/21/hinkley-point-c-dreadful-deal-behind-worlds-most-expensive-power-plant.

Watson, J. (2009) 'Technology assessment and innovation policy'. In I. Scarse and G. MacKerron (eds.), *Energy for the Future: A New Agenda*. Basingstoke: Palgrave, pp. 123–147.

Watts, M. (2008) *The Curse of the Black Gold*. New York: Powerhouse Press.

WCED (World Commission on Environment and Development). (1987) *Our Common Future: Report of the Brundtland Commission on Environment and Development*. Oxford: Oxford University Press.

Weale, A. (1992) *The Politics of Pollution*. Manchester: Manchester University Press.

Weaver, V. M. & Lerman, A. E. (2010) 'Political consequences of the carceral state'. *American Political Science Review*, 104(4): 817–833.

Weber, M. (1948) 'Politics as a vocation'. In *From Max Weber: Essays in Sociology*. London: Routledge and Kegan Paul, pp. 77–128.

Weber, M. (1978) *Economy and Society: An Outline of Interpretive Sociology*. Berkeley: University of California Press.

Weiss, L. (1995) *The Myth of the Powerless State*. Ithaca, NY: Cornell University Press.

Weiss, L. (2003a) 'Guiding globalisation in East Asia: New roles for old developmental states'. In L. Weiss (ed.), *States in the Global Economy: Bringing Domestic Institutions Back In*. Cambridge: Cambridge University Press, pp. 245–271.

Weiss, L. (ed.) (2003b) *States in the Global Economy: Bringing Domestic Institutions Back In*. Cambridge: Cambridge University Press.

Wells, R., Howarth, C., & Brand-Correa, L. I. (2021) 'Are citizen juries and assemblies on climate change driving democratic climate policymaking? An exploration of two case studies in the UK'. *Climatic Change*, 168: 1–22.

Westley, F. & Antadze, N. (2010) 'Making a difference: Strategies for scaling social innovation for greater impact'. *Innovation Journal*, 15(2).

Whitehead, M., Jones, R., & Jones, M. (2008) *The Nature of the State: Excavating the Political Ecologies of the State*. Oxford: Oxford University Press.

Whitfield, D. (2001) *Public Services or Corporate Welfare: Rethinking the Nation State in the Global Economy*. London: Pluto Press.

Wickham, A. & Gillespie, T. (2022) 'US sees up to £170 billion excess profits for energy firms'. Bloomberg, 30 August. www.bloomberg.com/news/articles/2022-08-30/uk-predicts-up-to-170-billion-excess-profits-for-energy-firms?in_source=embedded-checkout-banner.

Wigell, M. & Vihma, A. (2016) 'Geopolitics versus geoeconomics: The case of Russia's geostrategy and its effects on the EU'. *International Affairs*, 92(3): 605–627.

Willis, R. (2020) *Too Hot to Handle? The Democratic Challenge of Climate Change*. Bristol: Bristol University Press.

Wissenburg, M. (1998) *Green Liberalism: The Free and the Green Society*. London: University College London Press.

Wood, E. (2002) *The Origin of Capitalism: A Longer View*. London: Verso Books.

World Bank (2010) *World Development Report 2010: Development and Climate Change*. Washington, DC: World Bank.

World Bank (2012) *Inclusive Green Growth: The Pathway to Sustainable Development*. Washington, DC: World Bank.

Wright Mills, C. (1956) *The Power Elite*. New York: Oxford University Press.

Wu, F. (2015) 'China's puzzling energy diplomacy toward Iran'. *Asian Perspective*, 39(1): 47–69.

Yashar, D. (2005) *Contesting Citizenship in Latin America*. Cambridge: Cambridge University Press.

Ybarra, M. (2017) *Green Wars: Conservation and Decolonization in the Maya Forest*. Berkeley: University of California Press.

Yergin, D. (1991) *The Prize: The Epic Quest for Oil, Money and Power*. New York: Simon & Schuster.

Index

www.ingramcontent.com/pod-product-compliance
Lightning Source LLC
Chambersburg PA
CBHW080325070126
37842CB00022B/470

* 9 7 8 1 0 0 9 5 9 0 1 1 2 *